Q
1
.07
v.12
1997

Women, Gender, and Science
New Directions

Edited by Sally Gregory Kohlstedt and Helen E. Longino

Osiris VOLUME 12

A RESEARCH JOURNAL DEVOTED TO THE HISTORY OF SCIENCE AND ITS CULTURAL INFLUENCES

History of Science Society

The History of Science Society was founded in 1924 to secure the future of Isis, the international review that George Sarton (1884–1956) founded in Belgium in 1912. Osiris was founded by George Sarton in 1936, as a companion volume to Isis. The first series of Osiris was published in fifteen volumes between 1936 and 1968.

The History of Science Society launched the second series of Osiris in 1985. Osiris publishes annual volumes devoted to a single theme or topic of wide interest to the history of science community.

EXECUTIVE COMMITTEE

PRESIDENT
Frederick Gregory
University of Florida

VICE-PRESIDENT
Albert Van Helden
Rice University

EDITOR
Margaret W. Rossiter
Cornell University

TREASURER
Marc Rothenberg
Smithsonian Institution

EXECUTIVE SECRETARY
Keith R. Benson
University of Washington

COUNCIL

To serve through 1997
Paul Lawrence Farber
Oregon State University
Rachel Laudan
University of Hawaii
Albert E. Moyer
Virginia Polytechnic Institute and State University
Margaret J. Osler
University of Calgary
Arleen Tuchman
Vanderbilt University

To serve through 1998
Joan Cadden
Kenyon College
Mott T. Greene
University of Puget Sound
Anita Guerrini
University of California, Berkeley
Shirley Roe
University of Connecticut

To serve through 1999
Loren R. Graham
Massachusetts Institute of Technology
Jan V. Golinski
University of New Hampshire
Jane Maienschein
Arizona State University
Liba Taub
University of Cambridge
Mary Terrall
Harvard University

Former Presidents ex officio
I. Bernard Cohen
Harvard University
Marshall Clagett
Institute for Advanced Study
Charles C. Gillespie
Princeton University
Thomas S. Kuhn
Massachusetts Institute of Technology
Erwin N. Hiebert
Harvard University
John C. Greene
University of Connecticut
Richard S. Westfall
Indiana University
Robert P. Multhauf
Smithsonian Institution
Frederic L. Holmes
Yale University
Gerald Holton
Harvard University
Edward Grant
Indiana University
Mary Jo Nye
Oregon State University
Stephen G. Brush
University of Maryland
Sally Gregory Kohlstedt
University of Minnesota
David C. Lindberg
University of Wisconsin-Madison

Osiris

A RESEARCH JOURNAL DEVOTED TO THE HISTORY OF SCIENCE AND ITS CULTURAL INFLUENCES

EDITOR
MARGARET W. ROSSITER

MANAGING EDITOR
JON M. HARKNESS

MANUSCRIPT EDITOR
JOAN VANDEGRIFT

OSIRIS EDITORIAL BOARD

MOTT T. GREENE
University of Puget Sound
JOSEPH W. DAUBEN
Lehman College, City University of New York

PNINA ABIR-AM
University of Ottawa
JOHN H. WARNER
Yale University

KATHRYN M. OLESKO
Georgetown University

HSS COMMITTEE ON PUBLICATIONS

SEYMOUR H. MAUSKOPF
Duke University
JOHN SERVOS
Amherst College

ROBIN E. RIDER
University of Wisconsin–Madison

MICHAEL H. SHANK
Worcester Polytechnic Institute

EDITORIAL OFFICE
DEPARTMENT OF SCIENCE AND TECHNOLOGY STUDIES
CORNELL UNIVERSITY
726 UNIVERSITY AVENUE
ITHACA, NEW YORK, 14850, USA

SUGGESTIONS FOR CONTRIBUTORS TO OSIRIS

OSIRIS is devoted to thematic issues, often conceived and compiled by guest editors.

1. Manuscripts should be **typewritten** or processed on a **letter-quality** printer and **double-spaced** throughout, including quotations and notes, on paper of standard size or weight. Margins should be wider than usual to allow space for instructions to the typesetter. The right-hand margin should be left ragged (not justified) to maintain even spacing and readability.

2. Bibliographic information should be given in **footnotes** (not parenthetically in the text), typed separately from the main body of the manuscript, **double-** or even **triple-spaced,** numbered consecutively throughout the article, and keyed to reference numbers typed above the line in the text.

   a. References to **books** should include author's full name; complete title of the book, underlined (italics); place of publication and publisher's name for books published after 1900; date of publication, including the original date when a reprint is being cited; page numbers cited. *Example:*

   [1]Joseph Needham, *Science and Civilisation in China,* 5 vols., Vol. I: *Introductory Orientations* (Cambridge: Cambridge Univ. Press, 1954), p. 7.

   b. References to articles in **periodicals** should include author's name; title of article, in quotes; title of periodical, underlined; year; volume number, Arabic and underlined; number of issue if pagination requires it; page numbers of article; number of particular page cited. Journal titles are spelled out in full on first citation and abbreviated subsequently. *Example:*

   [2]John C. Greene. "Reflections of the Progress of Darwin Studies," *Journal of the History of Biology,* 1975, *8*:243–272, on p. 270; and Dov Ospovat, "God and Natural Selection: The Darwinian Idea of Design," *J. Hist. Biol.,* 1980, *13*:169–174, on p. 171

   c. When first citing a reference, please give the title in full. For succeeding citations, please use an abbreviated version of the title with the author's last name. *Example:*

   [3]Greene, "Reflections" (cit. n. 2), p. 250.

3. Please mark clearly for the typesetter all unusual alphabets, special characters, mathematics, and chemical formulae, and include all diacritical marks.

4. A small number of **figures** may be used to illustrate an article. Line drawings should be directly reproducible; glossy prints should be furnished for all halftone illustrations.

5. Manuscripts should be submitted to OSIRIS with the understanding that upon publication **copyright** will be transferred to the History of Science Society. That understanding precludes OSIRIS from considering material that has been submitted or accepted for publication elsewhere.

OSIRIS (SSN 0369-7827) is published once a year.

Subscriptions are $39 (hardcover) and $25 (paperback).

Address subscriptions, single issue orders, claims for missing issues, and advertising inquiries to *Osiris,* The University of Chicago Press, Journals Division, P.O. Box 37005, Chicago, Illinois 60637.

Postmaster: Send address changes to *Osiris,* The University of Chicago Press, Journals Division, P.O. Box 37005, Chicago, Illinois 60637.

Osiris is indexed in major scientific and historical indexing services, including *Biological Abstracts, Current Contexts, Historical Abstracts,* and *America: History and Life.*

Copyright © 1997 by the History of Science Society, Inc. All rights reserved. The paper in this publication meets the requirements of ANSI standard Z39.48-1984 (Permanence of Paper).∞

Hardcover edition, ISBN 0-226-30753-0
Paperback edition, ISBN 0-226-30754-9

Women, Gender, and Science: New Directions

Edited by Sally Gregory Kohlstedt and
Helen Longino

Osiris

A RESEARCH JOURNAL
DEVOTED TO THE HISTORY OF SCIENCE
AND ITS CULTURAL INFLUENCES
SECOND SERIES   VOLUME 12   1997

Acknowledgments	1
SALLY GREGORY KOHLSTEDT and HELEN LONGINO: *The Women, Gender, and Science Question: What Do Research on Women in Science and Research on Gender and Science Have to Do with Each Other?*	3
EVELYN FOX KELLER: *Developmental Biology as a Feminist Cause?*	16
ANN B. SHTEIR: *Gender and "Modern" Botany in Victorian England*	29
NINA E. LERMAN: *The Uses of Useful Knowledge: Science, Technology, and Social Boundaries in an Industrializing City*	39
ROBERT A. NYE: *Medicine and Science as Masculine "Fields of Honor"*	60
ALISON WYLIE: *The Engendering of Archaeology: Refiguring Feminist Science Studies*	80
DIANA E. LONG: *Hidden Persuaders: Medical Indexing and the Gendered Professionalism of American Medicine, 1880–1932*	100
ESTELLE COHEN: *"What the Women at All Times Would Laugh At": Redefining Equality and Difference, circa 1660–1760*	121
ELVIRA SCHEICH: *Science, Politics, and Morality: The Relationship of Lise Meitner and Elisabeth Schiemann*	143
MARGARET W. ROSSITER: *Which Science? Which Women?*	169
SANDRA HARDING: *Women's Standpoints on Nature: What Makes Them Possible?*	186
LONDA SCHIEBINGER: *Creating Sustainable Science*	201
NOTES ON CONTRIBUTORS	217
INDEX	219

Cover: This image first appeared in the program for a conference, held in May 1995 at the University of Minnesota, from which the papers in this volume originated.

Acknowledgments

Reflecting back on the workshop and conference that generated the essays for this volume of *Osiris,* we are acutely aware of the numerous contributions made by colleagues here at the University of Minnesota and, indeed, around the world. The intellectual excitement generated by that meeting exceeded everyone's expectations, and discussions suggested far-reaching intellectual and activist consequences.

In order to accommodate the interests of historians, philosophers, sociologists, biologists, physicists, engineers, and others, we created a local committee to help evaluate proposals, recommend chairs and commentators, and help envision the entire conference that was held in May 1995. To those who joined us at the moment of initiation and supported us with the gifts of time, imagination, and critical intellectual sustenance, we offer sincere gratitude: Nina Lerman, Naomi Scheman, Mary Lay, Shirley Nelson Garner, Estelle Cohen, Janet Spector, Janice Hogan, Susan Henderson, and Jacqueline Zita. We also thank other colleagues who helped us at particular stages to formulate the conference, read proposals, and organize sessions. The strong feminist and historical communities here at Minnesota undergird the successes we enjoyed, while individuals buoyed us through treacherous waters and added to our delight in the conference. Essential to the implementation of the conference were Lori Graven and Susan Burke of Professional Development and Conferences Services. The workshop benefited from the careful preparation and organizational skills of Clare Gravon and Karen Moon of the Center for Advanced Feminist Studies. Only their individual and collective attention to detail and good sense of humor allowed us to bring over four hundred scholars to campus and involve them in several dozen sessions and workshops as well as special events at the Weisman Art Museum and the Earle Brown Conference Center.

The workshop that produced most of the essays included in this volume was often intense, sometimes quite intimate, and inevitably challenging as we strove to listen across disciplinary and other boundaries, determined to learn from each other. All presenters were also commentators, and a few other student and faculty participants joined the group as well. Their preparation, sensitive commentary, and sage advice moved the conversations forward, and so we thank Pnina Abir-Am, Marianne Ainley, John Beatty, Ronald Giere, Barbara Laslett, Elaine Tyler May, Carolyn Merchant, Gianna Pomata, Naomi Scheman, and Sharon Traweek. The workshop was funded in significant part by National Science Foundation Grant #9123719. Contributions to the workshop and conference came as well from many departments and colleges at the University of Minnesota, including the Program in the History of Science and Technology, the Center for Philosophy of Science, the Studies of Science and Technology Program, the Center for Advanced Feminist Studies, the Institute of Technology, the College of Biological Science, the College of Liberal Arts, the College of Human Ecology, and the Medical School. We especially thank Ronald Overmann and Rochelle Hollander of the National Science Foundation, who understood the significance of the event and offered advice as we planned the meeting. Helen Longino is grateful to the Michael and Penny Winton Visiting Scholars Program in the College of Liberal Arts, which brought her to the University of Minnesota.

Coordination of the initial editorial work for this volume was very ably managed by Kerry Brooks. As the volume underwent preparation, we added to our debt of gratitude by soliciting advice from scholars who could help enhance the individual papers by a critical reading. These readers proved remarkably helpful, offering often extensive comments in very short periods of time. Such cooperation renewed our appreciation of the collegiality and commitment that seem remarkably pervasive in studies of women, gender, and science. We are pleased to acknowledge the cooperation of John Beatty, Mario Biagioli, Paula Findlen, Ruth Ellen Joeres, Peggy Sue Kidwell, Diana Long, Mary Jo Maynes, Theodore Porter, Ruth Sime, Bonnie Spanier, Janet Spector, Nancy Tuana, and John Harley Warner.

The editor of *Osiris,* Margaret Rossiter, was encouraging as we moved forward. Joan Vandegrift's excellent editorial hand probed for clarifications and polished prose. Always, of course, we used time owed to others in our lives as we planned and implemented the entire activity—and thus we thank David, Valerie, Kris, and Kurt, who were supportive and there when we really needed them.

The Women, Gender, and Science Question
What Do Research on Women in Science and Research on Gender and Science Have to Do with Each Other?

By Sally Gregory Kohlstedt* and Helen Longino**

THIS VOLUME FEATURES WORK by prominent historians and philosophers of science and technology on issues of gender and science and women in science. Our aim in organizing the workshop of which these papers are the result was to bring together scholars who work on gender and science, scholars who work on women's participation in the sciences, and scholars who work on both aspects to begin to explore the potential for synergy between these two pieces of a larger puzzle. As a consequence of so framing our topic, we brought into conversation many of the leading feminist scholars in history and philosophy of science. The workshop and this volume are thus occasions for collectively assessing where we are in the mid 1990s: what feminist scholars have contributed to our historical and philosophical understanding of the sciences and what new questions have emerged to demand our attention.

ACCOMPLISHMENTS TO DATE

A focus on the sexual divisions of labor in science that result as well in the gendered organization of scientific communities, together with more recent attention to the gendered nature of science itself, has characterized much of the research by feminist historians. Although these are interconnected issues, they have been pursued for the most part separately, by individuals and within disciplines. Between individuals and between disciplines there is relatively little dialogue, although there are occasional verbal barbs about those who do "mere history" and those whose "social construction loses the science."

Historians studying women and science were initially determined to recover the significant number of women ignored by conventional histories of science. Although work in science can be identified as early as ancient Egypt, and work in technology even earlier, much of the foundational scholarship concerned those exceptional

---

* Program in History of Science and Technology, University of Minnesota, Minneapolis, Minnesota 55455.
** Department of Women's Studies, University of Minnesota, Minneapolis, Minnesota 55455.

©1997 by The History of Science Society. All rights reserved. 0369-7827/97/1201-0001$02.00

women who, despite numerous obstacles, made significant contributions to science over the past four centuries.[1] Documenting their existence has been the first challenge, and, while such work continues, historians have also turned their attention to the circumstances, personal and external, that empowered these women scientists as well as to the factors that inhibited their achievement and satisfaction in science. Such work includes case studies, comprehensive histories, and biographies. A number of historians have recently addressed the ways in which private and public activities intersected, noting the essential support some women derived from family relationships even as the demands of those relationships constrained certain aspects of their productivity and recognition.[2]

Recognizing that, historically, women's lives have had dimensions different from men's, some investigators have traced the dynamics of women's work within the framework of domestic responsibility, uncovering as well the patterns of collaboration necessary for women to gain access to information and instrumentation. Still others have investigated the professionalization of science and technology, seeking to identify what counts as science at any given time and place and the roles of gender in such classification.[3] As women's temporal, social, and geographical locations have varied, so too have their individual relations to their operative communities and the definitions and institutions that are identified under the term *science*. Issues of nationality, class, and race join gender in sometimes unanticipated ways as participants and patrons in science engage in research and dissemination.

Gender as a significant variable has been ignored by many scholars studying the social context of science. Feminist historians, however, have argued not only that the Scientific Revolution marked a dramatic shift in views of "nature" but also that these changing perspectives had profound gender implications for intellectual women as well as for the characteristics ascribed to scientific inquiry and results. Furthermore, in the seventeenth and eighteenth centuries, a renewed interest in sex differences became embedded in taxonomical constructs and theories of natural history, leading to new definitions of sex differences and new ways of marking the social implications of sexual identity. This attention to the Scientific Revolution has

---

[1] H. J. Mozans, *Woman in Science* (1913; Cambridge, Mass.: MIT Press, 1974), provided an early survey; more information is found in such recent biographical dictionaries as Marilyn Bailey Ogilvie, *Women in Science: Antiquity through the Nineteenth Century: A Biographical Dictionary with Annotated Bibliography* (Cambridge, Mass.: MIT Press, 1986).

[2] Some important examples of investigations into empowering and inhibiting factors, dealing primarily with North American women scientists, include Margaret W. Rossiter, *Women Scientists in America: Struggles and Strategies to 1940* (Baltimore: Johns Hopkins Univ. Press, 1982); Rossiter, *Women Scientists in America: Before Affirmative Action, 1940–1972* (Baltimore: Johns Hopkins Univ. Press, 1995); Pnina G. Abir-Am and Dorinda Outram, eds., *Uneasy Careers and Intimate Lives: Women in Science, 1789–1979* (New Brunswick, N.J.: Rutgers Univ. Press, 1987); and Evelyn Fox Keller, *A Feeling for the Organism: The Life and Work of Barbara McClintock* (New York: Freeman, 1983). On the intersection of public and private activities see Helena M. Pycior, Nancy G. Slack, and Abir-Am, eds., *Creative Couples in the Sciences* (New Brunswick, N.J.: Rutgers Univ. Press, 1996).

[3] For explorations of collaboration see Ann B. Shteir, *Cultivating Women, Cultivating Science: Flora's Daughters and Botany in England, 1760–1860* (Baltimore: Johns Hopkins Univ. Press, 1996); and Helena M. Pycior, "Reaping the Benefits of Collaboration While Avoiding Its Pitfalls: Marie Curie's Rise to Scientific Prominence," *Social Studies of Science*, 1993, *23:*301–323. Concerning professionalization see the historiographical discussion in Sally Gregory Kohlstedt, "Women in the History of Science: An Ambiguous Place," *Osiris*, 2nd Ser., 1995, *10:*39–58.

been broadened to encompass the subtle and complex ideas about nature in relation to sex and sex differences prior to the sixteenth century.[4]

These inquiries into context have raised issues taken up in more philosophically oriented work, which has addressed three main areas. Feminists within the sciences have criticized the representation of males, females, sex, and sexual difference in various contemporary scientific theories. They have shown how in many cases the collection and organization of data and in other cases the interpretation of data were skewed by gender bias. This critical work has gone on in fields ranging from animal ethology to human neuroendocrinology. Philosophers, as well as scientists, have used these critiques to develop more general analyses of the structure of research programs on or involving gender and sex differences.[5]

A second area of work for philosophers has been study of the roles of gendered images and metaphors in scientific theorizing about ostensibly nongendered subjects—for example, interactions between nucleus and cytoplasm in the cell. Feminist scholars have drawn attention to the ways in which cultural gender constructs are naturalized and the natural world sexually dichotomized by such linguistic practices. They have also shown how alternative theoretical accounts are marginalized or silenced by the salience of gender, with its attendant metaphors of domination and subordination, attack, and defeat.[6]

The third major area of feminist conceptual inquiry has been methodological and epistemological. How has gender affected our conceptions of knowledge? Such investigations have included psychoanalytically grounded reflection on the complex interconnections between stereotypes of the ideal scientist and conceptions of the form of scientific knowledge. These reflections have prompted more general questions about the affective dimensions of natural knowledge, including such matters as the design and construction of experiments. Some scholars have focused on a primary medium of scientific knowledge and communication: language. They have

---

[4] Carolyn Merchant, *The Death of Nature: Women, Ecology, and the Scientific Revolution* (San Francisco: Harper & Row, 1980); Brian Easlea, *Science and Sexual Oppression: Patriarchy's Confrontation with Woman and Nature* (London: Weidenfeld & Nicholson, 1981); Londa Schiebinger, *Nature's Body: Gender in the Making of Modern Science* (Boston: Beacon, 1993); Ludmilla Jordanova, *Sexual Visions: Images of Gender in Science and Medicine between the Eighteenth and Twentieth Centuries* (Madison: Univ. Wisconsin Press, 1989); and Joan Cadden, *Meanings of Sex Difference in the Middle Ages: Medicine, Science, and Culture* (Cambridge/New York: Cambridge Univ. Press, 1993).

[5] For work on gender bias in scientific theories see Ruth Bleier, *Science and Gender: A Critique of Biology and Its Theories on Women* (New York: Pergamon, 1984); Ruth Hubbard, "Have Only Men Evolved?" in *Women Look at Biology Looking at Women: A Collection of Feminist Critiques,* ed. Hubbard, Mary Sue Henifin, and Barbara Fried (Cambridge: Schenkman, 1979), pp. 7–36; and Anne Fausto-Sterling, *Myths of Gender: Biological Theories about Women and Men* (New York: Basic, 1985). Among more general analyses of the structure of research programs see Helen Longino and Ruth Doell, "Body, Bias, and Behavior: A Comparative Analysis of Reasoning in Two Areas of Biological Science," *Signs: Journal of Women in Culture and Society,* 1983, 9:206–227; Lynn Hankinson Nelson, *Who Knows: From Quine to Feminist Empiricism* (Philadelphia: Temple Univ. Press, 1990); Alison Wylie, "Gender Theory and the Archaeological Record: Why Is There No Archaeology of Gender," in *Engendering Archaeology: Women and Prehistory,* ed. Joan M. Gero and Margaret W. Conkey (Oxford: Blackwell, 1991), pp. 31–54.

[6] See Gender and Biology Study Group, "The Importance of Feminist Critique for Intracellular Biology," *Hypatia,* 1987, 2(3):61–76; Evelyn Fox Keller, *Refiguring Life: Metaphors of Twentieth-Century Biology* (New York: Columbia Univ. Press, 1995); Bonnie Spanier, *Im/partial Science: Gender Ideology in Molecular Biology* (Bloomington: Indiana Univ. Press, 1995); and, on the marginalizing of alternative accounts, Merchant, *Death of Nature* (cit. n. 4).

reflected on the role of language, and the availability of certain discursive formations, in directing the formulation, acceptance, and rejection of theories.[7]

Anthropologists have illuminated the masculine qualities of the culture of contemporary research communities and the expression of that culture in ideals of knowledge. Other feminist scholars have directed attention to the cognitive practices involved in knowledge construction and the ways in which analysis of those practices has been limited by sociopolitical biases in philosophy. Still other feminists have concentrated on delineating what a proper feminist epistemological attitude toward the sciences ought to be. These positions range from the advocacy of a feminist standpoint to forms of postmodern skepticism.[8] Running through all these methodological and epistemological discussions has been a concern with such metaphysical issues as the construal of nature, reductionism and the various forms of antireductionism, and the character of causality.

Thus, at the stage at which we began organizing our workshop, three concepts had emerged as separate foci of investigation. *Feminism* operates as an explicit sociopolitical orientation informing the research and analysis of scholars of science and of scientists. Feminist scholars of science are attentive to histories of social and conceptual exclusion and marginalization, to patterns of androcentrism both in science and in historical, philosophical, and social studies of science. Feminist scientists are concerned to conduct their investigations in accordance with feminist principles, to resist androcentric currents of mainstream research communities, and in some cases to organize their intellectual production along theoretical lines identified with feminism. *Gender* is a structural category, articulated in relation to sexual difference, that organizes social and symbolic systems. As such it is a central category of analysis for feminist scholars. To study gendering in science is to study the masculinization and feminization of ideas, practices, and institutions as well as the ways the sciences have themselves construed gender as a topic of empirical investigation. Finally, *women*—as biological and social individuals—have been both subjects and objects of scientific research. The careers and contributions of individual women scientists, such as Marie Curie and Barbara McClintock, have been studied, as have the general patterns of female participation in the sciences.

All three categories have been problematized, their concerns multiplied. There are many forms of feminism shaping inquiry, from equity feminism to postmodern

---

[7] Evelyn Fox Keller, *Reflections on Gender and Science* (New Haven, Conn.: Yale Univ. Press, 1985), explores how gender has affected our conceptions of knowledge. For work focusing on language see Donna Haraway, *Primate Visions: Race, Gender, and Nature in the World of Modern Science* (London: Routledge, 1989); Keller, *Secrets of Life, Secrets of Death: Essays on Language, Gender, and Science* (New York: Routledge, 1992); and Barbara Laslett, Sally Gregory Kohlstedt, Helen Longino, and Evelynn Hammonds, eds., *Gender and Scientific Authority* (Chicago: Univ. Chicago Press, 1996).

[8] For a study of a contemporary research community see Sharon Traweek, *Beamtimes and Lifetimes: The World of High Energy Physicists* (Cambridge, Mass.: Harvard Univ. Press, 1988). For work on cognitive practices see Genevieve Lloyd, *The Man of Reason: "Male" and "Female" in Western Philosophy* (Minneapolis: Univ. Minnesota Press, 1984); Helen Longino, *Science as Social Knowledge: Values and Objectivity in Scientific Inquiry* (Princeton, N.J.: Princeton Univ. Press, 1990); Longino, "To See Feelingly: Reason, Passion, and Dialogue in Feminist Philosophy," in *Feminism in the Academy,* ed. Donna Stanton and Abigail Stewart (Ann Arbor: Univ. Michigan Press, 1995), pp. 19–45; and Nelson, *Who Knows* (cit. n. 5). On feminist epistemological attitudes see Hilary Rose, "Hand, Brain, and Heart: A Feminist Epistemology for the Natural Sciences," *Signs,* 1983, 9:73–90; and Sandra Harding, *The Science Question in Feminism* (Ithaca, N.Y.: Cornell Univ. Press, 1986).

feminism. Some scholars see the issue as fair treatment for women, while others envision dismantling and (possibly) reconstructing intellectual institutions and practices. Many understand that the issues are multilayered. The concept of "gender" is used differently by different scholars: some see gender as inherent in individuals, while others see it as a matter of social and conceptual relations. Thus, differences in scientific practice may be seen as a function of fundamental psychosocial formations or as situational. And the concept of "woman" has been similarly contested, with some arguing that it is possible to define "woman" biologically and others insisting that our concept of "woman," like that of "man," is a social construct, mutable under the pressure of changing circumstances. These fundamental theoretical tensions have found expression in feminist science studies as in feminist scholarship generally.

There are, clearly, areas of convergence and potential cooperation, as well as of tension, between the historical and philosophical work we have described. The relationship between past and present practices of scientific thinking about gender and sex difference is an obvious example. In other cases the potential for constructive interaction is less clear and has been insufficiently explored. But if we take the feminist theoretical and philosophical work to have shown ways in which scientific theories, methods, and self-definitions have been influenced by ideologies and practices of masculinity, it seems reasonable to ask how women who succeeded (or attempted to succeed) in the sciences saw themselves in relation to the masculinized aspects of their calling. To what extent did they ignore them? internalize them? To what extent did they develop or pursue nonstandard themes, use nonstandard methods, innovate in ways that depart from a purportedly universal gendered standard? What facilitates and what impedes such nonconformity? How can the philosophical work inform the work of historians studying the experience of individual women or groups of women in the sciences? Correlatively, how can studying the lives and works of women in science help reveal the gendered aspects of scientific content and methods? The time has come, we think, to articulate and understand the assumptions that might underlie the answers to questions like these and to investigate what connections might exist or be constructed among the research programs of our diverse participants—as well as what tensions might persist and why. Our contributors have deliberately complicated these questions, insisting that research on women in science is closely connected to research on gender while continuously challenging any simplistic notions about how that is so.

RETHINKING THE ISSUES

The issues of gender and science are nowhere more concretely explored than in the experiences of women in science, often particularly those women whose work and research in biology and related medical settings involve them in questions of sexuality and reproduction. Thus Evelyn Fox Keller's evocative and penetrating analysis of the life of the 1995 Nobel Prize winner Christiane Nusslein-Volhard provides a useful way to open the discussion of our problem: understanding how research on women in science and research on science and gender relate to one another. Nusslein-Volhard, a German developmental biologist, has over the course of her life both resisted and perpetuated gendered assumptions about women in science through her own pathbreaking career and her management of an important and highly productive laboratory. We thus confront at the outset a bittersweet reality: the striking contemporary success of a few women—and the evident self-confidence and assuredness that success brings—casts into sharp relief the persisting problems of many others. Keller also takes us to the heart of developmental biology to explore the understanding of gene action and the rhetoric surrounding it over the past century. Nusslein-Volhard's reorganization of the problem and subsequent research were sufficiently powerful to garner a Nobel Prize. Other essays in this volume, most evidently that by Elvira Scheich, also use scientific biography in ways that explore the experiences of successful scientists and the complex roles gender identity plays in the lives of those who enter what remain male-dominated arenas.

Turning to cultural life in Britain two hundred years ago, Ann Shteir reprises the early and ongoing interests of women in an area of natural science to which they had early access and in which they gained considerable expertise as herbalists and horticulturists. Botany enjoyed widespread attention in the late eighteenth century as a family and social activity. Women found it intellectually challenging during a period when Linnaean taxonomy gave a systematic impetus to the study of local plant life and British imperialism brought exotics to home and public gardens. The relative openness of botanical science to women was, however, short lived. Shteir describes the role of John Lindley in formulating the circumscribed ways in which women might participate in botanical culture—largely as illustrators, collectors, and popular writers. The result was more subtle than outright exclusion; instead, women's botanical activities were situated and restricted through rhetorical devices, institutional affiliations, and social prescriptions. So acceptable were the constraints that allowed women to be involved in specific ways—while at the same time cutting them off from prestigious assignments and professional memberships—that, Shteir argues, even British suffragists took for granted the patterns that were in place by the end of the nineteenth century. Such fine-grained analysis of particular scientific fields, as Margaret Rossiter points out in another essay, allows us to understand the immediate influences that shape the involvement of individual women; in this case, the analysis documents the erosion of opportunity for women in botany.

Technology transformed life in England and the United States in the nineteenth century. Nina Lerman notes that despite extraordinary and rapid changes in outlooks, techniques, and instrumentation, American institutions were adapted and readapted in ways that perpetuated old and sometimes introduced new gender stereotypes about skills for work and life. Attentive to race and class as well as gender, Lerman shows that those who had limited (or no) political and economic authority were pushed into categories where training and socialization maintained the status quo. Her essay provides a rare examination of technical education, analyzed here over three generations in nineteenth-century Philadelphia; she shows how even dramatic changes in content had surprisingly little impact on assumptions about training for boys and girls. While class and race stratified boys for future occupations, a persisting theme of domesticity marked the education of poor and middle-class girls from the 1830s through the 1880s. Lerman's analysis of actual course content marks the meanings of technology that emerged in education in Philadelphia and their role in urban society and economy.

Investigating yet another aspect of nineteenth-century culture, Robert Nye explores the traditional aristocratic codes of honor that became translated into middle-class professional life, particularly into medicine, in France and Britain. Traits defined as noble took on ever more exclusively male identity and also became fundamental in emerging professions, Nye suggests. In this context, professional codes of ethics—particularly those involving competition, social behavior, and allegiance to appropriate associations—played an elusive but effective role in establishing gendered boundaries. Not surprisingly, these behavioral norms coincide with more specific rules barring women from certain medical and scientific societies and related activities. Such exclusivity operates to limit participation and at the same time provides a social basis for cognitive authority.

While uneasy compromises nonetheless allowed a few exceptional women into male-dominated fields by the end of the nineteenth century, a hundred years later feminists and other scholars have challenged both their limited access to professional institutions and the authenticity of the established knowledge base. Alison Wylie provides a close look at recent events in another discipline, archaeology, established early in this century. Its goals paralleled those of European medical physicians whose masculine institutions established boundaries of participation and perpetuated gendered assumptions within the core of their theory and practice. Using questionnaires and interviews based on a highly focused conference, "The Archaeology of Gender," Wylie investigates the nature and impact of feminist critiques after a decade of continued efforts to open the doors of science to women, when a new generation of scholars challenged the entrenched claims to scientific authority and objectivity. Wylie examines the content critiques and, at the same time, equity challenges from those scholars who see a connection between outcomes of research and gendered assumptions of researchers. Her questions about this relationship are at the heart of our inquiry—and the answers are complicated by the rich diversity of feminist work lives and feminist theory. New studies rightly challenge old evidence and interpretations; yet reconstruction of the past remains incredibly complex. Wylie thus looks further for the emergence of feminist initiatives in archaeology and assesses the demographics of that interest. Arguing that there are two sources for the new critique—one identified with feminism external to the field, the other drawn to the excitement of new and provocative scholarship—she insists on the reciprocity of participation and content. Her conclusion provides an agenda that emphasizes, at its core, the importance of empirical accuracy and explanatory breadth, along with a rigorous reflexivity. She suggests that feminist studies provides a model for science studies because it is at once empirically grounded and epistemologically sophisticated.

Every author necessarily engages with the meanings of language and text: past and present, contextualized around women, framed by women, grounded in empirical data, related to experience, bound by abstraction, always elusive. Diana Long investigates the vocabulary of women's bodies and health by examining the use of particular words and subject headings in the *Index Catalogue of the Library of the Surgeon General's Office*. Focusing on three editions of the *Index Catalogue,* Long concentrates on the cross-references that give meaning to and inscribe the keywords relating to women's bodies and pathologies. Well aware of the power vested in the right to classify—in this case, power held by medical doctors—she follows the changing descriptive content and referent connections of such terms as *woman* and *gynecology* during the critical period when science became a dominant factor in American medicine. In particular, she traces the growing authority of gynecology from the 1880s to 1932, suggesting that the new discipline captured the organs of women and their diseases. Her discussion underscores the medicalization and narrowing of definitions that occurred as these powerful markers categorized and codified the authority of physicians; pointing, in her conclusion, to today's new information technologies, she cautions that "we cannot leave it to the experts to tell us the proper names for our bodies or our selves."

Of course, as Estelle Cohen reminds us, the authority of even powerfully placed and institutionally certified experts does not go uncontested in any period, particularly in instances where the knowledge at stake relates to women's bodies and experiences. Cohen's account of medical literature in the early modern period argues that well-positioned and literate women both challenged and contributed to medical understanding. Using textbooks and similar sources, Cohen identifies major theories and some controversies regarding female reproductive organs from about 1660 to 1760 and thus documents the critical discussion about women's anatomy, particularly as it positioned arguments about sexual difference in relationship to intellectual authority. Judith Drake's *Essay in Defense of the Female Sex* (1696) challenged those who argued that women's inferior status had a basis in nature; Drake provided evidence and interpretations that were part of a significant contemporary literature intent on enlarging women's intellectual and social domains. Nonetheless, as Cohen points out, these arguments would be ignored a century later, when assertions about women's status that had earlier been contested became a standard part of medical and scientific literature. The sources of the dilemma and the counterarguments to those for whom biology seemed destiny have roots that reach far back into the historical record. Like Drake, women and some men with expertise who contributed to theory and practice are also part of an ongoing critical dialogue about the nature of sex and gendered identity. Cohen, like Wylie, suggests that a commitment to empirical data played a role in the controversies about women's anatomy, and both suggest that a significant source of that commitment was personal experience.

In the twentieth century, the experience of women in Western science, as Keller's essay illustrates, is still that of outsiders, even for those who, in most ways, appear firmly established. Elvira Scheich's account of the geneticist Elisabeth Schiemann and the physicist Lise Meitner documents a friendship brought into tension by the particular ways in which science and politics intertwined in German culture before and during World War II. The vulnerabilities of both women had multiple explanations. Schiemann followed a highly personal ethical and moral code in opposing the Nazi regime and never acquired a position commensurate with her qualifications. Scheich's narrative and analytic account underscores the way in which, despite career complications, Schiemann linked her scientific and human sensibilities—a life in science involves more than science. In order to expand—and complicate—this point, Scheich positions Schiemann's story against the better-known experiences of Lise Meitner, whose career was also marked by issues of gender, politics, ethnicity, and scientific outlook. The early friendship of the two women was compromised by fundamental differences in their cultural backgrounds and their personalities as they confronted Nazi Germany. Despite Schiemann's brave stands during World War II, these differences were so great that the two women were unable to recapture their earlier close relationship after the war. The paired accounts reflect similar constraints, based on gender, that inhibited achievement while revealing the individual ways in which each woman, quite unselfconsciously for the most part, insisted on the real connections between moral attitudes and scientific practice.

Stories of individual women like Nusslein-Volhard and Schiemann highlight the intimate and public circumstances that enabled or hindered their careers. Margaret Rossiter's "Which Science? Which Women?" serves as a reminder that "local history" of particular fields of science, located in particular places and times, is fundamental to the enterprise of understanding how gender issues connect with larger demographic patterns. Drawing on the 1956–1958 survey *American Science Manpower*—which, despite its title, included a significant contingent of women—she presents the aggregate patterns of women's participation in the sciences and argues that proportionate numbers are ultimately very important for the individual women involved; being an exception rarely took women very far. Drawing on the careers of individual women scientists during this period as examples, she suggests that "women tend to be where the money is not" and points out that there was a dearth of status and reward not only for particular individuals but also across whole fields that were highly feminized. Urging scholars to undertake more studies of women in science by subdiscipline, Rossiter suggests that such comparative data would allow for better explanatory models of women's participation.

In a volume concerned with questions at the margin of our knowledge and understanding about women, gender, and science, every author contends with the issue of where we go from here in terms of science and gender studies. Again, the issues are multilayered: we recognize the need for deeper analytical studies, for broad-based comparative work, for more reflexive conceptual frameworks, for accounts that problematize early generalizations without discounting pioneering investigations, for studies of rhetoric and cognitive authority, for sensitive reports about the complexity of individual experiences within and because of science, and for reconceptualizations of science and technology themselves.

While all the essays in this volume implicitly comment on future agendas, two of them concentrate on particular issues within and surrounding science. Sandra Harding restates, updates, and geographically expands her early work in an essay entitled "Women's Standpoints on Nature: What Makes Them Possible?" Her answer involves taking a position within postcolonial cross-cultural studies of science, where she makes a plea for the value of local knowledge systems that are themselves complicated by gender and class experiences. Understanding nature, she argues, depends on the material and social practices of women and men particularly as these vary by geographical and cultural setting. Local science, regularities and irregularities in nature, and cultural differences frame her argument for standpoint theory in science studies.

Londa Schiebinger concentrates on a much-discussed issue among women activists in the 1980s and 1990s—namely, the concern about women's participation in science at rates below what might be expected from the size of the talent pool, despite intervention efforts over the past two decades. Pointing to statistics on Department of Defense funding for research and development, broken down by field, she suggests, provocatively and in parallel with the observations of Margaret Rossiter, that women's participation in a field is inversely proportional to its level of military funding. Thus awareness of issues of access and equity is fundamental to understanding the nature of the knowledge produced and certified, as Lerman, Wylie, and others also make very clear. Schiebinger goes on to argue that successful recruiting and retention of women in science is far more complicated than simply ensuring their academic preparation and an open-door policy. We must, she concludes, draw on the rich array of current feminist thinking and incorporate those insights about gender and science into an activist agenda that will include women and their experiences in a "sustainable science."

NEW QUESTIONS / FUTURE DIRECTIONS

It is clear that we have a variety of strategies for understanding how maleness is reproduced in the sciences: through the affect-laden stories and myths created by high-energy physicists; the sexualized representation of knowledge and its objects and other specific gendering practices in which scientists engage; and the rituals of honor in male societies to which Robert Nye has drawn our attention. We now need to understand the implications of the multiplicity of ways in which knowing is gendered—specifically, implications of the multiplicity of ways in which it is gendered male. These essays (Keller, Scheich, Wylie) show that there is no simple way to articulate global gender critiques onto the specificities of women's experiences in the sciences. Many women scientists ignore or do not resist the gendering practices that surround them, while others are acutely sensitive and resistant, and still others manage to be conscious of but successfully negotiate the treacherous gender shoals in which they work.

The increasingly fine-grained historical research represented by the essays of Cohen and Long shows the tenuousness of connections between sociopolitical ideologies of gender and the biological construction of gender. Wylie makes a similar point in relation to the archaeology of gender. Multiple constructions of gender and contestations of gender stability go back at least to the Renaissance. And now, while we see a miniresurgence of biological determinism in some domains,[9] we also see the multiple possibilities of combination and recombination offered in molecular biology, the surgical and pharmacological management of gender and sex transformation, and the playful gender bricolage performed independently of and in serious resistance to biological understandings of gender. Both the historical work and our current circumstances present new challenges to understanding the relations between models pursued in the sciences and sociopolitical ideologies. Continued sophisticated historical research may help us to see patterns of persistence and change—and also, perhaps, to understand the forces that make for the alignment of biomedical and sociopolitical models in one context and their detachment or opposition in others.

Focusing on the sciences, we need to think more about how to illuminate the interrelations of the multiple factors involved in knowledge production. Students of the sciences also need to understand the construction of cognitive authority. Here there are two related questions. Since the sciences were not always granted cognitive authority, how have they come to occupy such a position and what has been the role of rituals and models of masculinity in that positioning? What is the role of new feminist voices in the sciences in altering those patterns of scientific authority? Our contributors show the complexities of trying to address these questions. They remind

---

[9] Simon LeVay, *The Sexual Brain* (Cambridge, Mass.: MIT Press, 1993); and Richard Herrnstein and Charles Murray, *The Bell Curve: Intelligence and Class Structure in American Life* (New York: Free Press, 1994).

us that the sciences are diverse, constituted by a multiplicity of practices. Furthermore, the word *science* itself is used in various ways. Sometimes we mean systematic attempts to understand the natural world; other times we mean a set of institutionalized practices and relationships; and at still other times *science* is used as an honorific. Some of our contributors study this latter phenomenon. Lerman's account of the association of skills and cognitive abilities and gender in technical education shows the privileging of certain practices over others, while Rossiter shows how the feminization of a discipline leads to its devaluation and loss of scientific status. The study of the constructedness of scientific authority is in a certain tension with the aim of showing that certain local practices count as science, when this presupposes that we know what science is. The real problem, as the essays by Lerman, Rossiter, and Harding together demonstrate, is to understand patterns of distribution of cognitive authority—that is, to make visible the power relations that undergird and facilitate persistence and change in those patterns.

This volume represents our belief that we as editors and our contributors as scholars from different disciplines are enabled by our common interests to address issues across disciplinary boundaries, to forge new relationships among feminists engaged in science studies, and to move gender studies into closer relationship with the established disciplines. The essays we have collected here are rich in suggestions, specific in their evidence, and grounded in the complex discussion of gender in late twentieth-century cultural and academic life.

BIBLIOGRAPHY

Abir-Am, Pnina G., and Dorinda Outram, eds. *Uneasy Careers and Intimate Lives: Women in Science, 1789–1979.* New Brunswick, N.J.: Rutgers University Press, 1987.

Ainley, Marianne Gosztonyi, ed. *Despite the Odds: Essays on Canadian Women and Science.* Montreal: Véhicule Press, 1990.

Bleier, Ruth. *Science and Gender: A Critique of Biology and Its Theories on Women.* New York: Pergamon Press, 1984.

———, ed. *Feminist Approaches to Science.* New York: Pergamon Press, 1986.

Brush, Stephen. "Women in Science and Engineering." *American Scientist,* 1991, *79:* 404–419.

Cadden, Joan. *Meanings of Sex Difference in the Middle Ages: Medicine, Science, and Culture.* Cambridge/New York: Cambridge University Press, 1993.

Cowan, Ruth Schwartz. *More Work for Mother: The Ironies of Household Technology from the Open Hearth to the Microwave.* New York: Basic Books, 1983.

Easlea, Brian. *Science and Sexual Oppression: Patriarchy's Confrontation with Woman and Nature.* London: Weidenfeld & Nicolson, 1981.

Fausto-Sterling, Anne. *Myths of Gender: Biological Theories about Women and Men.* New York: Basic Books, 1985.

Gender and Biology Study Group. "The Importance of Feminist Critique for Intracellular Biology." *Hypatia,* 1987, 2(3):61–76.

Hall, Diana Long. "Biology, Sex Hormones, and Sexism in the 1920s." *Philosophical Forum,* 1974, *5:*81–96.

Haraway, Donna. *Primate Visions: Gender, Race, and Nature in the World of Modern Science.* London: Routledge, 1989.

———. *Simians, Cyborgs, and Women: The Reinvention of Nature.* New York: Routledge, 1991.

Harding, Sandra. *The Science Question in Feminism.* Ithaca, N.Y.: Cornell University Press, 1986.

———. *Whose Science? Whose Knowledge? Thinking from Women's Lives.* Ithaca, N.Y.: Cornell University Press, 1991.

Harding, Sandra, and Merrill B. Hintikka, eds. *Discovering Reality: Feminist Perspectives on Epistemology, Metaphysics, Methodology, and Philosophy of Science.* Dordrecht/Boston: Reidel, 1983.

Herrnstein, Richard, and Charles Murray. *The Bell Curve: Intelligence and Class Structure in American Life.* New York: Free Press, 1994.

Holloway, Marguerite. "A Lab of Her Own." *Scientific American,* November 1993, 269:94–103.

Hubbard, Ruth. "Have Only Men Evolved?" Pages 7–36 in Ruth Hubbard, Mary Sue Henifin, and Barbara Fried, eds. *Women Look at Biology Looking at Women: A Collection of Feminist Critiques.* Cambridge: Schenkman, 1979.

Jordanova, Ludmilla. *Sexual Visions: Images of Gender in Science and Medicine between the Eighteenth and Twentieth Centuries.* Madison: University of Wisconsin Press, 1989.

Kass-Simon, G., and Patricia Farnes, eds. *Women of Science: Righting the Record.* Bloomington: Indiana University Press, 1990.

Keller, Evelyn Fox. *A Feeling for the Organism: The Life and Work of Barbara McClintock.* New York: W. H. Freeman, 1983.

———. *Refiguring Life: Metaphors of Twentieth-Century Biology.* New York: Columbia University Press, 1995.

———. *Reflections on Gender and Science.* New Haven, Conn.: Yale University Press, 1985.

———. *Secrets of Life, Secrets of Death: Essays on Language, Gender, and Science.* New York: Routledge, 1992.

Koblitz, Ann Hibner. *A Convergence of Lives: Sofia Kovalevskaia, Scientist, Writer, Revolutionary.* Revised ed. New Brunswick, N.J.: Rutgers University Press, 1993.

Kohlstedt, Sally Gregory. "Women in the History of Science: An Ambiguous Place." *Osiris,* 2nd Series, 1995, *10:*39–58.

LaFollette, Marcel. "Eyes on the Stars: Images of Women Scientists in Popular Magazines." *Science, Technology, and Human Values,* 1988, *13:*262–275.

Laslett, Barbara, Sally Gregory Kohlstedt, Helen Longino, and Evelynn Hammonds, eds. *Gender and Scientific Authority.* Chicago: University of Chicago Press, 1996.

LeVay, Simon. *The Sexual Brain.* Cambridge, Mass.: MIT Press, 1993.

Lloyd, Genevieve. *The Man of Reason: "Male" and "Female" in Western Philosophy.* Minneapolis: University of Minnesota Press, 1984.

Longino, Helen. *Science as Social Knowledge: Values and Objectivity in Scientific Inquiry.* Princeton, N.J.: Princeton University Press, 1990.

Longino, Helen, and Ruth Doell. "Body, Bias, and Behavior: A Comparative Analysis of Reasoning in Two Areas of Biological Science." *Signs: Journal of Women in Culture and Society,* 1983, *9:*206–227.

Martin, Jane R. "Science in a Different Style." *American Philosophical Quarterly,* 1988, *25:*129–140.

Mozans, H. J. *Woman in Science.* 1913. Cambridge, Mass.: MIT Press, 1974.

Merchant, Carolyn. "Clio's Consciousness Raised." *Isis,* 1982, *73:*398–409.

———. *The Death of Nature: Women, Ecology, and the Scientific Revolution.* San Francisco: Harper & Row, 1980.

———. *Earthcare: Women and the Environment.* New York: Routledge, 1996.

Nelson, Lynn Hankinson. *Who Knows: From Quine to Feminist Empiricism.* Philadelphia: Temple University Press, 1990.

Newman, Louise Michele, ed. *Men's Ideas/Women's Realities: Popular Science, 1870–1915.* New York: Pergamon Press, 1985.

Norwood, Vera. *Made from This Earth: American Women and Nature.* Chapel Hill: University of North Carolina Press, 1993.

Ogilvie, Marilyn Bailey. *Women in Science: Antiquity through the Nineteenth Century: A Biographical Dictionary with Annotated Bibliography.* Cambridge, Mass.: MIT Press, 1986.

Pycior, Helena M. "Reaping the Benefits of Collaboration While Avoiding Its Pitfalls: Marie Curie's Rise to Scientific Prominence." *Social Studies of Science,* 1993, *23:*301–323.

Pycior, Helena M., Nancy G. Slack, and Pnina G. Abir-Am, eds. *Creative Couples in the Sciences.* New Brunswick, N.J.: Rutgers University Press, 1996.

Rose, Hilary. "Hand, Brain, and Heart: A Feminist Epistemology for the Natural Sciences." *Signs: Journal of Women in Culture and Society,* 1983, 9:73–90.

Rosser, Sue. *Biology and Feminism: A Dynamic Interaction.* New York: Twayne, 1992.

Rossiter, Margaret W. *Women Scientists in America: Struggles and Strategies to 1940.* Baltimore: Johns Hopkins University Press, 1982.

———. *Women Scientists in America: Before Affirmative Action, 1940–1972.* Baltimore: Johns Hopkins University Press, 1995.

Russett, Cynthia Eagle. *Sexual Science: The Victorian Construction of Womanhood.* Cambridge, Mass.: Harvard University Press, 1989.

Schiebinger, Londa. *The Mind Has No Sex? Women in the Origins of Modern Science.* Cambridge, Mass.: Harvard University Press, 1989.

———. *Nature's Body: Gender in the Making of Modern Science.* Boston: Beacon Press, 1993.

Science, 13 March 1992, *255:*1363–1388; 16 April 1993, *260:*383–432.

Shteir, Ann B. *Cultivating Women, Cultivating Science: Flora's Daughters and Botany in England, 1760 to 1860.* Baltimore: Johns Hopkins University Press, 1996.

Traweek, Sharon. *Beamtimes and Lifetimes: The World of High Energy Physicists.* Cambridge, Mass.: Harvard University Press, 1988.

Tuana, Nancy, ed. *Feminism and Science.* Bloomington: Indiana University Press, 1989.

Weisbard, Phyllis Holman, and Rima D. Apple, eds. *The History of Women and Science, Health, and Technology: A Bibliographic Guide to the Professions and the Disciplines.* Second ed. Madison: University of Wisconsin System, Women's Studies Librarian, 1993.

Wylie, Alison. "Gender Theory and the Archaeological Record: Why Is There No Archaeology of Gender?" Pages 31–54 in Joan M. Gero and Margaret W. Conkey, eds. *Engendering Archaeology: Women and Prehistory.* Oxford: Blackwell, 1991.

Zuckerman, Harriet, Jonathan Cole, and John Bruer, eds. *The Outer Circle: Women in the Scientific Community.* New York: W. W. Norton, 1991.

Developmental Biology as a Feminist Cause?

By Evelyn Fox Keller*

THE SITUATION OF WOMEN IN SCIENCE—once a major concern for feminist scholars of virtually all stripes—has for some time now been seen by many feminist scholars in the United States, especially in the more theoretical literature, as a relatively low-priority issue. A number of reasons account for this shift, all of them directly or indirectly related to the dramatic increase in both numbers of and opportunities for women in American science over the last two decades. Such strides have led some to conclude that equity issues are no longer major problems for women in science (at least *qua* women). But whatever our assessment of the extent to which problems endure for women scientists, most would agree that, by any measure, race has now become a more conspicuously visible barrier of exclusion than gender. Furthermore, and perhaps more importantly, success itself has underscored and made visible certain tensions that have inhered from the start between the aims of women scientists and those of feminist theory. The most widely publicized tensions (and the ones most readily exploited by an antifeminist backlash) are twofold: the first centers on the widespread supposition among scientists (male and female alike) that feminist scholars of science advocate a "feminine" science, the second on the perception of hostility in the feminist literature to science itself. Both readings are, of course, misreadings of the bulk of the "gender and science" literature, but not of all of it. And while some women scientists may embrace the notion that, as women, they will or should do a different kind of science, most find such a proposition deeply threatening to both their identity and their prospects as scientists, that is, to all their hard-won gains. Indeed, the fear that such a notion will be used to discredit either them or their work seems at times to be so acute that any question about the role of gender in science is automatically regarded with suspicion and seen as likely to be counter to their interests as scientists. The perceived hostility—or, at the very least, lack of sympathy—of many feminist critics of science provides further grounds for the almost-unbridgeable gap that has now arisen. In turn, feminists are rightly frustrated by the misreading of their work, as well as by the unresponsiveness of women scientists to their larger agendas of both social and scientific change. Empowering a few women was never imagined to be sufficient for either the kind or the magnitude of change we had in mind.

The days when one might have expected the needs and goals of women and femi-

---

* Program in Science, Technology, and Society, MIT, Cambridge, Massachusetts 02139.

Figure 1. Christiane Nüsslein-Volhard.

nists to accord, as it were, naturally, or even when one might have spoken of the needs and goals of either "women" or "feminists" in a single breath, are long since gone. The great strength of feminist scholarship over the last decade has been the deepening of its understanding of what I might call the "situatedness" of gender. We have become exceedingly wary of sentences that begin "Women are . . . ," realizing that just about the only way one can complete such a sentence is to say that women are people, situated by many social variables, and both adaptive to and resourceful in the face of the pressures and opportunities they encounter. But if we have learned to spurn facile assumptions of commonality, we need, for the same reasons, also to spurn facile assumptions of opposition. I take our task in this volume of *Osiris* to be just that: to go beyond assumptions either of a natural commonality or of an entrenched opposition between women scientists and feminist analysts of science and to seek to situate the "women, gender, and science" question. To that end, I want to put the central question, What does "women in science" have to do with "gender and science"? to some of my own research on the history of developmental biology and, as a way of situating the question even more concretely, to the particular role of an especially pivotal figure in that recent history, Christiane Nüsslein-Volhard, the first (and only) woman named to the position of director of a Max Planck Institute (MPI) for biological research and, most recently, a recipient of the Nobel Prize in Physiology or Medicine.[1] (See Figure 1.)

---

[1] Nüsslein-Volhard shared the prize, awarded on 9 October 1995, with Eric Wieschaus and Edward B. Lewis.

DEVELOPMENTAL BIOLOGY

Developmental biology claims the interest of feminist historians of science on three different grounds: it is a field in which women have historically been relatively numerous, and in which a number of women today are leaders; in large part because of its intimate association with reproduction, traces of implicit and explicit gender coding can be found in the historical structuring of the field and hence can be used to illustrate more general arguments about the symbolic work of gender in the natural sciences; and the fundamental problem of developmental biology resists resolution in terms of "master molecules" and seems to require, instead, conceptual models of just the kind that contemporary feminists have shown partiality to—that is, models of complex interactivity. Let me take these three claims to our interest in order.

Women in Developmental Biology

Despite the undeniable gains realized by women in American science over the past two decades, for most women scientists real equity seems to be a long way off. The gains have been conspicuously uneven: more in some fields than in others, more in some parts of the country than in others, and more in some institutions than in others. For example, at MIT—in the 1970s a leader in this arena—progress has been minimal over the last decade, and in some disciplines (e.g., biology) the evidence points to a certain amount of backsliding. Indeed, the consensus emerging from a recently organized caucus of senior women scientists at MIT is that "nothing has changed," except perhaps the level at which the exclusivity of a "men's club" makes itself felt. It is a matter of considerable interest to these women, who feel beleaguered and discouraged, that there are some areas in which the promise of full gender equity actually appears as a realizable goal. Developmental biology is a prominent example. The marks of success are not simply to be found in numbers, although numbers do tell part of the story, but in the status and visibility of women and, perhaps above all, in their public display of a new kind of confidence. In some ways, the actual numbers are the most elusive measures. The history of women in developmental biology is to be found mostly in individual stories, in impressionistic accounts ("there have always been more women in developmental biology than in other fields, especially in certain areas—like mouse developmental biology"), and in a few woefully incomplete cumulative records. The inadequacy of cumulative records derives partly from the fact that counting women in particular disciplines is a relatively recent activity, partly from the fact that "developmental biology" as a disciplinary label is itself fairly recent (dating only from the 1960s and still not employed as a separate category by the National Research Council), and partly from the failure of such records as do exist to tell us much if anything about the actual position of the women in the discipline. Thus, while the official record does provide some corroboration of more impressionistic accounts, a more interesting story is to be gleaned from a finer-grained analysis of particular laboratories, publication records, and conference proceedings. It is here that the recent success of women in developmental biology is most clearly in evidence. Today, women head a significant number of the major laboratories in the field, and they make up over one-third of the membership of professional societies and almost as high a proportion of the presenters of papers at major conferences. Indeed, it is the intellectual space occupied by women in developmental biology today that has led to the subjective impression among some biologists that developmental biology is a field now "dominated" by women, though their numbers are still well under 50 percent of practitioners by any objective count. In my reading, what is responsible for such impressions is not simply the novelty of so many women in positions of authority but, perhaps more importantly, the ability of some of these women publicly to inhabit that authority—to present themselves with a kind of assurance and self-confidence that I, at least, have in the past seen only in male scientists. It is the newness of this confidence that, to me, puts into stark relief—far better than statistics can do—the toll that past (and, in most fields, enduring) obstacles have taken on those women scientists who have managed to survive.

The question of how developmental biology came to be such an exemplary model is of course an important one, and one that has yet to be adequately explored. But any attempt to answer this question must begin by situating the history of developmental biology in the larger context of the history of twentieth-century biology and, simultaneously, situating the history of women in that field in the larger history of women in American culture and, especially, the successes of second-wave feminism. Let me therefore turn to the history of developmental biology, a history that involves not only the question of "women in science" but also that of "gender in science."

A Brief History of Developmental Biology

One hundred years ago, biologists defined inheritance as subsuming concerns about transmission along with those about development. The central question of developmental biology (then called embryology)—How does an egg cell develop into an organism?—was also the central problem of biology. But with the rise of the American school of (Morganian) genetics in the 1920s, what had been a single subject became split into two rival fields, genetics and embryology. Throughout the 1930s the two disciplines ran neck-in-neck, but by the advent of World War II embryology began a decline from which it did not recover. Only in the last fifteen or twenty years has that subject, and its question, returned to center stage.

Relations between the two disciplines in the prewar period are neatly captured by a drawing by the Swiss embryologist Oscar Schotte that depicts two views of the cell: as seen by the geneticist, the cell is almost all nucleus; but as seen by the embryologist, the nucleus is barely visible. In this drawing, nucleus and cytoplasm are employed as tropes for the two disciplines—each lends to its object of study a size in direct proportion to its own view of its importance.[2] (See Figure 2.)

But to speak of the rivalry between two disciplines, troped here by two separate domains of the cell, suggests the possibility of (and need for) coexistence. Geneticists, however, had a program for colonizing the cytoplasm and, with it, the discipline of embryology. That program is captured in a metaphoric field that I have elsewhere described as the "discourse of gene action."[3]

---

[2] See Klaus Sander, "The Role of Genes in Ontogenesis," in *A History of Embryology: The Eighth Symposium of the British Society for Developmental Biology,* ed. T. J. Horder, J. A. Witkowski, and C. C. Wylie (Cambridge/New York: Cambridge Univ. Press, 1985), pp. 363–395.

[3] Evelyn Fox Keller, *Refiguring Life: Metaphors of Twentieth-Century Biology* (New York: Columbia Univ. Press, 1995). The notion of "gene action" is by now so much a part of our language that it must be considered a dead metaphor and, like many other conspicuously dead metaphors—e.g., "the first three minutes," "genetic program"—increasing in power as it declines in vitality (or visibility).

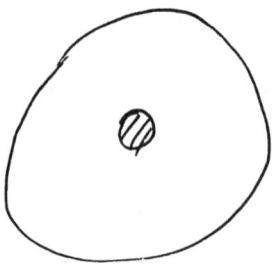 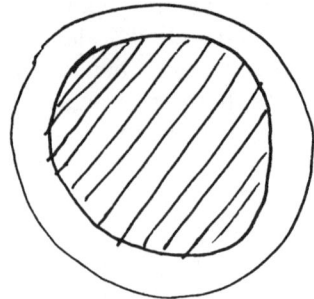

Figure 2. The cell in the view of the embryologist (left) and the geneticist (right); the nucleus is highlighted. Copied from a free rendering of a blackboard sketch by Oscar Schotte in the 1950s. (From Klaus Sander, "The Role of Genes in Ontogenesis" in A History of Embryology: The Eighth Symposium of the British Society for Developmental Biology, *ed. T. J. Horder, J. A. Witkowski, and C. C. Wylie [Cambridge/New York: Cambridge University Press, 1985], pp. 363–395, on p. 364.)*

By the discourse of gene action, I mean a way of talking about the role of genes in development, introduced in the 1920s and 1930s by the first generation of geneticists, that attributes to the gene a kind of omnipotence—not only causal primacy, but autonomy and, perhaps especially, agency. Development is controlled by the action of genes. Everything else in the cell is mere surplus. As H. J. Muller put it in 1926, "the great bulk . . . of the protoplasm was, after all, only a by-product of the action of the gene material; its 'function' (its survival-value) lies only in its fostering the genes, and the primary secrets common to all life lie further back, in the gene material itself."[4] The discourse of gene action actually evokes a Janus-faced picture of the gene in relation to the rest of the organism—part physicist's atom and part Platonic soul, at once fundamental building block and animating force. This way of talking not only enabled geneticists to get on with their work without worrying about what they did not know; it framed their questions and guided their choices, both of experiments worth doing and of organisms worth studying.

Nowhere is this more striking than in their reframing of the problems of embryology. Alfred H. Sturtevant, for one, was explicit. In 1932 he wrote: "One of the central problems of biology is that of differentiation—how does an egg develop into a complex many-celled organism? That is, of course, the traditional major problem of embryology; but it also appears in genetics in the form of the question, 'How do genes produce their effects?'" Between "the direct activity of a gene and the end product," he went on to argue, "is a chain of reaction." The task of the geneticist is to analyze these "chains of reaction into their individual links."[5]

This rephrasing of the embryologist's question guided research in developmental genetics for the next forty years. It encouraged the view that research on "gene

[4] H. J. Muller, "The Gene as the Basis of Life," in *Proceedings of the International Congress of Plant Sciences, Ithaca, New York, August 16–23, 1926* (Menasha, Wash.: Banta, 1929), pp. 897–921. The paper was presented to the Section of Genetics on 19 Aug. 1926.
[5] Alfred H. Sturtevant, "The Use of Mosaics in the Study of the Developmental Effects of Genes," *Proceedings of the Sixth International Congress of Genetics, Ithaca, New York, 1932* (Menasha, Wash.: Brooklyn Botanic Garden, 1932), pp. 304–307, on p. 304.

action" was primary, that developmental "chains of reaction" could be studied as well if not better in single-celled organisms as in higher organisms, and that cytoplasmic effects were at best of secondary interest—in Morgan's term, "indifferent." The phenomenal success of this research program, first in classical and, later, in molecular genetics, goes without saying. But it also had its costs—in the long eclipse not only of the discipline of embryology and its original problem, but also of a genre of experiments and even of organisms (the *Drosophila* embryo, e.g.). Over the last fifteen to twenty years, the problem of how an egg cell develops into an organism has returned to center stage. And with its return has come a change in discourse. As we have learned more about how genes actually work in complex organisms, talk about "gene action" has subtly transmuted into talk about "gene activation," with the locus of control shifting from genes themselves to the complex biochemical dynamics (protein–protein and protein–nucleic acid interactions) of cells in constant communication with each other. *Scientific American* glosses this shift as the "news" that "organisms control most of their genes."[6]

New metaphors abound. Fred Nijhout has even suggested that it would be better to think of genes "as suppliers of the material needs of development," as "passive sources of materials upon which a cell can draw."[7] His proposal may be extreme. But there is no question that a new way of talking is in the air, in keeping with the emergence of a new biology: molecular biologists seem to have "discovered the organism."

How did this happen? Certainly, the introduction of labeled antibodies and of new technologies for cloning and manipulating genes has been immensely significant, but this does not tell the whole story. Consider, for example, the work on maternal effect genes and cytoplasmic rescue in *Drosophila* begun in the early 1970s and later carried to such remarkable fruition by Christiane Nüsslein-Volhard and her colleagues. This work, establishing the critical role played by the cytoplasmic structure of the egg prior to fertilization, is widely regarded as pivotal in the recent renaissance of developmental biology. But it did not depend on new techniques. Indeed, Michael Ashburner writes that "it could have been done 40 years ago, had anyone had the idea.... All [it] required was some standard genetics, a mutagen, and a dissecting microscope, all available in the 30's."[8] So why had it not been done earlier? Ashburner says that no one had had the idea, but this is not quite right. Rather, I suggest, it was the motivation that had been missing. These experiments are immensely difficult and time consuming; one had to be confident that they were worth the effort. Or, to put it another way, there was no field in which the "idea" could have taken root. Earlier, the discourse of gene action had established a spatial map that had lent the cytoplasm effective invisibility and a temporal map that defined the moment of fertilization as origin, with no meaningful time preceding it. In this schema, there was neither time nor place in which to conceive of the egg's cytoplasm exerting *its* effects. Indeed, the preferred term for "maternal effects" was "delayed effects." As long as one believed that the genetic message of the zygote "produces"

---

[6] Tim Beardsley, "Smart Genes," *Scientific American*, Aug. 1991, pp. 87–95, on p. 91.
[7] H. F. Nijhout, "Metaphors and the Role of Genes in Development," *Bioessays*, 1990, *12*(9):441–446, on p. 441.
[8] Michael Ashburner, "Epilogue," in *The Development of* Drosophila melanogaster, ed. Michael Bate and A. M. Arias (Cold Spring Harbor, N.Y.: Cold Spring Harbor Laboratory Press, 1993), pp. 1493–1506, on p. 1499.

the organism, that the cytoplasm is merely a passive substrate, why would one go to all the trouble to investigate it? By the 1970s, however, the discourse of gene action had already begun to lose its hold. A number of different kinds of changes, above and beyond the obvious technical progress of molecular biology, contributed to its decline; here I will mention only three.

I have already referred to Oscar Schotte's invocation of the nucleus and cytoplasm as tropes for the disciplines of genetics and embryology. In his sketch, each discipline lends to its object of study a size reflecting not only its own view of its importance but also its self-attributions of agency, autonomy, and power. In addition, however, the nucleus and cytoplasm also came to stand as tropes for national importance, agency, and power; the former, as the domain in which American genetics had come to stake its unique strengths, was associated with American interests and prowess, and the latter with European and, especially, German interests and prowess. German biologists were often explicit about what they saw as the attempt by American geneticists to appropriate the entire field. In 1927, for example, V. Haecker described the field between genetics and development as the "no-man's land" of somatogenesis— "a border field which we have tilled for quite some time. . . . The Americans have taken no notice of this."[9] This tension persisted throughout the interwar years and was resolved only with the resounding defeat of Germany (and the virtual destruction of German biology) in World War II.

But the most conspicuous metaphoric reference of nucleus and cytoplasm is surely to be found in sexual reproduction. By tradition as well as by biological experience, at least until World War II, nucleus and cytoplasm are also tropes for male and female. Until the emergence of bacterial genetics in the mid 1940s, all research in genetics and embryology, both in Europe and in the United States, focused on organisms that pass through embryonic stages of development; and for these organisms, a persistent asymmetry is evident in male and female contributions to fertilization: the female gamete, the egg, is vastly larger than the male gamete, the sperm. The difference is the cytoplasm, deriving from the maternal parent (a no-man's land indeed); by contrast, the sperm cell is almost pure nucleus. It is thus hardly surprising to find that, in the conventional discourse about nucleus and cytoplasm, cytoplasm is routinely taken to be synonymous with egg. Furthermore—by an all-too-familiar twist of logic—the nucleus was often taken as a stand-in for sperm. Theodor Boveri, among others, argued the need to recognize at least some function for the cytoplasm on the grounds of "the absurdity of the idea that it would be possible to bring a sperm to develop by means of an artificial culture medium."[10] Many of the debates about the relative importance of nucleus and cytoplasm in inheritance thus inevitably reflect older debates about the relative importance (or activity) of maternal and paternal contributions to reproduction: activity and motive force were routinely attributed to the male contribution, while the female contribution was relegated to the role of providing a passive, facilitating environment. The egg is the body, the nucleus the activating soul.

But with the conclusion of World War II, the world began its irreversible slide

---

[9] V. Haecker, "Phänogenetisch gerichtete Bestrebungen in Amerika [Phenogenetic directed efforts in America]," *Z. Indukt. Abst. Vererb.*, 1926, *41*:232–238.

[10] Fritz Baltzer, *Theodor Boveri*, trans. Dorothea Rudnick (Berkeley: Univ. California Press, 1967), pp. 83–84.

out of modernism. The aftershocks of Hiroshima spread far and wide, transforming cultural landscapes along with political landscapes, the many spin-offs of the war (including, e.g., the computer) soon destabilizing the grounds of all the categories that had seemed so secure.

Change, of course, did not come overnight to biology. While embryology was no longer a thriving research enterprise after the war, the memory of that disciplinary struggle took time to abate. It also took time—roughly two decades—for German biology to rebuild. Finally, it took the women's movement to change our ideas about gender, and perhaps the hiatus occupied by bacterial genetics (where no one had to think about male and female contributions) for these changes to creep into biology. By the 1970s the entire world had changed, and so did what seemed natural ways to talk. Embryology was no longer a rival, Germany had become a friend, and gender equity was all the rage. And overlain on and interwoven with these "external" changes were, of course, the extraordinary developments internal to molecular biology, especially the techniques of recombinant DNA.

Many questions arise. For one: Did the change in discourse lead or follow our understanding of the complexity of regulatory dynamics? The answer is: Neither and both—they piggybacked off each other. The technical developments of molecular biology, working alongside and in interaction with changes in the way we talked and thought, soon effected dramatic changes in what we could know. The language and the science worked, as they always do, in concert and in mutual reinforcement.

But for us here, the central question is not about the relation between language and science, but about the relation between women and gender. What about the actual women in developmental biology? What, for example, about the fact that Nüsslein-Volhard, a major protagonist in this story, is a woman? And not only Nüsslein-Volhard. If one looks at the maternal effect mutants identified over the years, especially in the early years, one sees that more than half of them were identified by women. Why should this be so? Could it be that women are, after all, *naturally* drawn to the study of embryology? That they are *natural* allies of the egg? For the record, let me say clearly that I don't believe that women do have a *natural* affinity for embryology, *qua* women, any more than I believe that women have a *natural* affinity for nature.[11] Some women may be so drawn, but probably more as a consequence of the cultural insistence on equating women with reproduction, or with nature, and less because of their actual sex. But others will be propelled in just the opposite direction, in, as it were, natural rebellion against the coercion of cultural stereotypes. My guess is that the large number of women we see in developmental biology today has a lot to do with timing—that is, with the fact that the increase in the number of women entering biology coincided in time with the rise of developmental biology as a field. Some of it has to do with what I call the "Jewish violinist from Odessa" effect—that is, with the success of Christiane Nüsslein-Volhard and the women she trained. As to all the women who labored over the identification of maternal effect mutants in the earlier part of the century—well, as I've noted, that was hard, often back-breaking work, and widely assumed to be unrewarding. What more natural job to assign to women?

---

[11] Of course, some feminists (male and female) may be drawn to developmental biology by the apparent resonance between the demands of that subject and their own philosophical and political commitments to interactivity.

Situating Gender

By the time Nüsslein-Volhard enters the story in the 1970s, many changes had already begun. Let us, therefore, turn to the more specific case of Nüsslein-Volhard, and to the relevance of her particularly opportune disciplinary, national, and gender location. Nüsslein-Volhard stood at the intersection of multiple crossroads, able to make remarkably productive use of the ambiguities of her location in large part because of the timing of her intervention. The time was right for a molecular biologist to take on developmental problems, for a German biologist to win international acclaim, and for a woman scientist to make it big.

From her identity as a molecular biologist, Nüsslein-Volhard drew confidence, a kind of arrogance, and a cultural style. As a German, she had imbibed a tradition, shared by the French, of finding interest in complexity ("the more complicated the more interesting it was").[12] She cites Hans Driesch as an example. But for us, the most interesting point is her identity as a woman and her location at a moment in time when opportunities for women in science were just beginning to appear. And on all three axes of her fortuitous location, she has been simultaneously plagued and enabled by the ambivalences that location inevitably evoked. Here I will speak only of the ambivalence she displays toward gender issues and toward feminism.

To American women scientists, Nüsslein-Volhard is a heroine. Her role in their success is and has been significant in several ways: first, in the example she sets and, more substantively, in the women she has trained. Three of her first four postdocs were women, and at least two of them (Kathryn Anderson and Ruth Lehmann) have gone on to be leaders of the field.[13] Others who came later also owe a great debt to her mentorship (e.g., Leslie Stevens, Vivian Siegel, Helen Doyle, Mary Mullins), and even some senior women have found inspiration in her lab (e.g., Nancy Hopkins). Some of these might also note the generosity that accompanies her exacting demands or the unusually helpful and friendly atmosphere she has created in her lab (Nancy Hopkins, for one, says she has never seen another lab like it).[14] Also, because of the role her work has played in legitimizing (or in demanding) a more interactive framework, she might even qualify as a heroine among feminist analysts of science in the United States. But she is no heroine to German feminists. Those who know of her at all are more likely to see her as an enemy than as an ally. Her ambition, her phenomenal drive, her all-consuming investment in her research are anathema to a generation of feminist scientists in Germany who have become known for their

---

[12] Other differences in national style were also to her advantage; see Evelyn Fox Keller, "*Drosophila* Embryos as Transitional Objects," *Historical Studies in the Physical and Biological Sciences*, 1996, 26(2):313–346. The discussion that follows is taken from this essay. Unless otherwise attributed, quotations are taken from interviews I conducted with Nüsslein-Volhard in Tübingen in July 1994. I thank her for her patience and generosity.

[13] Of course, the work of Anderson and Lehmann has also contributed significantly to Nüsslein-Volhard's success. It could be said that all three were beneficiaries of an opportunity created by the much larger political and cultural transformation wrought by the contemporary women's movement. That transformation was responsible for the existence of a pool of talented young women scientists who, in the early 1980s, were just beginning their careers and were on the lookout for professional niches. It was also responsible for the existence of positions of responsibility in American universities when they were ready to move on.

[14] Nancy Hopkins, personal communication. Nüsslein-Volhard, for her own part, takes some pride in the particular way she runs her lab: "I am not afraid of admitting a distinct and perhaps more 'motherly' style, toward a more friendly, understanding, helpful, and familiar atmosphere in the lab." Christiane Nüsslein-Volhard to Evelyn Fox Keller, 6 Oct. 1995.

advocacy of a kinder, gentler, and more "relevant"—in a word, a "greener"—science. Fiercely opposed to genetic engineering, they see her as a member of the biotech establishment. And they complain bitterly of her intolerance of any interference with the scientific work brought about by family obligations of those in her lab. Even the day-care center she worked so hard to establish at the MPI for developmental biology in 1990 (one of the first in a scientific institute in what was then West Germany) meets with their disapproval because it is only partially subsidized by the Max Planck Society and the costs seem prohibitive to them.

In turn, Nüsslein-Volhard has her own complaints about women scientists in Germany: "They have such a hard time taking themselves seriously, being professional." "They so often give up because they don't want to work hard, they aren't really devoted to science.... They can't understand that one would just want to understand nature. It is not accepted here." Observing that, in the United States, there is now a real culture for women who "take themselves seriously," she notes that "here, it is still very lonely." And she thinks back to a time when it may have been different:

> Maybe there is some old tradition for professional women in Germany. If I think back to my grandmother, she had lots of women friends who were taken quite seriously—single women who did something. Or my teachers in school, they took us *very* seriously. I had an excellent education. I was at a school with only women, and we were taken very seriously.... I think up to when I was a post-doc in Basel, I didn't realize that it was a problem.

Of course, people always said that women had more trouble doing science than men, but "I didn't take it seriously. Why should I have more problems?"

Yet she did have problems, even if not in *doing* science. Her problems concerned recognition and finding a job. And she was exceedingly sensitive to the dangers (and at times the realities) of being overlooked. Nüsslein-Volhard may not have concerned herself with the politics around her, but she was well aware of the difficulties of women in the German academy and especially in science. Germany has consistently had one of the lowest percentages of women professors in all of Europe: as late as 1980, only 2.5 percent of professors were women, across all disciplines; and over the next decade, when the percentage of women professors was rising steeply in the United States, the numbers in Germany showed virtually no change. In biology, the situation looks especially discouraging: women account for over 50 percent of university graduates in biology, yet until Nüsslein-Volhard's appointment none had ever been made a director of a Max Planck Institute, and even today the number of women professors in biology is less than 3 percent of the total. Clearly, if she was really to "do" science, and not fall prey to the dismal statistics, she would have to do it exceedingly well. Still, to achieve her present stature, she needed more than determination and ability. Though she may have little use for feminists who want a kinder, gentler science, Nüsslein-Volhard has needed—and made good use of—that part of modern feminism that has fought so hard for equity and has even begun to have some impact on the German academy. In turn, her example has contributed enormously to such efforts both in Germany and in the United States.

But there is also another dimension to Nüsslein-Volhard's ambivalence toward feminism. If one's definition of feminism implies a primary loyalty to women, *qua* women, then Nüsslein-Volhard would seem not to be a feminist.[15] Quite simply, her ambition does not permit it. Nüsslein-Volhard is charming and personable, but she expects from others what she expects from herself and drives them just as hard. She is impatient with anything that interferes with the doing of "good science," be it slowness of temperament, domestic obligations, or the intrusion of personal problems, and complaints (from both sides) are legion. Blowups with women in her lab, especially in the early years, were common, and since then their numbers have tapered off. She says she would like to have more women in the lab but freely admits to difficulties with several who "did not work out." They have to be the right kind of women—like her, or like Kathryn Anderson or Ruth Lehmann. Or perhaps like her grandmother. Women with less drive and ability tend to be given short shrift.[16] Her relationship—or lack thereof—with Alice Bull, the woman who isolated the particular mutant, *bicaudal,* that gave Nüsslein-Volhard her start, is telling.

Alice Bull is, by temperament and by training, Nüsslein-Volhard's opposite. She had been a student of Donald Poulson (a *Drosophila* embryologist from the 1940s), and like many of Poulson's students, she had imbibed his passion for the *Drosophila* embryo along with his reticence about publishing. Furthermore, she came to maturity not at the height of modern feminism but, rather, at the lowest point in the century for women in American science, when opportunities were more restricted than at any other time before or since. Two letters—one from Ted Wright (another student of Poulson's), the other from Bull herself—tell a poignant story. When Wright received a copy of Nüsslein-Volhard's first manuscript on *bicaudal,* he wrote back: "I took the liberty of letting Alice Bull read your manuscript. She was, of course, extremely interested in your results and thinks you have done an excellent study. She is also quite envious, particularly since her heavy teaching load and responsibilities as chairman [sic] of the Biology Department at Hollins College has left her virtually no time to follow up her original observations." Two and a half months later, Bull wrote directly to thank Nüsslein-Volhard for sending her a reprint:

> I am very excited and pleased that you were able to increase the penetrance to the degree you achieved. Now the phenomenon can be really studied. Congratulations on your patience and the work.
> What are you planning to do next? . . . Next year I have a sabbatical leave from my teaching duties and so will have time for research. I should like to return to *bicaudal,* but do not wish to initiate any aspect of the study that you are already planning. So I shall appreciate learning what your plans are, and hope there may be a way we can collaborate on the next phases of the investigation. I am truly pleased you moved forward, recognizing the significance of this lucky mutant![17]

Alice Bull did come to Germany for her sabbatical (to Klaus Sander's lab) and paid a visit to Nüsslein-Volhard in Heidelberg, but a collaboration was not to be. By that time, Nüsslein-Volhard was in high gear, already embarked on the massive satura-

---

[15] This does not reveal a contradiction in Nüsslein-Volhard's personality or behavior so much as a tension that has inhered in the goals of feminism throughout this century. See, e.g., Nancy Cott, *The Grounding of Modern Feminism* (New Haven, Conn.: Yale Univ. Press, 1987).

[16] And so, of course, are men with less drive and ability. In this, Nüsslein-Volhard shows herself to be in full accord with the competitive mores of contemporary mainstream science.

[17] Ted Wright to Nüsslein-Volhard, 20 Sept. 1977; and Alice Bull to Nüsslein-Volhard, 4 Dec. 1977. Nüsslein-Volhard graciously permitted me to read through and photocopy the correspondence cited here during my visit in Tübingen in July 1994.

tion screen with her collaborator, Eric Wieschaus (now at Princeton). Bull was simply not in her league.

Finally, there is the matter of the consonance between Nüsslein-Volhard's intervention and the interactionist agenda of much recent feminist scholarship. Here we are dealing with gender neither as a biological nor even a social category,[18] but as what might be described as a cultural category—that is, with the cultural symbolic work of gender. In my discussion of the discourse of gene action, I argue that part of the strength of that discourse derived from the tacit association of nucleus (or gene) with sperm and of cytoplasm with egg, and I connect its decline (at least in the United States), in part, with both the changing valences of gender that were part of the cultural transformation wrought by the contemporary women's movement and the weakening of these gender associations enabled by two decades of biological focus on single-celled organisms.[19] Nüsslein-Volhard's work on the role of maternal effect mutants in disrupting the *anlagen* of the developing embryo was both facilitated by this shift and itself instrumental in restoring prominence to the informational content of the egg's cytoplasm in initiating gene activation. But once again, her ambivalence is in evidence. Although a focus on the informational content of the egg cell was explicit in her work from the start, much of her language conforms to this day to the framework of "gene action." By contrast, Kathryn Anderson, less ambivalently a feminist and someone who throughout her career made a point of studying only with women scientists, speaks unhesitatingly of her interest in "maternal control" (see, e.g., her 1989 paper entitled "*Drosophila:* The Maternal Contribution"); she even suggests this as a possible reason for the large number of women in the field.[20] Or note the article by Lynn Manseau and Trudi Schüpbach: "The Egg Came First, of Course!" Manseau and Shüpbach's title is, of course, a joke—but one that I doubt would be made by Nüsslein-Volhard.[21]

Perhaps it no longer matters. Once the linear narrative—beginning with fertilization and ending with maturity—is disrupted, as it now has been, it matters little where in the generational cycle one begins. The significant point is that the linear

[18] I use "social category" here to refer to the social roles of men and women.

[19] Keller, *Refiguring Life* (cit. n. 3). See also Scott Gilbert et al., "The Importance of Feminist Critique for Contemporary Cell Biology," *Hypatia*, 1988, *3*(1):61–76; and Gilbert, "Cellular Politics: Just, Goldschmidt, and the Attempts to Reconcile Embryology and Genetics," in *The American Development of Biology*, ed. Ronald Rainger, Keith R. Benson, and Jane Maienschein (Philadelphia: Univ. Pennsylvania Press, 1988), pp. 311–346.

[20] Kathryn Anderson, "*Drosophila:* The Maternal Contribution," in *Genes and Embryos*, ed. D. M. Glover and B. D. Harris (Oxford: Oxford Univ. Press, 1989), pp. 1–37; and conversation with Kathryn Anderson, 28 July 1992. Elsewhere I elaborate the reasons why I believe this is not a likely consideration for most women in contemporary developmental biology: Evelyn Fox Keller, "From Gender and Science to Language and Science" (Friday Night Lecture delivered at the Marine Biological Laboratory, Woods Hole, Mass., Aug. 1994). In brief, I argue that women biologists may have gravitated (or were relegated) to the study of development either because of the cultural equation of women and reproduction or simply because of the low status of that field. My own view is that the prominence of women in the field today has far more to do with the temporal coincidence of the increased number of women in biology and the resurgence of development as a promising area for research than with women's presumed interest in "maternal control."

[21] Lynn Manseau and Trudi Schüpbach, "The Egg Came First, of Course!" *Trends in Genetics*, 1989, *5*(12):400–405. At least, Nüsslein-Volhard would not make such a joke publicly. In private, however, she also speculates that there may be a special attraction for women in the very subject of development and embryos. Still, for her, as for virtually all the women developmental biologists I have spoken with, the most significant attraction by far is the presence of so many other women in the field and the sensation this brings of being a "wild-type": Nüsslein-Volhard to Keller, 9 Oct. 1995.

progression has been replaced by a circular one in which neither chicken nor egg can any longer be prioritized. And despite her extensive and multifaceted ambivalence, Nüsslein-Volhard was so placed in time and in both personal and cultural space that she was able to play a significant role in bringing this about.

Perhaps the real moral of Nüsslein-Volhard's story is to be found in her very ambivalence. She has not needed to be an unequivocal supporter either of feminism or of women in order to make an intervention of immense value to women in science, just as she does not need to be an explicit proponent of a new discourse in order for the work she has done to play a pivotal role in dislodging the discourse of gene action. Likewise, she has not needed to embrace feminist concerns in order to benefit from what such concerns might lead us to regard as victories. Gender matters to this story not because of her intent, but because of her situatedness, as a woman, in a field in which gender (now understood biologically, socially, *and* culturally) has mattered for a very long time, both for its practitioners and in the culture at large. Once again, gender matters for women in science not because of what they bring with their bodies, and often not even for what they may bring with their socialization, but for what the cultures of science bring to community perceptions of both women *and* gender—and, in turn, because of what such perceptions bring to community behavior.

Nüsslein-Volhard was an effective *bricoleur* in part because of the extent to which she was able to make opportune use of local alliances—for example, with those strains in feminism that accord with and those women who share her goals. Perhaps, as feminist analysts of science, we can learn to do the same. In developmental biology, and in Nüsslein-Volhard, we can find useful allies for some even if not all of our goals. Such strategic alliance may not be what some of us once hoped for, but it may be more realistic. Certainly it was, in this case at least, manifestly effective.

Gender and "Modern" Botany in Victorian England

By Ann B. Shteir*

DURING THE DECADES BETWEEN 1830 AND 1860, academic botanists, writers, and protoprofessionals in England worked to reshape popular and fashionable plant study into "botanical science." How, they asked, should botany be taught? Who were the ideal students of the new science? And what were the appropriate languages for this area of natural knowledge? These questions had resonance for different communities of interest, among them members of field clubs, fellows of the Linnean Society, popularizers, horticultural botanists, publishers of botanical and horticultural periodicals, adult students at mechanics' institutions, women plant collectors, and other devotees of Flora in her many forms. My study of women and botanical culture in England during the eighteenth and nineteenth centuries has shown me how essential it is to link research on the history of women and science with research on science and gender. The work of John Lindley—botany teacher, writer, and institutional power broker in early Victorian England—offers insights into how the march toward a "modernized" and "scientific" study of plants included strategies to defeminize botany. Gender, in fact, was integral to discipline formation in nineteenth-century botany. Through textual practices and other means, women and gender-tagged activities were placed into a botanical separate sphere, set apart from the mainstream of the budding science.

Botany was a popular and fashionable activity in eighteenth-century England. Part of Enlightenment science and of the taxonomic urge to collect and systematize nature in all its variety, botany enjoyed cultural cachet and social sanction as an activity that combined amusement and improvement. The simplicity of the Linnaean sexual system for naming and classifying plants according to the reproductive parts of flowers helped bring botany into prominence. During the later eighteenth century women had more culturally sanctioned access to botany than to any other science: they collected plants, drew them, studied them, and named them, taught their children about plants, and wrote popularizing books on botany. Botany came to be widely associated with women and was widely gender coded as feminine.

In the 1820s, however, new directions became apparent. A biography of Linnaeus that was published in 1827, for example, sought to correct representations of botany as a feminine activity and to make it palatable to boys. Sarah Waring's *A Sketch of the Life of Linnaeus,* a heroic biography about the influential Swedish botanist and his travels in Lapland, is written in the form of letters from a father to his son. The

---

* Graduate Programme in Women's Studies, York University, 4700 Keele Street, North York, Ontario M3J 1P3, Canada.

narrative focuses on a fifteen-year-old boy who considers botany to be "not a subject suited to . . . the stronger powers of [his] sex" and who is "rather prone to think lightly of women's pursuits, as unsuited to the dignity of the manly character." The boy is being guided toward medical training, and hence the father encourages him to learn about plants from his older sister, who lives at home and is "keenly alive to all the beauties of nature."[1] The father, brother, and sister in this narrative embody gendered features of botanical culture at that time. The sister's scientific engagement matches that of young women across late eighteenth- and early nineteenth-century England who read about various sciences in books and magazines and even received some formal science instruction in day schools. Their knowledge was situated and circumscribed, however, within gendered parameters. Thus, *A Sketch of the Life of Linnaeus* portrays a cultural field in which women give boys elementary training at home and then hand them over to men, who prepare them for adult responsibilities.

Waring produced her book during a time when a new social map of science was being drawn in England and new disciplinary boundaries of natural knowledge were being established. Specialist interest groups sprouted in London and the provinces; midcentury periodicals carried reports from subject-based groups including astronomical, chemical, entomological, geographical, geological, horticultural, statistical, and zoological societies. Practitioners, hobbyists, writers, and public lecturers all, in their various ways, reflected growing bifurcations in science culture between the generalist and the specialist, the popular and the academic, the "high" science of gentlemen in metropolitan learned societies and the "low" science of practitioners who diffused scientific knowledge for practical use. Activities within scientific culture that were associated with politeness and gentility were increasingly rejected, and utilitarian culture was on the ascendant.

In botany, a professionalizing trend took shape within the context of the Victorian romance of nature. David E. Allen has richly documented the world of Victorian naturalists, who went on excursions, gathered plants, studied specimens under microscopes, read journals and picture books, and attended gatherings of local naturalists' groups and the perambulating annual meetings of the British Association for the Advancement of Science.[2] An interest in plants and flowers satisfied diverse social, moral, religious, literary, and economic purposes. In the midst of industrializing England, enthusiasts indulged their taste for horticulture, floriculture, and botany. Albums of pressed flowers sat in breakfast rooms and drawing rooms, alongside cases filled with live and exotic specimens. Wax flowers, knitted flowers, paper flowers, and shell flowers, floral fabric and tile designs, and naturalistic wallpapers were part of the visual field. The Fern Craze of the 1840s–1860s, for example, blended aesthetics, science, and fashion. Enthusiasts, manifesting a particularly Victorian compulsiveness, collected ferns in the woods, bought tropical specimens from nurserymen, dried and pressed ferns, and made them a fundamental feature of the front parlor.

Among the friends of ferns and other flora during the first half of the nineteenth century, different communities of interest formed, diverged, and sometimes overlapped. Distinctions were being established between those with a more aesthetic,

---

[1] Sarah Waring, *A Sketch of the Life of Linnaeus* (1827), p. 6.
[2] See David E. Allen, *The Naturalist in Britain,* 2nd ed. (Princeton, N.J.: Princeton Univ. Press, 1994).

moral, and spiritual orientation to the study of nature and those with a more utilitarian or scientific approach. These approaches in turn shaped botanical education. Whereas some Victorians emphasized the social value and moral and spiritual benefits of botany, connecting it with general education and with natural theology, others shifted their focus to botany as a field for technical instruction. Hierarchies of value and authority emerged, such that the "botanist" was distinguished from the "botanophile," the "scientific Florist" from "the general reader," and "love of botany" from "love of flowers." During the years from 1830 to 1860, the direction of botanical culture, like that of scientific culture more generally, was toward stratification. The "strictly scientific" botanical community began to specialize. Tension between popularizing and professionalizing impulses in botany, along with tension about the gender identity of botany and botanists, is apparent in the work and writing of John Lindley, a central player in Victorian science culture. Lindley (1799–1865) was the first professor of botany at University College London, and he also served the (Royal) Horticultural Society in various administrative capacities for many decades. A ubiquitous and prodigiously energetic figure, he wrote voluminously about plants for audiences at various levels. Throughout his many areas of work, Lindley dedicated himself to putting botany on a new footing by cultivating interest in it as a science.[3] (See Figure 1.)

When Sir James Edward Smith, founder and president of the Linnean Society, died in 1828, an era in British botany came to an end. While many popular writers continued to rely upon the Linnaean sexual system as an accessible route to plant identification and arrangement, "scientific" botanists turned increasingly from taxonomy to physiology and morphology and from the Linnaean sexual system to the natural system of classification. The latter, promulgated by Continental botanists from Geneva and Paris, focused on morphological features of plants and natural affinities among plant groups. In the year of Smith's death, Lindley was appointed professor of botany at the new London university (established in 1826). He set out to depose the Linnaean system and establish the natural system in its place. Lindley clearly enunciated his chosen course for future work in plant science when, on Thursday, 30 April 1829, he delivered his inaugural lecture. He unequivocally declared that the science of botany should be about plant structure rather than identification and classification. Botany should move away from Linnaean ideas—he labeled them "stale," "static," and "superficial"—and should, instead, be studied according to the newer Continental mode.[4]

Lindley's advocacy of Continental botanical theories represented more than a botanist's decision about the shortcomings of a particular technical taxonomy. His call

---

[3] On John Lindley see Frederick Keeble, "John Lindley, 1799–1865," in *Makers of British Botany: A Collection of Biographies by Living Botanists*, ed. F. W. Oliver (Cambridge: Cambridge Univ. Press, 1913), pp. 164–177; and William T. Stearn, "John Lindley," in *Dictionary of Scientific Biography*, 18 vols. (New York: Scribners, 1970–1986), Vol. 8, pp. 371–373. Robert M. Hamilton has gathered and transcribed one thousand letters by John Lindley, many held in the Crease Collection of the British Columbia Archives and Records Service, Victoria, British Columbia. Available in photocopy, they provide an unparalleled resource for further work on a central figure in the history of modern science culture. See Robert M. Hamilton, *John Lindley (1799–1865), "Father of Modern Orchidology": A Gathering of His Correspondence Issued in Installments*, Pt. 1: *1818–36* (Orchid History Reference Papers, No. 17, 1994); Pt. 2: *1836–50* (Orchid History Reference Papers, No. 18, 1995); Pt. 3: *1819–65* (Orchid History Reference Papers, No. 19, 1996).

[4] John Lindley, *Introductory Lecture Delivered in the University of London on Thursday, April 30, 1829* (London: John Taylor, 1829).

Figure 1. Watercolor portrait of John Lindley by Charles Fox from 1834, the year of publication of Lindley's Ladies' Botany. *(British Columbia Archives & Records Service, PDP 45. Reproduced with permission of BCARS, Victoria, British Columbia.)*

for a new system also reflected the modernizing attitude of the self-styled "University of London." Founded to educate students excluded from Oxford and Cambridge on grounds of religion, wealth, or social class, it cultivated new styles of teaching and learning and appointed professors to teach subjects that had not been taught at other universities. Enlightened and secular reformers of the "Godless college," as the nondenominational university was called, represented all that was radical, secular, and commercial in imperial London. The founders and their supporters repudiated aristocratic ideals and polite knowledge, seeking instead, as Adrian Desmond put it, to "turn ... middle-class students into a professional elite, a new middle management." Lindley's botany, echoing the broader philosophy of the new university, also formed part of the agenda of those Victorian scientific naturalists, analyzed by Frank Turner, who opposed the Tory-Anglican alliance and wanted to define a new "man of science."[5]

Further, Lindley rejected Linnaean botany because of its social location in England as a polite activity and one widely gendered as feminine. In his inaugural lecture he declared his intention during the tenure of his professorship to "redeem one of the most interesting departments of Natural History from the obloquy which has become attached to it in this country." Lindley traced this "obloquy" to cultural connections between women and a class-marked culture of polite accomplishment: "It has been very much the fashion of late years, in this country, to undervalue the importance of this science, and to consider it an amusement for ladies rather than an occupation for the serious thoughts of man." Lindley stigmatizes the Linnaean system not only as polite knowledge but, particularly, as polite knowledge for women—"amusement for ladies." By contrast, he envisages a science of botany that would be worthy of the attention of "men of enlightened minds."[6] Lindley's chosen mission in his teaching and other botanical work became, therefore, to separate botany from the domains of politeness and accomplishment that for decades had linked botany, in his view, to women and to gentility. To this end, he delineated botany as utilitarian and dedicated himself to shaping a new kind of botanist who would be a scientific expert.

The exclusionary practices of self-defining elites are a powerful part of the history of women and science. John Lindley's distinction between botany as science and as polite accomplishment signaled a campaign in early Victorian England to defeminize the field by defining a scientific botany for middle-class men. His bifurcated identification of polite botany with women and botanical science with men illustrates the directions that botanical culture took during the succeeding decades. Recent studies have shown a similar pattern in the history of many disciplines at that time: these depict communities demarcating disciplinary practices, hiving off professional from amateur pursuits, distinguishing hierarchies of practice, and articulating appropriate levels of discourse.[7]

The gendered changes visible in institutional practices within Victorian botany also were evident in the textual practices and changing narratives of the time. The rich soil of Victorian culture nourished many discourses of nature. These included nature poetry and technical botanical nomenclature, and also the "language of flowers," a popular form of communicating emotions through emblematic and sentimentalized flower imagery. Within botanical print culture, periodicals, textbooks, and handbooks multiplied. Writers, editors, and publishers took cognizance of audiences with different levels of training, knowledge, and aspiration. For example, the *Phytologist: A Popular Botanical Miscellany,* a journal for field botanists, situated itself

---

[5] Adrian Desmond, *The Politics of Evolution: Morphology, Medicine, and Reform in Radical London* (Chicago: Univ. Chicago Press, 1989), pp. 26–27; and Frank Turner, "The Victorian Conflict between Science and Religion: A Professional Dimension," in *Contesting Cultural Authority: Essays in Victorian Intellectual Life* (Cambridge: Cambridge Univ. Press, 1993), pp. 171–200. For institutional features in the history of John Lindley's college see Negley Harte and John North, *The World of University College London, 1828–1978* (London: University College, 1978).

[6] Lindley, *Introductory Lecture* (cit. n. 4), pp. 17, 10.

[7] See the essays in Ellen Messer-Davidow, David R. Shumway, and David J. Sylvan, eds., *Knowledges: Historical and Critical Studies in Disciplinarity* (Charlottesville: Univ. Press Virginia, 1993).

between journals of "a general character" and "those of high scientific pretensions."[8] At the same time, though, that some science writers recognized the need to disseminate new topics and approaches to audiences eager for scientific knowledge, the demarcation of scientific botany from literary botany sharpened.

John Lindley was among many who both promoted science and also shaped representations of scientific fields and their practitioners. He wrote numerous books and presented many lectures for those not well versed in botany and disseminated new botanical knowledge to audiences with different levels of training and need. A contemporary wrote that he had "a happy knack of popularizing, and making clear the labour of others." At the same time, he set out in all his publications to delineate that which was appropriately botanical from that which, to his mind, did not accord with the "modern science of botany." Education was a central part of Lindley's project. During more than thirty years of teaching and writing he championed the natural system in lectures, books, periodical publications, and textbooks. His *School Botany* (1839), for example, explicated the natural method of classification—the "rudiments of Botanical Science"—for young men preparing for university entry. More detailed and comprehensive accounts were his *Introduction to Botany* (1832) and *Elements of Botany* (1841). He also wrote most of the articles on botany for the twenty-seven-volume *Penny Cyclopedia* (1833–1844), a project developed under the auspices of the radical Society for the Diffusion of Useful Knowledge. True to the anti-Linnaean theme of his inaugural lecture, the prospectus for one of Lindley's courses condemned almost all botanical books published before the nineteenth century and particularly requested students "not to furnish themselves with any introductory work by the late Sir James Edward Smith."[9]

A central feature in Lindley's cultural campaign to reconfigure the public profile of botany into a "serious" and utilitarian science was the erasure of links between botanical activities and polite accomplishment. Hence Lindley assiduously promoted botany as something different from "an amusement for ladies." Yet his efforts to modernize botany in this way did not mean that he excluded women as an audience. His *Ladies' Botany: or, A Familiar Introduction to the Study of the Natural System in Botany* (1834–1837) is a notable item on the roster of Lindley's writings, a two-volume elementary book about the "modern method of studying systematic Botany" for the "unscientific reader." *Ladies' Botany* is packed with information and material about the different "Tribes," or natural orders, of plants and is meant to be "an experiment upon the possibility of conveying strictly scientific knowledge in a simple and amusing form." Lindley explains in the preface that his aim was to do this "without sacrificing Science."[10] In an impressive display of visual instruction, lavish colored plates illustrate the more technical accounts.

Throughout his career as teacher, lecturer, and writer, Lindley worked to extend information about the new botanical systematics to new audiences, and *Ladies' Botany* indeed gives women readers of the early Victorian period access to serious,

---

[8] "Preface," *Phytologist*, 1841, *1*. See also Beverly Seaton, *The Language of Flowers: A History* (Charlottesville: Univ. Press Virginia, 1995).

[9] "The Late Dr. John Lindley, F.R.S., F.L.S.," *Journal of Botany*, 1865, *3*:338 ("happy knack of popularizing"); the proscription of Smith's writings is cited in William Gardner, "John Lindley," *Gardeners' Chronicle*, 1965, *158*:409.

[10] John Lindley, *Ladies' Botany: or, A Familiar Introduction to the Study of the Natural System in Botany*, 2 vols. (London: James Ridgeway, 1834–1837), Vol. 1, p. iii, Vol. 2, p. 2, and Vol. 1, p. v.

"scientific" botany. One reviewer commented that Lindley's book "must find its way into the library of every lady" and that it "will do more towards rendering the study of botany popular than any other which has appeared since botany became a science."[11] Lindley's text is more demanding and intellectually better informed than many of the introductory botany books for women written from the 1790s through his day.

Nonetheless, the genre and rhetoric of the book locate the woman reader in a botanical separate sphere. Lindley identifies the ideal audience for *Ladies' Botany* as those "who from their habits of life and their gentler feelings are the most sensible to the charms of nature," but who want to take their relationship to the vegetable world beyond "a vague sentiment of undefined admiration." He wants to teach women a language of flowers that differs from literary floral discourses of the 1830s. Lindley is quite specific about his preferred languages of nature. He writes:

> The power and wisdom of the Deity are proclaimed by no part of the Creation in more impressive language than by the humblest weed that we tread beneath our feet; but we must learn to understand the mysterious language in which we are addressed; and we find its symbols in the curious structure, and the wondrous fitness of all the minute parts of which a plant consists, for the several uses they are destined for. This, and this only, is the "language of flowers."[12]

Ladies' Botany did not aim to prepare women for contributing to new taxonomies based in plant morphology or undertaking research in plant physiology or microscopy. At a time when he was diligently working to shape botany as a modern science, Lindley represents female readers not as students themselves but as those who will be teaching their "little people." Gender and genre came together in Lindley's choice of the format for this elementary text. *Ladies' Botany* is organized as fifty letters to a mother who wants to teach her children about plants. By the 1830s the epistolary form had been used for decades to popularize science for women, children, and general readers. Most notably, Jean-Jacques Rousseau had used this format in the 1760s in his *Lettres élémentaires sur la botanique,* intended to teach a female friend about botany; Thomas Martyn translated and enlarged Rousseau's work for English audiences in the much-reprinted *Letters on the Elements of Botany* (1785). These works represent the female recipient of the letters as a mother attentive to the educational development of her children.

Botany became a discipline in part by means of books and disciplinary treatises that created representations of the field and demarcated types of activities. In a study of patriarchy and the sociology of professions, Anne Witz has identified demarcation strategies of professional closure through which boundaries were historically created and controlled in occupations such as medicine and nursing. These turn, she explains, "not upon the exclusion, but upon the encirclement of women within a related but distinct sphere of competence in an occupational division of labour."[13] Witz's findings have general application to the history of botanical science and help us understand John Lindley's textual and institutional strategies in the

---

[11] [John Claudius Loudon], *Gardener's Magazine,* 1834, 52:390. Indeed, *Ladies' Botany* was reprinted six times through 1865, and a German edition—*Botanik für Damen*—appeared in 1849.
[12] Lindley, *Ladies' Botany* (cit. n. 10), Vol. 2, pp. 2, 4–5.
[13] Anne Witz, *Professions and Patriarchy* (London: Routledge, 1992), p. 47.

professionalizing botanical culture of his day. During the 1830s Lindley endeavored through his writing to establish botany as a science rather than as an activity he stigmatized as "polite" and "feminine." While such reconfiguring is not necessarily antiwoman, the contrast between botany as "an amusement for ladies" and as "an occupation for the serious thoughts of man" narrowed the space for female botanists, whatever their social class. During the period from 1830 to 1860, botany was increasingly shaped as a science for men, and the "botanist" became a standardized male individual. In *Ladies' Botany* Lindley joined the cadre of botanical writers who addressed a female audience while also constructing an ideal reader for popular botany books. Committed to a view of the field as serious and specialized, Lindley defeminized botany. His elementary botany book positions the woman reader as informed but as engaged in science in a place apart from mainstream and increasingly professionalized pursuits.

In an earlier generation, during the period from 1760 to 1830, the gendered shape of botanical culture had given women access to botany as well as some discursive authority. Priscilla Wakefield's *Introduction to Botany* (1796), for example, was a basic textbook for two generations of readers. One of many popular science books written by and for women, it is an epistolary account that situates botany as an improving home-based activity shared between sisters and as part of valued family routines. The book embodies an Enlightenment approach to the moral and intellectual value of natural knowledge. It is a family-centered volume that teaches more than botanical systematics and that takes science education for young women seriously.[14] Such women-centered science books often invest mothers with substantial intellectual authority as teachers and knowers.

But whereas the gendered shape of botanical culture gave women access to botany during this earlier period, the same gendering was inverted after 1830 so as to restrict access to an increasingly "scientific" botanical practice. Women elbowed in, but then were elbowed out. The defeminized direction of botanical culture in turn shaped social practices for women in early and mid-Victorian botany. It shaped what they learned, how they practiced science, what they wrote, and how they positioned themselves in relation to audiences. While botanical brothers completed medical studies and established a place in the public world, sisters were at home, perhaps corresponding with clergymen-naturalists, perhaps engaging in botany as a "rational recreation," perhaps venturing a bit more deeply into plant physiology—or, having married and become mothers themselves, teaching botany to their children. The vocabularies of early and mid-nineteenth-century gender ideology shaped their scientific practices, and thus their botany was for the most part located in the breakfast room rather than the scientific society.

Mary Kirby's story nicely illustrates the convergence of social and textual practices in the professionalization of botany. Mary Kirby (1817–1893), working jointly with her sister Elizabeth Kirby, wrote many botany and natural history books for children and general readers during the 1840s to 1860s. From a prosperous Midlands manufacturing family, Kirby grew up interested in reading about science and attending science lectures. In her autobiography she recalled that as a young woman

---

[14] For excerpts from Priscilla Wakefield's *An Introduction to Botany* see Ann B. Shteir, "'The Pleasing Objects of Our Present Researches': Women in Botany," in *Women and History: Voices of Early Modern England,* ed. Valerie Frith (Toronto: Coach House, 1995), pp. 145–163.

she was already "deep in the study of botany": "ransacking" the beach during a family seaside holiday in Ramsgate, "searching for flowers and grasses and such like, in every hole and corner," and pressing plants under her mattress. Her first writing project was to compile and edit *The Flora of Leicestershire* (1850), a handbook that classified over nine hundred flowering plants and ferns in the county of Leicestershire according to the orders of the natural system and supplied details about habitats and localities. When their father died, Mary and Elizabeth Kirby wanted to take on tasks to ensure their future well-being and "soon began to plot and plan for book-writing." Publication of *The Flora of Leicestershire* did not lead Mary Kirby into a career as a writer of other field guides or mainstream technical botany books, however. Instead, identifying work compatible with conventions of gender and class in their day, Mary and Elizabeth Kirby fashioned themselves into a professional writing team that produced more than twenty books for young people, including many titles on botany and natural history.[15]

Family circumstances helped to shape Mary Kirby's career as a popular writer, but her story has wider resonance for women in botanical culture during the 1850s. After *The Flora of Leicestershire* was published, she received an "agreeable" letter from Sir William Jackson Hooker and noted "the sympathy [Hooker] expressed when any local effort was made to interest the public in the study of plants, or to make that study popular." As director of the Royal Botanic Gardens, Kew, Hooker contributed to the development of public, scientific, educational, and recreational botany in many ways.[16] His kindness and support were outweighed by other attitudes at that time, however. A professionalizing botanical science, embodied by John Lindley, did not make Mary Kirby feel welcome.

In a telling anecdote, Mary Kirby recalled spending a day with John Lindley in 1857, seven years after the publication of her *Flora of Leicestershire*. They met socially in Norwich, where Lindley and his wife and children had taken a summer house. Mary and Elizabeth Kirby had recently finished writing *Plants of the Land and Water*, a book for young readers that blends botanical information and "curious facts" about the uses of plants in different parts of the world. Mary Kirby recorded the meeting in her autobiography: "it was well for us [that] we had [completed our project], for the great doctor's influence was not calculated to encourage any work, except like his own, of the most scientific kind." The weather was inclement, and the party was forced to play indoor games. No botanical conversations developed. There was not, she reports, "much sympathy. . . . I suppose there was no 'elective affinity' between the great doctor and ourselves; for we felt constrained, and not at our ease in his presence."[17]

Mary Kirby's nonconversation with John Lindley illustrates a gulf that had opened in Victorian science culture by the 1850s between specialists and generalists, between academics and popularizing writers, between those who considered themselves "scientific" and those who were marginalized as "more literary." The gulfs in discourses of nature became gulfs in access and scientific practice. Certainly, gendered institutional and textual practices combined to shape the social, personal, and

---

[15] Mary Kirby, *"Leaflets from My Life": A Narrative Autobiography* (London: Simpkin & Marshall, 1887), pp. 40, 70.

[16] *Ibid.*, p. 148. On Sir William Jackson Hooker and nineteenth-century botany see Ray Desmond, *Kew: The History of the Royal Botanic Gardens* (London: Harvill, 1995), Chs. 10–13, esp. p. 222.

[17] Kirby, *"Leaflets from My Life,"* pp. 146–148.

professional practices of Mary Kirby, a Victorian woman in science. There were thresholds she chose not to attempt to cross. Within the gendered circumstances of her day, Kirby made pragmatic choices. Since the path toward botanical science was becoming increasingly professional, she took the less complicated, more welcoming, and also more lucrative path for women in Victorian science culture by becoming a popular science writer, joining the company of Anne Pratt, Margaret Gatty, Jane Loudon, Elizabeth Twining, and other productive authors of popular books about botany and other sciences for women, children, general readers, and the working classes.[18]

In later decades of the nineteenth century, when distinctions in science culture sharpened, many women took part in amateur and popular botany as leisure activities, collecting and drawing plants and bringing plant study into the family circle. At the same time, the scientific education of girls became a higher national and social priority. Some women studied for university-level local examinations and sought to step into the culture of specialized botany. In her essay "On the Study of Science by Women" (1869), the suffrage leader Lydia Becker asserted the importance of girls' science education. She opposed single-sex schools for girls and argued "on the principle of equality" that women should have access to coeducational laboratories and lecture halls. In the contestatory voice of a mid-Victorian feminist, Becker opposed any form of "botany for ladies." Her argument was based on her belief—at once theoretical and pragmatic—that recognition of any separate sphere hindered women's full intellectual development. Lydia Becker was herself an enthusiastic botanist, the author of *Botany for Novices* (1864), but she resisted in her work and her science writing any institutional or rhetorical model that represented women as different from, or complementary to, men. During the 1830s, John Lindley had worked to reconfigure a feminized botany into a modernized discipline for male experts. By the 1860s, this style of science had become normative, and Lydia Becker accepted and promoted a defeminized botany as a desideratum in her own scientific work and for women more generally.[19]

---

[18] See Ann B. Shteir, *Cultivating Women, Cultivating Science: Flora's Daughters and Botany in England, 1760 to 1860* (Baltimore: Johns Hopkins Univ. Press, 1996), Ch. 8.

[19] On Lydia Becker's botany see *ibid.*, pp. 227–231; and Ann B. Shteir, "Elegant Recreations? Configuring Science Writing for Women," in *Victorian Science in Context,* ed. Bernard Lightman (Chicago: Univ. Chicago Press, 1997).

The Uses of Useful Knowledge
Science, Technology, and Social Boundaries in an Industrializing City

By Nina E. Lerman*

IN 1824, IN PHILADELPHIA, PENNSYLVANIA, the newly formed Franklin Institute for the Promotion of Science and the Useful Arts held its first annual Exhibition of Manufactures. The managers awarded premiums for the most admirable objects on display and commended many others. At this and subsequent annual exhibitions, silver medals were awarded for products ranging from white lead to red earthenware, from iron ore made only with anthracite coal to silk spun only in Pennsylvania. At the first exhibition, the Pennsylvania Institution for the Deaf and Dumb was awarded two separate silver medals: one for a specimen of coarse cotton fabric, and one for a braided grass bonnet. The grass bonnet made by a Mrs. Hopkins of Lancaster and the split straw hats produced in two other Philadelphia schools were also commended. Thus the "perfection of workmanship" the managers sought to encourage was of many different types, and some of the "workmen" were women or even—as the managers phrased it in reference to residents of the Roman Catholic Orphan Asylum—"infant artizans."[1]

At first glance, "science and the useful arts" might appear to parallel the familiar late twentieth-century phrase "science and technology." Yet the range of products and processes included under the nineteenth-century rubric of "useful knowledge"—needlework as well as metalwork, spinning as well as mining—contrasts sharply with the late twentieth-century connotations of the term "technology." Although the Franklin Institute's carefully assembled "cabinet" of minerals bears little resemblance to modern laboratories and instruments, the cabinets and collections of nineteenth-century science are familiar to readers of *Osiris*. Straw bonnet making, on the other hand—a manufacture to which the Franklin Institute managers devoted substantial attention in their 1825 annual report—may seem to many readers a more surprising inclusion under the rubric of "technology."

This article has two tasks. First, as a historian of technology among scholars studying science, I find I add yet another dimension to an already interdisciplinary conversation. Before I can describe my own research and its bearing on "women, gender, and science," some background on approaches to "women, gender, and technology" is in order. Second, I turn to my own historical work on urban

---

* Department of History, Whitman College, Walla Walla, Washington 99362.
[1] "Report of Exhibition," *First Annual Report of the Franklin Institute* (1825), pp. 65–66, 86–88; and *Franklin Journal and American Mechanics' Magazine*, 1826, 1:2–5, 1826, 2:264.

industrialization and social boundaries. This study focuses on technical education, in which knowledge commonly labeled both "scientific" and "technological" is transmitted to children. Making comparisons within and among institutions offering such technical education raises questions not only of access to and ideas about various kinds of technological knowledge, but also about the role of *science* as a badge of white, male, middle-class identity, a badge of—in the language of the introduction to this volume of *Osiris*—both social and cognitive authority. This article explores programs offered in a single city in two periods: in the 1820s, when Philadelphia institutions from the Franklin Institute to the House of Refuge for juvenile delinquents sought new ways of preparing youths for productive adulthood in the early industrial city; and in the 1880s, by which time professional educators in the city's public schools had taken the task as their own. A brief tour of Philadelphia at midcentury highlights themes and provides transition between the two discussions.

WOMEN, GENDER, TECHNOLOGY, AND SCIENCE

Unlike women scientists, women technologists are ubiquitous. Scholars studying women, gender, and technology have long since pointed out that the task of writing a more complete history of technology begins simply with taking seriously the broad emphasis on "making and doing" set forth in the early postwar explorations of the field.[2] "Making and doing things" readily includes straw bonnet making; it includes both women's work and artisanal manufactures; it includes the tools of the Stone Age and the machines of the Space Age. By scholarly rather than popular definition, then, technology is not limited to a study of men, of machinery, or of Western cultures. On the contrary, if technology in the modern West has come to be defined as

---

[2] For an introductory tour of work on women, gender, and technology see Ruth Schwartz Cowan, "The 'Industrial Revolution' in the Home: Household Technology and Social Change in the Twentieth Century," *Technology and Culture,* 1976, *17*:1–24; Cowan, "From Virginia Dare to Virginia Slims: Women and Technology in American Life," *ibid.,* 1979, *20*:51–63; Joan Rothschild, ed., *Machina ex Dea: Feminist Perspectives on Technology* (New York: Pergamon, 1983); Judith McGaw, "Women and the History of American Technology," *Signs: Journal of Women in Culture and Society,* 1982, *7*:47–77; McGaw, "No Passive Victims, No Separate Spheres: A Feminist Perspective on Technology's History," in *In Context: History and the History of Technology,* ed. Stephen Cutcliffe and Robert Post (Bethlehem, Pa.: Lehigh Univ. Press, 1989), pp. 172–191; Judith Wajcman, *Feminism Confronts Technology* (State College: Pennsylvania State Univ. Press, 1991); and Cynthia Cockburn and Susan Ormrod, *Gender and Technology in the Making* (London: Sage, 1993). For more recent historical work and a bibliographical essay see Nina Lerman, Arwen Mohun, and Ruth Oldenziel, eds., *Gender and Technology,* Technol. Cult. (special issue), 1997, *38*(1) (hereafter cited as **Lerman et al., eds., Gender and Technology**). For a survey of similar arguments in archaeology see Alison Wylie's essay in this volume.

In the first volume of *Technology and Culture* (1959), Mel Kranzberg defined "technology" as "how things are commonly done or made" and "what things are done and made"; see Melvin Kranzberg, "At the Start," *Technol. Cult.,* 1959, *1*:1–10, on pp. 8–9. He was building on the work of Charles Singer and others. Brooke Hindle used the phrase "means of making and doing things" in his essay "The Exhilaration of Early American Technology" (1966), rpt. *Early American Technology: Making and Doing Things from the Colonial Era to 1850,* ed. McGaw (Chapel Hill: Univ. North Carolina Press, 1994), pp. 40–67. For a more recent discussion and a range of scholarship see the introduction and essays in McGaw's volume and Lerman et al., eds., *Gender and Technology.* Finally, it is important to note that according to this definition "engineering" is *part of* but not *synonymous with* "technology."

a masculine pursuit, then that association itself must become an object of study rather than an initial premise.[3]

Engineering offers ready parallels to science. Engineering, however, is only a small (albeit important) part of human technological activity. While the study of women in professional engineering closely parallels the study of women as professional scientists, the study of women constructing and repairing clothing or processing raw materials into a family dinner, like the study of carpentry and iron puddling, raises somewhat different questions.[4] In addition to the issue of how women fared in a male domain, the fundamental questions are about how gender boundaries have been drawn and redrawn across a truly enormous terrain. The examination of relationships between gender and knowledge becomes even more complex with the inclusion of technological knowledge, for by most accounts sewing and carpentry demand a different kind of knowledge than biology and physics. In addition, the knowledge involved in sewing and carpentry is, if anything, more embedded in its particular social context than is the fairly elite work of science. Indeed, many who study gender and technology are convinced that a full understanding of either gender or technology in the modern West demands analysis of the reciprocal relationships between them. Such relationships remain underexplored.[5]

---

[3] Compare the feminist broadening of "medicine" into "healing" as a means to consider women's activities and gender boundaries. For the importance of masculinity in studies of technology see Ruth Oldenziel, "Gender and the Meanings of Technology: Engineering in the U.S., 1880–1945" (Ph.D. diss., Yale Univ., 1992); Carroll Pursell, "Masculinity and the History of Technology," *Polhem,* 1993, *11*:206–219; McGaw, "No Passive Victims, No Separate Spheres"; and the bibliographic essay in Lerman *et al.,* eds., *Gender and Technology.* On European views of technology and other cultures see Michael Adas, *Machines as the Measure of Men: Science, Technology, and Ideologies of Western Dominance* (Ithaca, N.Y.: Cornell Univ. Press, 1989).

[4] Nineteenth-century educators recognized the latter comparisons clearly enough when they discussed school needlework in committees on "industrial arts." More recently, scholars studying technology and gender, recognizing that preparing food and making clothing have been labeled activities of consumption (or reproduction) rather than production and manufacture, have called for more detailed study of all aspects of what Ruth Schwartz Cowan has called "the consumption junction." See Ruth Schwartz Cowan, "The Consumption Junction: A Proposal for Research Strategies in the Sociology of Technology," in *The Social Construction of Technological Systems,* ed. Wiebe Bijker, Thomas P. Hughes, and Trevor Pinch (Cambridge, Mass.: MIT Press, 1987); see also the bibliographic essay and articles in Lerman *et al.,* eds., *Gender and Technology.* Manual training and industrial arts for girls and boys are discussed later in this essay.

[5] See Lerman *et al.,* eds., *Gender and Technology.* A feminist philosophy of technology has, as far as I know, yet to be developed—as does a sophisticated epistemology of sewing or carpentry. In my work I define the term "technological knowledge" broadly, so it includes both "skill" and "technical expertise." Following cognitive scientists such as Howard Gardner, I assume that technological knowledge involves a range of cognitive activities—what Gardner calls "intelligences." See the introduction to Howard Gardner, *Frames of Mind: The Theory of Multiple Intelligences* (New York: Basic, 1985). See also the introduction to Nina Lerman, "From 'Useful Knowledge' to 'Habits of Industry': Gender, Race, and Class in Nineteenth-Century Technical Education" (Ph.D. diss., Univ. Pennsylvania, 1993). This definition of technological knowledge includes the knowledge of users as well as that of designers. Technological knowledge has traditionally been examined in relation to scientific knowledge. Engineering knowledge, in particular, has received much attention. While there is a growing awareness of the place of "craft" in this discussion—noted as a newly emergent theme as early as 1985, in Staudenmaier's survey of the field—on the whole technological knowledge has been treated quite narrowly in the history of technology literature. See John Staudenmaier, S.J., *Technology's Storytellers: Reweaving the Human Fabric* (Cambridge, Mass.: MIT Press, 1985); Edwin Layton, "Mirror-Image Twins," *Technol. Cult.,* 1971, *12*:562–580; Layton, "Technology as Knowledge," *ibid.,* 1974, *15*:31–41; and Layton, "Through the Looking Glass, or News from Lake Mirror-Image," in *In Context,* ed. Cutcliffe and Post (cit. n. 2), pp. 29–41. See also George Wise, "Science and Technology," in *Historical Writing on American Science: Perspectives and Prospects,*

Even so, to anyone familiar with Western industrial gender systems it will hardly be surprising that in the 1820s plaiting straw to make hats was technological knowledge provided to women and girls, even when encouraged by local patricians, or that the Franklin Institute managers did not teach bonnetmaking to their sons and apprentices. The larger issue, and the one I want to address here, is about the changing meanings of terms like "science," "technology," and "useful knowledge," the changing meanings of particular kinds of useful knowledge, and the ways such meanings have interacted with social categories such as gender, race, and class (the meanings of which have also changed). As scholars studying gender have suggested, this kind of exploration demands attention to boundaries and to "others": to science versus not-science; to technology versus art, or craft, or nurture; to engineering "knowledge" versus artisanal "skill."

In this essay I will argue that, historically, theoretical and abstract approaches to making and doing things—including mathematics, science, quantification, drafting, and design—came to be treated in opposition to more specific kinds of artisanal knowledge and also to be associated with maleness, with whiteness, and with middle-class upward mobility. "Science" became a label to appropriate, as well as a knowledge to possess. Social and cognitive authority, in other words, reciprocally bolster each other. And if technologies called "scientific" have been associated with social categories connoting (and possessing) power, then ideas about technological knowledge will tell us something about the social, political, and cultural uses to which science has been put in American society.

As already suggested, I explore these questions by making comparisons between and among nineteenth-century institutions providing technical education to children. Education as a locus of study allows examination of the relationships between social structures and ideologies, on the one hand, and knowledge and ideas about that knowledge, on the other. Institutional reports provide extensive justifications for diverse types of education, as well as evidence of real programs providing access to some kind of training and credentials for real people, varying by time and place. Whether the knowledge acquired or the credential bestowed is the more valuable result, educational institutions have long existed both for what goes on inside them and for their differentiation of those who do and do not attend. Studying the education of children in a broad range of institutions provides a view of technological and scientific knowledge across boundaries of gender, race, and class.

The following discussion is drawn from a larger study of technical education in the city of Philadelphia in the nineteenth century. The present article does not pretend to a complete analysis of any one period or institution; rather, in highlighting the uses of science in technical education in different periods in the nineteenth century, it aims to sketch shifting ideas about technological knowledge, in particular about the kinds of knowledge associated with, and opposed to, science.

---

ed. Sally Gregory Kohlstedt and Margaret Rossiter (Baltimore: Johns Hopkins Univ. Press, 1985), pp. 229–246. The best recent accounts also focus on engineering knowledge: see Eugene Ferguson, *Engineering in the Mind's Eye* (Cambridge, Mass.: MIT Press, 1992); and Walter Vincenti, *What Engineers Know and How They Know It: Analytical Studies from Aeronautical History* (Baltimore: Johns Hopkins Univ. Press, 1990). Several promising avenues treat shopwork: Steven Lubar, "Representation and Power," *Technol. Cult.*, 1991, *36*(Suppl.):S54–S74 (this is a revised version of "Representing Technological Knowledge" [paper presented at SHOT Critical Problems Conference, session entitled "Knowing, Thinking, and Doing," Madison, Wisconsin, 1991]); and Robert Gordon, "Who Turned the Mechanical Ideal into Mechanical Reality?" *ibid.*, 1988, *29*:744–778.

"RAISED BY THEIR TALENTS": ARTISANAL KNOWLEDGE AND THE NEW MOBILITY

In the 1820s, even in a growing urban center like Philadelphia, artisanal work could still provide a path to respectable "independence": a man might not live in luxury, but he could call himself master and make his own way in the world. At the same time, however, some Philadelphians were constructing a new middle-class identity increasingly dissociated from craft work; in the industrializing city, new notions of upward mobility meant distance from workshop activities. Mobility was always possible in the young republic—especially in the eyes of those who sponsored educational and charitable institutions—but it was meted out in appropriate doses: children who might have been dependent on society could be rendered productive adults if they learned a trade; artisans might in turn become proprietors or go into business.[6] Both independence and mobility, of course, were perceived as male provinces—a woman's status was presumed to be defined by her father or husband. As a result, the rhetoric and usually the content of technical education for males and females, for middling and lower sorts, differed markedly. This section returns to the Franklin Institute and introduces the Walnut Street Charity School, run by the Philadelphia Society for the Establishment and Support of Charity Schools, and the Philadelphia House of Refuge, a reform school for juvenile delinquents.

The Act of Incorporation of the Franklin Institute for the Promotion of Science and the Useful Arts declared that its goals would be furthered "by the establishment of popular lectures on the sciences connected with them, by the formation of a cabinet of models and minerals, and a library, by offering premiums on all objects deemed worthy of encouragement, by examining all new inventions submitted to them, and by such other measures as they may judge expedient." Its members were to be drawn from "manufacturers, artizans, and persons friendly to the mechanic arts." While the managers formed the Franklin Institute at least partly on the model of mechanics' institutes such as those in New York and Glasgow, they soon developed loftier visions: in addition to the "volunteer" lectures in which members might present information of use to other members, they would establish professorships and a permanent course of lectures in each of four fields: natural philosophy, chemistry and mineralogy, architecture and civil engineering, and mechanics. Beginning in 1824, the institute sponsored the annual Exhibition of Manufactures; in 1826 it began publishing the *Franklin Journal,* which soon became heavily technical and scientific in its content. After some dispute with the U.S. Patent Office the institute also gained access to new patent records and disseminated news of inventions. In 1826, as well, the managers added a High School Department, for the purpose of extending to "citizens in moderate circumstances, the same advantages of education which are

---

[6] For extensive discussion of nineteenth-century middle-class definition see Stuart Blumin, *Emergence of the Middle Class: Social Experience in the American City, 1760–1900* (Cambridge: Cambridge Univ. Press, 1989); on business see also Patricia Cline Cohen, *A Calculating People: The Spread of Numeracy in Early America* (Chicago: Univ. Chicago Press, 1982). On artisans and proprietors see George Escol Sellers, *Engineering Reminiscences, 1815–1840,* ed. Eugene Ferguson (Washington, D.C.: Smithsonian Institution Press, 1965); Anthony Wallace, *Rockdale: The Growth of an American Village in the Industrial Revolution* (New York: Knopf, 1982); and Sean Wilentz, *Chants Democratic: New York City and the Rise of the American Working Class, 1788–1850* (Oxford: Oxford Univ. Press, 1984). For discussion of the educational and charitable community see Alan M. Zachary, "Social Thought in the Philadelphia Leadership Community, 1800–1840" (Ph.D. diss., Northwestern Univ., 1974).

now almost exclusively enjoyed by the children of the rich."[7] The Franklin Institute fashioned itself into, and remained for some years, the premier technical and scientific institution of the United States. It is worth noting that, although "ladies" were admitted to the lecture series and women submitted items for display at the annual exhibitions, most of the activity at the Franklin Institute took place in an entirely male environment.

Technical education for youth began with their admission to the lecture series planned for their elders. There were, initially, some problems with this approach: by the spring of 1827, the end of their second full season, the lectures were well attended, "but as they proceeded, much inconvenience was experienced from the indecorous conduct of a considerable number of boys, whose only object in attending must have been amusement, as many of them were wholly disinclined" to pay attention. Some of the senior members stopped coming, and over the next several years the managers issued a series of rules and restrictions. Eventually they resorted to that time-honored method of insuring students' attentiveness: the professors would quiz the youths before each lecture on the content of the previous one. "Thus," they reported, "an honourable emulation is excited among them, and instead of a place of amusement, the hall of the Institute has become to them what it should be, a place of instruction."[8]

Meanwhile, a far less problematic group had been included in the lecture audience: by late 1827 the managers had issued ladies' tickets at $2 per season. In London and Glasgow the practice had "been found to produce all the good consequences anticipated from such a measure; affording to those who are our earliest and most influential instructors, a mass of useful information, through the pleasing medium of rational amusement; whilst their presence stimulates to exertion, and tends to the promotion of order and decorum during the hours of the meeting."[9] Several notable differences from the treatment of members and boys emerge. "Amusement" was acceptable for females, but not for males; and whereas artisans would be improved *as artisans* by learning science, ladies learning science would help improve the men, by raising sons well prepared for further instruction and by promoting decorum in

---

[7] Franklin Institute, *First Annual Report* (1825) (cit. n. 1), pp. 7, 8; and *Address of the Committee of Instruction of the Franklin Institute of Pennsylvania, on the Subject of a High School Department to Be Attached to That Institution* [Philadelphia, March? 1826], p. 2. This text is hereafter cited as **Franklin Institute,** *Address* **(Mar.? 1826)**. (There were two similarly titled addresses printed that year; the Library Company of Philadelphia catalogues them as "March?" and "September?" respectively [see also note 12, below].) The founding and development of the Franklin Institute are ably recounted in Bruce Sinclair, *Philadelphia's Philosopher Mechanics: A History of the Franklin Institute, 1824–1865* (Baltimore: Johns Hopkins Univ. Press, 1974).

[8] Members were invited to purchase tickets for their sons and apprentices at $1 each for the season: *Franklin J.*, 1826, *1*:131. Membership cost $5 per year; the drawing school cost $5 for a ten-week term of two classes each week. Tuition in the drawing school included admission to the lectures. Thus, a member wishing to send his son or apprentice to drawing school had to have $10 he could spare. Weavers, in this period, might have made $5 per week if they were lucky enough to have more than a normal week's worth of work and ambitious enough to put in extra hours. Not surprisingly, of the more than five hundred men listed on the 1825 membership list, there was only one weaver; two made shoes, four were tailors, and eighty were merchants. The preponderance were more prosperous artisans and manufacturers of the sort one might call small businessmen. See Franklin Institute, *First Annual Report* (1825); and Sinclair, *Philadelphia's Philosopher Mechanics*. On wages see Philip Scranton, *Proprietary Capitalism: The Textile Manufacture at Philadelphia, 1800–1885* (Cambridge: Cambridge Univ. Press, 1983), pp. 123–124. For details of problems with boys in lectures see *Franklin J.*, 1828, *5*:74, 1829, *7*:76.

[9] *Franklin J.*, 1827, *4*:331.

the lecture hall. The lectures provided technical education at different levels for different groups: elevation for mechanics, instruction for youth, rational amusement for ladies.

During these early years some of the managers had concluded that lectures better suited adults than young people. Already they had established evening classes in mathematics and mechanical drawing, open to adults and youth, but these were deemed insufficient. The managers decided that only a High School Department would fill the need they saw and set about designing a course of study "such as is universally selected by the enlightened parent, whose wealth enables him to make a choice for his son."[10]

The rhetoric announcing the new school borrowed from a republican emphasis on opportunity:

> In this country, where permanent distinctions of rank are inconsistent with the spirit of our republican institutions, it is impossible to tell from the situation of the parent, what may be the destiny of the child. The system of education to be adopted, ought not, therefore, to presuppose that the pupils are to be necessarily mechanics or manufacturers, or that even if they are, their prospects in future life are to be confined within the walls of their workshops.

Accordingly, none of the courses offered was specifically vocational. The three-year curriculum included both "practical" education and preparation for college. In the view of the committee, this meant one to three years of writing, grammar, declamations, composition, rhetoric; ancient and modern geography and history, mythology, political economy, the constitutions of the United States and of Pennsylvania; arithmetic, algebra, geometry, trigonometry, surveying, mensuration; linear drawing, drawing in perspective; bookkeeping, stenography; natural philosophy, mechanics, chemistry, astronomy, natural history; and Greek, Latin, French, and Spanish. Only the best students would complete all of the offerings on schedule. Others would either take fewer courses or stay in school longer.[11]

In their high school, the managers at the Franklin Institute intended to offer opportunity at a modest price—tuition of $28 per year included "fuel," pens, ink, and slate pencils but not the required books and stationery—but such opportunity as might very well lead a boy out of his mechanic father's workshop. While the institute intended to encourage artisanal production generally, the content of its educational activities became increasingly removed from artisanal know-how. The technological knowledge offered to artisans was intended to "improve" them, but at the same time the message was clear that an improved artisan would no longer roll up his sleeves and work in a workshop. Improved artisans, including several influential members of the institute, were increasingly likely to be manufacturers, masters of an enterprise larger than a traditional shop.[12] This trend also meant that the artisanal men who worked in such shops, for wages, became increasingly unlikely to spare either

---

[10] Franklin Institute, *Address* (Mar.? 1826), p. 20.
[11] *Ibid.*, pp. 2 (quotation), 3–4.
[12] On the expenses covered by tuition see *Address of the Committee of Instruction of the Franklin Institute of Pennsylvania, on the Subject of a High School Department to Be Attached to That Institution* [Philadelphia, September? 1826], pp. 5–6. See Blumin, *Emergence of the Middle Class* (cit. n. 6), for discussion of occupational titles and status. Such an "improved" manufacturer would have to know the workings of his business, but that knowledge would not have been gained in school.

cash or the earning power of their sons for the pursuit of languages and natural philosophy.

Another view of education and upward mobility is offered by the Walnut Street School, established by the Philadelphia Society for the Establishment and Support of Charity Schools (PSESCS). Begun in 1799 as the Philadelphia Society for the Instruction of Indigent Boys, the society had at first run a weekly evening school and then, two years later, a day school. By the 1810s, at least some members of the society were avid supporters of the Lancasterian or monitorial movement, in which older students helped teach younger ones (allowing one teacher to handle a hundred or more students). Originally a system designed to provide cheap education to hordes of poor children, it was often justified, in the United States, as a democratic practice; the Franklin Institute's high school used a modified version of the system. The PSESCS managers explained: "All the children of a village or neighborhood may meet together on the same footing, be disciplined by the same rules, inspired by the same emulation, influenced by the same motives, impressed with the same moral sentiments, and be fitted for life on an equality that no other system affords." By 1817 the society was providing Lancasterian education for nearly seven hundred children in several schools.[13]

The standard school subjects in both England and the United States included reading, writing, arithmetic, and, for girls, needlework. The needlework was by and large such as a girl might need to maintain a household: plain sewing, marking, and knitting were basic domestic knowledge (if also sometimes a means of livelihood when no other source of income was available). Such needlework had long been a feature of girls' schooling, although in charity schools it stopped short of the usual schoolgirl's sampler.[14] Teaching schoolgirls to make straw bonnets, however, which a number of Philadelphia schools did in the 1820s, was an innovation prompted by a different philosophy.

Bonnetmaking was introduced on the girls' side of the Walnut Street School in 1823, in addition to the reading, writing, arithmetic, and sewing already taught. Not all girls participated; it seems to have been optional, and it cut down on time in other classes. The annual report for that year explains that the managers believed that bonnetmaking "would prove useful, as it would afford the pupils an opportunity of becoming acquainted with a business, by the aid of which, they would be enabled to provide for themselves a comfortable livelihood, and, perhaps, eventually introduce among the poorer classes of our population, an additional means of support, and

---

[13] *Manual of the System of Teaching Reading, Writing, Arithmetic, and Needlework, in the Elementary Schools of the British and Foreign School Society,* 1st American ed. (Philadelphia: Printed for the Philadelphia Society for the Establishment and Support of Charity Schools, 1817), pp. v–xi. In the annual reports of the PSESCS from the 1820s, the managers repeatedly emphasize the humbleness and quietness of their work, which was "not such as to excite applause; for its effects, though certain and of extensive influence, are produced silently and without display": Philadelphia Society for the Establishment and Support of Charity Schools, *Annual Report* [for 1828] (hereafter cited as **PSESCS,** *Annual Report* **[year]**). At least some of the managers were members of the Society of Friends (Quakers).

[14] Details on the charity school needlework curriculum are provided by the *Manual of the System.* Samplers, embroidered with flowers and verses in silk on linen, demonstrated a girl's mastery of her needle but also indicated that her family had some time and money to spare. See Betty Ring, *"Let Virtue Be a Guide to Thee": Needlework in the Education of Rhode Island Women, 1730–1830* (Providence: Rhode Island Historical Society, 1983).

thereby, considerably diminish the public burdens."[15] The managers, who referred to "pupils" but taught bonnetmaking, like sewing, only to girls, seemed not to know that members of poor families were likely already to be working at any tasks that paid or that spare time among the women of the "poorer classes" was a rare commodity indeed.

New plans for the Boys' Department followed a different approach. The same annual report described the managers' intentions to offer boys "the higher branches of an English education." The board had already restricted admission in the boys' school to those who knew how to read, but even so the teacher was still too busy to extend the curriculum much. The board believed that in a nation "where men are raised by their talents and virtuous actions, to the highest stations, it is an object of primary importance, that every child should partake of learning." They believed it was their duty not to permit the parent's poverty to be a "barrier" to the child, and they expected that students from the school could grow up to be "respectable citizens" given the chance.[16]

These innovations—bonnetmaking on the one hand and "higher branches" on the other—suggest a certain ambivalence on the part of the managers, which they not coincidentally manifested in strongly gendered terms. On the boys' side, teaching higher branches might produce "respectable citizens"; while on the girls' side, a new knowledge "among the poorer classes" might "diminish the public burdens." That the 1820s was a time of flux and contrasts is evident in several of the era's institutions—bonnetmaking was as paradoxical (and as short lived) as the Franklin Institute's monitorial high school teaching Greek, Latin, bookkeeping, and drawing—and that the "public burdens" should be gendered female is not inconsistent with the nature of nineteenth-century charity. But evidence from these two institutions makes clear the emergence of middle-class ideas linking mobility, assumed to be a male prerogative, with education, business, and science. Mobility was also increasingly disengaged from direct participation in artisanal production. Specific artisanal skills were appropriate for some but seemed to offer restricted opportunity rather than hope that the possessors might rise to the "highest stations." This new male middle-class knowledge, however, was distinguished from its female counterpart either by the uses to which it would be put or by outright denial: when women were granted access, it was for the good of their sons; but more often their education was simply limited. In this same period, according to Patricia Cline Cohen, arguments about women's education began to declare females incapable of learning mathematics, rather than simply assuming they did not need it.[17] The same managers who wanted to offer "higher branches" to boys advocated bonnets in preference to books for girls.

If the Walnut Street managers shared rhetoric with those of the Franklin Institute when they discussed "respectable citizens," their discussions of the "poorer classes" had more in common with reports from the Philadelphia House of Refuge. At that

---

[15] PSESCS, *Annual Report* [for 1823], p. 7. Bonnetmaking continued for several years; then sales fell off, and by 1830 it had disappeared from the curriculum. See subsequent annual reports.

[16] *Ibid.,* pp. 5–7.

[17] See Cohen, *Calculating People* (cit. n. 6), for discussion of attitudes about females and arithmetic in the early nineteenth century. On women's education see also Linda Kerber, *Women of the Republic: Intellect and Ideology in Revolutionary America* (Chapel Hill: Univ. North Carolina Press, 1980).

institution, a "home" for "juvenile delinquents" to which boys under twenty-one years of age and girls under eighteen could be committed by law or parent, provision for learning trades (for boys) and housewifery (for girls) was made to ensure the pupils' ability to participate appropriately in life beyond the institution. The refuge housed youths who would otherwise live on the streets, in the almshouse, or in prison.

Refuge managers intended to provide an environment in which potential criminals could learn to be productive and upstanding citizens. In this context, technical education had several purposes: in addition to providing a livelihood, education and employment were fundamental to the establishment of moral rectitude. As the managers put it, "Idleness is the parent of vice. The mind no less than material nature abhors a vacuw [sic]. If not furnished with useful reflections, it will dwell upon those which are pernicious. Hence the House of Refuge will be a place of never ceasing occupation, to every inhabitant." Most of that occupation would be some form of "Manual Labor," and at the House of Refuge, unlike in prison, the inmates would acquire knowledge of a trade. They would also receive basic schooling before and after a full day of work. As soon as they were sufficiently reformed, the children would be bound out as apprentices, a traditional practice grounded in British and colonial poor law. Children committed to the House of Refuge would be under its jurisdiction until they reached majority—age eighteen for girls, twenty-one for boys—sentenced to a wholesome environment throughout their childhood.[18]

The technical education at the House of Refuge, as opposed to the reading, writing, and ciphering of the schoolroom, was not of the formal classroom type found at the Franklin Institute or the Walnut Street School. Rather, it was conducted on the traditional model of apprenticeship, in which a child acquired skills as he or she assisted with the tasks of the workshop or household. The annual report for 1829 told its readers that the boys were engaged in bookbinding, basketmaking, wickerwork, shoemaking, tailoring, and carpenters' work. The girls performed sewing, washing, ironing, mending, cooking, and general housework. By May 1830 the managers could proclaim that all the clothing worn by the pupils was made within the house.[19]

Finding the right work for the boys was tricky enough that at several points there were more boys at the House of Refuge than jobs, and then even older boys ended up with simple tasks like picking oakum. In contrast, there was no difficulty employing the girls: they did all the housework for the institution.[20] For boys, the

---

[18] House of Refuge, *Address to the Citizens . . .* (Philadelphia, 1826), pp. 9–12.

[19] House of Refuge, *Annual Report* [for 1829] (Philadelphia, 1830); and House of Refuge, *Annual Report* [for 1830] (Philadelphia, 1831) (these reports will be cited hereafter as **House of Refuge, *Annual Report* [year]**).

[20] For the older boys, when there was work the assignments were taken seriously. In several cases a boy was reassigned because he was disinclined toward a particular kind of work. See House of Refuge, Minutes of Visiting Committee (HR-A201), 10 Jan., 18 Mar., 18 Sept., 3 Nov. 1829; and House of Refuge, Superintendent's Daily Log (HR-B-1), 7 Jan., 17 Mar. 1829. These documents are at the Historical Society of Pennsylvania, Philadelphia, in the House of Refuge/Glen Mills School collection; I thank C. D. Ferrainola of the Glen Mills School, Concordville, Pennsylvania, for permission to use and quote from these materials. The managers attended to the housework only rarely, as when the Visiting Committee ordered that "the steward will request the matron to put aside all work which is not absolutely necessary, until a sufficient number of shirts can be made to satisfy each boy with two per week, and each boy with an apron": House of Refuge, Minutes of Visiting Committee (HR-A201), 21 Apr. 1929.

schoolroom hours were the ones more consistently filled. Regular schooling for the girls, however, was evidently not the highest priority: the house had been open five months before the girls' schooling was rescheduled around the demands of housework. At that point the superintendent noted an improvement—twenty-two of twenty-five resident girls attended school that day.[21] The records do not indicate how few had attended before.

Thus, ideally, the successful boy committed to the refuge would acquire a rudimentary education and workshop-based craft knowledge and go out into the world as a respectable artisan. The successful girl would get married, having acquired the knowledge needed to run her own household. Of course, the refuge girls were also prepared to work in other people's households. The process of making dependent boys independent included, by definition, basic schoolroom education. Lower-class girls, never expected to achieve early nineteenth-century "independence" anyway, could make do without schooling if housework intervened.

Comparing the lots of the boys in the various institutions, we can see a hierarchy of technological knowledge assigned according to social hierarchies: artisanal knowledge might make better citizens of the poorest classes, but artisans themselves should learn scientific theory, mechanical drawing, and business techniques if they wanted to improve themselves. For girls, the ubiquitous emphasis on the indispensable tasks of housewifery masks a set of distinctions based on presumed family status—without the rhetoric of mobility. Science might well be appropriate "rational amusement" for those women whose sons or husbands needed science. Craft knowledge such as bonnetmaking would better fill the ostensible leisure time of poorer women. Although the respectable artisan still had his place in the social and technological hierarchies of the 1820s, as he did in the manufacturing enterprises of the urban economy, already science was becoming "useful knowledge" not only for its application to manufactures, but also as a badge of distinction for the emerging middle class and for a new kind of middle-class manhood in a new industrial order.

"TRAINED TO BUSINESS": SCIENCE, DOMESTICITY, AND MANUAL LABOR

By midcentury, amidst the tumult of a rapidly growing city, the social and technological order had in many ways stabilized. The shift from artisanal toward industrial production was reflected in an emphasis on "habits of industry" and a new respectability of wage work as a means, for men, of making a living. The respectability of men's white-collar work was also well established, and boys trained for the new middle class learned mathematics, science, and linear and perspective drawing. A generation earlier, working for another man could never have provided "independence," but now dependence had been limited to those who received charity, to those who pursued the service occupations, and to wives and daughters. Adult

---

[21] On the rescheduling of girls' schooling see House of Refuge, Minutes of Visiting Committee (HR-A201), 22 and 26 May 1829; and House of Refuge, Superintendent's Daily Log (HR-B-1), 26 May 1829. The boys' schoolwork was scheduled before breakfast and after supper. On the girls' improved attendance see House of Refuge, Minutes of Visiting Committee (HR-A201), 2 June 1829; and House of Refuge, Superintendent's Daily Log (HR-B-1), 19 June 1829. Related comments on schooling appear in House of Refuge, Minutes of Visiting Committee (HR-A201), 3 Apr., 22 May 1829.

independence, redefined, remained a central goal for educators of white boys of any economic background.

Ideas about race as well as class and gender were by midcentury entwined with ideas about appropriate work and economic status in the programs and reports of educational institutions. The House of Refuge, for example, opened a new Colored Department in 1850. Within the institution, technical education was gender appropriate and therefore similar on either side of the stone wall separating the races. Girls learned housewifery, and boys performed simple tasks like caning chairs. When children were apprenticed out after a year or two of reform, however, racial differences became more salient. Many boys of both races were apprenticed to farmers, and boys from the White Department were apprenticed to craftsmen such as carpenters and shoemakers. Nonfarming boys from the Colored Department were apprenticed to barbers or waiters. In this sense colored boys shared much with the girls: colored or white, a girl successfully apprenticed to "housewifery" was viewed as a "valuable servant."[22]

While all white boys in these institutions were trained for independence, they were certainly not trained in identical ways. Boys from the Girard College for Orphans—white, born in the United States, and never classed as "delinquent"—were rarely apprenticed to shoemakers, but most likely to printers or druggists. Where boys at the refuge had had a few hours of schooling before and after work, the most advanced portion of the Girard curriculum included geometry, algebra, trigonometry, natural philosophy, history, geography, grammar, French, Spanish, writing, bookkeeping, and architectural, mechanical, and perspective drawing.[23] Girard boys were educated for upward mobility, not unlike the "desirable young men to be trained to business" graduating with diplomas from Philadelphia's Central High School.[24]

The opposition of science and labor becomes even clearer when one reads the arguments about adding a workshop for the boys at Girard. By the end of the 1850s, some managers claimed that a workshop would produce healthy, well-rounded boys and would enhance their attractiveness in the apprenticeship market. To other directors, however, a workshop sounded suspiciously like manual labor and was therefore to be avoided. It took some years before the managers resolved the problem by hiring, in 1863, a "Professor of Industrial Science including Polytechnics." The curriculum mixed study of physics, chemistry, and anatomy with "applied mechanics" and "applied chemistry." The president of the board of directors reported that year that

---

[22] For apprenticeship data see, e.g., House of Refuge, *Annual Report* [for 1854] (Philadelphia, 1855), pp. 19, 52, and other annual reports from the 1850s. Excerpts of letters from masters were often printed in the annual reports. On servitude see also Faye E. Dudden, *Serving Women* (Middletown, Conn.: Wesleyan Univ. Press, 1983). For extensive discussion of the transitional period at midcentury see Nina Lerman, "'Preparing for the Duties and Practical Business of Life': Technological Knowledge and Social Structure in Mid-Nineteenth-Century Philadelphia," in *Gender and Technology*, ed. Lerman et al.

[23] Apprenticeships for 1854 are listed in Louis Romano, *Manual and Industrial Education at Girard College, 1831–1965: An Era in American Educational Experimentation* (New York: Arno, 1980), App. G, pp. 337–340; for the Girard curriculum see p. 94 n. 26.

[24] Philadelphia Board of Public Education, *Annual Report* [for 1850] (hereafter cited as **Board of Public Education, Annual Report [year]**), p. 118, quoted in David Labaree, *The Making of an American High School: The Credentials Market and the Central High School of Philadelphia, 1838–1939* (New Haven, Conn.: Yale Univ. Press, 1988), p. 20.

"those, therefore, who predicted that Girard College was to be leveled down to a manual-labor school have been mistaken." Even this solution proved short lived; within three years both president and professor were gone, and the issue remained inconclusively resolved until the early 1880s.[25]

Wage work for women raised its own complex issues. By the 1850s paid work outside the home was part of the economic life of a growing number of women, although they were generally excluded both from clerking activities and from learning the precise forms of industrial drawing, like drafting. Women taught the vast majority of Philadelphia's students and worked in textile mills, in addition to the more traditional domestic jobs like paid needlework or laundry.[26] Wherever they worked, however, women's pay was based on the assumption that women were supported by men, even though many of the women seeking paid work were doing so because they supported themselves and often their children. The better-paying jobs in industry were known as "skilled work" and also as "men's work"; they required training boys might acquire in shop apprenticeships or possibly in evening programs at several local institutes. Girls had access to no such opportunities. The rhetoric of educators and of employment kept women domestic and dependent always. Even when girls were learning industrial textile design at the Philadelphia School of Design for Women, supporters sometimes claimed that "these arts can be practiced *at home,* without materially interfering with the routine of domestic duty, which is the peculiar province of women." In practice, however, advanced students used the school's facilities after classes to execute paying jobs. Wood-block printing and lithography were hardly parlor activities.[27]

Continued comparison of institutional programs reveals layers of entwined ideologies about social categories, work, and technology. Manly work, by midcentury, was performed away from home, the female domain. White, manly work supported one's family but was not service, a distinction that helps explain the relative prestige of manufacturing work even when the worker could expect to have little control of the process. Middle-class, white, manly work was demonstrably abstract, precise, or quantified, in contrast to soft, intuitive, or even imprecise female thinking, to a

---

[25] On the proposed workshop see Girard College, *Twelfth Annual Report* [1859], quoted in Romano, *Manual and Industrial Education at Girard College* (cit. n. 23), p. 138; the new curriculum is described on p. 158. Apparently some Girard boys also learned shoemaking on campus, which Romano reports "had proved to be self-supporting." The president's remarks are quoted in Cheesman A. Herrick, *History of Girard College* (Philadelphia: Girard College, 1927), p. 232. By the 1880s "manual training" had become a respectable part of the high school curriculum; see the discussion later in this essay. See also Herrick, *History of Girard College,* Ch. 8; and Romano, *Manual and Industrial Education at Girard College,* Ch. 3, pp. 140–164.

[26] In the 1850s, fewer than 10 percent of Philadelphia's teachers were male; see Labaree, *Making of an American High School* (cit. n. 24), p. 98. On boys' high school education see *ibid.;* on girls' see John Trevor Custis, *The Public Schools of Philadelphia—Historical, Biographical, Statistical* (Philadelphia: Burk & McFetridge, 1897). Also useful on drawing is Peter Marzio, *The Art Crusade: An Analysis of Nineteenth-Century American Drawing Manuals, Chiefly 1820–1860* (Washington, D.C.: Smithsonian Institution Press, 1976).

[27] Letter of Sarah Peter, "At a stated meeting . . . held April 19, 1850," *Proceedings of the Franklin Institute of the State of Pennsylvania for the Promotion of the Mechanic Arts, Relative to the Establishment of a School of Design for Women,* Library Company of Philadelphia, p. 1; Philadelphia School of Design for Women, *First Annual Report* (Philadelphia, 1854), pp. 16, 17. For a history of PSDW see Nina de Angeli Walls, "Art, Industry, and Women's Education: Philadelphia's School of Design for Women, 1848–1932" (Ph.D. diss., Univ. Delaware, 1995).

range of stereotypes about black male passions, and to the experienced bodily knowledge that characterized the workingman's manual labor.[28] Science, symbolically, might now distinguish one from *multiple* "others." As the century progressed, "science" not only betokened content but also carried a new connotation—all the best of American progress.

"LABORATORY METHODS OF EDUCATION": MANUAL TRAINING FOR COLLEGE AND FACTORY

In the last decades of the nineteenth century urban America was, if anything, a more confusing and complex locus of growth and activity than at midcentury. Yet in some ways Philadelphia educators saw their world clearly. First and foremost, education was the realm of experts. Childhood learning should be guided by professionally trained educators. Increasingly, *school* education included all forms of "preparation for life," and various forms of technical education entered the public schools of Philadelphia and elsewhere. Here, too, educators might invoke clear understandings about the adult futures of many of their young charges and blend social and educational goals in a range of curricular channels and opportunities. Under rubrics ranging from manual training to industrial arts, girls were taught cooking and sewing and boys were taught various forms of drawing and shopwork. But similar labels often belied differences in content, traditional distinctions reinterpreted with the confident stratification of the new Industrial Age.

A brief examination of technical education programs in Philadelphia's public schools illustrates these alternatives and returns us to the discussion of "women, gender, and science" central to this volume. The well-known manual training movement was the invention of engineering educators mourning the loss of the "Yankee whittling boy" and setting out to train "the mind, the eye, and the hand together"— "the whole boy is put to school."[29] The movement focused at first on secondary-level schooling, where boys would learn not only high school–level academic subjects but also mechanical drawing, woodwork, and metalwork. Then, under the combined influence of professionalizing engineers and professionalized "schoolmen," manual training was adapted to the needs and circumstances of younger students and girls: cardboard construction, paper folding and cutting, sewing, and cooking were added to the standard shopwork methods. Proponents argued that manual training would improve all students, not just those planning careers involving shopwork. These claims of universal benefit meshed with the prevailing "common school" rhetoric, in which material was deemed appropriate to the public schools when it was considered relevant to all students. Proponents of manual training frequently reminded audiences that such training was not trades training and was not specific to the student's future vocation. This distinction, however, did not mean that "manual training" was practiced in a monolithic fashion. Technological knowledge for the "whole

---

[28] See David Roediger, *Wages of Whiteness: Race and the Making of the American Working Class* (London/New York: Verso, 1991), for a psychodynamic assessment of white workers' ideas about race.

[29] See, e.g., Calvin Woodward, "The Fruits of Manual Training" (1883), in *American Education and Vocationalism: A Documentary History,* ed. Martin Lazarson and W. Norton Grubb (New York: Teachers College Press, 1974).

boy" was provided primarily to white, middle-class males; for nonwhite, poor, or immigrant males and for females, technological knowledge was taught for either moral or vocational purposes.

Philadelphia's first manual training school, Central Manual Training School (CMTS), opened its doors in 1885. CMTS exemplified the original goals and methods of the national manual training movement. The three-year high school–level program, for boys only, emphasized drawing and shopwork alongside standard academic subjects in order to educate "men who combine in one person the thinker and the doer." CMTS prepared its students for business and industry or for college; many so-called Manual Boys eventually received degrees in engineering. As principal William Sayre explained to the entering class in 1890: "You must not think you are coming here to learn a trade, to be a blacksmith, or a carpenter, or to turn out doctors and lawyers. You are to make use of manual training as you do of algebra, as a means to an end. Manual training is only valuable as it brings out thoughts and mental action. The education of all the faculties, the head and the hand."[30]

This thoughtful side of manual training was enhanced by an emphasis on drawing. As the catalogue of the school explained in 1890, "From the conception of the idea to its expression in the concrete material, the drawing is the medium through which the mechanical processes are largely developed, and brought to a definite and practical form." Drawing had been a standard part of public school instruction at all levels since the 1870s. In the 1879 elementary course of study, as at the Normal School decades before, drawing was usually paired with penmanship. But drawing was also increasingly understood to be related to manual work: after a revision of the elementary school drawing curriculum, the 1881 drawing classes for teachers were organized by the Committee on Industrial Art Education. Even so, drawing maintained a status never reached by shopwork; the drawing classes at venerable Central High continued throughout this period.[31]

In 1890 CMTS boys spent half of their six hours in school each day on manual training: one hour for drawing and two more for shopwork. During the first two years the boys progressed from woodwork to cold metal to hot metal techniques. By the third and final year, a boy's shopwork had progressed to mechanical construction, culminating in a class project such as "a steam engine, a dynamo, or some other machine." As one manual training proponent explained in a talk to the American Society of Mechanical Engineers, the purpose of construction work was to show the boys that they were prepared to do such work and to demonstrate to them that even after preparation, new problems requiring thought could always arise.[32]

Despite the success of CMTS and despite their continued conviction that, indeed, the whole boy should be put to school, by 1894 Philadelphia's manual training proponents found themselves relying on an entirely different strategy to justify their program:

---

[30] Quoted in A. O. Michener, *A History of the Northeast Manual High School* (Philadelphia: Alumni Association of Northeast High School, 1938), p. 38.

[31] *Catalogue of the Manual Training Schools, 1890–91* (Philadelphia: Board of Public Education, 1890), p. 21. On the status of drawing in the new curriculum see "Drawing" and "Object Study" in revised curriculum, *Journal of the Board of Public Education* (Philadelphia, 1880), App. 3. On drawing classes at Central High see Labaree, *Making of an American High School* (cit. n. 24).

[32] *Catalogue of the Manual Training Schools, 1890–91*, p. 23. The address of Calvin Woodward cited in the text is quoted in Charles Bennett, *History of Manual Training and Industrial Education, 1870–1917* (Peoria, Ill.: Charles A. Bennett, 1937), p. 358.

> The shop instruction is simply part of the laboratory methods of education.
>
> The term "shop" in this connection is as much of a misnomer as is the term "manual training" when applied to the whole school.
>
> It would seem more fitting, therefore, in speaking of the shop, to call it a *laboratory,* a term which carries with it the educational significance of its work. The name, however, is so closely identified with the kind of instruction given, that it is not easy to change the nomenclature.

Whether to attract parents or convince board of education members that this was not a "trades school," the authority of university faculty and professional educators was insufficient; for middle-class high school boys the manual training curriculum had to be justified, rhetorically, as science.[33]

The boys at CMTS learned the principles and theories underlying complex technologies and had the opportunity to work with the machines they had studied. They also pursued academic courses in the sciences and humanities that prepared them for college, if they chose to go—and more than a few of them did so. CMTS students were an elite group both because their families could afford to let them attend school at an age when many boys went to work and because they had achieved the highest scores in their local grammar schools on the entrance exam. The school's curriculum was designed to teach them initiative in all things, partly by teaching them mastery of theory and machines. As the catalogue put it in 1890, the school intended "not to make mechanics, but to train boys for manhood."[34]

The other manual training school the board of education established was intended for a population very different from that of CMTS. The James Forten School had been a "colored" school, but by the end of the 1880s Italian, Polish, and Russian immigrants were moving into tenements left behind by any African Americans who could afford to move. In 1890 the board reopened the school as the James Forten Elementary Manual Training School, employing a specially hired cadre of teachers who went door to door throughout the neighborhood to encourage local children to attend.[35]

Forten's new curriculum was aimed primarily at foreign students. The president of the board explained that children who could not speak English could not profitably attend ordinary schools. He asserted that "a school in which elementary manual training should be combined with primary school work, in the English language,

---

[33] *Catalogue of the Central Manual Training School, 1894–95* (Philadelphia: Board of Public Education, 1894), p. 29. A decade later the principal was still arguing the point: "The 'drawing' of the exercise is the 'question stated,' and the concrete result in wood or metal is the educational product. Treated from this standpoint, the exercises become 'problems' in wood or metal, and the logical processes thus evolved make manual training rise to the level of scientific or mathematical studies as a means of mental development. The exercises cease to be mere mechanical imitations, and the trade school idea is banished." "Report of the Principal of Central Manual Training High School," in Board of Public Education, *Annual Report* [for 1905].

[34] *Catalogue of the Manual Training Schools, 1890–91* (cit. n. 31), n.p. It also explains, "In the changing conditions of the thing in hand during its construction, there is a constant necessity for creating new means to meet new requirements, and the directive skill thus involved makes manual training rise to the level of scientific or mathematical studies as a means of intellectual development" (p. 22).

[35] In 1892, 162 of 350 students (46.3 percent) were "colored"; the proportion remained just under half until the mid 1890s. It dropped to 43.9 percent in 1895, to 30 percent in 1896, and to 12.6 percent of 572 students in 1899. These data are drawn from Frederic Speirs, "The James Forten School: An Experiment in Social Regeneration through Elementary Manual Training," paper presented to the Civic Club of Philadelphia, 2 Mar. 1901.

would benefit the community by helping these children to a better life."[36] Manual training stood at the forefront of progressive educational reforms, so it is not surprising that progressive educators used manual training to educate immigrants. Even so, the close association in the minds of the reformers between manual training and better lives for immigrant children emphasizes its different purposes at Forten and CMTS.

These differences are evident both in the justifications given for the Forten curriculum and in its technological content. Hannah Fox, the new principal of Forten, reported in 1891 that "the object of the manual training work [was] not only the cultivation of the hand and eye, but also to teach habits of accuracy, neatness, dispatch, and obedience." Forten teachers promoted a Swedish woodworking method, known in the United States as "Sloyd." At Forten, Sloyd was meant, like high school–level manual training, to teach a boy to think; but in addition it would "teach a boy to be neat and orderly, to be careful and accurate, [and] to be honest and truthful," claims not made for the CMTS curriculum.[37] At Forten, honesty was the remedy for the new "subversive influences" of the immigrant population, "which in our early history were absolutely unknown." The pedagogy of Sloyd matched its purposes at Forten. In Sloyd each wooden object was referred to as a "model," which was chosen by the teacher. The students' task was to make careful copies. Variations on this system used paper and cardboard rather than wood, but in all cases each student produced an exact replica of the teacher's model.[38]

Some girls learned Sloyd, but it was mostly the domain of boys. Manual training for girls generally entailed cooking and sewing. Beginning in 1888, girls in selected public schools took cooking classes, using standard printed recipes and moving from simple to more complicated food preparation. The girls were eventually taught the "scientific branches of the work," including the composition of foods and their effects upon the body. At Forten, however, it was found "necessary to adapt the regular course of instruction": "The attention of these pupils is directed to the necessity of preparing food plainly and economically, to avoid waste, and of so utilizing material as to produce the best results—they are taught habits of cleanliness and neatness and a desire for such habits is created."[39] Educators clearly presumed that such habits were not taught in students' homes and that, unlike grammar school girls, elementary-level immigrant girls did not need the "scientific branches" of cookery.

Drawing, too, played a different role at Forten. Hannah Fox's description contrasts with the rhetoric employed at CMTS: "The intelligent construction of a working drawing, the reproduction in wood of the article drawn, together with the correct use

---

[36] Board of Public Education, *Annual Report* [for 1891], p. 17.

[37] *Ibid.*, p. 126; and Board of Public Education, *Annual Report* [for 1892], p. 137. The claim that Sloyd would promote honesty was echoed often, and occasionally far afield; in an article on "accuracy in clinical work," for example, the physician Richard Cabot argued, "An enthusiastic advocate of manual training in the public schools once said in my hearing that a boy who had had a thorough course in sloyd work would never tell a lie. In this obviously exaggerated statement there is, I think, this much of truth: such a boy will find it much *harder* in the future to lie." Cabot went on to discuss the importance of observation and data. Richard C. Cabot, "The Ideal of Accuracy in Clinical Work: Its Importance, Its Limitations," *Boston Medical and Surgical Journal*, 24 Nov. 1904, *151*:557.

[38] Isaac Sheppard, President of the Board of Public Education of Philadelphia, quoted in Board of Public Education, *Annual Report* [for 1891], p. 10. On Sloyd see, e.g., Everett Schwartz, *Sloyd or Educational Manual Training with Paper, Cardboard, Wood, and Iron for Primary, Grammar, and High Schools* (Boston: Educational Publishing Co., 1893).

[39] Board of Public Education, *Annual Report* [for 1892], p. 137.

and proper care of tools, must yield skill, we believe, that will be of service in almost any trade, and will also promote habits of neatness, accuracy, persistence, and concentration."[40] Again, manual training was taught in different ways because it was used for different social purposes. Forten teachers focused on "reproduction" of models and "correct use" of tools; CMTS teachers focused on understanding, exploration, and design. Similarly, the standard girls' cooking curriculum introduced "scientific" discussion of theory. Forten students, learning how to be American, were taught to follow directions. CMTS students were expected to issue them.

Manual training was also justified as particularly suitable for Forten children because it was vocationally appropriate. Forten students were given an education tailored to the factory jobs their teachers and the board assumed they would soon hold. Thus "moral" and "vocational" had overlapping meanings: the best "vocational" preparation for entry-level factory and manual jobs was the development of "moral" skills such as neatness, punctuality, and obedience. In cases where the student's vocation was easily predicted, training for that vocation could be enlisted on the side of morality. For these students vocational preparation was moral, and moral training was vocational.

Despite the nonvocational nature of the common school model, there was one other group of students who had been provided with vocationally oriented training early in the decade. In 1881, before the opening of CMTS or Forten, sewing was introduced in the Girls' Normal School. The Girls' Normal, originally established for the vocationally oriented purpose of training teachers, remained the city's only public school for girls who wished to continue their education beyond grammar school. By 1880, however, Philadelphia was experiencing a glut of teachers; part of the board's purpose in adding sewing to the curriculum was to provide the girls with alternative remunerative skills. The report on the subject, prepared jointly by the Committees on the Girls' Normal School and on Industrial Art Education, began broadly nonetheless: "The importance of all branches of study which are of practical value in connection with any of the industrial pursuits, will scarcely be questioned. Furthermore, we believe that all women should have a knowledge of the art of sewing, whether they do or do not turn that knowledge to practical uses."[41] We may deduce, in this case, that "practical" stands in contrast to "domestic." While the vocations of most grammar-school boys in the 1880s were considered open ended, girls' vocations were few and clearly defined. Subject matter "of practical value" to girls was therefore easy to identify and uncontroversial. Sewing was introduced for all grammar school girls by 1885; cooking—a more expensive undertaking—followed in 1887 at the Normal and in the following year (as we have seen) at selected grammar schools.

By 1897 the board had established cooking centers in seven locations for the use of grammar school girls, but although similar shop centers for boys had been recommended in 1893, funds were not allocated for them. The facilities at the Forten School, in its poor immigrant neighborhood, were used by students at other nearby schools, but not until 1909 did boys elsewhere take shop courses. Such budgetary decisions reflect the priorities of the decision makers; the "reform" of cooking for

---

[40] Board of Public Education, *Annual Report* [for 1894], p. 104.
[41] *Journal of the Board of Public Education* (Philadelphia, 1881), App. 48. A general high school, Girls' High School, opened in 1893.

girls was either more important to proponents or less objectionable to detractors than that of woodworking for boys. Reform rhetoric about cooking lessons stressed the usual arguments about the educational value of manual training, but also consistently mentioned the usefulness of the skills involved for the students learning them. All girls would need to cook as adults, but not all boys would need carpentry skills. Vocational value, and not moral or educational content, dictated the spread of grammar school cooking.

In fact, the shopwork at CMTS, especially for boys going on to work in industry or to study engineering in college, also had a vocational purpose. But in the particular context of late nineteenth-century class and gender relations, it could never be justified as such. Instead it was labeled "science"—an argument somewhat at odds with the manual labor connotations of training the hand along with the head and the eye. In a period of notable labor "unrest," it is perhaps not surprising that the "manual" part of manual training lost out, that as the school grew the boys spent less time in shopwork and more time on high school subjects. The difficulty can perhaps be located in the explanation of an advocate of Sloyd: "We no longer absolutely despise hard bodily labor as we did a century ago, when to do nothing was considered more honorable than to work; yet even to-day we attach a certain stigma to all forms of bodily labor. In the social world, the clerk ranks higher than the skilled artisan, and the workmen themselves are only too apt to consider that their labor is less honorable than that of their masters."[42] In the social world, he might have added, the factory operative ranks lower yet than the skilled artisan. As the example of the Forten School suggests, the new male "other" for the middle class had become a factory hand, not an artisan.

HIERARCHIES AND BOUNDARIES: THE USES OF USEFUL KNOWLEDGE

By the end of the century, when the early upheavals of industrialization had largely been worked out for the urban middle class, traditional patrician "separate spheres" concerns with gender roles had to some degree given way to the more pressing concerns of immigrant lifestyles and labor unrest. Protestant, middle-class, native-born women had rendered their domestic prerogatives powerful in urban reform; cooking, too, might now have its "scientific branches." And yet domesticity remained central in all discussions of female education. Social boundaries shifted with new urban configurations, but by no means were they erased from the institutions of modern education.

Of the many themes emerging from this discussion, several must be emphasized here. First, it should be clear that technological knowledge carried social meanings, which in turn influenced and were influenced by the social differences among people possessing that knowledge. The literary content of schooling, as well, represented far more than simply one's ability to read, write, and cipher or to read French or Latin. Schooling throughout the century was a badge of American respectability; educators increasingly succeeded in winning control over a system of credentials

---

[42] On the decreasing place of manual training see the *Catalogue of the Manual Training Schools* for 1890, 1894, 1898, and 1910. The academic work per week averaged 15 hours in 1890, 18.7 hours in 1910; manual training per week averaged 15 hours in 1890, 11.3 hours in 1910. The quotation is from B. B. Hoffman, *The Sloyd System of Woodworking* (New York: American Book Co., 1892), p. 25. The author was superintendent of the Baron de Hirsch Fund Trade Schools in New York City.

that was in turn supported by those who had access to them.[43] School not only inculcated social values but was a product of them; it carried meaning independent of the skills it taught, and the possession of such skills carried meaning independent of their day-to-day usefulness. Schooling had meaning in the social hierarchy; book learning and manual training alike had meanings in the knowledge hierarchy.

But beyond the simple respectability that attached to sending a child to school, familiarity with and reliance on written communications—drawings, words, and numbers—had become increasingly important during the century in business and manufacturing practice, as implied by the emergence of white-collar work as a separate category. These written forms had also become an increasingly important part of the transmission of technological knowledge and had gained status in perceived hierarchies of technological knowledge, as the leaders shaping the scientific, mathematical, and drawing-based curriculum of schools like Girard, Central High, and CMTS well knew. Such hierarchies informed and reconfigured each other; both school-based credentials and the use of precise abstractions became tools with which an individual or group could raise itself in the social order, and status in the social order made it easier to acquire both diplomas and familiarity with modes of technical expression, written and drawn.

Second, the examples presented here—and they are by no means the whole range available—demonstrate the breadth of activities we must include in the realm of the "technological" and invite further discussion of the cognitive and social authority of "science" in the nineteenth century. The separation of "science" from the "useful arts" became increasingly complete as the century progressed, suggesting that our modern definition of "science" is no less conditioned by the social, economic, and mechanical processes of industrialization than are our assumptions about "technology."[44] Those assumptions, after all, came partly from an active campaign by engineers to link their work with the mathematics and theory of science. We need not be bound by them.

Finally, crossing these social boundaries in the study of science itself is more complex: these boundaries have been part of the very definition of what counted as "science." The hierarchies illuminated here by comparisons in technical education across social boundaries can raise important questions for scholars interested in gender and science. These examples remind us that there are multiple masculinities and multiple femininities available within a culture; throughout the century distinctions were made in the education of different groups of boys or groups of girls. Have there been and are there, symbolically, multiple sciences too? In the institutions I have discussed, science was invoked sometimes for its content and sometimes for the

---

[43] On credentials see Labaree, *Making of an American High School* (cit. n. 24); Shan Nelson-Rowe, "Markets, Politics, and Professions: The Rise of Vocationalism in American Education" (Ph.D. diss., State Univ. New York, Stony Brook, 1988); and Michael B. Katz, *The Irony of Early School Reform: Educational Innovation in Mid-Nineteenth Century Massachusetts* (Cambridge, Mass.: Harvard Univ. Press, 1968).

[44] Indeed, the formal institutions of American science—as opposed to the useful arts—emerged with American industry in the 1840s and 1850s. As Sally Gregory Kohlstedt has suggested, these institutions do not mark the *beginning* of American interest in science, which was widely evident in a range of other forms throughout the decades of the early republic. See Sally Gregory Kohlstedt, "Parlors, Primers, and Public Schooling: Education for Science in Nineteenth-Century America," *Isis,* 1990, *81*:425–445.

prestige the label conferred. Further, the content of science provided part of the prestige.

These uses are entwined and entangled both in historical documents and in the present, but with care we may begin to make analytical distinctions. If "science" has meanings on many levels, then it must be treated in a way not unlike our treatment of gender: it has structures and institutions; it produces knowledge; it also functions symbolically, as a cultural product. As such, it demands sustained attention to borders, to boundaries, and to "others": to both science and not-science, and to the changing boundaries between them. In what ways are gender, race, and class intertwined or differentiated by the meanings of science? Which dimensions are salient when, and why? When we study knowledge historically, we depend on descriptions and accounts of that knowledge rendered in the past to make new accounts rendered in the present.[45] With "science," as with gender or race, we must find ways to cross the boundaries our sources impose on us; otherwise we confine ourselves to an understanding limited by the separate spheres and categories of another time.

[45] Both Joan Scott and Sandra Harding have discussed gender as identity, structure and institution, and representation. See Joan Wallach Scott, "Gender: A Useful Category of Historical Analysis," in *Gender and the Politics of History* (New York: Columbia Univ. Press, 1988); and Sandra Harding, *The Science Question in Feminism* (Ithaca, N.Y.: Cornell Univ. Press, 1986). Judy McGaw has argued for interrogating rather than accepting our sources' views of gender in "No Passive Victims, No Separate Spheres" (cit. n. 2).

Medicine and Science as Masculine "Fields of Honor"

By Robert A. Nye*

THIS ESSAY IS A PRELIMINARY ATTEMPT to consider aspects of medicine and science as cultural practices governed by masculine honor codes. I wish to establish the point that honor codes of great antiquity were transmitted remarkably intact to modern bourgeois culture, where they served as part of the fabric of male sociability among doctors, scientists, and other professionals throughout modern Europe.

My argument relies on establishing continuities in the honor culture between early modern and modern times. Therefore, I first outline briefly the history of honor codes in Western Europe and show how, notwithstanding its aristocratic and military origins, a culture of honor has been a prominent part of the deliberations and sociability of bourgeois gentlemen from early modern times. I then attempt to show how important elements of the honor culture—including the *point d'honneur*—were incorporated into middle-class professional life in the nineteenth century. In the professional and academic associations that flourished after 1800, honor codes served as a basis for male social relations and as guides for intraprofessional etiquette. Indeed, as I hope to show by the examples of nineteenth- and early twentieth-century French and British medicine, honor was an indispensable component of the informal and written ethical codes of all modern professional groups. However, I also wish to develop the point Mario Biagioli and Steven Shapin have made for early modern scientists: that because the possession of personal honor was also an important criterion for ascertaining and maintaining the reliability and truthfulness of gentlemen as witnesses to natural events, judgments about honor became an important part of the process of science itself.

A crucial aspect of this essay will be my attempt to understand better the implications of a masculine honor culture for women and for the gendering of scientific and medical practice in the modern era. I draw most of my examples about the influence of honor from my current work on French and British medical practice, paying particular attention to professionalization processes and professional sociability. Marina Benjamin has recently argued that gender issues have been given inadequate attention in the cultural history and sociology of both science and medicine.[1] I will there-

---

* Department of History, Oregon State University, Corvallis, Oregon 97331.
[1] Marina Benjamin, "Introduction," in *Science and Sensibility: Gender and Scientific Enquiry, 1780–1945*, ed. Benjamin (Oxford: Basil Blackwell, 1991), pp. 1–26, on pp. 6–7.

fore venture a partial explanation for this lacuna in a final section that deals with the history and sociology of modern scientific laboratory practice and Bourdieuian "field" theories. As I hope to suggest, it is no accident that gender blindness is an aspect of much recent research and writing in this field.

* * *

The honor codes that both stimulated and regulated male conflict and sociability permeated upper-class European and Anglo-American culture in the nineteenth century, as some recent work has revealed. Nor were such codes and their rituals confined to a narrow, aristocratic crust; we can say with some assurance that, in varying degrees, the boundaries of an honor culture expanded in the nineteenth century to include men of social origins far below that of the old service nobility, reaching down past the financial and industrial bourgeoisie into social milieus that produced liberal professionals and others whose career investments were made chiefly in educational capital.[2]

Despite its new egalitarian appeal, it is nonetheless important to recognize that a modern honor culture developed from aristocratic roots. In the late Middle Ages and through much of the early modern era the status of noblemen reposed on two different but closely related kinds of personal independence. One of these, derived from the military and service origins of the nobility, stressed the personal courage and virtue of the nobleman, for whom being either a lord or a lord's retainer entailed an endless and shifting demonstration of personal assertiveness, bravery, and truculence. This much-prized independence was mediated in practice, however, by intense bonds of personal loyalty and a discourse of chivalric etiquette that provided stability and solidarity in an otherwise unruly social order. So long as they endured, unambiguous demonstrations of loyalty were regarded as the highest expression of a man's virtue and the most reliable affirmation of the trust placed in him. A man of honor in this system was an exemplar of "prowess, loyalty, generosity, courtesy, and frankness."[3]

The second source of noble independence lay in a man's patrimony, which consisted not only in his ability to control his land and material assets but also his wife

---

[2] For France see Robert A. Nye, *Masculinity and Male Codes of Honor in Modern France* (New York: Oxford Univ. Press, 1993) (hereafter cited as **Nye, *Masculinity and Male Codes of Honor***). Kevin McAleer has treated Germany in *Dueling: The Cult of Honor in Fin-de-Siècle Germany* (Princeton, N.J.: Princeton Univ. Press, 1995); see also Ute Frevert, *Ehrenmänner: Das Duell in der bürgerlichen Gesellschaft* (Munich: Beck, 1991). Istvan Deak has written on Austria-Hungary in *Beyond Nationalism: A Social and Political History of the Hapsburg Officer Corps* (New York: Oxford Univ. Press, 1990). Anthony Simpson has treated the disappearance of dueling in England in "Dandelions on the Field of Honor: Dueling, the Middle Classes, and the Law in Nineteenth-Century England," *Criminal Justice History,* 1988, *9*:99–155. For the United States see Bertram Wyatt-Brown, *Southern Honor: Ethics and Behavior in the Old South* (New York: Oxford Univ. Press, 1982). See also, in general, V. G. Kiernan, *The Duel in European History: Honour and the Reign of Aristocracy* (New York: Oxford Univ. Press, 1988). Educational capital and its social implications have been discussed by Pierre Bourdieu in *Distinction: A Social Critique of the Judgement of Taste,* trans. Richard Nice (Cambridge, Mass.: Harvard Univ. Press, 1984).

[3] Maurice Keen, *Chivalry* (New Haven, Conn.: Yale Univ. Press, 1984), p. 2. On the instability of relations in a noble honor culture see Kristen Neuschel, *Word of Honor: Interpreting Noble Culture in Sixteenth-Century France* (Ithaca, N.Y.: Cornell Univ. Press, 1989); Jonathan Dewald, *Aristocratic Experience and the Origins of Modern Culture* (Berkeley: Univ. California Press, 1993); and Mervyn James, *Society, Politics, and Culture: Studies on Early Modern England* (Cambridge: Cambridge Univ. Press, 1986).

and progeny, who were human capital in the struggle to maintain and expand his social and political power and strengthen his autonomy with respect to peers and liege lord alike. If we follow Pierre Bourdieu's notion of "practical belief," personal identity for this class of men was a kind of "embodiment" expressed in and through the body and its gestures, which gave rise, in turn, to a group of enduring cultural myths about noble masculinity that effectively "naturalized" noble qualities.[4]

There is no doubt that these notions of masculine honorability were under more or less constant assault throughout early modern times: from above by state-building monarchs, and from below by ambitious bourgeois asserting a new variety of rational and instrumental personal autonomy based on the values of a commercial society. However, the core notions of *noble* honor nonetheless endured well enough to serve as the foundation for *masculine* honor in the modern era. R. W. Connell has argued that in the transition to the liberal-constitutional state, the "hegemonic" form of patriarchal masculinity, which "connected the exercize of authority with a capacity for violence (symbolized in the duel, and more systematically seen in the role of the landed gentry in military affairs)," gave way to another form of (no less "hegemonic") masculinity "organized around themes of rationality, calculation, and orderliness." Connell builds his case for a new, "gentler" masculine honor on Norbert Elias's thesis that the advance of civilization has entailed a repression or sublimation of violent impulses on a Freudian model, with the result that violent practices like dueling were exiled to the colonial frontiers and priority was given to science and "technical education" as privileged activities.[5]

However, if it is true, for various reasons, that "Mr. Gladstone, Mr. Rockefeller, and Mr. Morgan did not fight duels," dueling in fact flourished among gentlemen almost everywhere else in the West until the early 1920s, as Connell acknowledges elsewhere.[6] My point here is that the "capacity" for violence remained intact as an instrument of masculine authority well into the twentieth century, influencing social relations in a way that continued to seal off women from full participation in the public sphere. To be sure, the duel was neither frequent nor especially dangerous in its nineteenth-century version. However, its continued presence alerts us to the remarkable tenacity of a male honor culture for which the duel, and the elaborate rituals of the *point d'honneur*, were a last resort for the resolution of male conflict. Perhaps more to the point: even when the duel finally did disappear, the etiquette that had governed it remained an integral feature of male sociability, where it continued to evoke the aggression it once choreographed.

I have argued at some length elsewhere that the tumultuous personal relations of old regime nobles were regulated by a code of honor that laid out in some detail— first in oral culture, later in legalistic published form—the ways that one man could offend or insult another and the rights a man so insulted could claim in seeking to reestablish his tarnished honor. A man's friends were enjoined to negotiate an apology with the friends of his offender in order to find a face-saving formula that de-

---

[4] Nye, *Masculinity and Male Codes of Honor*, pp. 6–7, 20–21; and Pierre Bourdieu, *The Logic of Practice*, trans. Richard Nice (Stanford, Calif.: Stanford Univ. Press, 1990), pp. 68–78. See also Arlette Jouanna, *Ordre social: Mythes et hiérarchies dans la France du XVIe siècle* (Paris: Hachette, 1977).

[5] R. W. Connell, "The State, Gender, and Sexual Politics," *Theory and Society*, 1990, *19*:507–544, on pp. 521, 522.

[6] *Ibid.*, p. 522; and R. W. Connell, *Masculinities* (Oxford: Polity, 1995), pp. 191–193.

flected or defused the offense. Only when these efforts broke down did recourse to weapons occur, and even then there were strict formulas in place by the nineteenth century that mitigated the danger of the confrontation and encouraged reconciliation.[7]

Indeed, the *point d'honneur*, in the multitude of forms it took in Western societies, was embedded in a discursive and practical structure of male sociability that was far more concerned with elementary politeness than with conflict, with the proper verbal formulas appropriate to varying social situations, and with what one might call prescriptions for personal advance. A flood of modern advice manuals emerged at the end of the eighteenth century to smooth the path of sociability for *arrivistes,* and many of them deplored the duel as a vestige of a brutal and undemocratic past. Codes of etiquette seldom pronounced a judgment more severe than finding a behavior in bad taste; indeed, in a certain sense they encouraged insincerity by stressing the importance of superficial appearance over genuineness.[8]

Nonetheless, even where it was formally forsworn, the duel continued to stand as the highest and last resort in the hierarchy of social practices put in place to mediate individual competition and conflict in bourgeois society. The nub of an offense against a man's honor remained in the nineteenth and early twentieth centuries what it had been since the early Middle Ages: one man asserted something about another man—it could be about his character, his family, or his behavior—that offended him, to which the man responded by denying its truth, which in effect meant he was asserting that his accuser had lied.[9] This is what generally gave rise to dueling challenges, though occasionally intended or inadvertent physical contact could have the same effect. What was at stake was not so much the truth of the allegation or the accusation of lying as a man's willingness to back up his words with deeds—which testified, at the minimum, to the sincerity, if not the accuracy, of his views.

We have a remarkable example of the way this process worked in a nineteenth-century scientific society. In the spring of 1857 the young Swiss physiologist René-Edouard Claparède attended a session of the Société de Biologie during an extended trip to Paris. At this time the society had been in existence for only nine years, but it had already become the most active scientific society in France. On a previous visit Claparède had made some of his recent work on the muscle structure of infusoria—written, as it happens, in his native German—available to the society. On this visit the society's president asked Claparède to offer a brief summary in French of his findings to the members. While delivering his remarks he noticed an unmistakably hostile look on the face of a certain Dr. Rouget, a man he scarcely knew, who was a professor at the Ecole de Médecine. After Claparède returned to his seat, Rouget, who was sitting in front of him, turned and asked if he had published his work on infusoria. No, responded Claparède, but others, including Franz Leydig, had seen the same structures.

"What Leydig has seen is perfectly absurd," asserted Rouget. "What have you seen yourself?" he asked Claparède. Claparède showed him a sketch of the muscles in question, to which Rouget replied, "Sir, what you imagine to be fibers are in fact

---

[7] Nye, *Masculinity and Male Codes of Honor,* pp. 23–30, 127–147.
[8] Michael Curtin, "A Question of Manners: Status and Gender in Etiquette and Courtesy," *Journal of Modern History,* 1985, 57:395–423; and Nye, *Masculinity and Male Codes of Honor,* pp. 127–130.
[9] On this aspect of the duel see François Billacois, *Le duel dans la société française des XVIe–XVIIe siècles* (Paris: Ecole des Hautes Études en Sciences Sociales, 1986), pp. 127–136.

folds. All your German histologists are like that. They see fibers everywhere where there are only folds."

By his account, Claparède responded that in fact opinions among German histologists on that issue were very much divided and that, moreover, the "fold" interpretation had originated in Germany. Rouget then claimed to have observed muscle tissue of all varieties and to have seen nothing but folds, and he insisted that such must certainly be the case with infusoria.

When Claparède replied that this assertion was "questionable" [*discutable*], Rouget barked out, "How is it, *Monsieur l'Allemand,* that you permit yourself to question my observations?" "It is not," responded Claparède, "a matter of observations. Observations are exact, but there are two possible interpretations of them."

"Ah! Monsieur l'Allemand, you still doubt me? Then, please understand that when I tell you that I have made an observation, it is well and truly done, which I, as its author, know better than anyone else in the world. And if you persist in doubting that what exists here are folds, you will be obliged to choose between two slaps in the face or two sword thrusts in the belly!"

Rouget then returned to his desk and wrote out two notes—one detailing the nature of his grievances in the form of a *cartel,* an old-fashioned way of issuing a dueling challenge, and a request for two seconds—both of which he handed over to Claparède's neighbor, the eminent microscopist Gabriel Balbiani. The latter found no one willing to serve as Rouget's seconds, and the matter effectively ended there.

Claparède coolly summed up the incident, in the way men often did, in a letter to his mother, noting the absurdity of getting one's throat cut over the muscles of an infusoria, and dismissing the whole matter as a "vaudeville." But he could not resist observing the furor the incident had provoked at the Société de Biologie, where the etiquette of the matter was passionately discussed. "There is nothing astonishing in such scenes for the French," he concluded, citing incidents of the same kind that very week in the Académie de Médecine. "These are things one only sees in the Congress at Washington and the learned societies of Paris."[10]

This incident illustrates two of the points I wish to make about the place of a culture of honor in professional life in the nineteenth century. First, as an outsider to the Société de Biologie, Claparède was, in effect, being challenged—by one of the society's most pugnacious members, to be sure—to display his credentials as a scientist and as a man. Claparède's antagonist made much of his German (actually Swiss) origins, but it is important to understand that national and linguistic differences were only two of a number of possible designations of outsider status that might have provoked a surly challenge like Rouget's. Exotic educational, religious, racial, or class background could also serve as grounds for such action. Second, though the issue between the two men seemed to be about fine points of evidence and observation, it was easily, perhaps willfully, conflated with the question of personal integrity, becoming thereby a matter of personal honor. The potential for a violent incident lay just beneath the smooth surface of the activities of the Société de Biologie, and, notwithstanding Claparède's assertion about a Franco-American

---

[10] This account is taken from René-Edouard Claparède to his mother, Apr. 1858, in *Lettres de René-Edouard Claparède,* ed. Georges de Morsier (Basler Veröffentlichungen zur Geschichte der Medizen und der Biologie, 30) (Basel: Schwabe, n.d.), pp. 56–58. I owe this citation to the generosity of Joy Harvey. Here and elsewhere, translations into English are mine unless otherwise indicated.

nexus of such incidents, there were similar occurrences in all-male clubs and societies elsewhere in Europe throughout the nineteenth century.[11]

In the old regime, the presence of clear markers of class and status allowed men to navigate the troubled waters of honor with minimal danger, even in venues where noble and commoner coexisted in relative equality. However, in the new postrevolutionary public sphere, where there were not yet clear guidelines for ethical behavior, the male honor code provided the best model, *faute de mieux,* for personal and professional comportment. The code allowed men to negotiate the tangled terrain of offense and insult in civil society and to advance claims for the "truth" of what they wrote or spoke through their willingness to accept dueling challenges to defend it. A man who was not willing to resort to arms to protect his reputation had little authority in public debate. In brief, violence, or the threat of it represented in the form of dueling challenges, undergirded much of the structure of public discourse in the nineteenth century.[12]

* * *

A relatively new line of historical inquiry is now engaged in examining the origins of modern civility and the modern civic order by following the debates about the evolution of politeness and its institutionalization in salons, clubs, and other organizations, most of which seem to have been governed by particular conventions of decorum. The subject is highly complicated, not least because of the Wittgensteinian admonition that there is no determinative relationship between the formulation of a rule and its practice. However, if we at least inform ourselves of the rules (in this instance, the exigencies of honor codes) while focusing our attention on the practices of honor cultures, we may reach some useful conclusions about the gendered nature of the public sphere and of the organization of scientific and medical practices that are continuous with it.[13]

At the end of the eighteenth century there were nearly utopian hopes attached to

---

[11] Paul Broca, whose presence dominated the Société de Biologie in this era, provides ample proof in his own career for the ubiquity of masculine aggressiveness in professional and scientific education and proceedings. Broca wrote home about the "thrill of the fight" in the oral exams for hospital intern and extern, noting the shameless favoritism of the examiners, who shouted at and tried to intimidate the rivals of their protégés. He wrote of threatened duels with his chief competitors, and when he passed his exams he exulted that he had "carried off [his exams] at sword point": Francis Schiller, *Paul Broca* (Berkeley: Univ. California Press, 1979), pp. 29, 41–42, 44–45, 86. Sharon Traweek has discussed the importance of male genealogies of the sort referred to by Broca in the modern high-energy physics community: Sharon Traweek, *Beamtimes and Lifetimes: The World of High Energy Physicists* (Cambridge, Mass.: Harvard Univ. Press, 1988), p. 94. On chemical genealogies see Mary Jo Nye, *From Chemical Philosophy to Theoretical Chemistry: Dynamics of Matter and Dynamics of Disciplines* (Berkeley: Univ. California Press, 1994), pp. 19–23.

[12] William M. Reddy, "Condottieri of the Pen: Journalists and the Public Sphere in Postrevolutionary France (1815–1850)," *American Historical Review,* 1994, *99:*1546–1570. See also Nye, *Masculinity and Male Codes of Honor,* pp. 187–199; and McAleer, *Dueling* (cit. n. 2), pp. 43–84.

[13] Some recent work in this area is Anne Goldgar, *Impolite Learning: Conduct and Community in the Republic of Letters, 1680–1750* (New Haven, Conn.: Yale Univ. Press, 1994); Peter France, *Politeness and Its Discontents: Problems in French Classical Culture* (Cambridge: Cambridge Univ. Press, 1992); Dena Goodman, *The Republic of Letters: A Cultural History of the French Enlightenment* (Ithaca, N.Y.: Cornell Univ. Press, 1994); Mark Kingwell, "Politics and Polite Society in the Scottish Enlightenment," *Historical Reflections,* 1993, *19:*363–387; and Harold Mah, "The Epistemology of the Sentence: Language, Civility, and Identity in France and Germany, Diderot to Nietzsche," *Representations,* Summer 1994, pp. 64–84.

the emergence of a new "democratic" politeness that would be, in a Rousseauvian sense, more sincere than salon decorum and less influenced by the class order in which it was, at that time, embedded. As we know, no such uncoupling of class and systems of decorum occurred in the nineteenth century; but the salon system that Rousseau so despised was much weakened by the popularity of his critique, and, if it did not altogether disappear, it did not become a popular form for the middle or popular classes in the nineteenth century.[14]

The organization that appears to have replaced or at least supplemented the salon was the club. This kind of group, which appears to have been modeled on the organization and aims of eighteenth-century Freemasonry, has been all the rage ever since and has ramified to serve virtually every business, recreational, or professional purpose imaginable. Until women began to form their own clubs later in the century, clublife satisfied at least one aspect of Rousseau's critique of the "feminized" salon in restricting membership to men. Early in the century, however, entrance requirements appear to have been aimed not at the barring of women—who were in a certain sense beneath consideration, or perhaps even consciousness—but at the exclusion of a *certain kind of man*.[15]

Club sociability in the nineteenth century was usually regulated by statutes that laid out the criteria for membership, the obligations of members, and the conditions for abrogation of membership. These statutes were sometimes very explicit, recalling to members their duty to respect the dignity of others, to limit discussions to issues not likely to provoke controversy or conflict, and to defend the interests and solidarity of the club on pain of exclusion.[16] Almost all clubs maintained committees for adjudicating disputes between members or disciplining the wayward. In societies where dueling continued to flourish such committees served to defuse potentially dangerous (and embarrassing) encounters between clubmen, and where dueling had disappeared they nonetheless helped keep differences out of the public eye. Such committees were essentially modeled on the honor courts that continued to exist in military life, and they served the same function and dealt with the same kinds of issues relating to the personal honor of members.

Scientists and medical professionals and other members of the "liberal" professions were no different from the general run of middle-class man in wanting to join groups of men like themselves who were interested in the same kinds of things. Most of the great academies of science and medicine had been organized, of course, along royal, later national, lines long before clubs began to flourish. But we now have a generation of scholarship on the organization of middle-class scientific societies, academies, and associations in Europe and America and their role in promoting research, scientific publication, and the dissemination of scientific knowledge. From the outset these new kinds of organizations seem to have paid more attention to the behavior and reputation of members than did the older national and royal academies, to have been more concerned with the reputation of the group (rather than the glory

---

[14] Londa Schiebinger, *The Mind Has No Sex? Women and the Origins of Modern Science* (Cambridge, Mass.: Harvard Univ. Press, 1989), pp. 56–60.

[15] On the origins of clubs in France see Maurice Agulhon, *Le cercle dans la France bourgeoise, 1810–1848: Etude d'une mutation de sociabilité* (Paris: Colin, 1977).

[16] I have discussed some of these statutes for the French case in Nye, *Masculinity and Male Codes of Honor*, pp. 127–132.

of the monarch or the nation), and to have engaged in rather fierce competition for precedence and membership with other groups in their domain of activity.

In terms of our contemporary notions of professional ethics, there is little evidence that ethical considerations played much of a role in the activities of either scientists or liberal professionals. Instead, their clubs and organizations appear to have been content to operate under the aegis of the honor culture and of the honor code that governed masculine relations in the larger public sphere. The rather general statutes many of them adopted, and what we know about their criteria for admission and expulsion, suggest that they were informed in such matters by the tacit knowledge their members possessed in their capacity as men of a certain class. In other words, the "ethical" standard that guided them was really the ethos of the upper-class male honor culture adapted to the tasks at hand.

The anthropologist Julian Pitt-Rivers has argued that honor in the West has been not only the "fact of repute and precedence" but "at the same time a matter of moral conscience and a sentiment." The deliberations of honor, and therefore those of a company of honorable men, concerned not only *préséance* (the honor distributed by the monarch or head of state) but also *virtue,* which, for a group of men, meant the personal qualities that merited "the acclamation of the population, the recognition of honorable qualities by the public."[17]

Notaries, lawyers, doctors, and even engineers already operated under the authority of these corporate principles in the old regime, and they continued to do so in their postrevolutionary incarnations as members of professions. They took oaths to uphold the solidarity of the group, collected honoraria instead of fees for their services, and regularly proclaimed their disinterest, probity, discretion, and "delicacy" to their clients and the general public. In keeping with notions of honor as old as chivalry itself, the essential quality of an honorable man was held to be his independence, which guaranteed his disinterestedness and protected his prospective clients against the venalities of greed or collusion. Necessarily, perhaps, the concept of modern professional "independence" was directly modeled on older, feudal ideals. An independent man did not perform his services simply in order to live; he performed them freely—curing the sick, overseeing the legal affairs of families, building bridges—out of a kind of generosity that reflected on his personal virtue, in return for which he received the honoraria of grateful clients.[18]

We are tempted to see in the claims to independence of modern professionals a vast conceit of social and self-delusion; no doubt few men could claim this degree of economic, not to mention honorable, autonomy. However, the force of honor was such that the threatened loss of this cherished independence, even the appearance of its loss, could bring down the weight of shame upon a man. If a man was in debt, had relations with dishonorable individuals, had through stealth or collusion profited excessively from his position, betrayed the trust of clients or colleagues, or engaged in shameful behavior, then he was judged to have placed his reputation in the hands

---

[17] Julian Pitt-Rivers, "Introduction," in *Honor and Grace in Anthropology,* ed. J. G. Peristiany and Pitt-Rivers (Cambridge: Cambridge Univ. Press, 1992), pp. 1–18, on p. 5; and Pitt-Rivers, "La maladie de l'honneur," in *L'honneur: Image de soi ou don de soi: Un idéal équivoque,* ed. Marie Gautheran (Série Morales, 3) (Paris: Editions Autrement, 1991), pp. 20–36, on p. 25.

[18] On these points see Bruno Lefèbvre, "L'argent et le secret: Dégradations et recompositions," in *L'honneur,* ed. Gautheran, pp. 142–175, esp. pp. 147–148, 154.

of others. By thus falling into relations of dependence on men outside the group, he not only limited his own autonomy but imperiled the reputation of the entire profession, which could expel him for the offense. In the hierarchy of professions in nineteenth-century society, wrote the Durkheimian sociologist Paul Lapie, a profession earns public esteem not because its members are rich or particularly useful to us, but because "it confers, or appears to confer on those who exercize it, more independence and more power."[19]

This notion of personal independence provides us with an unusually clear opportunity to demonstrate the connections and differences between the honor cultures of early modern and modern Europe. Mario Biagioli and Steven Shapin have recently underlined the importance of independence as a foundation for truth claims about the natural world in the careers of Galileo and Robert Boyle. As both of them make clear, independence was one of the indispensable elements assuring the credibility of a man's observations and judgments and, therefore, his reliability as a witness to the events of the natural world. Before a man could even have his claims considered as knowledge he needed to be on equal footing with the community of men who warranted and legitimated such claims. If he was not born to the language, manners, gestures, or other conventions of the host of independent gentlemen, as Boyle was, a man needed, as Galileo did, to master them.[20]

In demonstrating the link between personal independence and networks of social and cultural power, both Biagioli and Shapin illuminate the influence of an honor culture on scientific life and activity. They have thus revealed the extent to which science, by restricting the capacity for independent truth-telling to gentlemen (and those who worked under their protection), excluded most of the rest of their contemporaries, not by erecting barriers against them, but on account of a quality they did not possess: honor. As Shapin has argued, this disqualification had important implications for women: "the relevant category of analysis was not the natural one of *biological endowment* and its expression but the situated cultural one of *dependence*. And dependence was a circumstance that was understood to affect biological

---

[19] Paul Lapie, "La hierarchie des professions," *Revue de Paris*, 15 Sept. 1905, no. 5, p. 394.

[20] Because he was not highborn, Galileo needed the protection of a noble patron to achieve the independence to make a career as a natural philosopher; he eventually found the protection and status he sought when he established himself in the court of Cosimo de Medici as a "philosopher," a term that avoided the utilitarian aspects of relations between client and patron typical at the time. In Biagioli's words, "It was by repressing the utilitarian dimensions of patronage (something to which Cosimo was bound by his honor) that Galileo could present himself as disinterested and objective and, consequently, could represent his findings as truthful": Mario Biagioli, *Galileo, Courtier: The Practice of Science in the Culture of Absolutism* (Chicago: Univ. Chicago Press, 1993), p. 87. Robert Boyle had the advantage of being born a gentleman in a society less hindered by the presence of princely absolutism; he thus received at birth the relative "freedom" to engage in independent thinking that Galileo spent much of his adult life trying to acquire. As Shapin has noted, those who possessed the power of free action in a society such as seventeenth-century England, where the vast majority of citizens were still constrained by bonds of economic or patronage obligations, enjoyed unusual ability to shape and define their culture. Out of their mutual regard for this independence, "understandings of free action figure in much reflection about whether or not a person may be safely trusted as a truth-teller. Persons giving a promise bind themselves to others; their word, as the commonplace has it, becomes their bond. To that extent, trusted persons make some set of their future actions predictable by agreeing to forgo a certain amount of free action. And, because those who trust them may forgo relevant precaution or skepticism, they facilitate the free actions of others. Thus free action appears as a problem to which trust is the solution": Steven Shapin, *A Social History of Truth: Civility and Science in Seventeenth-Century England* (Chicago: Univ. Chicago Press, 1994), p. 39.

males in much the same way that it worked on biological females."²¹ As I have already noted, such a formulation may minimize the extent to which early modern culture naturalized categories that we today define as social, since contemporaries appear to have believed that those without honor could not participate in an honor culture because of something they did not possess *by nature.*

* * *

Shapin and Biagioli discuss duels as an aspect of gentlemanly society. Shapin, particularly, shows how the disruptive and dangerous threat of the duel led gentlemen to develop forms of discourse that would prevent direct conflict (based on the charge of lying) by permitting "utterances to be skeptically regarded, to be modified, or even negated, *without the risk of violence.*" A similar strategy was adopted, as Biagioli shows, in Florentine scientific discourse by the refusal of participants to claim closure in natural philosophy disputes. Sublimated though it may have been in circumspection and circumlocution alike, the duel had nonetheless a genuine presence in the professional and scientific gatherings of early modern gentlemen and was no less powerful for being seldom resorted to.²²

As I have argued, the *point d'honneur* served as a gentlemanly endgame for resolving differences everywhere in Europe and America until the mid-nineteenth century, at which point it disappeared rather suddenly from Anglo-American culture. However, the duel not only persisted on the Continent but continued to broaden its social and cultural scope, especially after 1860 or so. By the 1880s hundreds of duels per year took place between upper-middle-class men in France, Germany, Italy, Russia, Spain, and Austria-Hungary. Except in Germany, where particularly dangerous forms were favored, the duel was far less dangerous than it had been in the earlier part of the century, but it was practiced far more frequently and in milieus further down the social hierarchy than had been the case in the old regime.²³ (See Figure 1.)

Honor had thus become more democratic in the course of the century, in the sense that more men could claim to possess it and could demonstrate a grasp of its procedures. It had also become less closely tied to the intimate concerns of caste and class and was more fully integrated into the fabric of civil society and public affairs. Nineteenth-century men probably felt slights to clan or extended family less keenly than eighteenth-century men had done, but they took umbrage more readily at slights to their individual persons and at insults to the corporate entities of modern life with which they had forged powerful bonds of emotional identity, whether nation, profession, party, or club. (See Figure 2.) Ute Frevert points out that in nineteenth-century Germany dueling challenges were a fairly common consequence of legal, medical, and scientific disputes; after duels between officers, academic duels were the most numerous kind. When Otto von Bismarck issued a challenge in 1865 to Rudolf Virchow in the Prussian diet, officer and academic squared off together.²⁴

---

²¹ Shapin, *Social History of Truth,* p. 87.
²² *Ibid.,* p. 113; Biagioli, *Galileo, Courtier* (cit. n. 20), p. 74.
²³ On the European statistics see Nye, *Masculinity and Male Codes of Honor,* pp. 134–137, 183–187.
²⁴ Ute Frevert, "Honour and Middle-Class Culture: The History of the Duel in England and Germany," in *Bourgeois Society in Nineteenth-Century Europe,* ed. Jürgen Kocka and Allen Mitchell (Oxford: Berg, 1993), pp. 207–240, on p. 231.

Figure 1. Ruffian and gentleman: the first public criticism of the duel. (Cover of L'Assiette au Beurre, 26 January 1907.)

Figure 2. "A glorious wound. Don't worry. In the absence of any blood, I've given you a little nick with my scalpel." (From L'Assiette au Beurre, 26 January 1907.)

The aristocratic *Standesehre* that permeated the academic and professional culture of Germany was more or less confined to central Europe; to the west and south a more democratic ethos prevailed. There was nothing elsewhere to compare with the ritualized university *Mensur* duel practiced in upper-class German fraternities, where men acquired facial scars—or lost an ear or a nose—to bear witness to the quality of their masculine courage. In France and Italy the prickliest sense of honor was felt, it would appear, by journalists and politicians trying to be read and heard in the tumult of democratic politics. What all European men of honor shared, however, was the need to match deeds to words, to put their honor (and their bodies) on the line as a kind of good-faith deposit for the assertions they made in public life. In France it became less and less common, for instance, for newspaper articles (not just editorials) to be unsigned. As the French journalist and dueler Edouard Drumont wrote in 1886, "Behind every signature everyone expects to find a chest."[25]

Indeed, anonymity was suspect. As one physician described homosexuals and other nonmanly men: "writing an anonymous letter is the most exact expression of their courage." Though it would be stretching a point to make a profession of fin-de-siècle journalism, it is clear that the swashbuckling style journalists favored simply magnified the ordinary problems women might have had making a living at it. In

---

[25] Edouard Drumont, in *Le Temps*, 23 Apr. 1886. See also McAleer, *Dueling* (cit. n. 2), pp. 119–158; and Peter Gay, *The Cultivation of Hatred*, Vol. 3: *The Bourgeois Experience: Victoria to Freud* (New York: Norton, 1993), pp. 9–34.

September 1890 the feminist Séverine wrote an article in *Gil Blas* that the Boulangist politician Gabriel Terrail judged insulting. Because his offender was an "ineligible" from the point of view of honorable reparation, Terrail issued a challenge to her male editor, who was badly wounded in the subsequent duel. Séverine's boldness was roundly condemned by other feminists because she had acted in a way that required a man to come to her defense. Her dilemma was thus a kind of catch-22: the independence she wanted and needed for full participation in male professional life could only be obtained by having already proved her independence as a free agent in the larger society—a quality denied her by the tutelage of legal and social dependency imposed on women generally.[26]

In a celebrated scandal of 1911, Marie Curie, arguably the most famous woman in France, was reduced to an impotent silence while her married lover, Paul Langevin, defended his own reputation in dueling-field heroics. The letters she had exchanged with Langevin the previous year were published by a xenophobic right-wing scandal sheet. Gustave Téry, the journalist responsible for this obscene indiscretion, used language about Langevin that provoked him to issue a dueling challenge and then had the temerity to write that Madame Curie was one of those women who wanted to enter male citadels if she could but fell back on "French gallantry" when obstacles arose. The scandal provoked a letter from the Swedish Academy of Sciences suggesting that Curie might not have been awarded the Nobel Prize had these events occurred earlier, and it effectively killed any chance she might have had to be admitted to the all-male French Academy of Sciences.[27]

It is important to understand that women were not the only ones facing this dilemma: Jews, foreigners, and lower-class men were also discriminated against in a variety of formal and informal ways. Encouraged by an unprecedented overcrowding in the last decades of the nineteenth century, many professions followed strategies of "occupational closure" to maintain or strengthen their claims to a monopoly of services in their respective fields. As Anne Witz has written about this period, "These strategies employ gendered collectivist criteria of exclusion vis-a-vis women and gendered individualist criteria vis-a-vis men. They serve to create women as a class of 'ineligibles' through excluding them from routes of access to resources such as skills, knowledge, entry credentials, or technical competence, thus precluding women from entering or practicing within an occupation."[28]

This strategy at least partly explains how, despite the lack of an outright prohibition, male professionals managed for years to lock out even the most determined women from full professional status. But Witz's formulation does not address either the overwhelmingly informal nature of this process or the fact that the pervasive "masculinization" of professional culture that took place within the professions—including science—in the nineteenth century was not aimed originally or particularly

---

[26] Louis Thoinot, *Attentats aux moeurs et perversions du sens génital* (Paris: Doin, 1898), p. 309. On the incident involving Séverine see Nye, *Masculinity and Male Codes of Honor*, p. 188.

[27] Susan Quinn, *Marie Curie: A Life* (New York: Simon & Schuster, 1995), pp. 316–327.

[28] Anne Witz, *Professions and Patriarchy* (London: Routledge, 1992), p. 46. See also Margaret W. Rossiter, *Women Scientists in America: Struggles and Strategies to 1940* (Baltimore: Johns Hopkins Univ. Press, 1982), pp. 73–99; Samuel Haber, *The Quest for Authority and Honor in the American Professions* (Chicago: Univ. Chicago Press, 1991); and Sandra Harding, *The Science Question in Feminism* (Ithaca, N.Y.: Cornell Univ. Press, 1986), pp. 58–81.

at women. It was aimed primarily at controlling the quantity and quality of professionals by admitting and retaining only a *certain kind of man,* which was also a way of exercising some control over the practices and discourses in the field.[29]

* * *

I propose to demonstrate these points by examining how this informal exclusion process operated within British and French medicine. In both cases there were formidable legal, educational, and institutional obstacles that limited access to "outsiders" and built solidarity in the ranks. However, I suggest here that the masculine codes that regulated professional sociability provided additional obstacles to both men and women ignorant of their inner workings. Not coincidentally, both British and French doctors were struggling in the late nineteenth and early twentieth centuries to formulate ethical guidelines that would allow the profession to discipline or expel those who violated the elaborate etiquette of professional courtesy and competition or who dishonored the profession by infamous behavior. Neither British nor French doctors enjoyed airtight medical monopolies with full police powers over members; nor did they desire such powers, even if the state had offered them. In the time-honored way, practitioners jealously guarded their independence, preferring less formal mechanisms for keeping the troops in uniform and in line.[30]

In Britain an independent, physician-staffed General Medical Council was created in 1858 as part of a wave of reforms in medical licensing and practice. The council's responsibility was to hear charges brought against physicians (by other physicians) regarding violations of professional ethics, including such things as practicing without a license, advertising, or "unethical" behavior (the last serenely undefined). There was no written code that might serve as some kind of statutory benchmark, hearings were closed, and no transcripts were published. If it was determined that an "infamous" act had occurred, a note was published to that effect in a few medical periodicals and the individual was struck off the medical register for a predetermined period of time. Unless the matter went to the courts, the precise nature and details of the offense were never revealed.

Procedures of this kind illustrate the extent to which medical professionals in the nineteenth century engaged in intraprofessional regulation in a relatively informal way, according to an honor code that physicians, as gentlemen, were supposed naturally to understand. As Margaret Stacey has put it, "until very recently, . . . the Council had much of the appearance of a London Gentleman's Club, concerned only that its members behave like gentlemen and that 'bounders' should be evicted."[31] Indeed, until recent times it appears as if the whole point of ethical surveillance was not to

---

[29] Ted Porter has discussed these operations of community "boundary-drawing" in science and other "technologies of trust" in *Trust in Numbers: The Pursuit of Objectivity in Science and Public Life* (Princeton, N.J.: Princeton Univ. Press, 1995), pp. 220–231.

[30] On the operation of this informal exclusion process in British medicine see Witz, *Professions and Patriarchy* (cit. n. 28), pp. 73–103. For both Europe and America see Thomas Neville Bonner, *To the Ends of the Earth: Women's Search for Education in Medicine* (Cambridge, Mass.: Harvard Univ. Press, 1992); for America see Haber, *Quest for Authority and Honor in the American Professions* (cit. n. 28).

[31] Margaret Stacey, "The British General Medical Council and Medical Ethics," in *Social Science Perspectives in Medical Ethics,* ed. George Weisz (Dordrecht: Kluwer, 1990), p. 175. See also Stacey, *Regulating British Medicine: The General Medical Council* (London/New York: Wiley, 1992).

protect patients but, rather, to safeguard the image of the profession and the interests of other practitioners.

The British Medical Association, to which the majority of British physicians belonged in the early twentieth century, employed a Central Ethical Committee to assure gentlemanly behavior among its own membership. Everything about the committee's procedures harked back to traditional gentlemanly practices. As late as 1950 the committee ruled that complaints must first be addressed by the complainant to the offender, demanding "*his* explanation"; only when this proved "unsatisfactory" might the charge be forwarded to the committee. Legal counsel was forbidden to a man against whom a complaint had been brought, though (as in adjudications of the *point d'honneur*) he could bring a friend with him to the hearing. The committee did not have the power to expel offenders from the profession and even hesitated to revoke association membership in most cases. Instead, it mobilized a host of informal mechanisms ranging from inviting disputants to seek an "amicable resolution," where "amends" or "regrets" were expressed, to urging "ostracism" and extending censure to members who maintained professional or friendly relations with offenders. When a physician from Pembrokeshire wrote to the committee complaining of another BMA member "canvassing"—poaching—his patients, the committee's secretary advised him to have their differences arbitrated at the branch office in Wales "or in clubs you both belong to." When action was unavoidable, a man was expelled from the association (though not the profession) and an "important notice" to that effect published in the association's official journal.[32]

As late as 1946 there were still no written ethical rules, and resistance to formal legal action remained strong. As one member wrote to the committee, the association could take more initiatives on its own, not as some official legal tribunal, "but rather much as the committee of a social club which has the power to get rid of a member who offends against the *recognized* code." Underlining the wholly masculine nature of this enterprise, he urged the committee to follow up the "important notice" with surveillance: "Is the 'important notice' merely a pious parental hope that we shall all be good boys or is it an official rule breach of which is disloyalty to the Association?"—this at a time when there were already a substantial number of women physicians![33]

In France physicians had, if anything, less ability than their English counterparts to control access to the profession or the professional comportment of colleagues. Until a law was passed in 1892 doctors were formally prohibited from organizing to promote their collective interests, with the sole exception of burial and mutual aid societies. Not only was the state unwilling to tolerate any restraints on the free exercise of medicine; it was also, in the opinion of most practitioners, insufficiently willing to prosecute charlatans, unlicensed midwives, or other paramedicals who drained away business from legitimate healers. An unprecedented growth of medical

---

[32] Minutes of the Central Ethical Committee, 3 Apr. 1950, SA/BMA D199 E10, Wellcome Library, London (emphasis added). However, if a man failed to forward his complaint when he did not receive satisfaction, then he "may himself come under consideration": procedural rules written in 1919 (copy), discussed at a meeting of the Ethical Committee, 8 Feb. 1944, SA/BMA D99 E10, Wellcome Library. Regarding expulsion see Secretary of Central Ethical Committee to Dr. J. H. Elliot, 21 May 1938 (copy), SA/BMA D177 E213, Wellcome Library.

[33] Letter of C. O. Hawthorne, 5 Feb. 1946; and discussion at meeting of 7 Feb. 1946, SA/BMA D199 E10, Wellcome Library.

specialists in the 1880s and 1890s created an overpopulation of practitioners, reducing medical incomes and stimulating unusual competition for clients, particularly in Paris. Despite the glut, the state-regulated medical faculties produced M.D.'s at ever faster rates, moving from 590 new doctors in 1889 to 1,152 in 1901. More ominously still, foreign doctors, particularly from eastern Europe, immigrated to France in considerable numbers in these years; these included a handful of fully trained women physicians.[34]

Practitioners met this crisis in two main ways. They organized, illegally at first, in medical syndicates (unions) to protect their interests, and they addressed the pressing issues of medical competition in huge medical congresses and in a flood of treatises on medical "ethics" (*déontologie*). The ethical discourse produced from these activities largely resuscitated the medical etiquette of earlier times, clarifying the proprieties of collegial relationships and presenting a united and uplifting front to the general public. Discipline was left to hundreds of regional and municipal syndicates, many of which published brief codes setting down the elements of professional ethics. As I have argued, these ethical *règlements* resembled those adopted throughout the century by male clubs of all kinds. They proscribed "unprofessional" behavior, outlined the protocols for consultancy and referrals, and in some cases convened "honor tribunals" to mediate disputes.[35]

Talk of honor abounded. One physician called for a virtuous crusade, "*à armes courtoises*" (with weapons of courtesy) and the formation of a "code that would have the force of moral law." Another urged his colleagues to "follow the cult of honor. In its general character it is superior to both law and morality because one does not reason it out so much as feel it, as one does with religion. The doctor must have a scrupulous kind of honesty [*honnêteté*] that he applies to every act in his life." This obsession with personal honor encouraged doctors to portray their profession as uniquely dangerous and to endow practitioners with qualities of great courage. Medicine was practiced on a "field of honor" as exigent of bravery as military combat; indeed, all the deontologies of the period make much of the courage, ardor, and virile steadfastness of the French doctor.[36]

---

[34] On the legal situation see Martha L. Hildreth, *Doctors, Bureaucrats, and Public Health in France, 1888–1902* (New York: Garland, 1987); Jacques Léonard, *La médecine entre les savoirs et les pouvoirs: Histoire intellectuelle et politique de la médecine française au XIXe siècle* (Paris: Aubier, 1981); and Pierre Darmon, *La vie quotidien du médecin parisien en 1900* (Paris: Hachette, 1988), pp. 105–106. On women's medical education see Bonner, *To the Ends of the Earth* (cit. n. 30), p. 75; and J. Poirier and R. Nahon, "L'accession des femmes à la carrière médicale," in *Médecine et philosophie à la fin du XIXe siècle,* ed. J. Poirier and J. L. Poirier (Creteil: Institut de Recherche Universitaire d'Histoire de la Conaissance des Idées et des Mentalités, 1977), pp. 25–46.

[35] I have discussed these issues in Robert A. Nye, "Honor Codes and Medical Ethics in Modern France," *Bulletin of the History of Medicine,* 1995, *69:*91–111. On the early history of medical etiquette see Robert Baker, Dorothy Porter, and Roy Porter, *The Codification of Medical Morality: Historical and Philosophical Studies of the Formalization of Western Medical Morality in the Eighteenth and Nineteenth Centuries* (Dordrecht: Kluwer, 1993).

[36] Joseph Grasset, quoted in *Comte rendu de la première session du congrès international de médecine professionelle et de déontologie médicale* (Paris: Masson, 1900), p. 310 (see also Grasset, *Principes fondamentaux de déontologie médicale* [Saint-Quentin: Lagnier-Larose, 1901], pp. 11–12); and Léon Cassine, *Le médecin dans la société actuelle* (Saint-Quentin: Baudry-Baudry, 1896), p. 3. See also Lucien Grellety, *L'héroisme médical* (Macon: Protat, 1900), pp. 4–11; Edouard Juhel-Reney, *Vie professionelle et devoirs du médecin* (Paris: Doin, 1892), pp. 33, 66–68; and Nye, "Honor Codes and Medical Ethics." On virility in particular Dr. Peinard argued that "the attributes of virility inspire, in general, respect in the weak, confidence in women, and the public will have only pity and suspicion

In general, praise of the desirable qualities of the "native" French doctor was designed to exclude both foreign and female physicians. Some deontologies were openly opposed to women in the profession, holding them to be lacking in energy, courage, judgment, personal authority, firmness, and that most honorable of qualities, independence, which consisted of "the conscience of the free man, so little compatible with the indecisiveness of a woman's inconstant nature." Though some conceded female physicians' place in the care of women and children, they were believed not to possess the requisite sangfroid for the surgical theater, and they were held to be given to an affected "primness and pedantry" that ill suited them for the rough-and-tumble of medical life.[37]

By the turn of the century, women everywhere in the West had begun to break down the formal barriers that had obliged them in earlier years to go "to the ends of the earth" in search of medical education, hospital experience, and certification. But no dramatic increases in the number of female physicians occurred over the next seventy-five years. Successful women M.D.'s were shunted into acceptably "feminine" areas of practice: public health, hygiene, gynecology, pediatrics, and obstetrics. The same patterns marked professional science as well. Margaret Rossiter has shown that the "growth" in the number of women scientists in the early years of the twentieth century was modest and that the percentage of Ph.D.'s in science awarded to women actually fell in most fields after 1932.[38]

The reasons for this are many and complex, but I suggest that one hitherto-unappreciated factor has been the exclusionary role played by the male honor culture in the multiple formal and informal settings where professional sociability controlled behavior, expectations, and opportunities. I have tried to establish the ubiquity and power of male honor codes in some of these settings, focusing on the fact that such codes had historically functioned to regulate masculine intraprofessional relations. However, when women began to enter science and the professions in significant numbers, these same mechanisms worked effectively to alienate and handicap them.

One can identify a kind of hierarchy of disincentives—ranging from brutal to subtle—firmly rooted in the practices of a masculine honor culture. The most obvious, especially where the duel was tolerated in public life until after World War I, was a tense atmosphere of watchful aggression where words were measured for their effects on the man behind them. In view of the fact that a willingness and ability to engage in violence was regarded as a warrant for the truthfulness (or at least sincerity) of public statements, it is likely that in such situations educated middle-class

---

of a limp and frail doctor not in the most flourishing and robust health": Peinard, *La profession de médecine* (Paris, 1902), p. 138.

[37] Peinard, *Profession de médecine,* pp. 38–40, on p. 38; see also Jean Pozzi, "Contre l'internat des femmes," *Revue Scientifique,* 3rd Ser., 1884, 8:536–538. On female physicians' "place" see Etienne Martin, *Précis de déontologie et de médecine professionnelle* (Paris: Masson, 1914), pp. 29–30; and Georges Morache, *La profession médicale: Ses devoirs, ses droits* (Paris: Alcan, 1901), p. 71.

[38] Women's efforts to obtain medical training have been chronicled in Bonner, *To the Ends of the Earth* (cit. n. 30). See also Mary Roth Walsh, *"Doctors Wanted: No Women Need Apply": Sexual Barriers in the Medical Profession* (New Haven, Conn.: Yale Univ. Press, 1977); Regina Markell Morantz-Sanchez, *Sympathy and Science: Women Physicians in American Medicine* (Oxford: Oxford Univ. Press, 1985), p. 182; and Rossiter, *Women Scientists in America: Struggles and Strategies to 1940* (cit. n. 28), pp. 129–133.

women would feel, at the minimum, discomfort, and at most, a thoroughgoing disenfranchisement.

However, as I have also suggested, where the *point d'honneur* either did not exist or had died out, its imprint on the forms of sociability remained. Thus "satisfaction," "making amends," the mediation of "differences," the premium put on deft but "frank" interchange, all remained important aspects of middle- and upper-class professional sociability, even though they were no longer ostentatiously underwritten by the threat of physical challenge. Might this not have stilled the voices of women, whose bodies could not unambiguously represent masculine notions of resolve, or who did not know or care to adopt the gestural repertory of assertiveness?

Further down the hierarchy, but no less redolent of violence, was the unholy trinity of smoking, drinking, and profanity, which were salient expressions of male exclusivity if not aggression. All flourished in male circles and societies, and there is excellent evidence that men fully grasped the gendered meanings they conveyed. One late nineteenth-century French male could think of nothing more praiseworthy to say about his club than that it was "a pseudonym for divorce, like the cigar."[39] In an example as symbolic as it is melodramatic, Sophia Jex-Blake, a pioneering medical graduate of the University of Edinburgh, described the experience of being locked out of the final examination hall by a group of male medical students "who stood within, smoking and passing about bottles of whiskey, while they abused us in the foulest possible language." Another medical pioneer, Mary Putnam Jacobi, who attended the Ecole de Médecine in the late 1860s, was prevented from becoming a hospital intern, which was then the royal road to medical eminence, by social rather than legal prohibitions. Interns lived in common quarters and socialized in a *salle de garde,* which was notorious, as Jacobi knew, for erotic drawings and a vulgar atmosphere.[40]

Other barriers were more subtle. Though offense or discourteousness was neither intended nor observed, women nonetheless felt isolated in local and regional medical societies—assuming, that is, that they gained admission at all. They did not rise to positions of leadership and did not feel as though they were an integral part of the group. This led to a growth, in late nineteenth-century America, of "parallel" women's medical societies, founded not simply out of rancor but because women desired a sense of professional solidarity they did not feel in groups of men. As Dr. Azuba King told the State Society of Iowa Medical Women in 1901: "Our professional brothers long ago recognized the truth: In union there is strength . . . let us profit by their example. The woman physician—alone either in city or town has an isolated professional life, the brother practitioner may be courteous and ethical—she is alone nevertheless."[41]

---

[39] As Margaret Rossiter has shown, cigar smoking was deployed as a "deliberately intimidating part" of the "masculinization" of late nineteenth-century American science, which only the most daring women challenged. See Rossiter, *Women Scientists in America: Struggles and Strategies to 1940,* pp. 92–94; quoted in Nye, *Masculinity and Male Codes of Honor,* p. 131. Sometimes, as Freud once said, a cigar was only a cigar. However, even when not serving as a metaphor for something else, cigars drove women away.

[40] Sophia Jex-Blake, quoted in Witz, *Professions and Patriarchy* (cit. n. 28), p. 90; and Joy Harvey, "La Visite: Mary Putnam Jacobi and the Paris Medical Clinic," in *French Medical Culture in the Nineteenth Century,* ed. Ann La Berge and Mordechai Feingold (Amsterdam: Rodopi, 1994), pp. 350–371, esp. pp. 355, 369 n. 21.

[41] Azuba King, quoted in Morantz-Sanchez, *Sympathy and Science* (cit. n. 38), p. 181; see also Walsh, *"Doctors Wanted: No Women Need Apply"* (cit. n. 38), pp. 262–264.

* * *

In conclusion, let me suggest that we need to think more about how masculine honor cultures have managed to sustain themselves in science and medicine despite the presence of increasing numbers of women. Leslie McCall has recently shown how Pierre Bourdieu's concept of the "field" may be adapted to provide a fully gendered understanding of the way specialized or technical fields "reproduce" particular practices in the form of a kind of "unconscious habitus" in which "quasi-bodily dispositions" function as incorporated (tacit) knowledge. I say "adapted" because in his recent work on academic and social "fields" Bourdieu often writes as though these fields are neutral with respect to gender. Bourdieu began his career as a sociologist studying masculine honor codes in Kabyle society in North Africa. His later notion of the "habitus" as a rule-bound self-perpetuating system appears to be based on the model of a male honor culture passed down from father to son. But he appears somehow to have "forgotten" that this fruitful concept was originally, indeed primordially, a masculine model and to have made it into a neutrally gendered device designed for more general kinds of social reproduction: of academic culture, aesthetic philosophies, taste, and the like.[42]

When gender is put back into the equation, a more interesting picture emerges. As McCall points out, when a specialized field has been historically dominated by men and is structured by the protocols of an oral honor culture, a man and a woman who enter it for the first time experience it differently. The man may proceed immediately to the tasks at hand, based on his knowledge and expertise, while the woman is reflexively aware of being in a social situation. For him the social is "natural" in the sense that it is gendered masculine and reflects his previous experiences. The woman, however, must work through a supplementary array of choices about identity and appropriate behavior because, as Elizabeth Fee has written, "in this process women internalize the cultural contradictions of gender in a constant, ongoing process of mediating opposing cultural demands."[43]

As I noted at the beginning of this essay, with some important exceptions much of the literature in the sociology of science or on science as practice is curiously uninterested in gender, though it is fantastically sensitive to the slightest hint of a variety of other factors that constrain or inflect the direction of scientific work. I think here of Bruno Latour and Steve Woolgar's *Laboratory Life*, a rich account of day-to-day experience in a molecular biology laboratory. Though the authors do not acknowledge this point, their account of lab life takes the almost caricatural form of an oral, face-to-face male honor culture. Though the "inscription" of "hard facts" is of great importance, it serves the larger purpose of "persuading" those outside the

---

[42] Leslie McCall, "Does Gender Fit? Bourdieu, Feminism, and Conceptions of Social Order," *Theory Soc.*, 1992, *21*:837–867. There are glimmers of understanding in the critical literature on this point. See Beate Krais, "Gender and Symbolic Violence: Female Oppression in the Light of Pierre Bourdieu's Theory of Social Practice," in *Bourdieu: Critical Perspectives*, ed. Craig Calhoun, Edward LiPuma, and Moishe Postone (Oxford: Polity, 1993), pp. 156–177; and Rogers Brubaker, "Social Theory as Habitus," *ibid.*, pp. 212–224.

[43] McCall, "Does Gender Fit?" and Elizabeth Fee, "Critiques of Modern Science: The Relationship of Feminism to Other Radical Epistemologies," in *Feminist Approaches to Science*, ed. Ruth Bleier (New York: Pergamon, 1986), pp. 42–56, on pp. 45–46. For an interesting account of how the geneticist Barbara McClintock negotiated this journey see Evelyn Fox Keller, *Reflections on Gender and Science* (New Haven, Conn.: Yale Univ. Press, 1985), pp. 158–176.

lab that "what they do is important, that what they say is true, and that their proposals are worth funding." By eavesdropping on conversations between scientists, Latour and Woolgar learn that "who had made the claim was as important as the claim itself." Indeed, in the aggressive atmosphere of high-stakes science, speakers evaluated scientific publications in terms of "the author's social strategy or their psychological makeup" and in light of the author's past work and "reputation."[44]

For Latour and Woolgar the scientific enterprise is a "quest for credit" amassed on the basis of "credentials" and on the "creditable" results of scientific research. Credit is extended on the basis of "trust," and what they specifically call the "*point d'honneur*" of a "credit receipt" could be withdrawn, in the form of lab time and space or access to equipment, when personal differences emerge. In this schema, credit is like honor, which may be acquired, threatened, or lost just as personal honor fluctuated in previous centuries. The ultimate aim is to gain the maximum amount of "independence"—a lab of one's own—and to avoid the fate of dependency— falling into the position of a salaried employee or technician. The "field" of the laboratory, in this account, is like a battlefield: "The tension of a battalion headquarters at war, or an executive room in a period of crisis, does not compare with the atmosphere of a laboratory on a normal day."[45]

Descriptions of this kind come easily to hand from other male scientists. Richard Lewontin writes that "what every scientist knows, but few will admit, is that the requirement for great success is great ambition. Moreover, the ambition is for a personal triumph over other *men,* not merely over nature. Science is a form of competitive and aggressive activity, a contest of man against man that provides knowledge as a side product. That side product is its only advantage over football." In another acknowledgment of the workings of honor, Carl Djerassi has one of the male scientists in his novel *Cantor's Dilemma* (1989) liken science to war and has his main character say to an adoring female companion, "Because of our mutual dependence and our need for absolute trust, once somebody's credibility in science is damaged, it can never be totally repaired. Most often it's gone for good."[46]

The object of Lewontin's remarks, James D. Watson's *The Double Helix,* is packed with battle metaphors—mediated, to be sure, with assurances about the "gentlemanly" restraints that keep science from being a vulgar free-for-all. The odd woman out in the "war" this book describes was, of course, Rosalind Franklin, who "was not about to play games with me" and whose retorts were especially feared because they had a way "of bringing back unpleasant memories of lower school" (where

---

[44] Bruno Latour and Steve Woolgar, *Laboratory Life: The Construction of Scientific Facts* (Princeton, N.J.: Princeton Univ. Press, 1986), pp. 69, 87–88, 164, 163–165. In a recent review of the literature on the sociology of science and science as practice, Michael Lynch devotes no more than a dozen lines to gender issues and interpretations, which he refers to as "feminist and other politicized modes of textual criticism": Michael Lynch, *Scientific Practice and Ordinary Action: Ethnomethodology and Social Studies of Science* (New York: Cambridge Univ. Press, 1993), pp. xiii, 83. One important exception is Sharon Traweek's *Beamtimes and Lifetimes* (cit. n. 11). See also, on this matter, the comments of Hilary Rose, "Gendered Reflexions on the Laboratory in Medicine," in *The Laboratory Revolution in Medicine,* ed. Andrew Cunningham and Perry Williams (Cambridge: Cambridge Univ. Press, 1992), pp. 324–342.

[45] Latour and Woolgar, *Laboratory Life,* pp. 194–195, 228, 231 n. 8, 228–229.

[46] Richard Lewontin, "'Honest Jim' Watson's Big Thriller about DNA," in James D. Watson, *The Double Helix: Text, Commentary, Reviews, Original Papers,* ed. Gunther Stent (New York: Norton, 1980), pp. 85–187, on p. 187 (emphasis added); and Carl Djerassi, *Cantor's Dilemma* (New York: Penguin, 1989), pp. 207, 113.

one's teacher was a woman). Indeed, "the thought could not be avoided that the best home for a feminist was in another person's lab." Watson's account of the race to determine the structure of DNA presents modern scientific research as squarely situated in a "field" with masculine rules of conduct that guide scientists in their behavior in the laboratory and in the informal discussions of common room and tennis court, rules that pioneer women scientists like Franklin either did not know or refused to follow.[47]

Sharon Traweek has written that junior women scientists often do not see how these gendered "rules" work against them "because they [have] not yet gotten to the career stage at which they would be defining fully independent research projects requiring their own command of significant resources."[48] The male authors I have just quoted seem to understand the rules well enough, but, as the examples given reveal, they regard them as somehow "natural" to science and so simply don't understand the extent to which they were and are still (en)gendered by a masculine code of honor. Indeed, were it not for the fact that scholars like Traweek have provided us with detailed studies of the masculine culture dominant in certain scientific and professional fields, we might well imagine that the war metaphors we have seen sprinkled through many of these descriptions of lab life were part of a deliberate gatekeeping operation designed to keep science a woman-free zone. As I noted in Bourdieu's case, however, mistaking the cultural for the natural is one of the deeper pitfalls on the road to universal truths.

I am aware of the lack of rigor in the term *practice* and of the difficulty of explaining how practices, scientific and otherwise, are constituted and, in the Bourdieuian sense, "reproduced" across time and space. But it seems unfruitful to me to mount a campaign of skepticism against practice as a useful concept in the history of medicine or science before we have fully deconstructed the reasons why practice has been treated as gender neutral in much of the recent literature. If we attend more thoroughly to the history of the wider social and cultural setting in which science, medicine, and other professions of "expertise" have developed, we will discover far more about the influential role gender plays in the dynamics of such rule- and practice-bound activities.[49]

---

[47] Watson, *Double Helix,* ed. Stent, pp. 13, 30, 95, 45, 15.

[48] Sharon Traweek, "Border Crossings: Narrative Strategies in Science Studies and among Physicists in Tsukuba Science City, Japan," in *Science as Practice and Culture,* ed. Andrew Pickering (Chicago: Univ. Chicago Press, 1992), pp. 429–466, on p. 443.

[49] See Harding, *Science Question in Feminism* (cit. n. 28), pp. 72–73. For some creative efforts of this kind see a recent issue of *Actes de la Recherche en Sciences Sociales,* Dec. 1994, *105,* on "Stratégies de reproduction et transmission des pouvoirs." For an example of this skeptical approach to the concept of practices see Stephen Turner, *The Social Theory of Practices: Tradition, Tacit Knowledge, and Presuppositions* (Chicago: Univ. Chicago Press, 1994).

The Engendering of Archaeology
Refiguring Feminist Science Studies

By Alison Wylie*

INTERNAL CRITIQUES: THE SOCIOPOLITICS OF ARCHAEOLOGY

In the last fifteen years archaeologists have been drawn into heated debates about the objectivity of their enterprise. These are frequently provoked by critical analyses that demonstrate (with hindsight) how pervasively some of the best, most empirically sophisticated archaeological practice has reproduced nationalist, racist, classist, and, according to the most recent analyses, sexist and androcentric understandings of the cultural past. Some archaeologists conclude on this basis that however influential the rhetoric of objectivity may be among practitioners, the practice and products of archaeology must inevitably reflect the situated interests of its makers. A great many others regard such claims with suspicion, if not outright hostility. They maintain the conviction—a central and defining tenet of North American archaeology since its founding as a profession early in this century—that archaeology is, first and foremost, a science and that, therefore, the social and political contexts of inquiry are properly external to the process of inquiry and to its products.[1]

The feminist critiques of archaeology on which I focus here are relative newcomers to this growing tradition of internal "sociopolitical" critique. Not surprisingly, they have drawn sharply critical reactions that throw into relief the polarized positions that dominate thinking about the status and aims of archaeology. And yet, I will argue, these feminist interventions do not readily fit any of the epistemic options defined in this debate; they exemplify a critical engagement of claims to objectivity

---

* Department of Philosophy, 315 Talbot College, University of Western Ontario, London, Ontario N6A 3K7, Canada.

[1] As in many social sciences, archaeologists have set enormous store in establishing the scientific credibility and authority of their discipline and its products in the last thirty years. In North America this took the form of widespread commitment to the proscience, explicitly positivist goals of the New Archaeology, which embody objectivist ideals in an especially stringent form. Reconstructive hypotheses were to be treated as the starting point, not the end point, of research, and any investigation of the archaeological record was to be designed (on a hypothetico-deductive model of confirmation) as an empirical test of these hypotheses; whatever their sources, they were to be confronted with evidence from the surviving record of the pasts they purport to describe and accepted or rejected on this basis. The expectation was that a rigorously scientific methodology would preserve archaeologists from the pernicious influence of standpoint-specific interests and power relations as they either operate within the field or impinge on it from outside; they would ensure that archaeology is "self-cleansing" of intrusive bias and therefore produces genuine (i.e., objective) knowledge of the cultural past. These developments are discussed in more detail in Alison Wylie, "The Constitution of Archaeological Evidence: Gender, Politics, and Science," in *Disunity and Contextualism: New Directions in the Philosophy of Science Studies,* ed. Peter Galison and David Stump (Palo Alto, Calif.: Stanford Univ. Press, 1996), pp. 311–343.

©1997 by The History of Science Society. All rights reserved. 0369-7827/97/1201-0006$02.00

that refuses reductive constructivism as firmly as it rejects unreflective objectivism. This is a strategic ambivalence that holds enormous promise and is typical of much feminist thinking in and about scientific practice. In this essay I first characterize what I will identify provisionally as the feminist initiatives that have emerged in archaeology since the late 1980s (qualifications of this designation come later) and then consider their larger implications. My immediate concern is how, within the rubric of feminist science studies, we are to understand the late and rapid emergence of an archaeological interest in questions about women and gender. This leads, in turn, to a set of reflexive questions about how to do feminist science studies.

Feminist Critiques in Archaeology

Critiques of sexism and androcentrism in archaeology fall into two broad categories that parallel analyses of other dimensions of archaeological practice (e.g., its nationalism, classism, and racism): "content" and "equity" critiques. In addition—and in this feminist critiques are distinctive—there is emerging a move toward "integrative" analyses that combine content and equity critiques.

Content Critiques. Two types of content critique can usefully be distinguished. The first draws attention to erasure, to ways in which the choice of research problem or the determination of significant sites or periods or cultural complexes leaves out of account women and gender even when they are a crucial part of the story to be told.[2] For example, Anne Yentsch delineates previously unacknowledged patterns of change in the ceramic ware of domestic assemblages that testify to the gradual transfer of women's productive activities (specifically, domestic dairy production) from the home to commercial enterprises whenever these became capable of industrialization; she argues that this largely unexamined process of appropriation of "women's work" is crucial for understanding the transformation of the rural economy in the northeastern United States through the eighteenth and nineteenth centuries. Similarly, Donna Seifert describes the difference it makes to our understanding of the archaeology of urban centers if we take seriously the presence of prostitutes, for example, in "Within Sight of the White House." And Cheryl Claassen draws attention to the rich insights that follow from a focus on the shellfishing activities associated primarily with women and children in the Shell Mound Archaic. To take a prehistoric example that I will discuss in more detail later in this essay, Pat Watson and Mary Kennedy argue that dominant explanations of the emergence of horticulture in the Eastern Woodlands share a common flaw: although women are presumed to have been primarily responsible for collecting plants under earlier gatherer-hunter/foraging subsistence regimes and for cultivating them when gourds and maize were domesticated, they play no role at all in accounts of how this profoundly

---

[2] These critiques closely parallel those that draw attention to the archaeological record of, for example, colonial and neocolonial domination in areas where archaeology has focused on the "eclipsed civilizations" or hominid origins of much earlier periods (e.g., in Latin America and Africa), that of slaves on plantation sites where the "great houses" and lives of landholding planters had been the primary focus of archaeological attention, and that of First Nations communities in areas long occupied by Euro-Americans that were not recognized because their patterns of settlement did not conform to the European model of nucleated villages. These examples are discussed in more detail in Alison Wylie, "Evidential Constraints: Pragmatic Empiricism in Archaeology," in *Readings in the Philosophy of Social Science,* ed. Lee McIntyre and Michael Martin (Cambridge, Mass.: MIT Press, 1994), pp. 747–766.

culture-transforming shift in subsistence practice was realized.[3] Watson and Kennedy say they are "leery" of explanations that remove women from the one domain granted them as soon as an exercise of initiative is envisioned.

Often, however, straightforward erasure is not the problem; and so a second sort of critique is required, one that focuses on how women and gender are represented when they are taken into account. From the outset feminist critics have emphasized that, although questions about women and gender have never been on the archaeological research agenda, archaeological research problems and interpretations are routinely framed in gendered terms.[4] The functions ascribed to artifacts and sites are often gender specific, and models of such diverse cultural phenomena as subsistence practices among foragers, social organization in agrarian societies, and the dynamics of state formation often turn on the projection onto prehistory of a common body of presentist, ethnocentric, and overtly androcentric assumptions about sexual divisions of labor and the status and roles of women. Women in prehistoric foraging societies are presumed to be tied to "home bases" while their male counterparts quite literally "bring home the bacon," despite extensive ethnohistoric evidence that women in such contexts are highly mobile and that their foraging activities are often responsible for most of the dietary intake of their families and communities.

More subtle but equally problematic are interpretations of large-scale cultural transformations that treat gender roles and domestic relations as a stable (natural) substrate of social organization that is unchanged by the rise and fall of states and is, therefore, explanatorily irrelevant. In another case that I will consider further, Christine Hastorf argues that the domestic units encountered in the highland Andes at the time of the Spanish conquest cannot be projected back into prehistory as if their form was a given. She offers compelling archaeological evidence that households and gender roles were substantially reshaped by the extension of Inka influence into these territories. In a parallel analysis, Elizabeth Brumfiel argues not just that the Aztec system of economic and political control changed domestic relations but that, given its basis in exacting tribute in the form of locally produced cloth, it depended fundamentally on the intensified and restructured exploitation of female (domestic) labor.[5] In these cases, critical (re)analysis reveals ways in which understanding has been limited not by ignoring women and gender altogether, but by conceptualizing them in normatively middle-class, white, North American terms.

Equity Critiques. Alongside these forms of content critique, there has grown up a

---

[3] Anne Yentsch, "Engendering Visible and Invisible Ceramic Artifacts, Especially Dairy Vessels," in *Gender in Historical Archaeology,* ed. Donna Seifert, special issue of *Historical Archaeology,* 1991, 25(4):132–155; Seifert, "Within Sight of the White House: The Archaeology of Working Women," *ibid.,* pp. 82–108; Cheryl Claassen, "Gender, Shellfishing, and the Shell Mound Archaic," in *Engendering Archaeology: Women and Prehistory,* ed. Joan M. Gero and Margaret W. Conkey (Oxford: Blackwell, 1991), pp. 276–300; and Patty Jo Watson and Mary C. Kennedy, "The Development of Horticulture in the Eastern Woodlands of North America: Women's Role," *ibid.,* pp. 255–275.

[4] See, e.g., Margaret W. Conkey and Janet D. Spector, "Archaeology and the Study of Gender," in *Advances in Archaeological Method and Theory,* Vol. 7, ed. Michael B. Schiffer (New York: Academic, 1984), pp. 1–38; and Spector and Mary K. Whelan, "Incorporating Gender into Archaeology Courses," in *Gender and Anthropology: Critical Reviews for Research and Teaching,* ed. Sandra Morgen (Washington, D.C.: American Anthropological Association, 1989), pp. 65–94.

[5] Christine A. Hastorf, "Gender, Space, and Food in Prehistory," in *Engendering Archaeology,* ed. Gero and Conkey (cit. n. 3), pp. 132–159; and Elizabeth M. Brumfiel, "Weaving and Cooking: Women's Production in Aztec Mexico," *ibid.,* pp. 224–253.

substantial and largely independent body of literature concerning the demography, institutional structures, funding sources, training, and employment patterns that shape archaeology. Feminist analyses of the status of women constitute some of the most fine-grained and empirically rich work of this sort.[6] These "equity critiques" document not only persistent patterns of differential support, training, and advancement for women in archaeology, but also entrenched patterns of gender segregation in the areas in which women typically work.

While such studies provide fascinating detail on ways in which women are marginalized within archaeology, rarely are they used as a basis for understanding how the content of archaeological knowledge is shaped. And although content critics provide compelling evidence that the silences and distortions they identify are systematically gendered, rarely do they make any connection between these and the gender imbalances in the training, employment, and reward structures of the discipline documented by equity critics. In general, sociopolitical critics in archaeology have tended to sidestep explanatory questions about how the silences and stereotypes they delineate are produced or why they persist.[7]

---

[6] Much of this "equity" literature appears in society or institution newsletters, in publications produced by in-house report series, or is circulated as informal reports and internal documents. Some of the more accessible and widely known of these studies and reports include Carol Kramer and Miriam Stark, "The Status of Women in Archaeology," *Anthropology Newsletter,* 1988, 29(9):1, 11–12; Joan M. Gero, "Gender Bias in Archaeology: A Cross-Cultural Perspective," in *The Socio-Politics of Archaeology,* ed. Gero, David M. Lacy, and Michael L. Blakey (Research Reports, 23) (Amherst: Dept. Anthropology, Univ. Massachusetts, 1983); and Gero, "Socio-Politics and the Woman-at-Home Ideology," *American Antiquity,* 1985, 50:342–350. A number of related studies are collected in Dale Walde and Noreen D. Willows, eds., *The Archaeology of Gender: Proceedings of the 22nd Annual Chacmool Conference* (Calgary: Archaeological Association, Univ. Calgary, 1991); Hilary du Cros and Laurajane Smith, eds., *Women in Archaeology: A Feminist Critique* (Canberra: Australian National Univ. Occasional Papers, 1993); Margaret C. Nelson, Sarah M. Nelson, and Alison Wylie, eds., *Equity Issues for Women in Archaeology* (Archaeological Papers, 5) (Washington, D.C.: American Anthropological Association, 1994); and Cheryl Claassen, ed., *Women in Archaeology* (Philadelphia: Univ. Pennsylvania Press, 1994). The collection edited by Nelson *et al.* includes reprints of a number of earlier and otherwise inaccessible reports, along with newer studies and overviews of work in a number of different national contexts and subfields of archaeology.

In discussing this literature it is important to note that women are perhaps the only traditionally excluded group (with the possible exception of men from working-class backgrounds) to gain sufficient levels of representation within archaeology to develop such critiques on their own behalf. Nevertheless, studies of the sociopolitics of archaeology document many other dimensions on which the demographic homogeneity of the discipline has been maintained. See, e.g., the discussion of recruiting and training practices in Jane H. Kelley and Marsha P. Hanen, *Archaeology and the Methodology of Science* (Albuquerque: Univ. New Mexico Press, 1988), Ch. 4. Thomas C. Patterson considers ways in which the interests of intranational elites have shaped archaeology in Patterson, "The Last Sixty Years: Toward a Social History of Americanist Archaeology in the United States," *American Anthropologist,* 1986, 88:7–22; Patterson, "Some Postwar Theoretical Trends in U.S. Archaeology," *Culture,* 1986, 11:43–54; and in Patterson, *Toward a Social History of Archaeology in the United States* (Orlando, Fla.: Harcourt Brace, 1995), he offers an analysis of the impact of the GI bill's educational support on the class structure of the discipline. Bruce G. Trigger explores the alignment of archaeology with nationalist agendas of various sorts in *A History of Archaeological Thought* (Cambridge: Cambridge Univ. Press, 1989).

[7] Typically these studies identify correlations, at a general level, between sociopolitical features of the discipline and of its products, offering an implicitly functional explanation for androcentric, nationalist, racist, or classist gaps and biases in content, but rarely do they supply an account of mediating mechanisms. Some important exceptions are reported in the landmark collection of essays, *The Socio-Politics of Archaeology,* ed. Gero *et al.,* that appeared in 1983. Working at a local, infrastructural scale, Martin H. Wobst and Arthur S. Keene argued that the fascination archaeologists

Integrative Critiques. There is one study, undertaken from an explicitly feminist perspective, that illustrates the potential fruitfulness of "integrative analyses": analyses that explore the link between workplace inequities and androcentric bias in the content of research. It is an analysis of Paleo-Indian research undertaken by Joan Gero. She begins by documenting a strong pattern of gender segregation: the predominantly male community of Paleo-Indian researchers focuses almost exclusively on stereotypically male activities—specifically, on large-scale mammoth- and bison-hunting practices, the associated kill sites and technologically sophisticated hunting tool assemblages, and the replication of these tools and of the hunting and butchering practices they are thought to have facilitated. Gero finds that the women in this field have been largely displaced from these core research areas; they work on expedient blades and flake tools and focus on edge-wear analysis. Moreover, in the field of lithics analysis generally, women are cited much less frequently than their male colleagues even when they do mainstream research, except when they coauthor with men. Not surprisingly, Gero argues, their work on expedient blades and patterns of edge wear is almost completely ignored, despite the fact that these analyses provide evidence that Paleo-Indians exploited a wide range of plant materials, presumably foraged as a complement to the diet of Pleistocene mammals. Gero's thesis is that these "social *relations* of paleo research practice" derail the Paleo-Indian research program as a whole: "women's exclusion from pleistocene lithic and faunal analysis . . . is intrinsic to, and necessary for, the bison-mammoth knowledge construct."[8] The puzzles that dominate Paleo-Indian research are quite literally created by the preoccupation with male-associated (hunting) activities. They turn on questions about what happened to the mammoth hunters when the mammoths went extinct: Did they disappear, to be replaced by small game and plant foraging groups, or did they effect a miraculous transformation as the subsistence base changed? These questions can only arise, Gero argues, if researchers ignore the evidence from female-associated tools that Paleo-Indians depended on a much more diversified set of subsistence strategies than acknowledged by standard "man the (mammoth/bison) hunter" models. This is precisely the sort of evidence produced mainly by women working on microblades and edge-wear patterns; it is reported in publications that remain largely outside the citation circles that define the dominant focus of inquiry in this area.

ARCHAEOLOGY AS POLITICS BY OTHER MEANS

When critiques of androcentrism and sexism appeared in archaeology in the late 1980s, debate about the implications of sociopolitical critiques was already sharply

---

have with "origins" research should be understood as, at least in part, a consequence of structural features of disciplinary practice: Wobst and Keene, "Archaeological Explanation as Political Economy," *ibid.,* pp. 79–90. Researchers who control the understanding of originary events or cultural formations must be acknowledged, in various ways, by all who work on later, linked periods and developments; they establish themselves as the "eye of the needle" through which all else must past. This line of argument has recently been extended and reframed in feminist terms by Margaret Conkey, in collaboration with Sarah H. Williams, "Original Narratives: The Political Economy of Gender in Archaeology," in *Gender, Culture, and Political Economy: Feminist Anthropology in the Post-Modern Era,* ed. Micaela di Leonardo (Berkeley: Univ. California Press, 1991), pp. 102–139.

[8] Joan M. Gero, "The Social World of Prehistoric Facts: Gender and Power in Prehistoric Research," in *Women in Archaeology,* ed. du Cros and Smith (cit. n. 6), pp. 31–40, on p. 37.

polarized. Some of the most uncompromising critics of the explicitly positivist "New Archaeology" of the 1960s and 1970s parlayed local analyses of the play of interests in archaeology into a general rejection of all concepts or ideals of objectivity. Through the early 1980s they insisted, on the basis of arguments familiar in philosophical contexts (underdetermination of theory by evidence, theory-ladenness, and various forms of holism), that archaeologists simply "create facts," that evidential claims depend on "an edifice of auxiliary theories and assumptions" that archaeologists accept on purely conventional grounds, and that there is, therefore, no escape from the conclusion that any use of archaeological data to test reconstructive hypotheses about the past can "only result in tautology."[9] The choice between tautologies, then, must necessarily be determined by standpoint-specific interests and the sociopolitics that shape them; archaeology is quite literally politics by other means.

With these arguments, some critics within archaeology broach what Bruce Trigger has described as a nihilistic "hyperrelativism" now familiar in many of the social sciences. Given critical analyses that "shatter" pretensions to objectivity, demonstrating that there is no "view from nowhere," no immaculately conceived foundation of fact, no transcontextual or transhistorical standard of rationality, it is assumed that epistemic considerations play no significant role at all.[10] What counts as sound argument and evidence (as "good reasons" for accepting a knowledge claim) is entirely reducible to the sociopolitical realities that constitute the standpoint of practitioners, or communities of practitioners, and the conventions of their practice. For a great many archaeologists, these conclusions were grounds for summarily dismissing postprocessualism and any aligned analysis that purports to bring into view the play of politics in archaeology. A dominant counter-response has been to call for a return to basics, to the real (empirical) business of archaeology. Not surprisingly, the feminist critiques that appeared in the late 1980s met with considerable skepticism.

What distinguishes the interventions of feminist critics in these debates is their refusal, for the most part, to embrace any of the polarized responses generated by this growing crisis of confidence in objectivist ideals. In most cases feminist critics in archaeology depend on painstakingly careful empirical analysis to establish their claims about gaps or bias in content, about inequities in the role and status of women in the field, and about the links between equity and content critiques. But however pervasive the androcentrism or sexism they delineate, and however sharply they criticize pretensions to neutrality and objectivity, they are deeply reticent to embrace any position approaching the hyperrelativism described by Trigger. They are clear about the social, political nature of the archaeological enterprise, and yet they do

---

[9] Ian Hodder, "Archaeology, Ideology, and Contemporary Society," *Royal Anthropological Institute News,* 1983, *56:*6; Hodder, "Archaeology in 1984," *Antiquity,* 1984, *58:*26; and Michael Shanks and Christopher Tilley, *Re-constructing Archaeology* (Cambridge: Cambridge Univ. Press, 1987), p. 111.

[10] Bruce G. Trigger, "Hyperrelativism, Responsibility, and the Social Sciences," *Canadian Review of Sociology and Anthropology,* 1989, *26:*776–797; Thomas Nagel, *The View from Nowhere* (Oxford: Oxford Univ. Press, 1986); and Richard Bernstein, *Beyond Objectivism and Relativism: Science, Hermeneutics, and Praxis* (Philadelphia: Univ. Pennsylvania Press, 1983). See also Alison Wylie, "On 'Heavily Decomposing Red Herrings': Scientific Method in Archaeology and the Ladening of Evidence with Theory," in *Metaarchaeology,* ed. Lester Embree (Boston: Reidel, 1992), pp. 269–288.

not consider the outcomes of inquiry or the criteria of adequacy governing practice to be reducible to the sociopolitics of practice.

Two lines of argument support this stance. For one thing, it is evident that, as a matter of contingent empirical fact, "reasons"—appeals to evidence and considerations of explanatory power, as well as of internal and cross-theory consistency—do frequently play a critical role in determining the content of archaeological interpretations and the presuppositions that frame them, including those embraced or advocated by feminists. That is to say, reasons can be causes; they shape belief and the outcomes of archaeological inquiry, although their form and authority are never transparent and never innocent of the power relations that constitute the social contexts of their production. For another, close scrutiny of archaeological practice makes it clear that, as Roy Bhaskar argued years ago, one crucial and much-neglected feature of science "is that it is *work;* and hard work at that. . . . [It] consists . . . in the transformation of given products." Most important, these "products" are built from materials that archaeologists do not construct out of whole cloth, whose properties they can be (disastrously) wrong about, and whose capacities to act or be acted upon can be exploited to powerful effect by those intent on "intervening" in the world(s) they study when these worlds are accurately understood.[11] Sociologically reductive accounts cannot make sense of these features of archaeological practice, including the practice of feminists and other critics in and of archaeology. Perhaps feminists have been more alert to these considerations because here, as in other contexts, they are painfully aware that the world is not (just) what we make it, and the cost of systematic error or self-delusion can be very high; effective activism requires an accurate understanding of the forces we oppose, conceptually, politically, and materially.

Most recently, the critics within archaeology who raised the specter of hyperrelativism have backed away from their strongest (and most untenable) claims.[12] They seem to have recognized that, insofar as they mean to expose systematic error and explain it (e.g., by appeal to the conditions that shape knowledge production), their own practice poses a dilemma: they bring social contingencies into view by exploiting precisely the evidential constraints and other epistemic considerations they mean to destabilize. They make good use of the fact that, as enigmatic and richly constructed as archaeological evidence may be, it does routinely resist appropriation in any of the terms compatible with dominant views about the past. This capacity of the world we investigate to subvert our best expectations can force us to reassess not only specific claims about the past but also background assumptions we may not have known we held, assumptions that constitute our standpoint in the present. As critics within archaeology have moved beyond reaction against the New Archaeology and have undertaken to build their own alternative research programs, they

---

[11] David Henderson, "The Principle of Charity and the Problem of Irrationality," *Synthese,* 1987, *73:*225–252 (reasons as causes); Roy Bhaskar, *A Realist Theory of Science,* 2nd ed. (Brighton, Sussex: Harvester, 1978), p. 57; and Ian Hacking, *Representing and Intervening: Introductory Topics in the Philosophy of Natural Science* (Cambridge: Cambridge Univ. Press, 1983).

[12] See, e.g., Ian Hodder, "Interpretive Archaeology and Its Role," *Amer. Antiquity,* 1991, *56:*7–18; and Christopher Tilley, "Archaeology as Socio-Political Action in the Present," in *Critical Traditions in Archaeology: Essays in the Philosophy, History, and Socio-Politics of Archaeology* (Cambridge: Cambridge Univ. Press, 1989), pp. 117–135.

tend to embrace epistemic positions that have much in common with those occupied by feminist critics and practitioners.

Parallels with Science Studies

A similar polarizing dynamic has long structured relations between the constituent fields of science studies. After decades of rancorous debate between philosophers and sociologists it is now unavoidable, although still far from being universally accepted, that sociological challenges (themselves much modified in recent years) cannot simply be set aside by philosophers as misconceived or irrelevant; the traditional philosophical enterprise of "rational reconstruction" must be substantially broadened and not only naturalized but "psychologized" and "socialized." The hallmark of postpositivist philosophy of science is a commitment to ground philosophical analysis in a detailed understanding of scientific practice (historical or contemporary), an exercise that has forced attention to the diversity and multidimensionality of the sciences. This, in turn, makes it increasingly difficult to sustain the faith that there is any distinctive, unifying rationality to be "reconstructed" across the historical and cultural particularity of the disciplines we identify as scientific.[13] At the same time, many sociologists of science now emphasize that science is work made hard, in part, by engagement with the "materiel" of its technology and subject domain; practice is conditioned by the sorts of considerations that have been central to epistemological analyses of science.[14]

One implication of these developments is that none of the existing science studies disciplines has the resources to make sense of the sciences on its own, in strictly philosophical, sociological, or historical terms. As Andrew Pickering puts the point, "Scientific practice . . . is situated and evolves right on the boundary, at the point of intersection, of the material, social, conceptual (and so on) worlds"; it "cuts very deeply across disciplinary boundaries."[15] The crucial challenge, now taken up on many fronts, is to develop genuinely interdisciplinary strategies of inquiry, and for this we need problems and concepts, categories of analysis, that escape the dichotomous thinking that has structured disciplinary studies of science to date, setting "epistemic"/"internal" (constitutive) considerations in opposition to "social"/"external" (contextual) factors. This is, fundamentally, the challenge of building an integrative program of analysis capable of explaining how the thoroughly constructed materials of science—for example, whatever counts as evidence in a given context—*can*, in fact, "resist" appropriation, sometimes quite unexpectedly and

---

[13] See, e.g., contributions to the symposium "Discourse, Practice, Context: From HPS to Interdisciplinary Science Studies," presented at the 1994 biennial meeting of the Philosophy of Science Association: Joseph Rouse, "Engaging Science through Cultural Studies," in *PSA 1994*, ed. David Hull, Micky Forbes, and Richard Burian (East Lansing, Mich.: Philosophy of Science Association, 1994), pp. 396–401; Vassiliki Betty Smocovitis, "Contextualizing Science: From Science Studies to Cultural Studies," *ibid.*, pp. 402–412; Andy Pickering, "After Representation: Science Studies in the Performative Idiom," *ibid.*, pp. 413–419; and Brian S. Baigrie, "HPS and the Classic Normative Mission," *ibid.*, pp. 420–430.

[14] See, e.g., Andrew Pickering, "From Science as Knowledge to Science as Practice," in *Science as Practice and Culture*, ed. Pickering (Chicago: Univ. Chicago Press, 1992), pp. 1–28; and Pickering, "Knowledge, Practice, and Mere Construction," *Social Studies of Science*, 1990, 20:682–729.

[15] Pickering, "Knowledge, Practice, and Mere Construction," p. 710.

decisively, and sometimes with the effect of transforming the values and interests that frame our research programs.

These questions have been central to feminist analyses of science from the outset. Given political and conceptual commitments that make corrosive hyperrelativism as uncongenial as unreflective objectivism, feminists have been exploring positions between, or "beyond," these polarized alternatives[16] throughout the period in which discipline-specific debates about the implications of hyperrelativism have run their course. Consider, for example, the efforts to articulate a viable standpoint theory made by Nancy Hartsock, Sandra Harding, and Donna Haraway; the multidimensional analyses of Evelyn Fox Keller; Helen Longino's treatment of the interplay between constitutive and contextual values in science; and innumerable critical and constructive programs of feminist analysis in the social and life sciences (e.g., Anne Fausto-Sterling's work on biological theories of sex difference and the range of feminist research in the social sciences analyzed by Shulamit Reinharz and anthologized by Mary Margaret Fonow and Judith Cook, Harding, and Joyce Nielsen).[17] It is a great loss to mainstream science studies that its practitioners have considered feminist work in these areas almost not at all, even when their own debates propel them in directions already well explored by feminist philosophers, historians, and sociologists of science.

I submit that the questions constitutive of these traditions of feminist research are worth pursuing not just because they are important for science studies and for archaeology, but because we badly need more nuanced critical appraisals of the fruits and authority of science if, as feminists, we are to exploit the emancipatory capacity that it may (yet) have. Despite their sometimes apocalyptic conclusions, the practice of archaeological critics, especially the feminists among them, demonstrates just how powerful systematic empirical inquiry can be as a tool for contesting the taken-for-granteds that underwrite oppressive forms of life.

GENDER RESEARCH IN ARCHAEOLOGY

Feminist initiatives appeared much later in archaeology than in such cognate fields as sociocultural anthropology and history. It was not until 1984, just over a decade

---

[16] I use Bernstein's language; see Bernstein, *Beyond Objectivism and Relativism* (cit. n. 10).

[17] Nancy Hartsock, "The Feminist Standpoint: Developing the Ground for a Specifically Feminist Historical Materialism," in *Discovering Reality: Feminist Perspectives on Epistemology, Metaphysics, Methodology, and Philosophy of Science,* ed. Sandra Harding and Merrill B. Hintikka (Dordrecht/ Boston: Reidel, 1983), pp. 238–310; Harding, "Why Has the Sex/Gender System Become Visible Only Now?" *ibid.,* pp. 311–324; Harding, *Whose Science? Whose Knowledge? Thinking from Women's Lives* (Ithaca, N.Y.: Cornell Univ. Press, 1991); Donna Haraway, "Situated Knowledges: The Science Question in Feminism and the Privilege of Partial Perspective," in *Simians, Cyborgs, and Women: The Reinvention of Nature* (New York: Routledge, 1991); Evelyn Fox Keller, *Secrets of Life, Secrets of Death: Essays on Language, Gender, and Science* (New York: Routledge, 1992); Keller, "Gender and Science," *Psychoanalysis and Contemporary Thought,* 1978, *1:*409–433; Keller, "A World of Difference," in *Reflections on Gender and Science* (New Haven, Conn.: Yale Univ. Press, 1985), pp. 158–179; Helen Longino, *Science as Social Knowledge: Values and Objectivity in Scientific Inquiry* (Princeton, N.J.: Princeton Univ. Press, 1990); Anne Fausto-Sterling, "Introduction," in *Myths of Gender: Biological Theories about Women and Men* (New York: Basic, 1985), pp. 9–12; Shulamit Reinharz, *Feminist Methods in Social Research* (Oxford: Oxford Univ. Press, 1992); Mary Margaret Fonow and Judith A. Cook, eds., *Beyond Methodology: Feminist Scholarship as Lived Research* (Bloomington: Indiana Univ. Press, 1991); Harding, ed., *Feminism and Methodology* (Bloomington: Indiana Univ. Press, 1987); and Joyce McCarl Nielsen, ed., *Feminist Research Methods: Exemplary Readings in the Social Sciences* (Boulder, Colo.: Westview, 1990).

Figure 1. Woman carrying antelope in burden basket. (William Endner Collection, G 495, Museum of Western Colorado. Al Ligrani Photo.) A drawing of this Mimbres bowl appears on the cover of Joan M. Gero and Margaret W. Conkey, eds., Engendering Archaeology: Women and Prehistory *(Oxford: Blackwell, 1991).*

ago, that the first paper appeared in Anglo-American archaeology that argued explicitly for the relevance of feminist insights and approaches to the study of gender. And it was another seven years before a book presented a substantial body of original work in the area. This took the form of a collection edited by Joan Gero and Margaret Conkey, *Engendering Archaeology: Women and Prehistory*,[18] which was the outcome of a small working conference convened by the editors in 1988 specifically for the purpose of mobilizing interest in the questions about women and gender posed by Conkey and Janet Spector in 1984 (see Figures 1 and 2). Most participants had never considered these questions and had no special interest in feminist initiatives.

The following year, the graduate student organizers of an annual thematic conference at the University of Calgary chose "The Archaeology of Gender" as their topic for the fall 1989 "Chacmool" conference. To everyone's surprise, the open call for papers advertising this meeting drew over a hundred contributions on a wide range of topics, a substantially larger response than had been realized for any previous

---

[18] Conkey and Spector, "Archaeology and the Study of Gender" (cit. n. 4); and Gero and Conkey, eds., *Engendering Archaeology* (cit. n. 3).

Figure 2. Participants in "Women and Production in Prehistory," the small working conference organized by Joan Gero and Meg Conkey that gave rise to Engendering Archaeology. *The conference was held at the Wedge Plantation in South Carolina, 5–9 April 1988.*

Russell G. Handsman   Alison Wylie   T. Douglas Price
Janet D. Spector   Prudence M. Rice
Cheryl P. Claassen   Patty Jo Watson   Ruth E. Tringham   Henrietta Moore   Thomas L. Jackson   Peter White
Christine P.   Joan M.   Margaret W.   Elizabeth M.   Susan   Irene
Hastorf   Gero   Conkey   Brumfiel   Pollock   Silverblatt

(Conference photograph generously provided by the organizers.)

Chacmool conference.[19] The only previous meetings on gender had been annual colloquia at the meetings of the Society for Historical Archaeology (beginning in

---

[19] Marsha P. Hanen and Jane Kelley undertook an analysis of the abstracts for papers presented at this conference with the aim of determining how wide ranging they were in topic and orientation. The results are published in Hanen and Kelley, "Gender and Archaeological Knowledge," in *Meta-archaeology,* ed. Embree (cit. n. 10), pp. 195–227. Chacmool conferences have been held at the University of Calgary every fall since 1966. They are sponsored by the archaeology undergraduate society of the Department of Archaeology, but graduate students and faculty are centrally involved in their organization. They have developed a strong reputation in North America and, increasingly, abroad as well-focused, congenial working conferences that have steadily increased in size and scope since their inception. The 1989 meeting represents something of a threshold, in which the number of submissions grew substantially, from the forty to sixty typical of previous years to more than a hundred, a pattern of growth that has been sustained by subsequent Chacmool conferences.

1988) and several Norwegian and British conferences and conference sessions.[20] The 1989 Chacmool proceedings were published two years later, and in the meantime at least five other widely advertised public conferences, and a number of smaller-scale workshops and conference symposia, were organized in Australia, North America, and the United Kingdom; several of these have produced published proceedings or edited volumes.[21] In an annotated bibliography of papers on archaeology and gender that were presented at conferences from 1964 through 1992, the editor/compiler, Cheryl Claassen, indicates that only twenty-four of a total of 284 entries were presented before 1988 and that only two of these appeared in print; more than half the entries are papers presented between 1988 and 1990, and fully 40 percent of those presented after 1988 have been published. So, despite the fact that little more than Conkey and Spector's 1984 paper was in print by the late 1980s, when various groups of enterprising organizers set about arranging archaeological conferences on gender, there seems to have been considerable interest in the topic that was, in a sense, just waiting for an outlet, an interest that has since taken hold across the field as a whole.[22]

The questions raised by these developments are conventional enough; they have to do with theory change, with why these initiatives should have appeared in the form they did and when they did, and with their implications for the presuppositions of entrenched traditions of research.[23] I have found these to be resolutely intractable questions, however, because the conditions shaping the emergence of gender research in archaeology are so multidimensional: a great many factors are at work, none of them separable from the others, and they operate on different scales, some

---

[20] These include a thematic conference held in Norway in 1979, the proceedings of which appeared eight years later: Reidar Bertelsen, Arnvid Lillehammer, and Jenny-Rita Naess, eds., *Were They All Men? An Examination of Sex Roles in Prehistoric Society* (AmS-Varia, 17) (Stavanger: Arkeologisk Museum I Stavanger, 1987). Also, several sessions on women and gender were organized for the annual meetings of the Theoretical Archaeology Group in the United Kingdom (in 1982, 1985, and 1987); see Karen Arnold, Roberta Gilchrist, Pam Graves, and Sarah Taylor, "Women in Archaeology," *Archaeological Reviews from Cambridge* (special issue), 1988, 7:2–8.

[21] Walde and Willows, eds., *Archaeology of Gender* (cit. n. 6) (Chacmool proceedings); Cheryl Claassen, ed., *Exploring Gender through Archaeology* (Monographs in World Archaeology, 11) (Madison, Wis.: Prehistory Press, 1992); Claassen, ed., *Women in Archaeology* (cit. n. 6); du Cros and Smith, eds., *Women in Archaeology* (cit. n. 6); and Seifert, ed., *Gender in Historical Archaeology* (cit. n. 3).

[22] Cheryl Claassen, "Bibliography of Archaeology and Gender: Papers Delivered at Archaeology Conferences, 1964–1992," *Annotated Bibliographies for Anthropologists*, 1992, *1*(2). See also the annotated bibliography compiled by Elisabeth A. Bacus *et al.*, eds., *A Gendered Past: A Critical Bibliography of Gender in Archaeology* (Technical Reports, 25) (Ann Arbor: Univ. Michigan Museum of Anthropology, 1993). Some earlier archaeological publications on women and gender include Anne Barstow, "The Uses of Archeology for Women's History: James Mellaart's Work on the Neolithic Goddess at Catal Huyuk," *Feminist Studies*, 1978, *4*(3):7–17; Alice Kehoe, "The Shackles of Tradition," in *The Hidden Half: Studies of Plains Indian Women*, ed. Patricia Albers and Beatrice Medicine (Washington, D.C.: Univ. Press America, 1983), pp. 53–73; several important contributions by Alice Kehoe, Sarah Nelson, Patricia O'Brien, Pamela Bumstead, *et al.*, to *Powers of Observation: Alternative Views in Archeology*, ed. Nelson and Kehoe (Archaeological Papers, 2) (Washington, D.C.: American Anthropological Association, 1990); Rayna Rapp, "Gender and Class: An Archaeology of Knowledge Concerning the Origin of the State," *Dialectical Anthropology*, 1977, *2*:309–316; and Janet D. Spector, "Male/Female Task Differentiation among the Hidatsa: Toward the Development of an Archaeological Approach to the Study of Gender," in *Hidden Half*, ed. Albers and Medicine, pp. 77–99.

[23] The formulation of these questions is discussed in more detail in Alison Wylie, "Feminist Critiques and Archaeological Challenges," in *Archaeology of Gender*, ed. Walde and Willows (cit. n. 6), pp. 17–23.

highly local while others are quite general. Indeed, nothing brings home more forcefully the need for an *integrative* program of feminist science studies than grappling with the complexities of these recent developments in archaeology. What follows is a provisional and, most important, a *syncretic* account of the conditions responsible for the "engendering" of archaeology; fully integrated categories of analysis remain to be formulated. My aim is to illustrate why none of the familiar strategies for explaining science is adequate taken on its own. This will inevitably raise more questions than I can answer but will allow me to specify, in the conclusion, some of the tasks at hand in reframing science studies.

Theoretical and Methodological Considerations

When Conkey and Spector argued the case for an archaeology of gender in 1984, they suggested that the dearth of such work was to be explained by the dominance of an especially narrow, ecologically reductive conception of culture that was associated with the New Archaeology. In an effort to make archaeology scientific, attention had been diverted from all types of "internal," "ethnographic" variables; gender dynamics were just one casualty of a general preoccupation with interactions between cultural systems and their external environments, associated with the conviction that "internal" variables are both inaccessible and explanatorily irrelevant. Initially this explanation seemed persuasive; I have argued for it myself.[24] The difficulty, however, is that a great many of those who subscribed to the scientific ideals of the New Archaeology never did give up an interest in the social structures and internal dynamics of the cultural "systems" they studied; they showed great initiative in devising strategies for documenting, in archaeological terms, such inscrutables as interaction networks, kinds and degrees of social stratification, and modes of community and household organization (and changes in all of these over time). Given this, the real question is, Why did these more expansive New Archaeologists not turn their attention to gendered divisions of labor and organizational structures?

This lacuna is especially puzzling when we recognize that the New Archaeology and its most stringently ecologistic models were decisively challenged at the turn of the 1980s, initiating a decade of wide-ranging exploration in which archaeologists reopened a great many questions that had been set aside by more orthodox New Archaeologists.[25] According to the "theoretical and methodological constraint" model, research on gender and critiques of androcentrism should have appeared with these other initiatives at the beginning of the 1980s, rather than a decade later. In fact, some early critics of the New Archaeology did explicitly advocate "feminist" initiatives as an example of just the sort of politically self-conscious archaeology they endorsed. Few pursued these suggestions, however, and several of these critics have since been sharply criticized by Norwegian and British feminists who argue that their own practice was often not just androcentric but quite explicitly sexist.[26]

---

[24] Alison Wylie, "Gender Theory and the Archaeological Record: Why Is There No Archaeology of Gender?" in *Engendering Archaeology,* ed. Gero and Conkey (cit. n. 3), pp. 31–54.

[25] See, e.g., Colin Renfrew's baleful account of the proliferation of "isms" in Renfrew, "Explanation Revisited," in *Theory and Explanation in Archaeology,* ed. Renfrew, M. J. Rowlands, and B. A. Segraves (New York: Academic, 1982), pp. 5–23.

[26] Examples of early interest in feminist approaches include contributions to *Ideology, Power, and Prehistory,* ed. Daniel Miller and Christopher Tilley (Cambridge: Cambridge Univ. Press, 1984):

In retrospect, it seems that the new generation of archaeologists shared with their predecessors a number of (largely implicit) presuppositions; despite other differences, they all tended to treat gender as a stable, unchanging (biological) given in the sociocultural environment. If the social roles that biological males and females occupy can be assumed to be the same across time and cultural context—to be "naturally" theirs—gender is not a variable that can be relevant in explaining cultural change. The question, Why not before? then becomes, Why now? Why would this particular set of taken-for-granteds come to be seen as problematic now? Here the complexity of the explanandum outstrips the explanatory resources afforded by standard categories of philosophical analysis.

Sociopolitical Factors

My thesis is that nothing in the theoretical content, intellectual history, methodological refinement, or evidential resources of contemporary archaeology can explain why an interest in questions about women and gender should have arisen (only) in the late 1980s. Sociopolitical features of the research community and its practice play a central role in determining the timing, the form, and the impact of the feminist critiques and research programs on gender that have begun to challenge the entrenched androcentrism of archaeology. In order better to understand these factors, I undertook a survey of everyone who participated in the 1989 Chacmool conference and did interviews with a number of those I identified as "catalysts": those who had been instrumental in organizing this and related conferences and in producing the publications that drew attention to the need for and promise of feminist initiatives in archaeology. My immediate aim was to determine what factors had converged in creating the substantial constituency of archaeologists who were ready and willing to attend a conference on gender despite the lack of visible work in the area.

At the outset I assumed that the emergence of feminist initiatives in archaeology had followed roughly the same course as in other closely affiliated disciplines (e.g., sociocultural anthropology, history, paleontology): they appeared when a critical mass of women entered the field who had been politicized in the women's movement and were therefore inclined to notice, and to be skeptical of, the taken-for-granteds about gender that had hitherto structured archaeological interpretation and the research agenda of the field. In archaeology a significant increase in the representation of women was not realized until after the mid 1970s. I expected, then, that participants in the 1989 Chacmool conference would prove to be predominantly women drawn from the first professional cohorts in which women were strongly represented and that they would have been attracted to the topic of the conference because of prior involvement in feminist activism and scholarship. This account would suggest

---

Mary Braithwaite, "Ritual and Prestige in the Prehistory of Wessex c. 2200–1400 B.C.: A New Dimension to the Archaeological Evidence," pp. 93–110; and Ian Hodder, "Burials, Houses, Women, and Men in the European Neolithic," pp. 51–68. For criticisms of this work see Ericka Engelstad, "Images of Power and Contradiction: Feminist Theory and Postprocessual Archaeology," *Antiquity,* 1991, *65:*502–514; and Roberta Gilchrist, "Review of *Experiencing Archaeology* by Michael Shanks," *Archaeol. Rev. Cambridge,* 1992, *11:*188–191. In the latter discussion Gilchrist draws attention to a notorious passage in which Shanks likens archaeology, specifically excavation, to striptease—each "discovery is a little release of gratification"—pretty clearly reaffirming dominant assumptions that the subject position of the archaeologist is normatively gendered male.

that the 1989 Chacmool conference afforded participants an opportunity to integrate preexisting feminist commitments with professional interests in archaeology.

In the event, 72 percent of the 1989 Chacmool participants responded to the survey, providing me with enormously detailed answers to a lengthy list of open-ended questions about their background training and research interests, their reasons for attending the conference, their involvement with feminist scholarship and activism, and their views about why gender research should be emerging in archaeology in the late 1980s. Preliminary analysis suggests that my initial hypothesis captures the experience and motivations of most of the "catalysts" but not of conference participants. The survey results do bear out my hypothesis about the demographic profile of contributors to the Chacmool program but confound my assumptions about their backgrounds and why they attended this first public conference on "The Archaeology of Gender."

Those who attended the 1989 Chacmool conference were disproportionately women, and these women, more than the men, were drawn from cohorts that entered the field in the late 1970s and early 1980s, when the representation of women in North American archaeology doubled. Altogether 80 percent of submissions to the conference were made by women; this more than inverts the ratio of women to men in North American archaeology as a whole, where women make up roughly 36 percent of practitioners.[27] And while the average age of men and women at the time of the conference was very similar (forty-three as compared to forty years), the men were more widely distributed across age grades; altogether 60 percent of the women (twice the proportion of men) were clustered in the twenty-six to forty age range. Combined with information about their education and employment status, this suggests that, as I had expected, the majority of those who attended the conference were middle-ranked professional women who would have completed their graduate training and achieved some measure of job security by the mid to late 1980s, just when the first stirrings of public interest in questions about women and gender began to appear in archaeology. Moreover, most of these women made it clear that the call for papers tapped an existing interest in questions about gender; only a fifth reported ever having attended a Chacmool conference in the past (over half of the men reported being regular or previous attendees), and virtually all said the main reason they attended the 1989 Chacmool conference was the topic.

The survey responses also make it clear, however, that an avowed interest in questions about gender does not necessarily reflect a feminist standpoint. Nearly half of the women (and more of the men) said explicitly that they do not identify themselves as feminists, and many of those who embraced the label recorded reservations about what it means. Although three-quarters of respondents (both men and women) said they had a prior interest in research on gender, altogether two-thirds described the Chacmool conference as opening up a new area of interest for them, and less than half reported any previous involvement in women's studies or familiarity with femi-

---

[27] Counts of the membership lists for the Society for American Archaeology and the Archaeological Institute of America show that, before 1973, women never made up more than 13 percent of the society's members; in 1973 their representation jumped to 18 percent and by 1976 to 30 percent. Altogether 36 percent of SAA members were women in the fall of 1988, when the Chacmool call for papers was distributed, a level of representation that has been stable in the field since then. See, e.g., Kramer and Stark, "Status of Women in Archaeology" (cit. n. 6); and Patterson, *Toward a Social History of Archaeology* (cit. n. 6), pp. 81–82.

nist research in other fields. These results are consistent with Marsha Hanen and Jane Kelley's analysis of the conference abstracts, which reveals what they describe as a "dearth" of references to feminist literature, authors, influences, or ideas.[28] Most striking, just half of the women and a quarter of the men who responded to the survey indicated any involvement in women's groups, in action on women's issues, or in "feminist activism," and most described their involvement as limited to "being on a mailing list" or "sending money," usually to women's shelters and reproductive rights groups. Very few had been involved in any direct action or frontline work with the agencies and groups they supported. No doubt this level of involvement in the women's movement (broadly construed) is substantially higher than is typical for North American archaeologists. Even so, it does not support the hypothesis that the majority of participants in the Chacmool conference on "The Archaeology of Gender" had been independently politicized as feminists and had welcomed this conference as a first public opportunity to integrate their feminist and archaeological commitments.

The results of this preliminary analysis suggest, then, that the expanded cohort of women entering the field at the turn of the 1980s brought to their work in archaeology a standpoint of sensitivity to gender issues—no doubt in some sense a gendered standpoint—but not an explicitly feminist standpoint. Hanen and Kelley describe this orientation as a largely untheorized and apolitical "grass roots" interest in questions about gender relations and categories.[29] It would seem that the 1989 Chacmool call for papers resonated with a latent awareness of the contested and contestable nature of gender roles, considered both as a feature of daily life and as a possible topic for investigation in archaeology. Indeed, for many the conference seems to have been attractive because it provided an opportunity to engage these questions at arm's length, on the relatively safe (or at least familiar) terrain of archaeological inquiry. And for some this scholarly interest proved to be politicizing: a number of respondents noted, in their survey returns and in subsequent correspondence, that their work on the "archaeology of gender" has put them in touch with feminist scholarship in other fields and has led to an involvement in women's groups active on issues such as workplace equity, sexual harassment, reproductive rights, and violence against women. By contrast, almost all who played a role as catalysts had already been politicized as feminists and then brought this explicitly feminist angle of vision to bear on the programs of research in which they were engaged as archaeologists.

In these two rather different senses, then, the appearance of gender research in archaeology in the last few years seems to reflect a growing awareness, among relatively young professionals in the field, of the gendered dimensions of their experience, perhaps provoked by the fact that the gender composition of their own cohort disrupts the status quo. And perhaps, as amorphous and ill-defined a standpoint as this is, it was sufficient to incline (some) members of this cohort, especially the women, to greater awareness of and skepticism about the androcentrism inherent in extant research programs. Much remains to be done to determine what constitutes this "grass roots" standpoint of gender sensitivity, how it is articulated in archaeological contexts, how it relates to the gender politics of the larger society, and how it

---

[28] Hanen and Kelley, "Gender and Archaeological Knowledge" (cit. n. 19).
[29] Ibid.

shapes archaeological practice; evaluation and refinement of this hypothesis will depend, in part, on further analysis of the survey responses and, in part, on comparative analysis (within archaeology and across fields). But if this line of argument is plausible, it was a distinctive self-consciousness about gender relations that put these new participants in a position to think differently about their discipline and their subject matter, to identify gaps in analysis, to question taken-for-granted assumptions about women and gender, and to envision a range of alternatives for inquiry and interpretation that simply had not occurred to their older, largely male colleagues—colleagues whose gender privilege (as men working in a highly masculinized disciplinary culture) includes an unquestioning fit between their gendered experience and the androcentrism that partially frames the research traditions in which they work.

Content Analysis and the Role of Evidence

If it is accepted that sociopolitical factors are centrally responsible for the emergent (archaeological) interest in women and gender as a research subject, broader questions about epistemic implications immediately arise. My thesis is that although such examples make it clear that the standpoint of practitioners affects every aspect of inquiry—the formation of questions, the (re)definition of categories of analysis, the kinds of material treated as (potential) evidence, the bodies of background knowledge engaged in interpreting archaeological data as evidence, the range of explanatory and reconstructive hypotheses considered plausible, and the array of presuppositions held open to systematic examination—they also demonstrate that standpoint does not, in any strict sense, determine the outcomes of inquiry. The results produced by those working from a gender-sensitive standpoint are not explicable, in their details, in terms of the angle of vision or social location that constitutes this standpoint. Consider, briefly, two examples that illustrate this point.[30]

In their critique of theories about the emergence of horticulture in the Eastern Woodlands, mentioned earlier, Pat Watson and Mary Kennedy begin with a conceptual analysis that draws attention to the conspicuous absence of women in accounts of how this transition was realized, even though they are accorded a central role in plant collection (before) and cultivation (after).[31] One explanatory model identifies male shamans as the catalysts for this transition; their interest in manipulating plant stocks resulted in the development of cultigens. In another, the plants effectively domesticate themselves by an "automatic" process of adaptation to conditions disrupted by human activities (in "domestilocalities"). As Watson and Kennedy point out, women passively follow plants around when they are wild and passively tend them once domesticated but play no role in the transition from one state to the other. The authors then deploy collateral evidence to show that this failure to recognize women as potential catalysts of change carries substantial costs in explanatory elegance and plausibility. The automatic domestication thesis must counter ethno- and paleobotanical evidence that the key domesticates appeared very early in environments that were by no means optimal for them, evidence that suggests that some human intervention must have been involved in the process of domestication. Like-

---

[30] The analysis of these examples has been developed in more detail in Wylie, "Evidential Constraints" (cit. n. 2).
[31] Watson and Kennedy, "Development of Horticulture" (cit. n. 3).

wise, the shaman hypothesis must ignore the implications of presuming that women were involved full time in the exploitation of the plants that later became domesticates, as well as ethnohistorical evidence that shamanism is by no means a male preserve and that women in foraging societies often hold the primary expertise about plant and animal resources that informs group movement and other subsistence-related decision making.

Whatever standpoint-specific factors might have put Watson and Kennedy in a position to notice the common incongruity in these explanatory models (the disappearing women), what makes their analysis compelling is their identification of internal contradictions in the logic of these models and their use of collateral evidence to call into question the assumptions that underlie these contradictions. They grant their opponents the assumptions they make about sexual divisions of labor in foraging and horticultural societies but point out that the archaeological record does not, in fact, deliver any evidence that, interpreted subject to these assumptions, would indicate that men mediated the transition to horticulture. And they make use of independent paleobotanical evidence to call into question the plausibility of "automatic domestication" accounts that deny human agency any substantial role in the transition. In neither case are the presuppositions of Watson and Kennedy's (re)interpretation of the evidence dependent on the assumptions about women's capacities that they criticize or embrace.

In a project that moves beyond critique, also mentioned earlier, Christine Hastorf relies on a similar strategy, exploiting independent background knowledge and sources of evidence to reassess the way in which women's labor and domestic units are conceptualized in state-formation theories for the highland Andes.[32] She compares the sex ratios and lifetime dietary profiles of skeletal material recovered from burials in the Montaro Valley through the period when the Inka first made their imperial presence felt in this region. She found that the dietary intake of men and women was undifferentiated until the advent of Inka influence but then diverged sharply on the isotope value associated with the consumption of maize. Comparing these results with patterns of change over time in other aspects of the sites, she found independent evidence of intensified production and increasingly segregated work areas related to the processing of maize. To interpret these findings she relied on ethnohistoric sources that establish the association of women with maize processing and beer production and suggest that Inka rule involved negotiating with local men as the heads of households and communities and extracting them from their households to serve as conscript labor on Inka construction projects. These multiple lines of evidence suggest that the gendered organization of domestic units was significantly altered by Inka rule; the hierarchical, gender-differentiated divisions of labor and consumption patterns now familiar in the region were established when local communities were incorporated into a state system. This means that gender relations and household organization cannot be treated as a stable substrate that predates, and persists as a given through, the rising and falling fortunes of states; state formation in the Andes depended on a fundamental restructuring of household-based social relations of production.

As in Watson and Kennedy's case, nothing in the social and political factors that may have informed Hastorf's interest in questions about gender determines that she

---

[32] Hastorf, "Gender, Space, and Food in Prehistory" (cit. n. 5).

should have found such striking divergence in the dietary profiles of men and women or such congruence in patterns of change over time in several materially and inferentially independent aspects of the archaeological record. The presuppositions that Hastorf uses to construct data as evidence are not the same as those that define the questions she asks or the range of hypotheses she entertains; they may be radically theory-laden, but they are not laden by the same theories that are tested against this evidence or frame her research program. To put the point more generally, feminist practitioners exploit the fact that androcentric assumptions about gender roles generally lack the resources to ensure that archaeological data will conform to androcentric, presentist expectations; these assumptions do not deliver, along with reconstructive hypotheses, the linking principles necessary to establish evidential claims about the antecedent conditions that produced the contents of a specific archaeological record.

There is nothing unique to feminist or gender-sensitive research in this respect. The limited independence of facts of the record from the background assumptions that establish their import as evidence is the primary methodological resource that archaeologists use to assess the credibility of claims about the past in most contexts of inquiry.[33] It is in this that the capacity of evidence to resist our expectations resides. We can exploit this potential in any number of standpoint-specific ways; critics of racism, sexism, nationalism, and classism in archaeology use it to bring into view taken-for-granteds that we should be questioning. That they should do so is no doubt overdetermined by a range of social, theoretical, political, and empirical factors, but exactly how they proceed and what they find out—where or, indeed, whether they locate incongruities that open a space for critical engagement—is also very much a function of the evidence they engage when they assess their own interpretive hypotheses and the background assumptions, the auxiliaries, on which they rely. It is this capacity of even quite remote subjects of inquiry to act back on us that we must keep in view when negotiating polarized debates about the implications of recognizing the limitations and partiality of our sciences.

CONCLUSIONS

I draw four forward-looking conclusions concerning the tasks that face the proponents of a genuinely interdisciplinary, integrative program of feminist science studies.

1. Critiques that bring into view the pervasive ways in which social and political factors shape inquiry, including those foregrounded by feminist critics of science, should not be the *end* of discussion about such epistemological questions as what constitutes evidence and "good reasons" in a given context of scientific practice. Rather, they should be the beginning of a new kind of discussion, which feminists are especially well situated to carry forward.

2. To set discussion on a new footing, we must break the grip of the presupposition (held by objectivists and relativists alike) that objectivity is an all-or-nothing affair, that it is something we have only if the process and products of inquiry are (implausibly) free of any social or political entanglements and something we lose irrevocably

---

[33] This analysis is developed in more detail in Wylie, "Evidential Constraints" (cit. n. 2); and Wylie, "Constitution of Archaeological Evidence" (cit. n. 1).

if there is any evidence that science reflects the standpoint of its makers. We must also give up the view that "neutral" investigators are best fitted to maximize the cluster of (often sharply divergent) virtues we associate with "objectivity."[34] We need accounts of knowledge production, authorization, credibility, and use that recognize that the contextual features of social location (standpoint) can make a *constructive* difference in maximizing these epistemic virtues, including quite pragmatic virtues such as reliability under specific ranges of application (a capacity to "travel"[35]) and intersubjective stability. The contributions of feminist researchers (both critical and constructive) make it clear that diverse standpoints can greatly enhance the likelihood of realizing specific sorts of empirical accuracy or explanatory breadth and may ensure that a rigorously critical perspective will be brought to bear (or, indeed, that detachment will be preserved) in the evaluation of claims or assumptions that members of a homogeneous community might never think to question.

3. These proposals have concrete implications for research practice. According to current objectivist wisdom, we can best safeguard the authority of science and of specific scientific claims by eliminating from the processes by which we evaluate knowledge claims any hint of contamination from social or political context. But from the foregoing, it follows that a commitment to objectivity may require direct consideration of the sociopolitical standpoint of inquirers in the adjudication of knowledge claims as an integral part of scientific inquiry.[36]

4. Finally, these observations have implications for feminist science studies. They suggest a need for analyses of science that are at once empirically grounded (historically, sociologically, and in the sciences themselves) and epistemically sophisticated, that work "right at the boundary" (as Pickering has put it) between the existing science studies disciplines, and that bring together equity and content critiques. They suggest, further, that feminist science studies must incorporate a normative as well as a descriptive component and that science studies practitioners, most especially feminists, should deliberately position themselves as "insider/outsiders" with respect to the sciences they study. The work of a great many feminist theorists of science already exemplifies this hybrid stance.[37] Indeed, this active engagement with the sciences may be one reason why feminist practitioners and analysts of science have resisted the categories imposed by debates between philosophers and sociologists, constructivists and objectivists in their various fields of (metascientific) practice.

---

[34] See, e.g., Elisabeth Lloyd, "Objectivity and the Double Standard for Feminist Epistemologies," *Synthese,* 1996, *104:*351–381.

[35] Haraway, *Simians, Cyborgs, and Women* (cit. n. 17).

[36] Feminist researchers move in this direction when they insist on the need for rigorous reflexivity, in the sense explicated by Fonow and Cook and by Mies: Mary Margaret Fonow and Judith A. Cook, "Back to the Future: A Look at the Second Wave of Feminist Epistemology and Methodology," in *Beyond Methodology,* ed. Fonow and Cook (cit. n. 17), pp. 1–15; and Maria Mies, "Towards a Methodology for Feminist Research," in *Theories of Women's Studies,* ed. Gloria Bowles and Renate Duelli Klein (New York: Routledge & Kegan Paul, 1983), pp. 117–139.

[37] See, e.g., the works of Keller, Fausto-Sterling, and Haraway cited in note 17, above, and the collaborative work of Helen Longino and Ruth Doell: "Body, Bias, and Behavior: A Comparative Analysis of Reasoning in Two Areas of Biological Science," *Signs: Journal of Women in Culture and Society,* 1983, *9:*206–227.

Hidden Persuaders
Medical Indexing and the Gendered Professionalism of American Medicine, 1880–1932

By Diana E. Long*

HIDDEN PERSUADERS are difficult to discuss. This essay introduces an analysis of medical indexing that may help us to identify an unnoticed discourse that reinforced the sexism of professional American medicine after 1880. That discourse was produced in a new institution of the period, the *Index Catalogue of the Library of the Surgeon General's Office,* which, by providing subject headings to guide its readers along the right path of medical thinking, also provided them with an education in gender.

The *Index Catalogue* was a guide to the holdings of the Library of the Surgeon General's Office. This United States government bureau was in fact, and later was named, the National Library of Medicine.[1] The initial three series of this catalogue (to 1932), indexed by subject headings, designated and specified "Women" in gendered terms that signaled their marginal place in medicine. This essay will analyzethese sexist rubrics from our contemporary perspective, suggest new mapping techniques that allow us to see the coherence of these terms, and discuss the circumstances that made their cultural import invisible to the men who compiled the catalogue and the women who sought entrance into the world of medicine.

INDEXING

Subject indexes are not just lists of words that help the reader find information. Because we think of them as "just words" and look "through," not "at," the subject headings in an index, we ignore their educational power. This is a great mistake for feminists, who must look at words attentively if we want to see their sexism—as Joan Marshall did in considering the headings used by the Library of Congress (LC) in the 1970s. Only with such insights can we go on to propose an alternate lexicon, as did Marshall, who opened up a new approach to "women in LC terms," and Paula

---

* University of Southern Maine, 84 Bedford Street, Portland, Maine 04103.
[1] The Library of the Surgeon General was named the Army Medical Library in 1922, the Armed Forces Medical Library in 1952, and the National Library of Medicine in 1956.

©1997 by The History of Science Society. All rights reserved. 0369-7827/97/1201-0007$02.00

Treichler, who with Cheris Kramarae authored a *Feminist Dictionary* of radically subversive terms.[2]

Marshall's analysis of sexism in indexing was written for library personnel. She states that indexing is more than the simple assignment of words to literature; it requires a subtle and precise understanding of both the literature being placed under subject headings and the subject headings that host the literature. Furthermore, as Marshall notes in the introduction to *On Equal Terms,* indexing is a psychological game in which the editor makes guesses about both the uses to which the reader will put the literature and her or his thought processes and lexicon. Marshall does not make this comparison, but the indexer works like the advertising artist who moves the reader or viewer to make a purchase by a seductive reinforcement of what he or she already knows and feels but has not yet quite articulated. In short, indexing provides the perfect conditions for sex bias and, in Judith Butler's felicitous phrase, "gender trouble."[3]

Marshall summarizes the trouble with the LC headings as their representation of the general reader as "American/Western European, Christian, white, heterosexual and male."[4] From this narrow base, the Library of Congress (which was modernized in the same era that launched the *Index Catalogue*) treated women as a mythical "Woman" in its headings, made men a universal, excluded the female attributes of terms, transmitted the old stereotypes of active men and passive women, and in general demeaned women with gender markers of their "special" human condition.

All of this could be avoided, Marshall claims, by following six rules that lessen the chance that the indexer will forget women or describe them as inferior. I will analyze these rules as an introduction to the stereotypes of the *Index Catalogue* (*IC*).[5]

That index appeared in three series. Series I, edited by John Shaw Billings, was published in sixteen volumes from 1880 to 1895; Series II, edited by Robert Fletcher, in twenty-one volumes from 1896 to 1916; and Series III, edited by Fielding H. Garrison, in ten volumes from 1918 to 1932.[6] These editors chose a subject heading that represented, as Billings put it, "the center of the subject [of each publication]" as they surveyed the cards of the 1.8 million items that they indexed be-

---

[2] The clever distinction between "looking through" and "looking at" is made by Richard Lanham in his defense of rhetoric for the postmodern age: Richard Lanham, *The Electronic Word: Democracy, Technology, and the Arts* (Chicago: Univ. Chicago Press, 1993), p. 5 and *passim.* See also Joan Marshall, *On Equal Terms: A Thesaurus for Nonsexist Indexing and Cataloging* (New York: Neal-Schuman, 1977). Ruth Dickstein, Victoria A. Mills, and Ellen J. Waite, *Women in LC's Terms* (Phoenix, Ariz.: Oryx, 1988), records the new, "nonsexist" terminology. "Nonsexist" is a problematically negative designation; see Paula Treichler, "From Dictionary to Discourse: How Sexist Meanings Are Authorized," in Francine Wattman Frank and Treichler, *Language, Gender, and Professional Writing: Theoretical Approaches and Guidelines for Nonsexist Usage* (Chicago: MLA, 1989), pp. 51–80. See also Cheris Kramarae and Paula Treichler with Ann Russo, *Feminist Dictionary* (London: Pandora-Routledge, 1985).

[3] Marshall, *On Equal Terms,* introduction; and Judith Butler, *Gender Trouble: Feminism and the Subversion of Identity* (New York: Routledge, 1989).

[4] Marshall, *On Equal Terms,* p. ii.

[5] I quote the six rules from *ibid.,* pp. v–vi.

[6] All three series were published by the Government Printing Office, Washington, D.C. Claudius Mayer and others edited a fourth series, from "A" to "Mn," until 1950, when the library discontinued the *Index Catalogue*. This series is conceptually very different from the first three; its cultural and professional politics deserve a separate discussion.

tween 1880 and 1932.[7] They often used words that appeared in the titles as subject headings; but primarily they looked for words that placed the work in the right part of medical discourse, in the same way that a call number placed it on the right shelf of the library. After all the cards were headed they were sorted by subject headings or subheadings. At this point the editors had the opportunity to "re-head" the cards to make each subject heading of a manageable size or bring it into accordance with their understanding of medical thinking and medical readers.

The editorial perspective of the indexers (speaking for the "general reader") was as gendered as that at the Library of Congress. The heading "Women," which appeared in all three series of the *Index Catalogue,* displayed its gender in complex ways.[8]

MARSHALL'S RULES FOR NONSEXIST INDEXING

1. "The authentic name of the ... groups should be established ... or the name preferred by the group should be established."

Assuming, as Marshall does, that "Women" is the authentic name for the gender, the *Index Catalogue* made the progressive decision.[9] In Series I, II, and III the heading used is "Women," not "Woman," although the literature indexed under the heading in all three series uses both terms. In Series I, the English literature refers to "Woman" in 67 percent of the books and 55 percent of the articles. By Series III, 63 percent of book titles still use "Woman," but only 23 percent of the article titles do so.

In all three series, however, women authors are marked as female by the inclusion of their first names and, in some cases, their married status. Neither the first name of a man nor the fact of his married status is given, although a "great doctor" like William Osler is occasionally designated as, for example, "Professor Osler."[10]

2. "Subdivisions should consider the connotation, in addition to the denotation, of the working and structure of the subdivision. Avoid words which connote inferiority or peculiarity."

The subheadings of the heading "Women" tell a remarkable story of rising concern about the so-called New Woman at the turn of the century, when Series II was in preparation. The editor of that series designates bad female behavior as "criminal" or "degenerate and defective" and pathologizes "sexual frigidity" and "sexual perversions." But the medical index also identified these pathologies in men, except for "sexual frigidity," and Garrison rejected even this term in favor of "sexual life of Women" in Series III.

This medical mosaic of women was created one word at a time. Each bibliographic heading was a piece of the mosaic, a chance to choose one contemporary word as the proper term for a medical audience. Table 1 lists all of the subheadings chosen for "Women" from 1895 to 1932. Table 2 lists subheadings that the in-

---

[7] Fielding H. Garrison, *John Shaw Billings: A Memoir* (New York: Putnam, 1915), p. 220.

[8] In this essay I capitalize the word that is the subject heading, e.g., "Women," and leave the words of the subheadings in lowercase, e.g., "diseases of Women."

[9] "Females" was specifically rejected in Series I with the phrase "See Gynaecology, Sex, and Women."

[10] E.g., Series II, Vol. 21, p. 226, referring to his article "on medical women's work."

Table 1. Subheadings of "Women," Series I–III

Series I (1895)	Series II (1916)	Series III (1932)
Women	Women	Women
	Anatomy and anthropometry of	
	Bearded	
	Beauty of	
	Clothing of	
	Criminality in	
	Degenerate and defective	Defective, delinquent, and criminal
Diseases of*	Diseases of*	Diseases of
	Education of*	Education of
	Ethnic and temporal status of	
	Fertility and infertility of	
	Frigidity of, sexual	
	Gymnastics for	Gymnastics for
	Hygiene of	Hygiene of
	Insurance and insurability of	
	Legal and social position of	
	Longevity and mortality of	
	Married, occupations of	
	Morality and responsibility of	
Occupations of	Occupations of*	Occupations of
	Physical examination of	
	Pregnant, charitable care and protection of	
	Psychology of*	Psychology of
	Sexual life of	Sexual life of
	Unmarried	
	Women as dentists	
	Women in medicine and science	Women in medicine and science
	Women as pharmacists	
Women as physicians		
		Women and athletics

*Indicates subcategories not shown here.

dexers of Series II deemed problematic; in these cases they shared their uncertainties with the reader. The left-hand column reminds the reader of some discourse about women—"feeble-minded," "over-educated," and "sexually perverse"—that "he" might expect to find in the *Index Catalogue*. The right-hand column lists the proper designation for "Women" in *IC* terms. We should pay special attention to these public choices.

Feminists might see these choices of words about women as healthy and progressive: the names of specific diseases replaced the term "sexual perversions," "hygiene in [the] education of Women" replaced the hostile term "over-educated Women," and the general "occupations of Women" replaced the division into charity work and employment. The editors' grouping of women as a homogeneous sex, however,

Table 2. Choices of Subheadings for "Women", Series II (1916)

Possible Subheading	See (instead)
Women	Women
Charitable and social avocations of	Occupations of
	Women in medicine
Education of, sexual	Hygiene of
	Sexual life of
Employment of	Occupations of
Feeble-minded	Degenerate and defective
	Prostitution
Insanity in	Hebephrenia
	Jealousy
Over-educated	Education of, hygiene in
Sexual perversions in	Masturbation in the female
	Nymphomania
	Sapphism
	Sexual instinct, inversion of
	Sexual instinct, perversion of

NOTE.—All indented headings are subheadings of "Women."

without regard to differences between individuals, points to a whole new set of problems that Marshall addressed by denouncing *all* forms of discrimination. She did so because she detected racist, classist, and colonialist markers along with the sexism of the Library of Congress catalogue. We are reminded of these characteristics of professional medicine by the *Index Catalogue* subheading "charitable care and protection of pregnant Women" in Series II (1916). The condescension in this elitist medical approach contrasts with the nearby subheading "occupations of Women," which takes the lives of the women, not the responsibilities of the professionals, as its subject.

3. "The wording and structure of headings for minority or other groups should not differ from headings for the majority. Avoid all *as* and *in* constructions to describe practitioners of an activity."

The indexers of the *Index Catalogue* straightforwardly ignored this principle. The very heading "Women" is gender biased, as there is no comparable term for men. The term "Man (See Also Anthropology, Apes, human Body)" obviously referred to the species.[11] The catalogue likewise listed the special studies only of women—whether "Gynaecology,"[12] in all three series, or "Feminism," which first appeared in Series II as a reference to hirsute women and then in Series III as a social movement (there is no comparable reference to masculinism).

[11] Only in the fourth series did "female Human" and "male Human" make their appearance, as part of a new indexing scheme centered on biologico-social sex as dimorphism. On this conceptual shift see Diana Long Hall, "Biology, Sex Hormones, and Sexism in the 1920s," *Philosophical Forum*, 1974, 5:81–95.

[12] The medical indexers used the British spelling in Series I and II, the American spelling in Series III.

Some of the subheadings for women did refer to general headings found elsewhere in the *Index Catalogue:* anatomy, anthropology, crime, diseases, education, fecundity/fertility, hygiene, insurance, marriage, occupations, physical examination, pregnancy, psychology, sexual instinct, and perversions of the sexual instinct ("Sexual Life" did not become a heading until Series IV) are all *IC* subject headings. But the editors held on to special fantasies and prejudices about female sexuality, as shown by the subheadings "nymphomania," "prostitution," and "frigidity."

The catalogue quite deliberately uses "in" and "as" subheadings for women, with just the effect that Marshall warns against: the women in these fields seem out of place and abnormal. These fields appear in Table 1 as subheadings of "Women," areas in which the medical indexers would not welcome their competition: "Women as dentists," "as physicians," "as pharmacists," "in medicine and science." Women "in science" do not really seem to be scientists. Women "as physicians" seem to be passive fillers of the position rather than active participants in professional life.

4. "Be specific and current. Do not use previously established terms to cover new topics."

This library rule ensures that the reader has the most up-to-date vocabulary as well as information available. The *Index Medicus,* the monthly publication of the national medical library that accompanied the *Index Catalogue* from the beginning, values such present relevance above all. The indexing of historical and current material in a single catalogue for each generation required a complex approach to vocabulary that the indexers of Series I–III never clearly articulated. They followed their understanding, as Billings put it, of the "center" of the subject and of the needs of the current reader. This led them to reify, as Marshall warns us not to do, the sexist prejudices in the "best" of the old literature for their contemporaries and for all future users of the *Index Catalogue*.

5. "Do not use subsuming terminology."

The editors of the *Index Catalogue* constantly and deliberately specified the traits of women, but not those of men, as subheadings. I have already discussed the use of "women as" and "women in" subheadings. In the same spirit, the indexers described the "female" version of body parts as subsets of the "real thing." The most striking case is the construction of "Genitals" as a male term, for which "female Genitals" is a subheading, in Series I–III.

6. "Do not allow huge files of undifferentiated cards to accumulate under a heading."

This did not happen in the case of "Women," which was never a very large subject heading: 39 pages in Series I, 34 pages in Series II, and 7 pages in Series III. By comparison, the ever-fascinating subject of the "Uterus" covered 220 pages in Series I, 292 pages in Series II, and 102 pages in Series III.

Subjecting the *Index Catalogue* to Marshall's rules reveals a text gendered in complex ways. The editors were clearly aware of the need to treat "Women" (and hence women) with respect and serious attention. The headings and subheadings often represent women as people with occupations and even sexual lives, and they avoid the entrapments of demeaning abstractions like "feeble-minded Women" and new prejudices such as "over-educated Women." But the indexers' representation of working and professional women included, in the literature chosen and the headings that organized it, condescending and voyeuristic studies of charitable cases or exotic women with a different "ethnic and temporal status" (as Series II put it). And the terms of female sexuality were typically pejorative ("nymphomania") or subordinates of those for male sexuality.

MAPPING THE SUBJECT HEADINGS INTO "FIELDS" OF TERMS

Marshall's analysis of sexism opens our eyes to the biases of "Women" in *IC* terms. The terms alone, however, did not guide the reader's mind down the correct cultural and medical path. After all, one could interpret "nymphomania" or "charitable" in many ways, depending on the context. I argue in this section that the *Index Catalogue* did indeed have such a context: the field of terms generated by the cross-references between the medical subject headings.

Marshall did not discuss the cross-references of the LC subject headings, but what the *Index Catalogue* called "See Also" references from the subject headings were another opportunity for the indexer to make cultural choices for his "general reader." They allowed the indexer to use "word associations" to enlarge the reader's understanding of a subject, to introduce medical personnel to the complex possibilities in the standard lexicon of modern medicine. They put otherwise isolated terms from medicine, science, and popular culture into a meaningful whole, a field of terms. And they did it without "looking like" meaningful discourse, education, or propaganda.

Cross-references are crucial to all indexes. They were especially important in the *Index Catalogue* because of Billings's notion that each work should get only one subject heading. Since most works address more than one topic, the reader could discover the extra meanings of a heading only by investigating the cross-references. For example, "Women," in Series II, tells the reader to "See Also" the subject heading "Man and woman"; there he or she would find five books and two articles that have information on "Women" as part of the gender relations of "Man and woman." (Havelock Ellis's book *Man and Woman* was the most influential of these works.)[13]

This cross-reference, by itself, was meaningful. The indexer, the authors of those works, and the reader collaborated in establishing gender difference as an important part of the medical word "Women." Cross-references joined together to form a map can tell us even more about the medical mentality. A map of "Women" and its cross-references in Series I is especially instructive (see Figure 1).

Linked in this picture, the words associated with "Women" are clearly more than signposts to medical bibliography. This particular map represents a woman in a Victorian story; she is confined to sex, marriage, prostitution, and generation—with her pelvis under the watchful eye of the gynecologist. Or, as the president of the Gynecological Society put it in 1900: "Many a young life is battered and forever crippled in the breakers of puberty; if it crosses these unharmed and is not dashed to pieces on the rock of childbirth, it may still ground on the ever-recurring shallow

---

[13] The library owned and indexed four copies of this book by Havelock Ellis, two indexed under this heading and one under the heading "anatomy and anthropology of Women" in Series II, and one indexed in Series I under the heading "sexual life of Women." Possession of different editions of books allowed the editors to subsume them under varied headings.

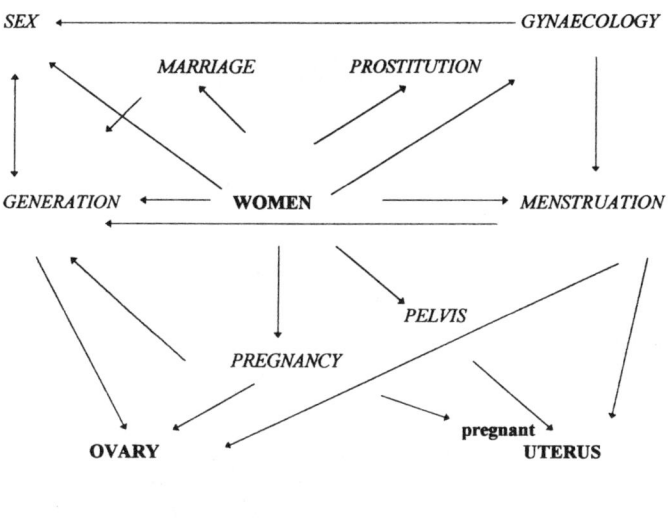

Figure 1. "Women" and its cross-references, plus "Ovary" and "Uterus." (Compiled from Index Catalogue of the Library of the Surgeon General's Office, *Series I.*)

of menstruation, and lastly, upon the final bar of the menopause ere protection is found in the unruffled waters of the harbor beyond the reach of sexual storms."[14]

What happened to this story as the *Index Catalogue* progressed? It was not repeated in any later series. Series II, we have seen, directed the reader from "Women" to the literature on "Man and woman." Series III had no cross-references from "Women." Yet the Series I "picture" of women is there to influence all users of this bibliographic aid who want to follow the subject headings for "Women" and the literature on women up to 1895.

MEDICAL GENDER IN THE *INDEX CATALOGUE:* THE "DISEASES OF WOMEN"

A far more continuous narrative in the representation of the "diseases of Women" allows us literally to follow the "changing of the medical mind" on gender from

---

[14] This medical description of women is quoted in Charles E. Rosenberg and Carroll Smith-Rosenberg, "The Female Animal: Medical and Biological Views of Woman and Her Role in Nineteenth-Century America," *Journal of American History,* 1973, *60:*332–356, on p. 336. In the company of medical men, Somerset Maugham revealed, academics could really get nasty about women: "The Professor of Gynaecology ... began his course of lectures as follows: Gentlemen, woman is an animal that micturates once a day, defecates once a week, menstruates once a month, parturates once a year and copulates whenever she has the opportunity." W. Somerset Maugham, *Writer's Notebook* (1894), quoted in Maurice B. Strauss, *Familiar Medical Quotations* (Boston: Little Brown, 1968), p. 661.

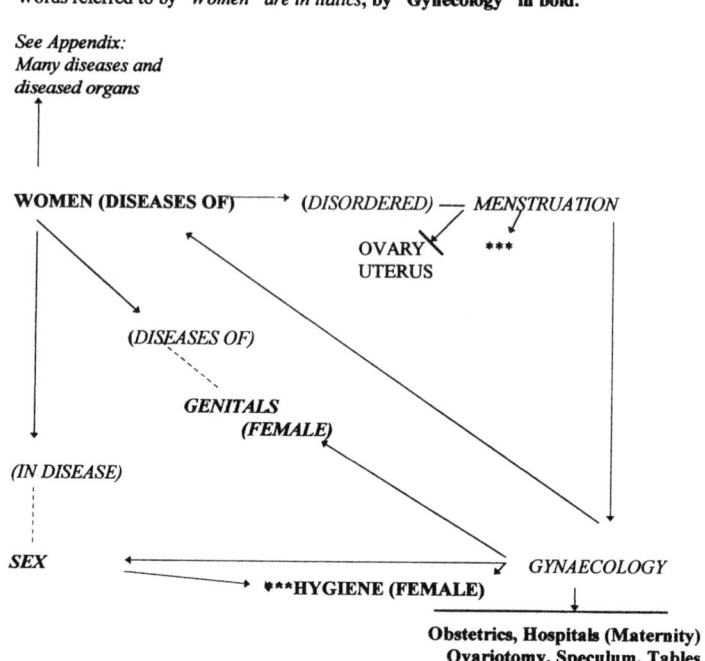

Figure 2. "Gynaecology" and "Women (diseases of)." (Compiled from Index Catalogue of the Library of the Surgeon General's Office, *Series I.*)

1895 to 1932. "Diseases of Women" can refer either to women's ailments or to a section of medicine. The two meanings are represented in the *Index Catalogue* by the fact that "diseases of Women" is a subheading of "Women" and a cross-reference from "Gynaecology." The relationship of the two terms, with arrows again indicating cross-references is quite complicated (see Figure 2).

The complication is that both "Gynaecology" and "diseases of Women" refer to the same terms of medical theory and practice. The gynecologist, in the nineteenth century, was not the only practitioner who had responsibility for the "diseases of women"; all physicians had this area of knowledge as part of their repertoire. The map, in this reading, is a moving picture of a struggle between two medical practices, one general and the other specialized.

In Figure 2, which depicts the subject headings used in Series I, the struggle looks fairly balanced, with "diseases of Women" and "Gynaecology" both pointing to their shared interest in the "female Genitals," "Sex," and "Menstruation" as well as to their specialized resources. "Diseases of Women," as the Appendix shows, pointed the reader to literature on many diseases and diseased organs. This category designated specific disease processes. "Gynaecology," by contrast, referred to its special allies, the obstetricians, its tools (speculum and tables), its place of practice (hospitals), and its controversial surgical intervention (ovariotomy).

Why did the indexers choose these terms to specify "Gynaecology"? Billings, Fletcher, and Garrison left few explanations of their choices, and those they did offer were generally pragmatic: the number of cards they had to fit into the catalogue, the words in the titles of the works indexed, and the simultaneous importance and drudgery of just getting the job done.[15]

Advertently or no, these terms point the reader to the struggles of gynecology for legitimacy and hegemony in the American (and international) medical arena. The winners and losers in this struggle are well known. Midwives lost out to obstetricians as practitioners. The latter had control not only of hospital privileges but of a rhetoric of self-justification and legitimization that placed the new science of gynecology at the center of professionalism and appealed to modern women.[16] The reader of Series I, published from 1880 to 1895, could not have predicted the outcome of this struggle, which continued within medicine in the United States until the specialists worked out their monopoly of certification with the formation of a specialty board in 1935.[17] But the attentive consumer of the subject headings in Series III could have seen which way the wind was blowing. Figure 3 maps the headings "diseases of Women" and "Gynecology" in Series III (1918–1932). The number of references in boldface type, those from "Gynecology," show that the balance of attention has shifted decidedly to the specialty field. "Diseases of Women" no longer designates many specific diseases, and it no longer has contact with the literature on the female genitals.

This comparison of the cognitive fields for women's diseases in Series I (Figure 2) and Series III (Figure 3) both deepens and modifies our view of the sexism in the *Index Catalogue*. Individual subject headings, however biased, always took their meaning in part from the field of terms with which they were associated. Those associations, along with the terms themselves, educated the reader about the medical culture of gender and the place of women.

Where did this culture, as represented by the shift from "diseases of Women" to "Gynecology" in the early twentieth century, place women? This lexical shift displaced women in two ways. First, it quite literally separated women from their diseases. Women were the subject in Series I; in later catalogues they neither "headed" the medical issues nor, as people, interested the medical practitioner. The scientific frame of mind that fragmented the "woman in the body" and constructed the world of "organs without bodies" may have aimed at specialization but arrived at something closer to psychosis.[18]

Second, women lost direct association with much of their medical literature and

---

[15] Fielding Garrison alludes to all these pressures in his descriptive chapter "The Index Catalogue and Index Medicus," in *John Shaw Billings* (cit. n. 7), Ch. 5.

[16] Judith Leavitt balances the professional politics with the interests and desires of women in her history of American childbirth, *Brought to Bed: Childbearing in America, 1750–1950* (Oxford: Oxford Univ. Press, 1986). She focuses on technology as the strong suit of the new gynecology; but the rhetorical changes form a parallel story. Ornella Moscucci has shown us just how complex the struggle was in England to "fashion a recognizably modern profession" on territory formerly held not only by midwives but also by general practitioners and surgeons. Her model takes into account the ambition of the medical elites, the technological innovations of the practitioners, and the gendered attitudes inherent in both. See Ornella Moscucci, *The Science of Women: Gynaecology and Gender in England, 1800–1929* (Cambridge: Cambridge Univ. Press, 1990), pp. 204–205.

[17] Paul Starr, *The Social Transformation of American Medicine: The Rise of a Sovereign Profession and the Making of a Vast Industry* (New York: Basic, 1982), pp. 223, 357.

[18] See Emily Martin, *The Woman in the Body* (Boston: Beacon, 1988); and Rosi Braidotti, "Organs without Bodies," in *Nomadic Subjects: Embodiment and Sexual Difference in Contemporary Feminist Theory* (New York: Columbia Univ. Press, 1994), pp. 41–57.

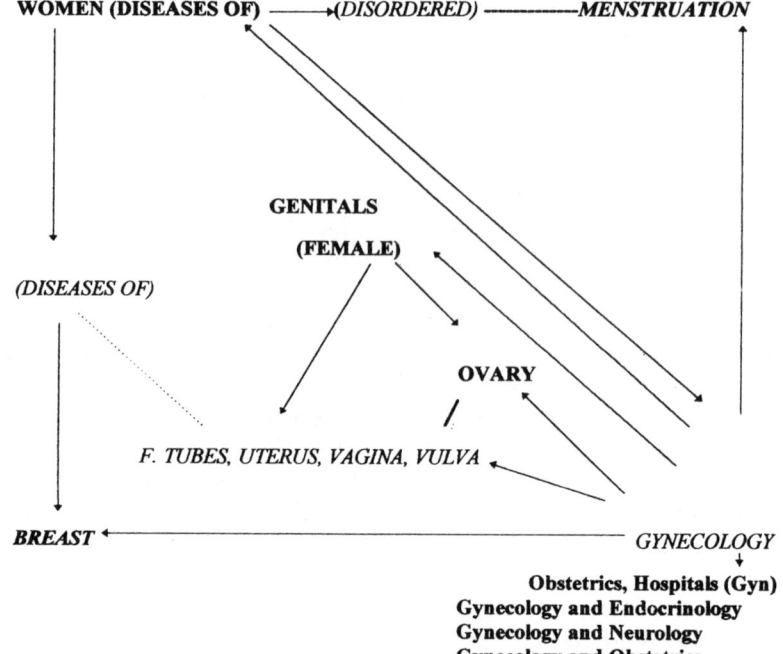

Figure 3. The balance shifts to "Gynecology." (Compiled from Index Catalogue of the Library of the Surgeon General's Office, Series III.)

with the details of their sickness and health. In Series I and Series II, "diseases of Women" was highly subdivided—by cases, causes and pathology, classification, diagnosis and semiology, popular treatises, prevention, quackery, and treatment (including "with animal extracts," "by artificial hyperaemia," "by electrotherapy," "by heat," "by hydrotherapy and balneotherapy," "with ichthyol," and "by light, radium, and Roentgen rays"). By Series III, "diseases of Women" had no subheadings and contained only fifty-six entries, in contrast to the 2,109 entries in Series II.

The literature traditionally assigned to the heading "diseases of Women" was deliberately moved to "Gynecology." This is one occasion when we have specific evidence of a decision: a handwritten note from the editor in the National Library of Medicine copy of Series I (above the entry for "diseases of Women") announces that "Women, Diseases of, the subdv. [subdivision] transferred to Gynaecology, excluding Women, Diseases of, causes of."[19] The author of the note is unidentified, but the changes in subject headings it called for were made after the "W" volume of Series II and before the "G" volume of Series III—that is, between 1916 and 1926.

Occasionally we see the editors making their culturally significant choices. And occasionally they shared with each other the metaphors that guided their selection. Usually such conversations took place in person, at their desks or in their clubs; occasionally we have some record of what they thought they were doing, the games

---

[19] Series I, Vol. 16, pp. 548–549.

they were playing with their readers. The editor of the third series, Fielding Garrison, tells this story on his predecessor, Robert Fletcher:

> Fletcher, after an experience of many years, likened the *Index-Catalogue* to a vast metropolitan hotel containing story after story of rooms and suites of rooms of all sizes and prices adapted to the tenants of every degree of income and worldly place. In such a caravansary, some subjects like Labour, Surgery, Water Supply, etc., are old wealthy patrons having a permanent claim upon apartments of vast extent occupying an entire floor. Others, such as Arteriosclerosis, Bacteriology, Parasitology, Pellagra, Poliomyelitis, were once poor and needy, but, having come up in the world acquire extensive suites, with room perchance for even maid and courier.[20]

THE CONSTRUCTION OF AN *INDEX CATALOGUE* FOR AN AUTHORITATIVE PROFESSION AND A GYNECOLOGICAL SPECIALTY

Fletcher's hotel metaphor for the *Index Catalogue* reveals something of the atmosphere in the "old library" of medicine, as the librarian and the editor of the *Index Catalogue* struggled to put together their (approximately) yearly volumes of indexed bibliography.[21] Fitting the published literature to subject headings and including just the right amount of information in the right place surely was a challenge. The metaphor acknowledges that the work affects the balance of power and social relations in medicine. But it denies the human agency that made the choices and expended the labor. In Fletcher's image the subject headings are personified as actors engaging in a Darwinian struggle for space in the medical mind and on the medical bookshelves.

The subject headings, however, did not struggle by themselves; they populated the rooms and suites of Fletcher's hotel through the choices of the editors,[22] and those choices took place in the context of a community that used and welcomed their representations of all aspects of medicine, including those pertaining to women and gender.

No one paid much attention to the Library of the Surgeon General's Office until John Shaw Billings created its *Index Catalogue*. Surgeon General Joseph Lovell began accumulating books in his office in 1836 but had neither the funds nor the interest to put together a larger collection until after the Civil War. Then he found that he had unexpended hospital funds and an assistant who took to the task of collecting with a vision and energy that astonished all.

John Shaw Billings rapidly collected books and articles to form the kernel of what would become the National Library of Medicine. The Surgeon General's library had

---

[20] Garrison. *John Shaw Billings* (cit. n. 7), pp. 220–221.

[21] For a nostalgic, authoritative, and engaged view of the "old library" see Frank Bradway Rogers, "The Old Library in Washington, 1836–1961," in *Past, Present, and Future of Biomedical Information* (Bethesda, Md.: National Library of Medicine, 1986), pp. 16–27. Rogers was the leader of the "modernizers" who discontinued the *Index Catalogue* and discarded its card catalogue to clear the way for other finding aids, a new classification defined in terms of professional criteria, dramatic new technologies, and an enlarged staff including influential women like Estelle Brodman, Jane Doe, and M. Ruth MacDonald. See Wyndham Miles, *A History of the National Library of Medicine: The Nation's Treasury of Medical Knowledge* (Bethesda, Md.: National Institutes of Health, 1982), p. 336 and *passim*.

[22] Compare the construction metaphor of Cuddon: "To me making a dictionary has seemed much like building a sizable house singlehanded." J. A. Cuddon, *A Dictionary of Literary Terms* (Garden City, N.Y.: Doubleday, 1977), quoted in Treichler, "Dictionary to Discourse" (cit. n. 2), p. 60.

fifty thousand books and fifty-seven thousand pamphlets when Billings published the first volume of the *Index Catalogue* in 1880. Robert Fletcher joined him in 1876 to assist in producing the first series. Fletcher became editor of Series II when Billings left the library in 1895 to become director of the New York Public Library. Fielding Garrison joined the happy band as an assistant in 1891; he in turn became editor of the *Index Catalogue* from 1912 until his departure for Johns Hopkins in 1930. By 1932, these men had overseen the collection and indexing of almost two million items of medical literature in forty-seven quarto volumes indexed by author and subject headings.[23]

The band was not always happy doing this work of bibliographic production. The daily grind of producing accurate records on so many publications was enormous, work that made Billings "always sad" but fulfilled by his "labor of love." Those who evaluated the first volume of the first series could only say that they were grateful for his organization of the tidal wave of literature.[24]

The *Index Catalogue,* however, did not just serve the library needs of the profession. The first series generated a reputation for Billings and for his index that can only be called a mythology. The authors of this mythology were the elite, scientific doctors from the universities and from the new specialties, notably William Henry Welch in pathology and Alexander Jacobi in pediatrics. Jacobi said of Billings, in private and in public: "He was not really 'one of us,' no practitioner, no consultant, not often seen in medical societies. I believe there are many of the younger men who never saw him. But all knew him; knew he was above us. . . . Everyone knew he had rendered and was constantly rendering, services, unique and such as nobody else could render or imitate."[25]

Welch astonished his eager audience in the library, and later in print, with the judgment that the library and its index were the most important American contribution to medicine in the nineteenth century, greater even than anesthesia or asepsis or surgery. This story, as authorized by a later librarian of the Surgeon General's Office, Everett E. Hume, has all the marks of a good myth: it is local, vivid, and surprising. Hume set the stage: "On the last visit he paid to Washington, not long before his final illness, [Welch] was sitting in the Librarian's office smoking one of his black cigars, when he fell into one of those reminiscent moods so enjoyed by his friends and pupils." Welch named the four greatest contributions of America to medicine in the nineteenth century, concluding with "'the Army Medical Library and its *Index Catalogue* and (he added slowly), this library and its catalogue are the most important of the four.' . . . I was so struck by this pronouncement, that I reduced it to writing immediately after the doctor had left."[26]

Billings's "cool, impersonal self" may have been indifferent to such hyperbole, but he believed as strongly as Welch and Osler in the importance of heroes and

---

[23] The preface of Vol. 1 of each series (1880, 1896, 1918) contains data on the number of books and articles indexed.

[24] Miles, *History of the National Library of Medicine* (cit. n. 21), pp. 176, 252 (Billings's attitude); and *Library Journal,* 1880, p. 5 (review of Series I, Vol. 1).

[25] Jacobi's remark of 1913 first appeared in a private letter to Fielding Garrison; it is quoted in Garrison, *John Shaw Billings* (cit. n. 7), p. 393.

[26] E. E. Hume, "John Shaw Billings as an Army Medical Officer," *Bulletin of the Institute for the History of Medicine* (John Shaw Billings Memorial Number), 1938, 6:266–267.

models of excellence.²⁷ These myths were part of the late nineteenth-century cultural and political struggle to upgrade American medicine, to make it harder, more competitive, and more uniformly scientific. This was a Sisyphean task, one that required the combined political and cultural efforts of many institutions and individuals in science, medicine, government, and business. It succeeded. The lobbying efforts of scientific doctors, promoters of an American Medical Association, and other interested parties resulted by 1920 in a profession unified around standardized requirements for all phases of medical education and medical life, from the prerequisites for medical school to the qualifications of a legitimate practitioner. Every state in the union passed some kind of medical licensing law between 1870 and 1900. Only "regular" doctors—those trained in institutions dedicated to science and to mainstream medical practices—could certify births and deaths, treat the sick, and speak for the medical profession; all others became suspect as "quacks."²⁸

This successful transformation required stories that inspired leaders in Congress and business, as well as medicine and science, to make the effort. In addition, as William Bynum has pointed out, this successful social movement also required a large-scale response from what Billings called "the good average practitioner." William Henry Welch in America, like Louis Pasteur in France and Robert Koch in Germany, inspired the emulation of hundreds of young men keen to join medicine as regular doctors in spite of the effort required.²⁹ The new medicine justly claimed to be both valuable and accessible.

The *Index Catalogue,* too, represented both excellence and accessibility. Billings tried in his collecting to make the library a commons of all the legitimate contributions of the field and succeeded by 1896 in possessing "75% of all publications." But the indexes were selective, according to Garrison. Fletcher indexed all the articles from the better journals for the monthly *Index Medicus,* but Billings aimed to "make [the *Index Catalogue*] a repository of the very best and most select material, but of no other." He hoped thus to provide the profession with the "dignity" of excellence.³⁰

It is important to notice that it was excellence and dignity that the profession desired in 1880, not science per se. The new scientific institutions of the period were scientific, medical, and health care centers. The Johns Hopkins Medical School and other elite medical schools developed hospitals, schools of nursing, and schools of public health along with medical schools that both taught medicine and promoted

---

²⁷ Garrison, *John Shaw Billings* (cit. n. 7), p. 210. The word *excellence,* denoting both a superior condition and a competitive atmosphere, is central to discourse about the Johns Hopkins Medical School. See Victor Turner, *Heritage of Excellence* (Baltimore: Johns Hopkins Univ. Press, 1974).

²⁸ A fine introduction to this story is Ronald L. Numbers, "The Fall and Rise of the American Medical Profession," in *Sickness and Health in America: Readings in the History of Medicine and Public Health,* ed. Judith Walzer Leavitt and Numbers, 2nd ed. (Madison: Univ. Wisconsin Press, 1985), pp. 185–196.

²⁹ Garrison, *John Shaw Billings* (cit. n. 7), p. 188. William Bynum, *Science and the Practice of Medicine in the Nineteenth Century* (Cambridge: Cambridge Univ. Press, 1995), describes the formation, by World War I, of an Anglo-American medical community of doctors who wanted to be like Pasteur, Koch, or William Henry Welch.

³⁰ Editorial, *Library J.,* 1896, *3:*107–108; Fielding H. Garrison to the Surgeon General, Garrison Papers, 209/4G, National Library of Medicine, Bethesda, Maryland; and Garrison, *John Shaw Billings,* p. 216. Presumably the reported figure meant 75 percent of all contemporary medical publications, but Billings was equally eager to have the entire historical record at his library.

medical science. And the culture that made them so special and effective in teaching and promoting medicine as a profession was not just technical, although it set new, higher, and much more expensive standards for technical work. Billings, Welch, and Osler were at the center of conversation about all the policy issues associated with science. They were influentials who could persuade members of Congress, scientists, or humanists with equal ease.[31]

John Shaw Billings was both a lobbyist for this culture—as far abroad as the Internation Medical Congress in London in 1885—and its beneficiary. His elite colleagues, notably Welch and Jacobi, intervened in Congress and the profession to ensure that his index got the extraordinary funding that it needed, about $1,000 a volume for the forty-seven volumes that appeared between 1880 and 1932. In return, the country was promised not only a history and index of all the contributions to medicine, but also a cultural monument to the military and to American society.[32]

Both elite and democratic, Billings's index was just the tool that the growing profession needed to increase its dignity and power. Leaders and "wanna-bes" alike had access to the literature, with its record of the promise as well as the achievement of the profession. For a man like Thomas Cullen the *Index Catalogue* was an integral part of the thrilling and rewarding path that led directly from his student days at Johns Hopkins to his leadership in his field. And it was a path that, from the beginning, integrated reading and scholarship with socialization as a physician.

> In January 1892 I became an intern in the Department of Gynaecology, under that wonderful surgeon, Howard Atwood Kelly. Dr. Kelly ran into many interesting and unusual cases and suggested that his assistants publish these.
> We adopted his suggestion and before long some of us found that much time could be saved by running over to the Surgeon General's Library in Washington to look up the literature on a given subject. . . . Frequently, before going to Washington, we would consult the *Index Catalogue* and later the *Index Medicus,* to see what had been written on a given subject. Upon reaching the library, we would go to the reading room and write out on separate cards the books that we desired.

Cullen continued to integrate this medical institution into his repertoire as he moved up the professional ladder, so that "during the years I wrote five books and three volumes of short articles. The literature for all of the books and nearly all of the separate monographs was furnished me by the Surgeon General's Library." In these publications, Cullen contributed to new understanding of the cancer, adenomyoma, and myomata of the uterus. He combined embryology, anatomy, and pathology in a way characteristic of the new gynecology of the Kelly school at Hopkins, where he

---

[31] On the medical profession's use of science as justification see John Harley Warner, "The History of Science and the Sciences of Medicine," *Osiris,* 2nd Ser., 1995, *10:*164–193; and Susan E. Bell, "Gendered Medical Science: Producing a Drug for Women," *Feminist Studies,* 1995, *21:*469–498. See also Starr, *Social Transformation of American Medicine* (cit. n. 17), p. 116. The classic account of a medical influential is Donald Fleming, *William Henry Welch and the Rise of Modern Medicine* (Boston: Little, Brown, 1954).

[32] Fielding Garrison reinforced this work of the *Index Catalogue* with his *History of Medicine,* 4th ed. (Philadelphia: Saunders, 1929), which arranged the best of the indexed literature by topic and presented his checklist of the greatest works of medicine of all time. The first edition, more limited in scope, appeared in 1913.

became professor of clinical gynecology in 1900 and succeeded Kelly as professor of gynecology in 1932.[33]

Cullen's success epitomized the intended effect and effectiveness of the *Index Catalogue*. As one institution in a complex of interrelated intellectual and professional centers, the *Index Catalogue* gave detail and depth to the new medical culture. A commons of all the legitimate contributions to that new culture, the index was both based on and the source of medical discourse that was intellectually exciting and professionally progressive.[34]

THE EFFECT OF THE *INDEX CATALOGUE* ON WOMEN IN MEDICINE AND SCIENCE

All professionals welcomed the *Index Catalogue*, but not all professionals benefited equally from its scholarship and cultural work. Women, I have suggested, were both misrepresented and denigrated by the choices of subject headings. They had very little opportunity to choose those headings, as they became librarians much later in this military institution than in civilian libraries.[35] The first woman to work in the library came as a staff helper in 1905, and women successfully competed with male clerks for jobs during and after World War I. By 1927 they held well-paid positions, and Florence Garrison, sister of the editor, had risen to the responsible job of chief of indexers. Fielding Garrison referred to her as the "real prime mover and backbone of the old *Index Medicus,* doing all the drudgery on it and managing the finances." Beatrice Bickel, a Swiss librarian, was appointed chief librarian in 1931. She was thus authorized to do subject heading after Fielding Garrison resigned as editor.[36] It could well have been she who compiled the headings under "Women" in Series III.

The women on the staff of the library did not eliminate or even publicly discuss the gender bias inherent in the headings for "Women" and the cognitive maps of subject headings. Nor did medical women comment on this sexism, these hidden persuaders. Why?

Women in American medicine in the late nineteenth century had their own reasons for welcoming the *IC*, however costly that acceptance might ultimately prove. As Regina Morantz-Sanchez tells the story, women moved into medicine in consonance with their new image of themselves as capable and autonomous contributors to the public world, as part of the first wave of American feminism in the mid-nineteenth century. The Women's Medical College of Philadelphia was created in 1850, followed by other schools of education and women's medical societies and centers. By the time the first series of the *Index Catalogue* was completed in 1895,

> women physicians could congratulate themselves for a measure of achievement which offered ample opportunity for pride and satisfaction. . . . In numbers alone their ranks

---

[33] Thomas Cullen, quoted in Miles, *History of the National Library of Medicine* (cit. n. 21), pp. 171, 201. Biographical data on Cullen come from *American Men of Science* (New York: Science Press, 1938).

[34] Note the similar role of dictionaries as described in Treichler, "Dictionary to Discourse" (cit. n. 2), p. 51.

[35] I will not consider here the gendered psychology and politics of library work in this military medical establishment. For an introduction to the feminization of library work see Dee Garrison, *Apostles of Culture: The Public Librarian and American Society, 1876–1920* (New York: Free Press, 1979), Pt. 4: "The Tender Technicians."

[36] Miles, *History of the National Library of Medicine* (cit. n. 21), pp. 247, 249 (quotation), 256. Bickel was never the head of indexing, but Miles suggests (p. 256) that she did challenge the work of a later Librarian, Claudius Mayer.

> had increased by several thousand: in 1900 they comprised close to five percent of the profession, over seven thousand strong. Visionary women like Elizabeth Blackwell, Mary Putnam Jacobi, Ann Preston, Marie Zakrzewska, and Mary Harris Thompson could point proudly to the achievements of their own institutions. Even more heartening was the progress of medical coeducation.... Crowning these achievements in 1893 was the opening of the Johns Hopkins Medical School as a coeducational institution.[37]

In addition, 75 percent or more of women doctors were regular physicians, and most hospital training programs and state and local medical societies admitted women.

Women had their female societies, but they, like men, recognized that there was only one medical profession and that it was defined by exciting new leadership and institutions, including the *Index Catalogue* and Fielding Garrison's historical studies based on it. There was no path except the path of real medicine recorded in the literature; women must struggle to get into the male profession and to enlarge their place within it. A nonconforming woman might end up publicly denounced, like "Dr. Bertha C. Day, a mail-order medical faker specializing on the diseases of women," who appears in Series II of the *Index Catalogue* under the rubric "quackery in the diseases of Women."[38]

Margaret Rossiter has detailed the "struggles and strategies" of American scientific women for advancement and success in the cultural space between the great doctors and modern quackery. Penina Migdal Glazer and Miriam Slater summarize these strategies as "superperformance, innovation, segregation, and subordination," all compromises with the rules set by male leaders like Billings, Welch, and Jacobi and the standards set by the *Index Catalogue* and associated institutions.[39]

The *Index Catalogue* and Garrison's histories based on it were at the center of the new professional medical mainstream. The catalogue was a carrot and a stick, a call to measure up to and be part of "the very best and most select material" in medicine. American medical women could point with pride to their excellence. In time, they received positions and awards that were recorded in the historical record. In 1929 Maud Slye was cited in Garrison's list of outstanding discoveries of all time for her work on cancer, starting in 1914. He also singled out another twenty-two American women as "talented women . . . investigators." He mentioned

> the Americans Mary Putnam Jacobi who won the Paris faculty medal for her thesis on acid and neutral fats (1870), the late Mme. Dejerine (neurology), Maude Slye (cancer), Florence Sabin (hematology), Alice Hamilton (industrial medicine), Gladys Dick (scarlatina), Dorothy Reed (Hodgkin's disease), Ruth Tunnicliff (measles, meningitis), Margaret Lewis (mitochondria), Alice C. Evans (Brucella), Anna Williams (diphtheria), Martha Wollstein (serology), Louise Pearce (experimental medicine), Lydia and Louise Rabinovich (bacteriology; resuscitation), Clara Jacobson (trophic nerves), Mary Swartz Rose (food chemistry), Lydia De Witt (pathology), Kay Daniels (nutrition), Katherine

---

[37] Regina Morantz-Sanchez, *Symapthy and Science: Women Physicians in American Medicine* (Oxford: Oxford Univ. Press, 1985), p. 232.

[38] Series II, Vol. 21, p. 203.

[39] Margaret W. Rossiter, *Women Scientists in America: Struggles and Strategies to 1940* (Baltimore: Johns Hopkins Univ. Press, 1982); and Penina Migdal Glazer and Miriam Slater, *Unequal Colleagues: The Entrance of Women into the Professions, 1890–1940* (New Brunswick, N.J.: Rutgers Univ. Press, 1987). The latter study of the lives of nine prominent professionals in education, medicine, science, and psychiatric social work indicates that all these women, over the span of their work lives, tried to get in by hard work, by the clever choice of an underpopulated or opportune niche, by the cultivation of a "women's field," or by serving the needs of men in an important field.

M. Howell (serology), Nina Simmonds (biochemistry), Josephine B. Neal (meningitis, encephalitis), Miss N. M. Stevens (embryology.)[40]

Women measuring their success in and contributions to the profession could also point to the listing of their work in the *Index Catalogue*. For women as a group, some sections of the catalogue presented a pleasing view of female success. Under "Women," most notably, women could see that they formed a fair portion of the publishing scholarly community. In Series I (1895), summarizing past publication, only twenty American women published twenty-one papers in a subject heading of some thirty-nine pages. But in the second series, summarizing the literature from 1894 to 1916, 112 American women authored about 5 percent of all the publications listed and a full 20 percent of the American contributions. In subheadings of "Women" other than "diseases of Women," women published 31 percent of the American contributions.[41]

By 1916, however, it was becoming evident to feminists that something had gone very wrong and that their hopes for fair play and an equal opportunity would go unfulfilled in the cutthroat competition of the new American science and medicine. During the period of publication of Series II, 1896–1916, the number of women regular physicians declined, along with the number of women in regular medical schools. Only the Women's Medical College of Pennsylvania remained as a single-sex school.[42]

In this context, the separation of women's subjects in the *Index Catalogue* might have lost both its symbolic and its professional usefulness. Women, whether from fatigue, fear of backlash, or changed priorities, published less on "women's issues" than they had in the early days of professional feminist scholars. In a period when the medical sciences were taking shape as competitive team efforts requiring substantial funding, women tried to join the new research teams and integrate their talents within the wider opportunities of the medical culture.[43] Yet the *Index Catalogue* remained a place where one could see the contributions of individual women and of the community as a whole. On the subject of "Women," Series III, summarizing the literature from 1916 to 1932, listed fifty-six women responsible for about 8 percent of the publications. In the literature, at least, women were moving ahead.

In hindsight, feminists can see the limitations of this victory and the restricted options and strategies of these ambitious women. In hindsight, we can see that as long as women could succeed only by divorcing themselves from their sex and from their gender, they could always be marginalized as special or dangerous. As Glazer and Slater point out, even the most successful women, like Dorothy Reed and Florence Sabin at Johns Hopkins, lacked the resources to participate fully in the new medical culture themselves, much less to help the women of the next generation. No matter how important their work or how acceptable their individual contributions

---

[40] Garrison, *History of Medicine*, 4th ed. (1929) (cit. n. 32), p. 801.
[41] I have used the place of publication to establish the nationality of authors unless what I know of an author's biography indicates otherwise.
[42] Morantz-Sanchez, *Sympathy and Science* (cit. n. 37), Ch. 9.
[43] On the ambivalent position of women in the research teams of the 1920s see Rossiter, *Women Scientists in America: Struggles and Strategies to 1940* (cit. n. 39), Ch. 7; and Diana Long Hall, "Academics, Bluestockings, and Biologists: Women at the University of Chicago, 1892–1932," *Annals of the New York Academy of Sciences*, 1979, *323:*300–320.

to medicine, women always played against a background in which they did not look like experts, or like scientists.[44]

Women in American medicine in the Progressive Era, 1890–1920, were extraordinarily resourceful in their strategies and struggles. They both bargained for fair play and challenged stereotypes.[45] They did so, however, from a doubly subordinate position. Not only were they dubious newcomers in a man's world; they were also the object of study in that world. Like men, they were patients; but unlike men, they were special patients that occupied two special places in the medical literature and the medical mind. They were "Women," with their own diseases, occupations, and psychology. And they were also the object of "Gynecology," a special discipline that was replacing what it called the vague and inferior diagnosis and treatment of women by laymen and general practitioners with precise and therapeutic studies such as those by Thomas Cullen. The *Index Catalogue* did not create this situation, but it did acknowledge and legitimate it. The heroes at the National Library of Medicine could literally move the "diseases of Women" from the "Women" suite to the "Gynecology" suite in the word hotel, and no one would register or challenge the move. "Gynecology" was simply "coming up in the world."

CONCLUSION

Women did not look like the authors of medical expertise in the laboratory, classroom, or hospital. Nor, this essay argues, did "Women" look like normal subjects of medicine in the headings of the *Index Catalogue of the Library of the Surgeon General's Office* (1880–1932). They looked like special objects. The prejudices inherent in these headings reveal a medical world that never had women in mind as typical authors or readers of the literature. They made the work of women less visible than it deserved to be and made women themselves oddities.

This discounting of women in the medical index did not happen in a vacuum. Just as the index itself was situated at the intersection of the new medical education, the recruitment of regular physicians into a more dignified profession, and the new possibilities for publication, its effect depended on the shared assumptions of the authors who wrote the works catalogued and the readers looking for the literature. In many ways the indexer stood as a sort of traffic cop at the intersection of these two groups of medical participants. Billings claimed that he made no active decisions about medical thought but was simply the "hod carrier" of materials for intellectual and political life. This was a popular view in the medical library profession in the 1940s, when Helen Field quoted S. I. Hayakawa to assert that the indexer, like "*the writer of a dictionary, is a historian, not a law-giver.*" Yet the man at the intersection, if not a law-giver, certainly held a sign. He educated as well as informed the readers about what indexers call the "controlled vocabulary" of the field. And he had the power, as Jane Doe told the medical librarians in 1943, to "take the mind along paths it might not take of itself."[46]

The power of naming and word association was especially strong in a new field

---

[44] Glazer and Slater, *Unequal Colleagues* (cit. n. 39), pp. 209–245.

[45] Rossiter, *Women Scientists in America: Struggles and Strategies to 1940* (cit. n. 39), introduction.

[46] Hume, "John Shaw Billings" (cit. n. 26), p. 260; Helen Field, "Subject Headings and the Growing Library," *Bulletin of the Medical Library Association*, 1942, p. 363 (Field's emphasis); and Jane Doe, "A Critical Review of Existing Medical Subject Heading Lists," *ibid.*, 1948, *36:*87.

such as scientific medicine in the late nineteenth and early twentieth centuries. The persuasiveness of the professional leaders, the faith of the followers in their heroes, and the vulnerable situation of women created special conditions that left no one to challenge the cultural work of the "golden indexers" (as one student remembers them from library school).[47] Helen Field, Jane Doe, and other professional indexers noticed the problem in the 1940s, and the "linguistic turn" of feminist reform since the 1970s has emphasized its importance. The challenge this awareness presents is especially important as indexing goes on-line and the Internet provides keyword searches of global information. In these new situations we need to be clear about our lexical choices, about who is making them and in what context. The history of medical indexing suggests that we cannot leave it to the experts to tell us the proper names for our bodies or our selves.

[47] Christine Ruggere, medical librarian at the College of Physicians of Philadelphia, personal communication, 1986.

Appendix. Cross-References from "Women (diseases of)"

Series I (1895)*	Series III (1932)
Gynaecology	Gynecology
Obstetrics	
Medicine (popular) etc.	
Hospitals (maternity, etc.)	
Lithotomy in the female	
Clothing	
Genitals (female, glands of)	
Ovary	
Uterus	
Bladder (displacements of)	
Calculus (urinary) in the female	
Chlorosis	
Coccygodynia	
Gonorrhea in the female	
Insanity in women	
Menstruation (disordered) etc.	
Nymphomania	
Rectocele	
Sterility	
Syphilis in the female	
Variocele in the female	
Venereal diseases in the female	
Sex in disease	
Bladder (diseases of) in the female	
Breast (diseases of)	Breast (diseases of)
	Fallopian tubes (diseases of)
Genitals (female, diseases of)	
Nervous system (diseases of) of uterine origin, etc.	
Pelvis (diseases of)	
Urethra (female, diseases of)	
Uterus (diseases of)	Uterus (diseases of)
	Vagina (diseases of)
	Vulva (diseases of)

*This category includes "systematic treatises on gynaecology of A.D. 1800 and subsequently."

"What the Women at All Times Would Laugh At"
Redefining Equality and Difference, circa 1660–1760

By Estelle Cohen*

DURING THE EARLY MODERN CENTURIES learned men redefined themselves as intellectuals or men of letters, constituting themselves a new priesthood in the international Republic of Letters, while defining learned women as something entirely different: as immodest, indecent, aberrant, and distinctly undesirable creatures.[1] That much is widely known. Learned women, on the other hand, while ridiculing patriarchal and liberal theorists from Jean Bodin to Robert Filmer and John Locke, insisted that the most critical anatomy proves their equality with men. Taking their cue and many of their lines from the (usually unattributed) work of François Poullain de la Barre, they also urged other women to study their own anatomy.[2] By the end of the eighteenth century, however, the force of such arguments

---

*Center for Philosophy of Science, University of Minnesota, Minneapolis, Minnesota 55455.

I want to thank audiences who heard earlier versions of this essay in Minneapolis, Montreal, and Ottawa for their helpful questions and comments; the editors of this volume for their support and patience; and two very special people: Dr. Eleanora Gordon, of Wynnewood, Pennsylvania, who offered a congenial working space at the earliest stages of this project; and Steve Lelchuk, of the Minnesota Center for Philosophy of Science, who has responded cheerfully and intelligently to repeated requests for assistance.

[1] On the new intellectuals of the early modern period see Robert Mandrou, *From Humanism to Science, 1480–1700,* trans. Brian Pearce (New York: Penguin, 1978); and E. J. Hundert, "A Cognitive Ideal and Its Myth: Knowledge as Power in the Lexicon of the Enlightenment," *Social Research,* 1986, *53*:133–157. For an outstanding analysis of one woman intellectual's efforts to play an *active* role in the Republic of Letters, to participate in the *production* of knowledge, see Mary Terrall, "Émilie du Châtelet and the Gendering of Science," *History of Science,* 1995, *33*:283–310. Paula Findlen's interpretation of the rather different fate of Laura Bassi and other female scholars in Italy nonetheless concludes that learned women were no more than "spectacles of learning, rather than intellectuals in their own right," in the eighteenth century: Findlen, "Translating the New Science: Women and the Circulation of Knowledge in Enlightenment Italy," *Configurations,* 1995, *3*:167–206, on p. 205; and Findlen, "Science as a Career in Enlightenment Italy: The Strategies of Laura Bassi," *Isis,* 1993, *84*:441–469. Lorraine Daston's essay "The Naturalized Female Intellect," *Science in Context,* 1992, *5*:209–235, which argues that women intellectuals of the late seventeenth and eighteenth centuries were viewed as absurdities, abominations, or at best wonders (pp. 227–230), is essential reading on the subject, despite my disagreement with some of her statements about the period before 1800. Another very useful study is Elizabeth Colwill, "Laws of Nature/Rights of Genius: The *Drame* of Constance de Salm," in *Going Public: Women and Publishing in Early Modern France,* ed. Elizabeth C. Goldsmith and Dena Goodman (Ithaca, N.Y.: Cornell Univ. Press, 1995), pp. 224–242.

[2] To my surprise, I first encountered the injunction to women to seek knowledge of their bodies in anatomy books in the work of a Dutch physician working in London from 1693: Bernard Mandeville, *The Virgin Unmask'd* (London, 1709), p. 123. He pointed out that to read anatomy books required

had diminished, although they recur throughout the nineteenth century in both Western Europe and the United States, and new models of knowledge and scientific method had significantly undermined the authority of women's own narratives of their bodily experience.

My study of a range of medical literature from around 1660, much of it slighted, misrepresented, even deleted in later accounts of the period, suggests that these learned women were indeed wise women. That is, arguments for a biological foundation for gender inequality, which grew increasingly strident during the final decades of the eighteenth century, could not be reliably grounded on recent anatomy lessons. And we have only begun to recover the history of feminist efforts to use the new anatomy to contest what patriarchal theorists referred to as "the empire of the father."[3] During the eighteenth century there continued to be an enormous range of ways of imagining the body; although some could be traced to the teachings of the ancients, most were of more recent provenance. Two things in particular deserve attention: the emergence and development of new ways of imaging the body in seventeenth- and eighteenth-century Europe, and the fact that these new technologies had limited immediate impact on the diverse ways in which the body was construed—or at least did not have the kind of effect we (moderns) would consider appropriate. I refer in particular to the medical practices of microscopy, dissection, and preservation of anatomical specimens, on the basis of which significant numbers of anatomists, physicians, and midwives contested received ideas about menstruation and uterine pathology. Most significantly, perhaps, following the rediscovery and renaming of the ovaries in mid-seventeenth-century Leiden by Reinier de Graaf and others, some influential accounts of generation accepted women's active and essential, if not principal, role in reproduction—at a time when patriarchal theorists

---

no more skill, time, or trouble than the completion of an intricate piece of filigree work. Eventually, I traced this notion to François Poullain de la Barre, *De l'égalité des deux sexes: Discours physique et moral, où l'on voit l'importance de se défaire des préjugez* (Paris, 1673). Poullain explained that it requires more intelligence to learn to do embroidery or needlework well than to learn the sciences, or, as he put it in his second book, published a year later, "It isn't as hard to become a Philosopher as it is to become an Upholsterer": Poullain, *De l'éducation des dames pour la conduite de l'esprit dans les sciences et dans les moeurs: Entretiens* (Paris, 1674), p. 241.

[3] There is an impressive literature on patriarchalism in early modern England and France. See, e.g., Gordon Schochet, *Patriarchalism in Political Thought* (Oxford: Blackwell, 1975); Susan Dwyer Amussen, "Gender, Family, and the Social Order, 1560–1725," in *Order and Disorder in Early Modern England*, ed. Anthony Fletcher and John Stevenson (Cambridge: Cambridge Univ. Press, 1985), pp. 196–217; D. E. Underdown, "The Taming of the Scold: The Enforcement of Patriarchal Authority in Early Modern England," *ibid.*, pp. 116–136; Carole Pateman, *The Sexual Contract* (Oxford: Polity, 1988), esp. Ch. 4; Pateman, "'God Hath Ordained to Man a Helper': Hobbes, Patriarchy, and Conjugal Right," in *Feminist Interpretations and Political Theory*, ed. Mary L. Shanley and Pateman (University Park: Pennsylvania State Univ. Press, 1991), pp. 53–73; Melissa A. Butler, "Early Liberal Roots of Feminism: John Locke and the Attack on Patriarchy," *ibid.*, pp. 74–94; Sarah Hanley, "Engendering the State: Family Formation and State Building in Early Modern France," *French Historical Studies*, 1989, *16:*4–27; Hanley, "Family and State in Early Modern France: The Marriage Pact," in *Connecting Spheres: Women in the Western World, 1500 to the Present*, ed. Marilyn Boxer and Jean H. Quataert (New York: Oxford Univ. Press, 1988), pp. 53–63; Hanley, "Social Sites of Political Practice in France: Lawsuits, Civil Rights, and the Separation of Powers in Domestic and State Government, 1500–1800," *American Historical Review*, 1997, *102:*27–52; Jeffrey Merrick, "Royal Bees: The Gender Politics of the Beehive in Early Modern Europe," in *Studies in Eighteenth-Century Culture*, Vol. 18, ed. John W. Yolton and Leslie E. Brown (East Lansing, Mich.: Colleagues, 1988), pp. 7–37; and Merrick, "Fathers and Kings: Patriarchalism and Absolutism in Eighteenth-Century French Politics," *Studies on Voltaire and the Eighteenth Century*, Vol. 308 (Oxford: Voltaire Foundation, 1993), pp. 281–303.

derived male superiority and authority at least in part from men's presumed generative powers.[4]

Among a number of reasons one could offer for the often skeptical, sometimes hostile, reception of the new optical data are the following: the tenacity of cultural biases about sexual difference, particularly the long-standing assumption of women's inferior and limited role in sexual reproduction; the influence of social anxieties about population, public opinion, political obedience, and gender hierarchy; and the persistence of analogical reasoning as a mode of understanding that, because of its conviction that truth was essentially metaphorical, was less concerned than we would be by failure to find empirical evidence. In addition, although the new scientific instruments and techniques, aided by new technologies associated with print, now brought the body's interior as well as its surface into view in ways never possible before, many in the scientific community doubted their usefulness or reliability. Learned opinion around 1700 still contested the link between visualization and knowledge widely presumed to exist in later periods and emphasized the variety of ways in which seeing is deceiving. If anything, the new visual data appear to have reinforced doubts about how much was known or could be known about generation. Therefore, questions about the cognitive authority of these images and the social authority of their producers, about the production and reproduction of scientific knowledge in societies characterized by profound disagreement over the sources of authority, need to be addressed in any investigation of these new scientific practices.[5] I remain convinced that the meaning and impact of images of the body widely available in print in the seventeenth and eighteenth centuries are far from self-evident.

The new biomedical theories of sexual difference that developed from the end of the eighteenth century, I would argue, owed little, if anything, to the anatomical research of the previous century. We err seriously—and with only the thinnest evidential warrant—insofar as we continue to assume that science *must have* provided the data so clearly desired by ideologues and politicians of left and right, liberal and royalist, socialist and evangelical tendencies in the decades on either side of 1800. However much ideologists of domesticity, of unambiguous sexual identity, and of female inferiority and infirmity claimed scientific support for their points of view

---

[4] I discuss these events in Estelle Cohen, "The Body as a Historical Category: Science and Imagination, 1660–1760," in *The Good Body: Asceticism in Contemporary Culture*, ed. Mary G. Winkler and Letha B. Cole (New Haven, Conn.: Yale Univ. Press, 1994), pp. 67–90; and Cohen, "Regendering 'Hysteria' in Nineteenth-Century Medical Textbooks," paper presented at the Tenth Berkshire Conference on the History of Women, University of North Carolina, Chapel Hill, June 1996. Among recent studies that contribute to our understanding of seventeenth- and eighteenth-century debates about sexual difference and generation see esp. Lorraine Daston and Katharine Park, "The Hermaphrodite and the Orders of Nature: Sexual Ambiguity in Early Modern France," *GLQ: A Journal of Lesbian and Gay Studies*, 1995, *1*:419–438; Catherine Wilson, *The Invisible World: Early Modern Philosophy and the Invention of the Microscope* (Princeton, N.J.: Princeton Univ. Press, 1995); and Edward G. Ruestow, *The Microscope in the Dutch Republic: The Shaping of Discovery* (New York: Cambridge Univ. Press, 1996).

[5] Recent work on Robert Hooke and Antoni van Leeuwenhoek has in fact addressed some of these questions. See esp. Michael Aaron Dennis, "Graphic Understanding: Instruments and Interpretation in Robert Hooke's *Micrographia*," *Sci. Context*, 1989, *3*:309–364; Steven Shapin, "Who Was Robert Hooke?" in *Robert Hooke: New Studies*, ed. Michael Hunter and Simon Schaffer (Woodbridge, Suffolk: Boydell, 1989), pp. 253–285; Edward G. Ruestow, "Images and Ideas: Leeuwenhoek's Perception of the Spermatozoa," *Journal of the History of Biology*, 1983, *16*:185–223; and K. van Berkel, "Intellectuals against Leeuwenhoek," in *Antoni van Leeuwenhoek, 1632–1723*, ed. L. C. Palm and H. A. M. Snelders (Amsterdam: Rodopi, 1982), pp. 187–209.

or social programs, wide-ranging investigation of controversies about sexual anatomy and embryology between roughly 1660 and 1760 calls all such claims into question. Just as eighteenth-century politicians who bemoaned an imagined population decline were unperturbed by evidence to the contrary,[6] so, too, eighteenth-century arguments in defense of gender inequality could not draw sustenance from the new anatomy. But that made no apparent difference to the appeal of such arguments. Moreover, if recent anatomy lessons became either embarrassing or inconvenient, it was relatively easy to ignore or discredit them.

Medical historians, through their own politics of exclusion, have made it extremely difficult to discern and reconstruct this process. That is, narratives of medical history either recited in lectures and preserved in collections of carefully written lecture notes (a valuable commodity even in the eighteenth century) or published in increasingly authoritative medical textbooks, especially from the beginning of the nineteenth century, either omitted other stories altogether, slighted the work of particular others, or misrepresented the findings of those whose credibility could no longer be denied. Recent scholarship makes clear the extent to which nineteenth-century medical writers and translators read back into earlier periods disease entities and categories of difference that had only been formulated in their own time.[7] If indeed it is the case that biomedical "explanations" of gender hierarchy that emerged toward the end of the eighteenth century could have derived little comfort or warrant from the previous century's anatomical debates, we ought to be redirecting our energies away from a futile search for that alleged warrant toward an analysis of the claims for its existence.

Attempts to ground social differences between the sexes on presumed anatomical differences were in fact widely contested during the century after 1660. Therefore, I wish to argue that there is much work to do before we can feel confident that we understand the full range of seventeenth- and eighteenth-century scientific opinions about sexual difference and their likely relevance for broader political and cultural debates about marriage, reproduction, and sexual identity in this period. Moreover, the multiplicity of discourses about women's minds and bodies in the scientific literature leads one to wonder what literate women would have been likely to learn about themselves from a variety of texts available to them at this time. In addition, we need to acknowledge not only the extent to which scientists may have been prepared to displace inherited systems of thought about bodies—Galenic homologies as well as Aristotelian opposites—but also the fact that their willingness to interrogate ancient theories did not produce general agreement about either the most reliable methods of investigation or the most probable lessons to be drawn from the new

---

[6] Carol Blum, "Of Women and the Land: Legitimizing Husbandry," in *Early Modern Conceptions of Property*, ed. John Brewer and Susan Staves (New York: Routledge, 1995), pp. 161–169.

[7] I survey this development in nineteenth-century gynecology and psychiatry in Cohen, "Regendering 'Hysteria' in Nineteenth-Century Medical Textbooks" (cit. n. 4). For a model study of this phenomenon see Helen King, "Once upon a Text: Hysteria from Hippocrates," in *Hysteria beyond Freud*, ed. Sander L. Gilman *et al.* (Berkeley: Univ. California Press, 1993), pp. 3–90. One noteworthy example of an influential course in the history of anatomy that significantly distorted that history is the series of lectures presented by Alexander Monro *primus*, who taught medical students and surgical apprentices at the University of Edinburgh for more than three decades. I have used the lecture notes taken by David McBride in April 1750, which are housed in Edinburgh University, Special Collections: MSS Lectures. I discuss Monro's lectures in Cohen, "Body as a Historical Category" (cit. n. 4), pp. 86–87.

anatomy. In this essay I will examine discussions of sexual equality and difference from around 1670 that referred explicitly to recent anatomical research and then went on to insist that the new anatomy thoroughly discredited ancient scientific traditions still offered as evidence for female inferiority and grounds for female subjection. Because the work of both François Poullain de la Barre and Judith Drake is central to this analysis, I further wish to emphasize their importance for the history of gender and science in the period of the Enlightenment.[8]

Significant numbers of informed commentators in the late seventeenth and eighteenth centuries rejected the view that female biology provided a sound basis for female subjection, arguing instead that women's "understanding appears in every way similar to that of men," that there is "no natural impediment in the structure of our bodies" either, and that "all the researches of anatomy have not yet been able to show the least difference [apart from reproductive organs] between *Men* and *Women*.[9] One physician urged women to read medical books, claiming that knowledge of their own anatomy would permit "inward government" of their bodies.[10] Another, however, noting the lack of agreement among physicians and their tendency to perpetuate myths about women, exclaimed with undisguised glee that fables abound about the menses, which, "tho' recounted by many grave, and some great Authors, I reject, . . . and have only recited . . . to shew what things have been superstitiously taken up upon Credit, without sufficient Examination by Men of great Authority, who have been prevail'd upon to believe, *what the Women at all times would laugh at.*"[11]

Scientific arguments about female anatomy and physiology in the period around 1700 were as likely to contest dominant social attitudes as to support them; that is, an important body of scholarly opinion rejected both old and new theories, both popular and learned traditions, that continued to represent women as inferior and defective versions of men. Examination of a range of texts suggests that scientific writings, like other kinds of public discourses, offered different, often ambivalent,

---

[8] The debate on the Enlightenment's legacy for women has continued almost unabated since Mary Wollstonecraft first announced her views on the subject in *A Vindication of the Rights of Woman* (1792). I will list only a few recent studies that, in my view, more than repay the attention they demand: Joan Wallach Scott, *Only Paradoxes to Offer: French Feminists and the Rights of Man* (Cambridge, Mass.: Harvard Univ. Press, 1996); Lieselotte Steinbrügge, *The Moral Sex: Woman's Nature in the French Enlightenment*, trans. Pamela E. Selwyn (New York: Oxford Univ. Press, 1995); Madelyn Gutwirth, *The Twilight of the Goddesses: Women and Representation in the French Revolutionary Era* (New Brunswick, N.J.: Rutgers Univ. Press, 1992); Erica Harth, *Cartesian Women: Versions and Subversions of Rational Discourse in the Old Regime* (Ithaca, N.Y.: Cornell Univ. Press, 1992); and Michèle Le Doeuff, *Hipparchia's Choice: An Essay Concerning Women, Philosophy, Etc.*, trans. Trista Selous (Oxford: Blackwell, 1990).

[9] Émilie du Châtelet, from the preface to her unpublished interpretative translation of Bernard Mandeville's *Fable of the Bees* (1735), quoted in translation in Esther Ehrman, *Mme. du Châtelet: Scientist, Philosopher, and Feminist of the Enlightenment* (Leamington Spa: Berg, 1986), p. 61, and available in the original French in Ira Wade, *Studies on Voltaire, with Some Unpublished Papers of Mme du Châtelet* (Princeton, N.J.: Princeton Univ. Press, 1947), p. 135; Judith Drake, *An Essay in Defence of the Female Sex* (hereafter cited as **Drake, Essay**) (London, 1696), p. 12; and "Sophia," *Woman Not Inferior to Man* (London, 1739), p. 24.

[10] Mandeville, *Virgin Unmask'd* (cit. n. 2), p. 123. It is worth noting that Mandeville used a conventional idiom (a dialogue between an older and a younger woman) to propose emancipatory strategies for women.

[11] James [and Judith] Drake, *Anthropologia Nova; or, A New System of Anatomy*, 2 vols., 2nd ed. (London, 1717) (hereafter cited as **Drake, New System of Anatomy**), Vol. 1, pp. 176–177 (emphasis added). This text also appeared in 1707, 1727, and 1750.

and sometimes contradictory ways of construing female nature. Well-known, highly regarded, and widely read scientific writers confessed that there were a number of important questions about women's bodies that they could not answer, indicating their uncertainty, for example, about how conception takes place and about the causes of menstruation. To be sure, discussions of the limits of knowledge and of new ways of knowing were very much a seventeenth-century enterprise. From a late twentieth-century perspective, however, it is particularly instructive to note the extent to which medical theorists and practitioners freely admitted uncertainty, even ignorance, at this time. Although the acceptability of uncertainty in medicine was clearly related to the growing conviction of the sufficiency of probable knowledge, it also contrasts markedly with the ways in which medical theories were represented in later periods.

René Descartes's mind-body dualism was interpreted by his own and succeeding generations as legitimating the public careers of learned women, who then went on to argue, with others, that recent anatomical findings confirmed women's intellectual equality with men. That is, Cartesian women, and numbers of Cartesian men as well, took the separation of mind from body as a way of making physical differences between the sexes less significant and of asserting the equality of the sexes in rationality and will.[12] Analysis of the arguments of egalitarian theorists who invoked reproductive and brain anatomy in support of their claims, while ignoring the angry debates about the conclusions that could be drawn from the new anatomy, is long overdue. My inclination to highlight the positive readings of Cartesian dualism for women intellectuals underscores the importance of recovering the competing interpretations of Descartes's work in the seventeenth and eighteenth centuries.

Feminist discourse has long resisted claims that to be equal men and women must be the same.[13] As far back as the late seventeenth century, feminist writers recognized that male and female were not fixed or stable identities but were relational and constructed.[14] Similarly, seventeenth-century accounts of the differences between male and female sexual anatomy—by Reinier de Graaf, a Dutch physician, Jane Sharp, an English midwife, and Pierre Dionis, a French surgeon-accoucheur,

---

[12] See esp. Ruth Perry, "Radical Doubt and the Liberation of Women," *Eighteenth-Century Studies*, 1985, *18:*472–494; Harth, *Cartesian Women* (cit. n. 8); Margaret Atherton, "Cartesian Reason and Gendered Reason," in *A Mind of One's Own: Feminist Essays on Reason and Objectivity*, ed. Louise M. Antony and Charlotte Witt (Boulder, Colo.: Westview, 1993), pp. 19–34; Carolyn C. Lougee, *Le paradis des femmes: Women, Salons, and Social Stratification in Seventeenth-Century France* (Princeton, N.J.: Princeton Univ. Press, 1976); and Catherine Gallagher, "Embracing the Absolute: The Politics of the Female Subject in Seventeenth-Century England," *Genders*, 1988, *1:*24–39.

[13] I owe this argument to Joan Wallach Scott's article on Olympe de Gouges: Scott, "French Feminists and the Rights of 'Man': Olympe de Gouges's Declarations," *History Workshop Journal*, Autumn 1989, *28:*1–21. Recent attempts to contextualize and historicize the equality/difference conundrum include, first of all, Scott, "Deconstructing Equality-versus-Difference; or, The Uses of Poststructuralist Theory for Feminism," *Feminist Studies*, 1988, *14:*33–50 (a different version of this essay appeared in Scott, *Gender and the Politics of History* [New York: Columbia Univ. Press, 1988], Ch. 8); Scott, *Only Paradoxes to Offer* (cit. n. 8); Claire Goldberg Moses, "'Difference' in Historical Perspective: Saint-Simonian Feminism," in *Feminism, Socialism, and French Romanticism*, ed. Moses and Leslie Wahl Rabine (Bloomington: Indiana Univ. Press, 1993), pp. 17–84; and Gisela Bock and Susan James, eds., *Beyond Equality and Difference: Citizenship, Feminist Politics, and Female Subjectivity* (London/New York: Routledge, 1992).

[14] See, e.g., Mary Astell, *Reflections upon Marriage* (London, 1700, 1703, 1706, 1730), now available in a modern edition, ed. with an introduction by Bridget Hill (Aldershot: Gower/Maurice Temple Smith, 1986); *Female Rights Vindicated; or, The Equality of the Sexes Morally and Physically Proved* (London, 1751, 1758); and Catherine Macaulay, *Letters on Education* (London, 1787, 1790).

for example—clearly did not conclude that their views provided grounds for social and cultural arguments about female inferiority. On the contrary: like feminist writers (François Poullain de la Barre, Judith Drake, Olympe de Gouges, and Anna Doyle Wheeler, most notably) who labored to ground claims for equality on the recognition of differences, not sameness, they stressed that women's anatomical differences in no way diminished their worth. In other words, seventeenth-century medical opinions could be—and indeed sometimes were—cited in attempts to *collapse* traditional social and cultural hierarchies that privileged men. If medical thought and practice at times interacted with other aspects of early modern culture and society in ways that were complicitous, on many other occasions they interacted in ways that were clearly contestational.

At the end of the eighteenth century Gouges reiterated the view that the sexes were differentiated only for the purposes of reproduction, that all members of a species had been endowed by "nature" with similar, but not necessarily identical, faculties. By that time, however, the medical opinions that could have supported her rejection of fixed, categorical distinctions between male and female, opinions that had been widely publicized in a variety of texts up to about 1760, had already been submerged. Was there, then, a period when female was not defined by absence and passivity in important scientific texts, when male and female were construed as neither homologous nor mutually exclusive, neither different versions of the same model nor oppositional yet complementary?[15] If there was such a time, and I obviously believe that there was, why have we learned so little about it from historians of medicine and science?

Among a growing number of medical books around 1700 that disputed a variety of opinions about women's bodies, James Drake's *Anthropologia Nova; or, A New System of Anatomy* deserves to be singled out. Reprinted four times between 1707 and 1750, this two-volume text, which included some of de Graaf's diagrams of the female reproductive system, was recommended by Herman Boerhaave of Leiden, teacher of anatomy and medicine to students from many Western European countries and the North American colonies in the early eighteenth century, on account of its accuracy. Moreover, the importance of Drake's *New System of Anatomy,* not only for eighteenth-century medical education but for wider discussion of sex and reproduction as well (Laurence Sterne, for example, assumed that the readers of *Tristram Shandy* would be able to identify "Dr. Drake"), is not conveyed in standard histories of science and medicine. The text was posthumously published and edited by the author's sister Judith Drake, an unlicensed medical practitioner; she may well have written at least the chapter on generation, which was never listed in the contents by the publishers. In this chapter Drake insisted that at present the causes of generation are not sufficiently understood. The author summarized recent developments in embryology, including Antoni van Leeuwenhoek's microscopic findings, about which she remained doubtful. That is, like many others, Drake had confirmed the observation of microscopic organisms, which looked like tadpoles, in seminal fluid, but she

---

[15] I take this model from Thomas Laqueur's provocative and useful study, *Making Sex: Body and Gender from the Greeks to Freud* (Cambridge, Mass.: Harvard Univ. Press, 1990), which in my view overlooks many of the complexities, varieties, and continuities in debates about women's bodies before the nineteenth century. On Olympe de Gouges see esp. Scott, "French Feminists and the Rights of 'Man'" (cit. n. 13); Scott, *Only Paradoxes to Offer* (cit. n. 8), Ch. 2; and Harth, *Cartesian Women* (cit. n. 8), pp. 213–239.

was not convinced that these beings were preformed fetuses contained in the semen.¹⁶

Drake was one of many who rejected both the animalculist and the ovist versions of the preformationist hypothesis; neither, she pointed out, accounts for mixed generation in animals or the fact that children often resemble both parents. Such observations, Drake argued, prove that both sexes contribute to conception and heredity. Moreover, the attempt to account for these facts by alleging that the uterus "may have so much effect on the foetus as to alter the figure of the animal" contained in the sperm (a position adopted by Leeuwenhoek, among others) "is so poor, so unphilosophical a shift, that it is not worth an Answer; and they might with as good Authority persuade me, that an Orange-Tree transplanted from *Sevil* to *England* would bear Apples, and . . . *vice versa*." It is worth pointing out that not all animalculists shared Leeuwenhoek's notion of the mother's possible influence on the fetus. James Blondel angrily denounced such claims, referring specifically to the argument that the mother's imagination can alter the body of the fetus:

> By what Right has the Mother's Fancy any Influence upon the Body of the *Foetus*, which comes from the *Semen virile* and which is, in respect to her, but a *Passenger*, who has taken there his Lodging for a short time? If the Father could not cause, by the Strength of Imagination, any change in the Animalcule which was originally in his Body: I desire to know why the Mother should plead that Priviledge in Exclusion to the Father?¹⁷

In fact, an ancient tradition, Hindu as well as Greek, had associated birth deformities with the mother's mind or body. One wonders whether its revival in the seventeenth and eighteenth centuries was intended to counteract new, rather different claims for women's contribution to generation. Moreover, it is sometimes argued that the appeal of preformationist hypotheses in this period had much to do with the fact that generation carried connotations of divine creation. From this point of view, epigeneticists could be viewed as impious on the grounds that they assigned too much activity and intelligence to matter.¹⁸ Perhaps more to the point, resistance to a version of epigenesis that specifically stressed the prominent role of women in reproduction may have derived from the perception that this theory attributed agency, activity, intelligence, and will to *female* matter.

Drake particularly emphasized the contribution of the female to conception: "Generation cannot [take place] without an Egg rightly disposed, . . . a Concession which I think is at this time universal." Ignoring the representations, by Leeuwen-

---

¹⁶ Drake, *New System of Anatomy*, Vol. 1, pp. 185–187. By far the best account of Leeuwenhoek's contribution to these debates is Ruestow, "Images and Ideas" (cit. n. 5). I learned of Boerhaave's recommendation, and much else, from Antonie M. Luyendijk-Elshout, Professor Emerita of the History of Medicine at the University of Leiden.

¹⁷ Drake, *New System of Anatomy*, Vol. 1, p. 187; and James Blondel, *The Strength of Imagination in Pregnant Women Examined* (London, 1727), p. 47. Blondel is cited in Julia Epstein, *Altered Conditions: Disease, Medicine, and Storytelling* (New York: Routledge, 1995), p. 148. Epstein's book offers an excellent discussion of eighteenth-century debates on birth deformities in relation to the mother in Ch. 5. I discuss embryology in the seventeenth and eighteenth centuries in Cohen, "Body as a Historical Category" (cit. n. 4).

¹⁸ See, e.g., L. W. B. Brockliss, "The Embryological Revolution in the France of Louis XIV," in *The Human Embryo*, ed. G. R. Dunstan (Exeter: Univ. Exeter Press, 1990), pp. 158–186; and Shirley Roe, *Matter, Life, and Generation: Eighteenth-Century Embryology and the Haller-Wolff Debate* (Cambridge: Cambridge Univ. Press, 1981).

hoek and others, of ova as mere fantasy or sham, she declared that the existence of true ova in the ovaries of women is agreed on all sides, is indeed incontestable! Drake referred repeatedly to the writings of de Graaf, whom she labeled "the most industrious and accurate Inquirer" into the female body, both to affirm the existence of eggs in the ovaries of "all sorts of [female] animals whatsoever" and to cast doubt on the existence of the hymen. De Graaf, after all, "confesses that he always sought it in vain."[19]

The consensus Drake was so keen to celebrate was remarkably fragile and short lived, as far as I can tell. Not all medical writers who acknowledged the existence of eggs in women's ovaries accepted de Graaf's explanation of ovarian function as Drake had done. Like those who continued to prefer a two-seed theory that emphasized the weakness of female seed, they denied women an equal share in the business of reproduction. Moreover, even adoption of the new name *ovaria* for what many still called female *testes* and acceptance of their essential role in conception did not always signify agreement with the account of generation developed by the Leiden group of anatomists—not even within the university's walls. For example, in a series of treatises on female reproductive anatomy and the formation of the human fetus, Charles Drélincourt, professor of medicine at Leiden from 1668 to 1697, agreed that the existence of eggs in women's ovaries was incontestable. Nonetheless, his theory of generation assigned women merely a passive and nutritive role, reserving the active and material contribution to men. He appears to have argued that the fetus is formed by the father's substance and nourished by that of the mother. On the whole, Drélincourt's adversarial style makes it difficult to interpret his texts; it is far easier to be clear about what he rejects than about what he proposes. At the same time, his extensive experiments on animals appear to have taught him to distinguish between the ovum and the ovarian follicle.[20]

De Graaf's earlier work on rabbits also enabled him to draw this distinction, which he duly recorded in Chapter 16 of his volume on female reproductive anatomy (*De mulierum organis* [1672]). Although some of his contemporaries apparently noticed, others either failed to notice or simply did not read his book. An erroneous tradition soon developed—one that has persisted until our own time—to the effect that de Graaf had mistaken the entire follicle for the ovum. As it happens, some of de Graaf's most aggressive critics themselves acted on this assumption and therefore

---

[19] Drake, *New System of Anatomy*, Vol. 1, p. 187; this reiterates the point made on p. 184. References to de Graaf are on pp. 150, 164, and 177. Although de Graaf's former teacher and one-time adversary IJsbrand van Diemerbroeck made much the same claim about the role of ova in generation in an anatomy textbook used by several generations of students on the Continent and available in an English translation as well, and many others agreed, debates about the presence of eggs in human females and their precise role in reproduction remained unresolved. See IJsbrand van Diemerbroeck, *The Anatomy of Human Bodies* (1672), trans. William Salmon (London, 1694), p. 158. Controversies about the hymen's existence were of course related not only to the growing obsession with preserving, collecting, and displaying parts of the female sexual anatomy but especially to continuing anxiety about female virginity. Giovanni Bianchi, a noted eighteenth-century Italian physician (and correspondent of Laura Bassi), mocked both of these attitudes in a superbly ironic tale of a female cross-dresser in which he casually claimed to have collected whole shelves of jars filled with hymens, which he invited his readers to view. See Giovanni Bianchi, *Historical and Physical Dissertation on the Case of Caterina Vizzani*, trans. anon. (London, 1751), for a delightful read.

[20] Charles Drélincourt, *De conceptione adversaria* (Leiden, 1685), in *Opuscula medica omnia* (The Hague, 1727), pp. 427–450, esp. pp. 445–446. For contemporary discussions of this text see *Nouvelles de la République des Lettres*, mai, oct. 1685, in Pierre Bayle, *Oeuvres diverses*, facsimile of 1737 ed. (Hildesheim: Olms, 1964), Vol. 1, pp. 292–293, 393–395.

were able to argue that the structure was too big to pass through the (Fallopian) tube on its way to the uterus. Although a Dutch edition of de Graaf's complete writings appeared in 1686 and a French edition in 1699, the full text of his *Treatise on the Organs of Generation in Women* has been available in English only since 1972, three hundred years after its initial publication—and then only as a supplementary issue to the *Journal of Reproduction and Fertility!*

Controversies about ova and ovaries and about the formation of the fetus more generally continued to flare up, particularly during the next half century, sometimes with a vehemence impossible to understand without considering the ideological consequences of assigning women an equal or active role in reproduction.[21] After all, as Evelyne Berriot-Salvadore points out, this "was more than a dispute between schools; the moral status of women depended on its outcome." Noting that many generations since Aristotle have persisted in evaluating differently the contribution of men and women to generation, she explains: "At stake, in effect, was man's legitimate power in the family and in society." While the issue remained a thorny one, with resolution nowhere in sight at the end of the eighteenth century, one medical practitioner dismissed the dispute about the relative contribution of men and women to conception and heredity as irrelevant to the practice of medicine. In a letter to William Osborne, Thomas Denman commented:

> Upon this subject . . . the imagination hath been indulged with a freedom not very consistent with the dignity of philosophy.
>
> If we were able to discover the essential properties of the male *semen,* the precise share which the male and female contribute towards the formation of the *embryo,* and the part where the effect is produced, the advantages which would thence accrue in practice, do not appear. . . . It is happy for us that those things which are beyond the comprehension, or which elude the observation of men of plain understandings, are of the least importance in practice.[22]

Given the diverse opinions and lively disagreements that characterized discussion of these issues among male physicians and intellectuals in this period, it would be useful to attempt to recover women's views of these matters, particularly the views of those women we can identify as medical practitioners. The writings of midwives, for example, often contested men's exclusive claims to intellectual authority, especially with reference to women's bodies. A particularly interesting example, and one that illustrates the curious amalgam of credulity and criticism in many of these books, is *The Midwives Book; or, The Whole Art of Midwifery Discovered,* by Jane

---

[21] Nor were these disputes confined to learned treatises written in Latin. Further study of these controversies, as well as of the ways in which they were communicated (whether they circulated in small-format vernacular books that women could read, for example), is needed. Similarly, the important question of de Graaf's lack of institutional, corporate, and *regenten* support in the Dutch Republic cries out for investigation. My forthcoming book, *Constructing Biology as Social Knowledge: Gender, Reproduction, and the State, ca. 1660–1900,* will address these topics, examining in particular the revealing attacks on those medical commentators dismissed as *"ovaristes"* by their adversaries.

[22] Evelyne Berriot-Salvadore, "The Discourse of Medicine and Science," in *A History of Women in the West,* Vol. 3: *Renaissance and Enlightenment Paradoxes,* ed. Natalie Zemon Davis and Arlette Farge (Cambridge, Mass.: Harvard Univ. Press, 1993), p. 365; and Thomas Denman to William Osborne, 1 Nov. 1788, published in Denman's popular text *Introduction to Midwifery* (London, 1790), pp. 185–187.

Sharp. First published in 1671, this work had gone through four editions by 1725, when it appeared in a cheaper edition with a slightly altered title but identical contents. What is most obvious in this extraordinary volume addressed to her "Sisters," the midwives of England, are the lengths to which Sharp was prepared to go to dispel the myths currently purveyed in popular books, such as those falsely attributed to Aristotle. The ancients, she charged, and Galen in particular, could not have had knowledge of human bodies that was dependent on dissection: "The inside of men or women they saw not, and so were ignorant of the difference between them." She debunked the alleged authority of learned as well as popular traditions about multiple births; and she stressed the fact that women are not merely men turned outside in and inverted, contesting both the assumption of homologous structures, which represented women as inferior versions of men, and the recurrently popular myth of Tiresias, who, it was said, had been changed from male to female and back again, and who, Sharp explained derisively, "because he had been of both sexes, . . . was chosen as the most fit judge to determine the great Question, which of the two, Male or Female, find most pleasure in . . . copulation."[23]

Sharp's treatise underlines the mistaken tendency of too many accounts in the history of medicine and sexuality to assume that popular, prescriptive writings somehow sum up the medical opinion of the time. Manuals like those falsely attributed to Aristotle, Nicolas Venette's *Mysteries of Conjugal Love Reveal'd* (first edition, 1687), medical dictionaries, and other such compendia written for a lay readership, as well as the numerous others signed "A Woman's Doctor" or "A Physician," are no more reliable as evidence for current medical theories than are sermons or newspaper advertisements. Moreover, the ancient belief that women's reproductive organs were inferior because they were inverted and internal versions of male organs was bound to be undermined by the accounts of seventeenth- and eighteenth-century medical writers like Sharp who emphasized the differences and the (at least) equal importance of female sexual anatomy to reproduction.

The problem of identifying other kinds of women medical practitioners before the nineteenth century—let alone their opinions, published or otherwise—is an immense one. We are only now beginning to discover the extent to which early modern sources of various kinds document the existence of women practitioners of medicine outside midwifery,[24] in large part because later interpreters—readers, compilers, and

---

[23] Jane Sharp, *The Midwives Book; or, The Whole Art of Midwifery Discovered* (London, 1671), pp. 68, 69–70, 82. In an important article entitled "Women's Medical Practice and Health Care in Medieval Europe," which appeared in *Signs: Journal of Women in Culture and Society,* 1989, *14:*434–473, Monica H. Green pointed to the dearth of serious, comprehensive histories of premodern midwifery. Four years later, a splendid collection of essays on early modern midwifery appeared: Hilary Marland, ed., *The Art of Midwifery: Early Modern Midwives in Europe* (London: Routledge, 1993).

[24] In addition to Green, "Women's Medical Practice," see esp. Monica H. Green, "Documenting Medieval Women's Medical Practice," in *Practical Medicine from Salerno to the Black Death,* ed. Luis García-Ballester *et al.* (Cambridge: Cambridge Univ. Press, 1994), pp. 322–352; Doreen Evenden Nagy, *Popular Medicine in Seventeenth-Century England* (Bowling Green, Ohio: Bowling Green State Univ. Popular Press, 1988), esp. Ch. 5; Linda Pollock, *With Faith and Physic: The Life of a Tudor Gentlewoman, Lady Grace Mildmay, 1552–1620* (London: Collins & Brown, 1993; New York: St. Martin's, 1995); Margaret Pelling, "Knowledge Common and Acquired: The Education of Unlicensed Medical Practitioners in Early Modern London," in *The History of Medical Education in Britain,* ed. Vivian Nutton and Roy Porter (Amsterdam/Atlanta, Ga.: Rodopi, 1995); Pelling, "Medical Practice in Early Modern England: Trade or Profession?" in *The Professions in Early Modern*

archivists—appear to have buried some of this evidence. There is no question that traditional historiography underrepresents the medical practices of women. I suspect that this tendency not to see or identify such women increased during the course of the eighteenth century. The work of recovering female medical practitioners in the early modern period, therefore, will entail not the discovery of new documentation so much as a new way of reading and seeing either familiar or at least readily available texts and images: we need to learn *to notice what others have not seen.*

Although women apothecaries and surgeons were likely to encounter new, more sustained challenges from around 1700 than earlier, their presence and their acceptability in particular circumstances were still assumed.[25] My discussion will focus on a document that seems to me to illustrate the extent to which women's medical practices in premodern Europe are likely to have been unnoticed, unrecorded, and therefore unacknowledged by many generations of historians and catalogers. I refer to a letter written by Judith Drake, already identified as the editor, and possibly coauthor, with her physician brother James, of a two-volume anatomy text called *Anthropologia Nova; or, A New System of Anatomy* (first edition, 1707).[26] Addressed to Sir Hans Sloane, president of the Royal College of Physicians, in 1723, this letter was filed in the British Library manuscript collections with James Drake's papers and attributed to him—even though he had been dead some sixteen years at the time of its writing.[27] Moreover, the text is nonsensical if assumed to have been written by James, and the signature is not his either. It would appear, then, that later generations of librarians, particularly from the latter part of the eighteenth century, were inclined to regard the existence of women practitioners of medicine as unlikely—perhaps inconceivable—and that their uninformed, biased, and anachronistic assumptions continue to restrict our knowledge of the medical practices of women.

Judith Drake's letter to Sir Hans Sloane was written in reply to a summons from the Royal College of Physicians Board of Censors, which had acted on a complaint she characterized as "the aspersions of a malicious informant." She went on to plead in her defense that she was only treating women and children, a type of practice obviously sanctioned even without a license, as indicated by a variety of sources from the sixteenth to eighteenth centuries: "I did not suspect that the applying of a few medicines (and those not in acute distempers) among my own Sex and Little Children, w'd render me obnoxious to . . . the College." (Of course, she would surely have realized that this was the sensible thing to say in the circumstances, whether it was true or not.) Drake then insisted that she had "never either put my hand to a bill or pretended to a fee" for services, which presumably could have constituted a

---

England, ed. Wilfred Prest (Brighton, Sussex: Croom Helm, 1987), pp. 90–128; Elaine Hobby, *Virtue of Necessity* (London: Virago, 1988), pp. 165–189; Patricia Crawford, "Printed Advertisements for Women Medical Practitioners in London, 1670–1710," *Society for the Social History of Medicine Bulletin,* Dec. 1984, *35:*66–70; and A. L. Wyman, "The Surgeoness: The Female Practitioner of Surgery, 1400–1800," *Medical History,* 1984, *28:*22–41.

[25] Thus, e.g., Margaret Cavendish's play *The Convent of Pleasure* (first published in 1668) depicted a community of women in which the contribution of women physicians, surgeons, and apothecaries was specifically foregrounded.

[26] These volumes, as I have already indicated, were reprinted four times between 1707 and 1750 and were used by several generations of Boerhaave's European and North American students at the University of Leiden.

[27] British Library, Sloane MS 4047, fols. 38, 39.

breach of practice warranting censure. Much of the rest of the letter is devoted to undermining the informant's credibility. For example:

> I hope it will not pass without remark, that the Gentleman who now raises this clamour, this Zealous Agent for his Mistress, neither objected against the price (which he all along knew) nor the success of the medicines, till they came to be pay'd for, and the only Poison (as he terms it) I administer'd was to his Ears—in a demand for Money. . . . [Given that] whatever came from me has [been alleged to have] . . . all those poisonous Qualitys, he has [nonetheless] thrice allowed his Mistress to send for Medicines.

Finally, to drive home the same point yet again, she concluded, "I believe you will allow that when a man permits that to be taken by his Friends which he calls poison, he must not wonder if we reflect upon [his] . . . want of sense or veracity."[28] This letter, written when Judith Drake was an old woman, confirms that she had been an unlicensed medical practitioner for a period of years, possibly decades.

Judith Drake was also the author of an *Essay in Defense of the Female Sex*, which went through three editions in 1696 and 1697 and at least two more by 1750. This angry little book, which some of its readers imagined could not have been written by a woman, roundly denounced those who pretended that women's subject status had a basis in nature. Drake compared the experience of Dutch and English wives (a familiar motif) and also highlighted the apparently more equal condition of men and women among the rural laboring classes.[29] Her attack on male domination and on the prevailing social categories that distinguished men from women was a political critique that contested the alleged grounds of female subjection and powerlessness. Masculine identity in the early modern period was associated with particular social and economic opportunities from which women were often, perhaps increasingly, excluded, as well as with privileged access to a particular kind of education. Studying Latin, for example, became "a way of achieving masculinity." The feminist critique of classical traditions in this period was, first of all, an attack on traditions of thought and language that represented women as naturally domestic and men as properly political. Drake engaged with revered traditions, with male intellectual authority, and then went on to ridicule male ideals, mocking the scholar and the country gentleman in particular. Her characterization of the uselessness of scholars was intended to deflate any pretensions they may have had to honor as well as to learning: "Talk to them of the present and their native country, and they hardly speak the language of it and know so little of the affairs of it that as much might reasonably be expected from an animated Egyptian Mummy. . . . They hang so incessantly upon the . . . strings of Authority that their Judgments . . . become altogether crampt and motionless for want of use."[30]

---

[28] *Ibid.*

[29] Drake, *Essay,* pp. 15–17. See the second and subsequent editions (1696, 1697, 1721) of this work for Judith Drake's reply to those who doubted that a woman could write such a clever book (that is, who found the style too "masculine") and for her brother's verses written especially for the occasion (in part to shift the burden of authorship from his shoulders, for this too was attributed to him!).

[30] Mary Ann Clawson, *Constructing Brotherhood: Class, Gender, and Fraternalism* (Princeton, N.J.: Princeton Univ. Press, 1989), p. 48 (on studying Latin); and Drake, *Essay,* pp. 28–29. On gender relations in seventeenth-century England see Susan Dwyer Amussen, *An Ordered Society: Gender and Class in Early Modern England* (Oxford: Blackwell, 1988).

Arguing that male domination was secured by means of conquest, usurpation, and subterfuge, Drake further explained that one cannot learn anything about women from books, particularly history books, because their authors were men, and "as men are parties against us their evidence may justly be rejected." Thus did late seventeenth-century feminist writers like Drake turn the tables on men who would scorn learned, unmarried, deviant women; where they really scored, of course, was in their contempt for the masculine models normally deemed most worthy. Nonetheless, throughout this text, Drake was careful to ground statements about sexual equality on "learned" opinion, however disdainful she may have been about classical (male) scholarship: "I have heard some learned Men maintain . . . all Souls are equal, and alike, and that consequently there is no such distinction, as Male and Female Souls. . . . Neither can [a distinction of merit or ability] . . . be in the Body, (if I may credit the Report of learned Physicians) for there is no difference in the Organization of those Parts, which have any relation to, or influence over the Minds." The revised and extended conclusion to the fifth edition of the *Essay*, which was probably published posthumously in 1750, notably recorded a learned woman's exasperation and profound anger:

> Thus . . . does it . . . fully appear, how falsely we are deem'd, by the *Men,* [to be] wanting in that Solidity of Sense which they so vainly value themselves upon. Our Right is the same with theirs to all *publick Employments;* we are endow'd, by Nature, with Geniuses at least as capable of filling them as theirs can be. . . . Our *Souls* are as *perfect* as theirs, and the *Organs* they depend on are generally *more refined.* However, if the Bodies be compared to decide the Right of Excellence in either Sex; we need not contend: the Men themselves I presume will give it up. They cannot deny but that we have the Advantage of them in the internal Mechanism of our Frames: since in us is produced the most beautiful and wonderful of all Creatures. . . .
>
> I would therefore exhort all my Sex to throw aside idle Amusements, and to betake themselves to the Improvement of their Minds, that we may be able to act with that becoming Dignity our Nature has fitted us to . . . and compel [Men] to confess . . . that the worst of us deserve much better Treatment than the best of us receive.[31]

Equally familiar to her contemporaries was Mary Astell's *Reflections upon Marriage* (1700, 1703, 1706, 1730). The preface added to the third and fourth editions of Astell's treatise was particularly scathing of those (liberal political theorists like John Locke, who remained unnamed) who retained domestic tyranny while rejecting royal absolutism: "For if Arbitrary Power is evil in itself, and an improper Method of Governing Rational and Free Agents, it ought not to be Practis'd anywhere. . . . If *all Men are born free,* how is it that all Women are born slaves?" Insisting that neither the laws of nature nor the Scriptures justify women's subjection, Astell explained how girls and women are kept ignorant: "Laughter and Ridicule that never-failing Scare-Crow is set up to drive them from the Tree of Knowledge. But if in spite of all Difficulties Nature prevails, and they can't be kept so ignorant as their Masters wou'd have them, they are star'd upon as Monsters."

---

[31] Drake, *Essay,* pp. 23 ("justly rejected"), 11–12 ("all Souls are equal"); and Drake, *Essay* (1750?), pp. 147–149. Note the similarity of the first quoted passage to Poullain's formulation in 1673: "everything which men say [referring on this occasion to historians] about women should be suspect because they are both judges and litigants": François Poullain de la Barre, *The Equality of the Sexes,* trans. Desmond M. Clarke (Manchester: Manchester Univ. Press, 1990) (hereafter cited as **Poullain,** ***Equality of the Sexes,* trans. Clarke**), p. 80.

As Mary Terrall points out in her essay on Émilie du Châtelet's ambivalent but persistent efforts to penetrate the masculine sanctuary of scientific practice: "Ridicule was a frequently used weapon against all sorts of intellectual projects, and women who aspired to wisdom and rationality were especially vulnerable to dismissal by ridicule."[32]

Astell summoned the memory of Descartes, who had contrasted the attentive, critical reading of women and children who "do not dare to judge without examination" to the unreflective habits of the "Learned" who "continue wedded to their own Opinions, because they will not take the trouble of examining what is contrary to their receiv'd Doctrines." She then disclosed what she understood to be the underlying reasons for denying women's capacity to reason: "if Reason is only allow'd us by way of Raillery, and the secret Maxim is that we have none or little more than Brutes, 'tis the best way to confine us with Chain and Block to the Chimney-Corner, which probably might save the Estates of some Families and the Honor of others." Her conclusion called for a new "Millennium" when "a Tyrannous Domination which Nature never meant, shall no longer render useless if not hurtful, the Industry and Understandings of half Mankind!"[33]

The emphasis on intellectual equality in the work of both Drake and Astell was in fact characteristic of feminist literature during the decades on either side of 1700. Many of their arguments actually had a common source: the writings of a radical Cartesian philosopher whose application of Descartes's methodical doubt had produced a comprehensive critique of social assumptions about sexual inequality. The importance of François Poullain de la Barre (1647–1723) to the history of feminist thought is only now beginning to be appreciated, but the probable impact of his work on his own and succeeding generations is still vastly underrated.[34] His relevance here relates to the importance he attached to the findings of the new anatomy.

Apart from defending women's equal (or superior) capacity to learn science, practice medicine, and fill public offices, Poullain was probably responsible for developing and circulating a number of arguments that were to become almost common currency in debates about sexual equality up to about 1780. Among these were the following: reading science requires less time and intelligence than doing needlework; lawyers, physicians, and philosophers mistake custom for nature in their assumptions about women; scholars take literally what the ancients often said in jest,

---

[32] Astell, *Reflections upon Marriage* (cit. n. 14), 3rd ed. (1706), preface, n. p.; and Terrall, "Émilie du Châtelet and the Gendering of Science" (cit. n. 1), p. 300.

[33] Astell, *Reflections upon Marriage,* 3rd ed. (1706), preface, n.p.

[34] There is now a substantial literature on François Poullain de la Barre (his name is sometimes spelled Poulain; both spellings are correct). Most useful are Desmond M. Clarke's introduction to and superb translation of Poullain's major treatise, *De l'égalité des deux sexes* (1673) (cit. n. 2): Poullain, *Equality of the Sexes,* trans. Clarke. See also Daniel Armogathe, "De l'égalité des deux sexes, 'la belle question,'" *Corpus: Revue de Philosophie,* 1985, *1*:17–26; Geneviève Fraisse, "Poulain de la Barre, ou le procès des préjugés," *ibid.,* pp. 27–41 (also available in Fraisse, *La raison des femmes* [Paris: Plon, 1992]); Christine Fauré, "Poulain de la Barre, sociologue et libre penseur," *ibid.,* pp. 43–51; Paul Hoffmann, *La femme dans la pensée des lumières* (Paris: Ophrys, 1977), pp. 291–308; Harth, *Cartesian Women* (cit. n. 8), pp. 135–139; Lougee, *Paradis des Femmes* (cit. n. 12), pp. 18–21; Fauré, *Democracy without Women: Feminism and the Rise of Liberal Individualism in France,* trans. Claudia Gorbman and John Berks (Bloomington: Indiana Univ. Press, 1985), pp. 66–74; Madeleine Alcover, "The Indecency of Knowledge," *Rice University Studies,* 1978, *64*:25–39; and Ellen McNiven Hine, "The Woman Question in Early Eighteenth-Century French Literature," *Studies on Voltaire and the Eighteenth Century,* Vol. 116 (Oxford: Voltaire Foundation, 1973), pp. 65–79.

according reverence in particular to those who disparaged women; men's opinions about women are suspect "because they are both judges and litigants: . . . The opinions of a thousand authors against women . . . should be considered as nothing more than a tradition of prejudices and errors."[35]

Poullain declared that "physical explanations . . . prove indubitably that the two sexes are equal both in body and mind," an opinion he later modified in women's favor: "Women have an intellect just like ours," to be sure, but they "can claim superiority with respect to the body, . . . [for] it is clearly the women who conceive us and form us." Again and again we are told that anatomy lessons teach us that the minds of men and women are the same and, therefore, are equally capable of reasoning: "Since the mind does not work differently in one sex than in the other, it is equally capable of the same things in each one. . . . The head . . . is . . . the place where the mind exercises all its functions. Our most accurate anatomical investigations do not uncover any difference between men and women in this part of the body." Moreover, physicians who distinguish between male and female temperaments in such a way as to make it appear that women are "completely different" and "inferior in everything" offer "only feeble conjectures which occur to the minds of those who judge things on the basis of appearances and prejudices."[36]

His utterly dismissive treatment of Aristotle's opinions on women (as they were understood in the seventeenth century) and even his notion that women contribute more to generation than men were to be taken up by others (Pierre Dionis, for example); but only Poullain went so far as to reverse the ancient claim that females are failed males: "One would be just as correct as those philosophers if one said that men are imperfect women!"[37] I know of no other writer in this period who actually drew this logical inference.

We know of four, possibly five, editions of *De l'égalité* (1673, 1679, 1690?, 1691, 1692) and one English translation (1677) in this period, but the number of imitations, loose translations, and treatises heavily indebted to Poullain was probably far greater than is currently known. For example, Gabrielle Suchon's book on the intellectual capacity of women, published in 1693 under the pseudonym G. S. Aristophile, referred to Poullain's treatise on sexual equality in its preface without naming him, which is not surprising. Even if his authorship of *De l'égalité* had become common knowledge by 1693, which is unlikely, there were good reasons for a former nun writing in post-1685 France to avoid explicit reference to him: Poullain was a Huguenot ex-priest who had fled Paris for Geneva in 1688. The full title of Suchon's *Traité de la morale et de la politique* explained the purpose of her book, which was to demonstrate that persons of the female sex have been deprived of liberty, knowledge, and authority even though their natural intellectual capacities fully equip them to participate in all three. Acutely aware of the deprivations suffered by women forced into either marriage or the convent, Suchon labored to equip women with an arsenal of arguments with which to defend themselves against the "servile constraint, dumb ignorance, and base and degraded subordination" that would otherwise be their fate. Although she cautioned her readers against violent resistance, her positive, or at least ambiguous, notice of the feats of the Amazons

---

[35] Poullain, *Equality of the Sexes,* trans. Clarke, pp. 86–88, 98, 109, 21, 68, 89, 33, 80–81.
[36] *Ibid.,* pp. 51, 88, 109, 118–119, 115–116.
[37] *Ibid.,* p. 132.

highlights the allusive strategies required of audacious writers throughout the Republic of Letters around 1700.[38]

Well known are the English tracts of 1739 and 1740 by "Sophia, a Person of Quality," which borrowed freely from Poullain's *De l'égalité* and are therefore sometimes mistakenly described as translations. They were reprinted in 1743 and again in 1750 under another title. Adaptations and reprints of the "Sophia" treatises continued to appear under various titles up to at least 1780. Less well known is the fact that in 1750 and 1751 these tracts reentered the French language, so to speak, under a false imprint (Londres) and different titles. The 1750 title, *La femme n'est pas inférieure à l'homme*, reproduced precisely the title of the 1739 treatise, while the 1751 title, *Le triomph des dames*, loosely translated that of the 1750 edition— although not all readers have noticed. Apart from the later versions of the "Sophia" tracts, the last of the adaptations of *De l'égalité* in English of which I am aware appeared in London in 1751 and 1758 under the title *Female Rights Vindicated; or, The Equality of the Sexes Morally and Physically Proved*. This version even included Poullain's conclusion that since women lack only a beard, we might "with as much reason . . . say . . . that Men are but imperfect Women." In fact, this anonymous treatise comes closest to rendering accurately Poullain's most radical pronouncements about women's equality with men and its foundation in "the most critical anatomy."[39]

It is impossible to estimate accurately Poullain's readership during the century after *De l'égalité* first appeared in 1673, given the many guises in which his thoughts (or words) appeared. But it is clearly *not* the case that Poullain had few readers, as Timothy Reiss and Madeleine Alcover claim. Apart from the various editions, translations (including translated excerpts published in journals), and adaptations I have traced, there are obvious debts to *De l'égalité* in the writings of Astell, Drake, Bernard Mandeville (*The Virgin Unmask'd*), and, doubtless, others who wrote, often anonymously, in defense of sexual equality.[40]

The fact that Poullain's egalitarian ideas made no actual difference to the lives of most eighteenth-century women, that they failed to shift deeply entrenched biases and cultural practices, cannot be taken as evidence that they went unnoticed. After all, their application in practice is quite another matter, as Poullain well realized.[41] It is particularly instructive, therefore, to note the conservative uses to which Poullain's

---

[38] Modern French editions of parts of Gabrielle Suchon's two books have appeared recently: *Traité de la morale et de la politique: La liberté* (1693), ed. Severine Auffret (Paris: Des Femmes, 1988) (see esp. pp. 219–223; the quotation is from p. 221); and *Du célibat volontaire ou La vie sans engagement* (1700), Vol. 1, ed. Auffret (Paris: Indigo & Côté-Femmes Editions, 1994).

[39] *Female Rights Vindicated* (cit. n. 14), pp. 117 ("imperfect women"), 59–60, 90–91.

[40] See Timothy J. Reiss, *The Meaning of Literature* (Ithaca, N.Y.: Cornell Univ. Press, 1992), p. 98; and Alcover, "Indecency of Knowledge" (cit. n. 34), p. 34. Joan DeJean argues persuasively that seventeenth-century female writers often viewed anonymity as a defensive strategy: DeJean, "Lafayette's Ellipses: The Privileges of Anonymity," *PMLA*, 1984, *99*:884–902. See also Kathryn Shevelow, *Women and Print Culture* (London: Routledge, 1989), pp. 41–42, 50–51.

[41] Although Poullain did not imagine that he could effect the social and political changes he advocated, he hoped to change men's minds. Therefore, when the anticipated rebuttal of *De l'égalité* failed to appear, he wrote one himself two years later (*De l'excellence des hommes, contre l'égalité des sexes* [1675]), although he was careful to use this occasion to articulate his views on sexual equality once again. In case Poullain's readers failed to notice the explanation for writing yet another book on the subject that he offered in his preface, Pierre Bayle's *Dictionnaire historique et critique* (1st ed., 1697) would have made Poullain's intentions clear to a large readership (article on "Lucrèce Marinella").

injunction to women to study science would be put roughly a hundred years later. Denis Diderot's plan for his daughter's education included anatomy lessons using the latest wax models—the better to equip her for marriage and motherhood, he explained. Diderot was probably a more complex figure than I am about to allow, but I cannot help noticing how well he answers to the description of "a sane man of letters" borrowed by an early nineteenth-century publisher from Diderot himself (a self-portrait?): "A sane man of letters can be the lover of a woman who writes books, but he should only be the husband of a woman who sews shirts."[42]

For seventeenth- and eighteenth-century women intellectuals and feminist writers, the demand for intellectual equality and its justification by reference to women's natural capacities were central to discussions of all forms of equality. Ancien régime debates about intellectual equality were political debates precisely because speech and authorship were understood to confer wide-ranging power and authority. Mental subordination was especially insufferable, as Mary Robinson emphasized in a plea to her "unenlightened country-women," *A Letter to the Women of England, on the Injustice of Mental Subordination* (1799): "Shake off the trifling, glittering shackles, which debase you. . . . Let your daughters be liberally, classically, philosophically, and usefully educated; let them speak and write their opinions freely; let them read and think like rational creatures; expand their minds, and purify their hearts, by teaching them to feel their mental equality with their imperious rulers." As is well known, this was hardly a typical proposal for educating women at the end of the eighteenth century. More characteristic of this period, particularly in France, were the schemes that invariably stressed women's roles as wives and mothers and their responsibility for "the moral regeneration of the nation." The *femmes savantes* applauded by Poullain—who, as he put it, "have had to overcome the indolence in which they were reared, renounce the pleasures and idleness to which they had been reduced, . . . overcome the unfavorable ideas which ordinary people have about learned women, apart from those which they have about the female sex in general"—found even fewer champions after 1770 than they had in the previous hundred years.[43]

It is worth considering whether violent reactions to women in public, to women authors and political activists in particular, during the final years of the eighteenth century had anything to do with the perceived impact of egalitarian ideas like those distilled from the work of Poullain de la Barre. Certainly the language of some of those who denied women's capacity to reason altogether and who sought to redefine sexual difference in the period around 1800 appears to have been aimed precisely at some of the earlier defenses of sexual equality. For example: "Despite what has been claimed, the mind and the heart have a sex just as the body does and both are

---

[42] On Diderot's plan for his daughter's education see Eva Jacobs, "Diderot and the Education of Girls," in *Women and Society in Eighteenth-Century France*, ed. Jacobs *et al.* (London: Athlone Press, 1979), pp. 93–95; the remark about the "sane man of letters" is cited in Geneviève Fraisse, *Reason's Muse: Sexual Difference and the Birth of Democracy*, trans. Jane Marie Todd (Chicago: Univ. Chicago Press, 1994), p. 16.

[43] "Anne Frances Randall" [Mary Robinson], *A Letter to the Women of England* (London, 1799), in a collection of texts edited by Vivian Jones: *Women in the Eighteenth Century* (London: Routledge, 1986), p. 242; Jean H. Bloch, "Women and the Reform of the Nation," in *Women and Society in Eighteenth-Century France*, ed. Jacobs *et al.*, pp. 3–18, on p. 16; and Poullain, *Equality of the Sexes*, trans. Clarke, pp. 69–70.

dependent upon the body: the moral and the physical are so closely linked that they are in fact one."[44]

The fact that advocates of sexual equality in the seventeenth and eighteenth centuries often supported their arguments by reference to the new anatomy may well have influenced the kind of reception given to the anatomy lessons publicized by de Graaf and Drake (among others), as well as their representation and repression in anatomy lectures, textbooks, and dictionaries of science and medicine, particularly from around 1750. There was always more than one way to interpret the new anatomy, even in the seventeenth century; in fact, the range of possible readings is positively baffling to the twentieth-century reader. At the same time, it does appear that eighteenth-century commentators were increasingly likely to perceive the new anatomy as having created (however unintentionally) uncertainty, ambivalence, even indeterminacy regarding sexual difference, thereby undermining the grounds for male domination in household and society.

Aggressive efforts to reassert fixed biological differences between the sexes and to reemphasize the ideology that viewed the patriarchal household and the patriarchal state as facts of nature were partly a consequence of women's political transgression during the revolutionary era. Predictably, concern to reestablish order and authority in the political arena was bound to entail a less than tolerant attitude to scientific disputes that threatened to destabilize further notions of gender identity that were already unstable. Moreover, because these controversies had been published in small-format vernacular books that women could read, some of which circulated widely during the eighteenth century, irresolution of particular questions about women's minds and bodies could be construed as politically and morally dangerous. Therefore the years around 1800 were characterized by a deliberate effort to substitute definition for indeterminacy and to codify a more comprehensive dimorphism based on biological differences than had ever existed before.[45]

A widely shared view at this time was that of the Jacobin deputy André Amar, reporting to the National Convention on behalf of the Committee of General Security at the end of October 1793. Explaining why women should not "exercise political rights and meddle in affairs of government," he announced that

> the private functions for which women are destined by their very nature are related to the general order of society; this *social order results from the differences between man and woman*. Each sex is called to the kind of occupation which is fitting for it; its action is circumscribed within this circle which it cannot break through, because nature, which has imposed these limits on man, commands imperiously and receives no law.

Another deputy protested that women should be allowed to assemble peaceably: "Unless you are going to question whether women are part of the human species,

---

[44] Quoted in Fraisse, *Reason's Muse*, trans. Todd (cit. n. 42), p. 19. For an authoritative account of the selection of traditions in the history of medicine and a careful reading of many of the medical texts central to debates on the interdependence of the mind and the body see Elizabeth A. Williams, *The Physical and the Moral: Anthropology, Physiology, and Philosophical Medicine in France, 1750–1850* (Cambridge: Cambridge Univ. Press, 1994).

[45] On gender dimorphism in the revolutionary period see esp. Gutwirth, *Twilight of the Goddesses* (cit. n. 8), an outstanding study of the interplay of visual and verbal texts in late eighteenth-century France.

can you take away from them *this right which is common to every thinking being?*"⁴⁶ Concluding that public order was at stake, the Convention outlawed all women's political clubs and popular societies. When a deputation of women appeared before the Commune of Paris two weeks later, protesting the Convention's decree and appealing for support from the Council, they were denounced by Pierre Gaspard Chaumette, speaking for the municipal legislators, as "denatured women" and "*viragos*" whose actions were "contrary to all the laws of nature." Once again nature's decrees were invoked to affirm women's irreducible difference, which then became the grounds for categorically differentiating the social destinies of the sexes and for imposing laws and policies that presumably would establish the very differences between men and women alleged to exist in nature: "Since when it is permitted to give up one's sex? Since when is it decent to see women abandoning the pious cares of their households, the cribs of their children, to come to public places, to harangues in the galleries, at the bar of the Senate? Is it to men that nature confided domestic cares? Has she given us breasts to feed our children?"⁴⁷

Although debates about sexual difference and equality were neither resolved nor suspended by these arguments or the policies they sanctioned, the political goals of the new republics (on both sides of the Atlantic) at the end of the eighteenth century entailed reconceiving women as nonrational beings. Increasingly, this project involved redefining women as persons governed by their reproductive functions and, to some extent, by sexual organs that were thought to influence their entire being. Reendowing women's minds with sex followed easily from the assumption, shared by a number of important late eighteenth-century medical writers, that the sexes were distinguished by their *total* anatomy and physiology, not by their generative organs alone.⁴⁸

The appeal to nature's decrees in political rhetoric was hardly new, as Poullain de la Barre had pointed out more than a hundred years earlier, when he explained that lawyers use the law to subject women to men and "then say that it is nature which assigned the lowest functions in society to women and kept them out of public office." He continued: "[Because lawyers] have attributed to nature a distinction which derives only from custom, . . . one would embarrass them seriously if they were

---

⁴⁶ Extracts from the debate on women's clubs are translated in *Women in Revolutionary Paris, 1789–1795,* ed. Darline Gay Levy, Harriet Branson Applewhite, and Mary Durham Johnson (Urbana: Univ. Illinois Press, 1979), pp. 213–217; quotations are from pp. 215, 217 (emphasis added). For useful discussion of these proceedings and their broader context see Scott, *Only Paradoxes to Offer* (cit. n. 8), pp. 47–53; Suzanne Desan, "'Constitutional Amazons': Jacobin Women's Clubs in the French Revolution," in *Recreating Authority in Revolutionary France,* ed. Bryant T. Ragam, Jr., and Elizabeth A. Williams (New Brunswick, N.J.: Rutgers Univ. Press, 1991), pp. 11–35; Gutwirth, *Twilight of the Goddesses,* Ch. 7; Elizabeth Colwill, "'Just Another *Citoyenne?*' Marie Antoinette on Trial, 1790–1793," *Hist. Workshop J.,* Autumn 1989, 28:63–87; and Susan P. Conner, "Public Virtue and Public Women: Prostitution in Revolutionary Paris, 1793–1794," *Eighteenth-Cent. Stud.,* 1994–1995, 28:221–240.

⁴⁷ Levy, Applewhite, and Johnson, eds., *Women in Revolutionary Paris,* p. 219.

⁴⁸ Fraisse, *Reason's Muse,* trans. Todd (cit. n. 42), esp. pp. 21–26, 99–101, 163–164, 167–178. On attempts to assign women a fixed sexual identity and to make the psychic dependent on the physical see, e.g., Williams, *Physical and the Moral* (cit. n. 44), Ch. 2; Fraisse, *Reason's Muse,* trans. Todd, Ch. 3; Michèle Le Doeuff, "Pierre Roussel's Chiasmas: From Imaginary Knowledge to the Learned Imagination," *Ideology and Consciousness,* 1981–1982, 9:39–70; Ludmilla Jordanova, *Sexual Visions: Images of Gender in Science and Medicine between the Eighteenth and Twentieth Centuries* (Madison: Univ. Wisconsin Press, 1989), Ch. 2; and Jordanova, "Naturalizing the Family: Literature and the Bio-Medical Sciences in the Late Eighteenth Century," in *Languages of Nature,* ed. Jordanova (London: Free Association Books, 1986), pp. 86–116.

forced to explain intelligibly what they mean by 'nature' in this context, and to explain how nature distinguishes the two sexes in the ways they imagine." What was new at this time was the apparently acute anxiety of a newly empowered group of men to redefine sexual difference in terms that would furnish a legitimate foundation for denying women citizenship. How much, one wonders, did their inflamed rhetoric and enraged behavior owe to the fact that women revolutionaries had in fact succeeded in acting as citizens during the early years of the French Revolution? How important was the feared impact of the public discourse that had contested the alleged grounds for male supremacy during the previous hundred years? The alarm and hostility voiced by Nicolas-Edmé Restif de la Bretonne in 1796 may have been extreme, but it was not unrepresentative: "And so, I repeat to this century filled with error and folly, which seeks, despite nature, to confuse the two sexes in every way, man bears a greater resemblance to the male pig than to the woman who carries him in her womb, and in whose womb he places his son."[49]

Writing at the beginning of the revolutionary era, the British historian Catherine Macaulay had mocked "the notion of a sexual difference in the human character, ... which a close observation of Nature, and a more accurate way of reasoning, would disprove." Closely observing events across the waters in 1791 and 1792, Mary Wollstonecraft penned a lengthy plea for sexual equality. A French translation appeared within months of the publication of her *Vindication of the Rights of Woman* in 1792, as did two American editions; the following year the *Vindication* was printed in Dublin, and German, Dutch, and Italian translations soon followed. At the beginning of her treatise Wollstonecraft demanded, "If women are to be excluded, without having a voice, from a participation of the natural rights of mankind, prove first . . . that they want reason."[50] (See Figure 1.)

However exalted the authority claimed for nature's laws by revolutionary ideology, many women remained unconvinced and unintimidated. Among these were those revolutionary women who persisted in intervening in the course of political events. In addition, important women intellectuals in France published detailed replies to this rhetoric.[51] During succeeding decades, a number of well-known intellectuals and political activists continued to defend sexual equality by reference to recent research in anatomy and physiology despite the political success of those who had declared that medical evidence proved women's incapacity to reason and govern. Joseph Jacotot, for example, an influential educational theorist writing in the early decades of the nineteenth century, remained convinced that women's intellectual powers were undiminished by their anatomical and physiological differences from men. The Irish feminist Anna Doyle Wheeler, widely known through her public lectures on women's issues and her various publications, including the coauthored *Appeal of One Half the Human Race Against the Pretensions of the Other Half— Men—to Retain Them in Political and Thence in Civil and Domestic Slavery* (1825),

---

[49] Poullain, *Equality of the Sexes*, p. 82; and Nicolas-Edmé Restif de la Bretonne, cited in Gutwirth, *Twilight of the Goddesses* (cit. n. 8), p. 174.

[50] Macaulay, *Letters on Education* (1790) (cit. n. 14), p. 204; and Mary Wollstonecraft, *A Vindication of the Rights of Woman* (1792; London: Penguin, 1992), p. 88.

[51] Reprints of texts by Marie-Armande Gacon-Dufour (1787), Olympe de Gouges (1791), Constance de Salm (1797), Albertine Clément-Hémery (1801), and Fanny Raoul (1801) are now available in *Opinions de femmes de la veille au lendemain de la Révolution française*, ed. with a preface by Geneviève Fraisse (Paris: Côté-Femmes, 1989).

Figure 1. Mary Wollstonecraft (1759–1797), by John Opie. (Reproduced by permission of the Tate Gallery, London.)

in a talk on women's rights at Finsbury Square, London, in 1829, referred to the testimony of anatomists in terms that are strikingly familiar: "All the researchers of anatomy have not been able to prove a difference in the brain of either [sex]. Both [sexes] receive the same impressions, arrange and preserve ideas, form memory and imagination; judge, compare and analyse." She went on to explain why knowledge and a "useful education" have been withheld from women: "In every instance, where we find women sharing equal advantages of education with man, there is little or no difference in mental energy; and I fear, to this well authenticated fact, may be ascribed the hateful and unjust policy of denying all useful education to them. *Knowledge is power* say men; to keep women our slaves, we must keep them ignorant."[52]

---

[52] On Jacotot see Jacques Rancière's preface to Fraisse, *Raison des femmes* (cit. n. 34), p. 11; Anna Doyle Wheeler's lecture at Finsbury Square was published in the first numbers of the *British Cooperator* in April and May 1830, pp. 12–15 and 33–36, respectively. See Dolores Dooley, *Equality in Community: Sexual Equality in the Writings of William Thompson and Anna Doyle Wheeler* (Cork: Cork Univ. Press, 1996), for an outstanding study of two early socialist-feminists. "All the researchers" is quoted in Barbara Taylor, *Eve and the New Jerusalem: Socialism and Feminism in the Nineteenth Century* (London: Virago, 1983), p. 27; and "in every instance" is cited in Dooley, *Equality in Community*, p. 242.

Science, Politics, and Morality
The Relationship of Lise Meitner and Elisabeth Schiemann

By Elvira Scheich*

LISE MEITNER AND ELISABETH SCHIEMANN were both among the first women in their academic fields. Meitner was involved in the creation of modern physics; she is especially well known for her work with Otto Hahn and Fritz Straßmann, which led to the discovery of nuclear fission. Max Planck supported her career in spite of his reservations about women in science. He was impressed by her scientific abilities and her extraordinary determination. Meitner came from a Jewish family in Vienna and was forced to leave Germany in 1938. She went to Stockholm and spent the last years of her life in Cambridge, England. Her friend Schiemann lived in Berlin almost all her life. Her father had been a professor of European history, specializing in Russian history, culture, and politics, and a counselor to Kaiser Wilhelm II. Schiemann worked for nearly two decades with Erwin Baur, who held the first chair for genetics in Germany. She dedicated the largest part of her work to the history of cultivated plants, efforts later funded with the help of Fritz von Wettstein. She was one of the few German biologists who made no secret of her criticism of Nazi politics, especially its anti-Semitism.[1]

TWO FRIENDS

Meitner and Schiemann met for the first time in 1909, when both were on their way to work on the S-Bahn in Berlin-Dahlem. They soon initiated a friendship that would last sixty years. The two women had many interests in common: they went to conferences together, but also to concerts and on hiking tours; they were part of the scientific community in Berlin and of the newly founded institutes in Berlin-Dahlem; and Meitner was a regular guest in Schiemann's family home, while Schiemann

---

* Zionkirchstr. 54, D-10119 Berlin, Germany.

I am grateful to the Hamburger Institut für Sozialforschung for supporting my research on Lise Meitner and Elisabeth Schiemann.

[1] On Meitner see Renate Feyl, "Lise Meitner (1878–1968)," in *Der lautlose Aufbruch—Frauen in der Wissenschaft* (Darmstadt: Luchterhand, 1981), pp. 162–186; Charlotte Kerner, *Lise, Atomphysikerin: Die Lebensgeschichte der Lise Meitner* (Weinheim/Basel: Beltz, 1986); and Ruth Sime, *Lise Meitner: A Life in Physics* (Berkeley: Univ. California Press, 1996). Two short biographies of Schiemann, written by former students and colleagues, have appeared: Hermann Kuckuck, "Elisabeth Schiemann, 1881–1972," *Berichte der Deutschen Botanischen Gesellschaft*, 1980, *93*:517–537; and Anton Lang, "Elisabeth Schiemann: Life and Career of a Woman Scientist in Berlin," *Englera*, 1987, *7*:17–28.

Figure 1. Elisabeth Schiemann (left) and Lise Meitner on a summer excursion in the outskirts of Berlin. *(Courtesy of Churchill Archives, Cambridge.)*

accompanied Meitner on visits to the Plancks. (See Figure 1.) Both felt obligated to the women's movement (although they were not activists), and they shared the conviction that access to education was a major goal that would further the liberation of women. Faced with the misogyny of academic life, they recognized the fragility of their own careers and the necessity for networks among women in science. In 1909 both were around thirty years old and had struggled for some years to reach the positions they held. These were still very low in the university hierarchy and, accordingly, paid poorly (many male colleagues of the same age had already secured chairs or were applying for professorships), but Meitner and Schiemann were happy about the success they had achieved.[2]

During World War I both women were staunch German patriots, convinced that Germany had to defend itself against foreign aggressors. Their male colleagues went to the front. Meitner decided to do the same and worked as an X-ray assistant at a military hospital in the Ukraine. Schiemann had become responsible for maintaining research and teaching at her institute and was not free to leave. In their correspondence Meitner expressed her thoughts and feelings in the face of the realities of war, her wish to help the injured soldiers of all nations, and her concern about her friends and colleagues at the western front. After her return to Berlin and to her experiments at the Kaiser Wilhelm Institute for Chemistry in 1916, however, she was not critical of Fritz Haber's research on poison gas. Her only problem with his group was the

---

[2] See Elisabeth Schiemann, "Freundschaft mit Lise Meitner," *Neue Evangelische Frauenzeitschrift,* 1959, *1* (offprint). My main source for this article was the correspondence between Meitner and Schiemann, which began in 1911 and ended with Meitner's death in 1968; it is to be found with the Lise Meitner Papers at the Churchill Archives, Cambridge (hereafter cited as **Meitner Papers**).

threat it posed to her own work as it took over more and more of the institute. She endorsed all means to bring the war to an end, an outcome still tantamount, in her mind, to a German victory.[3]

Things changed after the war. In November 1918 Meitner wrote one of her longest letters to Schiemann, detailing the news from Berlin. Berlin was the center of the revolutionary uprising that swept over postwar Germany; the monarchy had broken down, and information was becoming available on the political and military strategies that had led to the prolongation of the war and on the unwillingness to compromise that resulted in a disastrous defeat. Meitner took the side of the Social Democrats, advocating the establishment of a parliamentary democracy with the full participation of intellectuals and women. She wrote, "But the middle classes too have to fulfill their duties and we women also.... Well, dear Elisabeth, don't mind, if you consider my opinions wrong. I have indeed the honest aspiration to know the objective truth, whether it is in accordance with my wishes or not, and I expect the same of you."[4] Schiemann did not agree—either with Meitner's new political insights and convictions or with the course of political developments in Germany. To her the Hohenzollern monarchy still represented Germany's culture and the best of its values. Like most German academics, she remained deeply skeptical toward the Weimar Republic.

This disagreement between the two friends was not an incidental personal difference. Schiemann's family came from the Baltic provinces and her father was a Prussian professor, while Meitner grew up as the daughter of an Austrian lawyer and her family was of Jewish descent. Meitner's hopes for a democratic Germany as part of a cosmopolitan, humanistic, and ethical global society were typical for assimilated Jews in Germany during that period (Meitner, like many others, strongly wished that Austria would become part of Germany). They imagined the "true" Germany: Germany as it should be, not as it was. Jewish intellectuals saw German culture as an expression of universal human values: rationality, science, knowledge, truth. The two friends did not disagree upon this point; the difference was that one held that this ideal was yet to be achieved, while the other sought it in the past.

The difference in Meitner's and Schiemann's stances after World War I suggests that race, as well as gender, played a role in their world views and their self-positioning as academic women. However, gender and race are not universal categories; they have to be specified in a given context—here, Germany during the interwar period. So situated, these categories can be used as probes into a network of meanings connecting science, politics, and morality. What is provided by the cultural and social surroundings of these two women? What shifts occur as they interact with the field of meaning that surrounds science?

REPRESENTING AMBIVALENCE

In mapping the field of meaning that links science, politics, and morality, I draw on Zygmunt Bauman's book *Modernity and Ambivalence*.[5] Bauman's work has

---

[3] See Sabine Ernst, *Lise Meitner an Otto Hahn: Briefe aus den Jahren 1912 bis 1924* (Stuttgart: Wissenschaftliche Verlagsgesellschaft, 1992).
[4] Lise Meitner to Elisabeth Schiemann, 29 Nov. 1918, Meitner Papers. Here and elsewhere, translations into English are mine unless otherwise noted.
[5] Zygmunt Bauman, *Modernity and Ambivalence* (Cambridge: Polity, 1991).

contributed to the recognition that the horrors of Nazism were not a fall from the state of modernity. What had seemed to be the particularity of racism against the Jews turns out to be general traits rooted in the modern political order. In his penetrating reflections on the social order and the elimination of difference, Bauman links the structure of modern thought with the experience of those beyond the pale of this order and investigates the motives and causal connections that sustained their advocacy of modernity, reason, and universal cultural values. His writings provide a rich framework that can be employed to study the relation of race and gender, two categories of otherness.

The modern national state is an artificial social order, created by humans and, hence, potentially alterable. The collective identity of a nation needs constantly to be reinforced; the grounds of its self-constitution are inherently unstable and thus can easily be jeopardized. Assimilation, the way strangers and outsiders are accommodated within liberal political culture, ultimately enhances the dominance and the superiority of the established culture and the otherness of the stranger. While political discrimination is directed against the collective of outsiders, cultural assimilation is seen as a matter of individual efforts, acts of self-improvement and self-transformation that are doomed to fail. The majority of German Jews, however, did not view themselves as different or as strangers.

Bauman's analysis draws attention to the social and political contradictions inherent in stigmatizing. The stigma points to a difference, stereotyped and conceived as essential and unchangeable. "An otherwise innocuous trait becomes a blemish, a sign of affliction, a cause of shame." The different ones are marked with bodily signs that draw attention to their putative inferiority, even dangerousness. As the manifestation of an inner truth set forth by nature, inherited and unchangeable, the stigma of otherness annuls acquired cultural characteristics. Thus it undermines modern beliefs in the ameliorating role of education and in individual responsibility, self-improvement, and self-determination. The burden of proof is placed on the stigmatized, who have to demonstrate the absence of a distinctive feature. "The bond between signs and inner truth may be denied, but cannot be broken." In the case of assimilated German Jews, no visible signs of difference were given by nature or class; their differences were the creation of racial theories and politics.[6]

In modern political thought, the constitution of society is grounded on its separation from nature. The definition of universal human values is a cornerstone in the Enlightenment program to rationalize every aspect of human life. The laws of nature—rightly understood—were to be employed to improve the natural and social conditions underwriting the progress of humanity. Scientific principles, important features of modern thought and modern forms of knowledge, are held to be unrelated to moral responsibility and personal relations. Classification, division, and boundaries, the designation and separation of strangers and outsiders, are integral to the establishment of order. Founded on the basis of universal cultural values, the modern political effort to establish order sought to eliminate whatever differed or was unfit, uncontrollable, or reluctant, uncertain or paradoxical. Otherness and ambivalence were cast in negative terms, as chaos or waste. Exclusion and elimination of the recalcitrant, then, became a mere question of technology. "Having emancipated pur-

---

[6] *Ibid.*, pp. 67, 68. On assimilated German Jews see Gertrud Koch, *Die Einstellung ist die Einstellung* (Frankfurt am Main: Suhrkamp, 1992).

poseful action from moral constraints, modernity rendered genocide possible."[7] Moreover, the tendency to dehumanize and naturalize otherness, denying its bearers political and civil rights, was strengthened by the fact that the German nation was understood (as is still the case in the 1990s) as a community defined by descent rather than by territory. In racial theories the German *Volk* was seen as a superorganism, whose health could be secured only by the extirpation of otherness.

Representing otherness, indefiniteness, and existential and intellectual ambivalence, the Jews were at the core of the set of contradictions that characterize modernity. Their experience of estrangement, marginalization, exclusion, and expulsion linked them to the situations and standpoints of the modern intelligentsia. Rootlessness and alienation, in intellectualized form, became cosmopolitanism and universalism—calling into question the concrete, specific, and unequivocal and discerning the particularism of any system of absolutes. "The standpoint of the exile is the only cognitive determinant of universally binding truth."[8] This new intellectual and political understanding of objectivity had ambiguous results. On the one hand, it yielded the insight that being different, a stranger, is an essential characteristic of the human condition and indeed its only universal feature. On the other hand, adherence to universal and absolute values led to a turn to the inner life and frequently resulted in an intellectual remoteness that distanced critique from social practice. The experience and epistemological standpoint of the outsider made recognition of the antinomies of modern thought and modern life possible: order, the absolute, and transparency gave way to pluralism, relativism, and ambiguity; the Enlightenment values of spontaneity and freedom were inverted.

Bauman's analysis is congruent in many respects with the feminist analysis of the role of women in modern society. Women have been denied full political rights by emphasizing and naturalizing their difference from men. Their bodies have been described and inscribed as well as stigmatized and used. In the discourse of gender, women represent the other and embody ambiguity; the images of women are contradictory and threatening to the identical male self. However, the otherness of women does not refer directly beyond culture. Women represent nature, but they cannot simply be expelled from culture and society. The bodily differences that set women apart from men are bound to the natural and hence the social reproduction of human life in a very fundamental way, individually and collectively. Women's straddling of the divide between the natural and the social sits uneasily with modern thinking; the modern way of perceiving the self in the world has never come to terms with sexuality and the fact that we are all born of woman. Within the culture of universalism women may signify chaos, but they cannot signify waste; they embody culture's foundations in nature—not rootlessness, but the roots. In modernity, women lead a double existence, in and outside the social; simultaneously acting out the absence and presence of the signs of femininity is a condition of their social life.

This essay goes on to examine the relations of universality and difference from the vantage point of women's struggles to participate in modernity and in science. I will focus on debates among German intellectuals after World War I and their

---

[7] Bauman, *Modernity and Ambivalence*, p. 48. The dismissal of morality was a salient feature of the role of the sciences during the Nazi period; see Peter Weingart, Jürgen Kroll, and Kurt Bayertz, *Rasse, Blut und Gene* (Frankfurt am Main: Suhrkamp, 1988).
[8] Bauman, *Modernity and Ambivalence*, p. 85.

differing attitudes toward modernization, on how that shaped their views about women, and, finally, on how women academics perceived themselves.

PARTICIPATION IN MODERNITY

The outcome of the Great War had been devastating for Germany—economically, politically, and individually. Some 2.7 million disabled veterans needed care; 6 million demobilized soldiers awaited reintegration. The defeat and its aftermath—especially the sense of humiliation shared by the vast majority of the nation that had begun the war in a rapture of enthusiasm—erected nearly insurmountable obstacles to the restoration of a civil society. The natural sciences were not untouched by the disastrous effects of Germany's wartime politics: the boycott of German science by Allied scientists and the economic crisis of the immediate postwar years severed ties to the international scientific community for years to come.

The first two decades of the twentieth century had been marked by fast-paced social changes that followed rapid industrialization and urbanization; the war effort accelerated the processes of modernization still further. For German society in general, and its intellectuals in particular, reactions to the ways of modern life varied widely. Conservatives interpreted modernization as an erosion of German "culture" and saw traditional values and forms of life being undermined by "machines and masses." They opposed parliamentary democracy and party politics on the grounds that the nation as a whole should be the focus of concern. Their concepts of *Bildung* and of the university aimed at developing comprehensive knowledge and "pure" science unsullied by practical and political interests. Others welcomed modernism and rationalization, which made it possible to dispense with notions of introspective authenticity. Like the conservatives, they employed the rhetoric and ideas of the philosophy of life (*Lebensphilosophie*), but they reached opposite conclusions.[9] The modernist avant garde perceived the artificiality of the social as its natural condition. They valued anonymity, alienation, and indifference in social relationships as liberating and welcomed the chance to redesign social life and its technocratic management. They consistently advocated materialism and positivism, analytical and pragmatic thinking; they called for the application of scientific research to social life and favored orienting institutions of higher learning toward the interests of the state and industry. Theirs was a culture of doers, builders, and inventors in which science was held to eliminate cumbersome beliefs and restrictions and to open up new ways of approaching the fundamental problems of its disciplines.[10]

---

[9] "Bildung is generally translated as 'cultivation.' It was an educational ideal which emphasized not simply the nurture of intellect, but the development of the whole person. . . . The aim of bildung was to acquire a 'complete view of the world,' to grasp the 'essence of the whole world's structure'": Jonathan Harwood, *Styles of Scientific Thought: The German Genetics Community, 1900–1933* (Chicago/London: Univ. Chicago Press, 1993), pp. 276–277. The conservatives recognized divisions in the outer manifestations of both natural and social life, a fracturing that threatened their true inner unity, whereas the modernists accepted fragmentation and the loss of wholeness as genuine, inevitable, and final.

[10] The literature on the central features of modernization is extensive. Among the works most important for my understanding of this period see Peter Ulrich Hein, *Die Brücke ins Geisterreich: Künstlerische Avantgarde zwischen Kulturkritik und Faschismus* (Reinbek bei Hamburg: Rowohlt, 1992); Corona Hepp, *Avantgarde: Moderne Kunst, Kulturkritik und Reformbewegungen nach der Jahrhundertwende* (Munich: DTV, 1987, 1992); Helmut Lethen, *Verhaltenslehren der Kälte: Lebensversuche zwischen den Kriegen* (Frankfurt am Main: Suhrkamp, 1994); and Fritz K. Ringer,

At the beginning of the century numerous women discovered new orientations and lifestyles that offered escape from traditional gender roles. At first sight the case of women in science is puzzling: university education and careers became possible for women when the pragmatic attitudes of modernists and technocrats who accepted outsiders prevailed, yet the women scientists who took advantage of these opportunities came mainly from families of the educated middle classes (*Bildungsbürgertum*) and clung to conservative values and ideals of comprehensive understanding.[11] However, neither conservatives nor modernists were ready fully to accept women—in society or in science. Gender roles had been rendered obsolete during the war; in reaction, conservatives turned back to the old conceptions of women as mothers, the domestic heart and soul of the nation, while in modernist discourse on gender a shift becomes visible as a result of their understanding of human nature and human society.[12] Conservatives had sought to develop the individual's complexity through education (*Bildung*), and their conception of gender relations was embodied in a complementary extension of the individual, the couple. Modernist personalities were constructed as antipoles: a "cold persona" of functional adaptation and change, whose actions were unconstrained by moral restrictions, was set against a "creature" reduced to an organic substratum, a bare, needy, driven bundle of reflexes in constant fear, indistinguishable from an animal, at the mercy of others in a time that knew no compassion. Modernist literature designed male and female protagonists, both cold and creature-like, yet sexuality made a difference, tipping the balance: only one aspect could predominate. The brutish natural force of sexual attraction caused an irreducible disunity; equality between men and women was not possible. Thus women could be seen only as calculating and deploying their sexual

---

The Decline of the German Mandarins: The German Academic Community (Cambridge, Mass.: Harvard Univ. Press, 1969). On the sciences see Michael Eckert, *Die Atomphysiker: Eine Geschichte der theoretischen Physik am Beispiel der Sommerfeldschule* (Braunschweig/Wiesbaden: Vieweg, 1993); Harwood, *Styles of Scientific Thought;* Bettina Heintz, *Die Herrschaft der Regel: Zur Grundlagen Geschichte des Computers* (Frankfurt am Main: Campus, 1993); Herbert Mehrtens, *Moderne—Sprache—Mathematik: Eine Geschichte des Streits um die Grundlagen der Disziplin und des Subjekts formaler Systeme* (Frankfurt am Main: Suhrkamp, 1990).

[11] The inner conflicts for women caught between these two worlds could become unbearable; see, for a case study, Gerit von Leitner, *Der Fall Clara Immerwahr: Leben für eine humane Wissenschaft* (Munich: Beck, 1993). On the new opportunities for women see Sigrun Anselm and Barbara Beck, eds., *Triumph und Scheitern in der Metropole: Zur Rolle der Weiblichkeit in der Geschichte Berlins* (Berlin: Dietrich Reimer, 1987); Heide Schlüpmann, *Unheimlichkeit des Blicks: Das Drama des frühen deutschen Kinos* (Frankfurt am Main: Stroemfeld/Roter Stern, 1990); Inge Stephan, Sabine Schilling, and Sigrid Weigel, eds., *Jüdische Kultur und Weiblichkeit in der Moderne* (Cologne/Weimar/Vienna: Böhlau, 1994); and Gisela von Wysocki, *Die Fröste der Freiheit: Aufbruchsphantasien* (Frankfurt am Main: Syndikat, 1980).

[12] Women had filled traditionally male positions during the war. The trauma of defeat had particularly wounded males' sense of self, which in Germany more than elsewhere was shaped by military ideals and education. On modernist discourse on gender see Christina von Braun, *Nicht Ich—Ich Nicht: Logik, Lüge, Libido* (Frankfurt am Main: Neue Kritik, 1985), esp. pp. 324–356; Braun, *Die schamlose Schönheit des Vergangenen: Zum Verhältnis von Geschlecht und Geschichte* (Frankfurt am Main: Neue Kritik, 1989); Silvia Bovenschen, *Die imaginierte Weiblichkeit: Exemplarische Untersuchungen zur kulturgeschichtlichen und literarischen Präsentationsformen des Weiblichen* (Frankfurt am Main: Suhrkamp, 1979); Ute Frevert, *Ehrenmänner: Das Duell in der bürgerlichen Gesellschaft* (Munich: DTV, 1995); Klaus Theweleit, *Männerphantasien* (Frankfurt am Main: Stroemfeld/Roter Stern, 1977); and Nike Wagner, *Geist und Geschlecht: Karl Kraus und die Erotik der Wiener Moderne* (Frankfurt am Main: Suhrkamp, 1987). On science see Karin Hausen, "Warum Männer Frauen zur Wissenschaft nicht zulassen wollten," in *Wie männlich ist die Wissenschaft,* ed. Hausen and Helga Nowotny (Frankfurt am Main: Suhrkamp, 1986), pp. 31–40.

attractiveness or as ruled by instinct. "The problematic man is shown on the run through a gallery of female figures."[13]

Organizations of middle-class and academic women concentrated upon education for girls and women, professionalization of women's work, and rationalization of the living conditions of women. They held that the "coldness" of abstract thinking, of economic and technological rationality, had to be remedied by the emancipation of women and "female culture."[14] They aligned the strategies of modernization with the traditional values of the educated middle classes. The resulting mélange of discordant and partly contradictory elements was double edged, both liberating and repressive. The feminist voices that merged into the nationalist frenzy at the beginning of the Great War, into the German *Volksgemeinschaft,* located women squarely within a family: they were mothers and sisters of the soldiers and dispassionate, reasonable, and active daughters embracing and advocating the paternal order. The self-presentation of these women often hints at a thoroughly elite consciousness and a novel form of emancipated female authoritarianism. It is significant that the women so depicted were without sexuality.[15] Their acquiescence in this image left these women helpless in the face of new surges of sexism and misogyny. Encircled by various ideological images of femininity, the feminist project of constructing the "new woman" was inevitably burdened by the deep-rooted tensions that characterized Weimar democracy as a whole and its intellectual framework in particular.

The controversies about the form of politics and the roles of science and morality in Germany after World War I cannot be directly reduced to patterns of left or right party politics. The National Socialists built their political power base on a mixture of seemingly opposed ideological elements; their appeal transcended political affiliations and thus reached people from vastly different social backgrounds. The establishment of the National Socialist state occurred through a series of almost imperceptible steps rather than in a singular turn; it was accompanied by a swelling

---

[13] Lethen, *Verhaltenslehren der Kälte* (cit. n. 10), p. 43.

[14] On women's organizations see Bärbel Clemens, *"Menschenrechte haben kein Geschlecht!" Zum Politikverständnis der bürgerlichen Frauenbewegung* (Pfaffenweiler: Centaurus, 1988); Hildtraud Schmidt-Waldherr, *Emanzipation durch Professionalisierung?* (Frankfurt am Main: Materialis, 1987); and Irene Stoehr, "'Organisierte Müttelichkeit': Zur Politik der deutschen Frauenbewegung um 1900," in *Frauen suchen ihre Geschichte: Historische Studien zum 19. und 20. Jahrhundert,* ed. Karin Hausen (Munich: Beck, 1983), pp. 221–249. The feminists' slogan of "spiritual motherliness" transformed the idealized unity of the couple from a private to a political idea, and they understood the complementarity of men's and women's qualities, abilities, and tasks as a model for society on all levels. In setting "motherliness" against "machinery," as "life" against "death," these feminists used traditional gender concepts in order to overturn traditional stereotypes by applying female activity and self-determination to the realms of the state and high culture. See Barbara Brick and Christine Woesler, "Maschinerie und Mütterlichkeit," *Beiträge zur Feministischen Theorie und Praxis,* 1981, 5:61–68. On the reception of Georg Simmel's "Philosophie der Geschlechter: Das Relative und das Absolute im Geschlechter-Problem" see Annemarie Wolfer-Melior, "Weiblichkeit als Kritik," *Feministische Studien,* 1985, 2:62–78; and Inka Mülder-Bach, "'Weibliche Kultur' und 'stahlhartes Gehäuse': Zur Thematisierung des Geschlechterverhältnisses in den Soziologien von Georg Simmel und Max Weber," in *Triumph und Scheitern in der Metropole,* ed. Anselm and Beck (cit. n. 11), pp. 115–140.

[15] The elimination of sexuality from this image of women might have seemed a necessity; self-determination was apparently to be gained only through emotional independence. But when sexlessness became a model for professional women, it fostered the bond to rigid forms of paternal authority. See Ulrike Prokop, "Die Sehnsucht nach der Volkseinheit: Zum Konservatismus der bürgerlichen Frauenbewegunng vor 1933," in *Die Überwindung der Sprachlosigkeit: Texte aus der neuen Frauenbewegung,* ed. Gabriele Dietze (Darmstadt: Luchterhand, 1979), pp. 176–202.

undertow of demoralization and political apathy.[16] The well-known antifeminism of the Nazis was an old vintage. Their ideology added little to the conservative image of women; their leadership was solely male and their politics made it abundantly clear that this would not change.[17] The majority of women were either uninterested in or reacted with resignation to political developments. The associations of the women's movement disbanded when confronted with the process of forced alignment (*Gleichschaltung*) by which the Nazis secured their control over many organizations and institutions in German society.[18]

The gates to National Socialism were much narrower for academic women than for their male colleagues, but they were not nonexistent—unless the experience of expulsion or the promptings of individual conscience rendered them so. The values held by many educated women—egalitarianism, internationalism, and pacifism—were directly opposed to the politics of the Nazis. Moreover, women's emancipation was regarded by right-wing ideologists as the cause of racial degeneration; in particular, academic women without children were targets of calumny. In the first year of the National Socialist regime two laws directed against academic women were passed: one limited the number of women students at the universities to 10 percent, and the Law on Reinstatement of the Permanent Civil Service (Gesetz zur Wiedereinführung des Berufsbeamtentums) made it possible to discharge married women, so-called double earners, from state service. Without exception, this second law applied to women who were of Jewish descent or married to Jews. In the twelve years of the Nazi regime eight of the fourteen women lecturers at the University of Berlin were forced to resign or to emigrate for political or "racial" reasons. Elisabeth Schiemann and Lise Meitner were among them.[19]

---

[16] The Nazis echoed the conservative rhetoric of authenticity and mixed in a nationalist—*völkischer*—ideology, making it difficult for conservatives to pinpoint differences from their own positions. To the modernists the Nazis promised a renewed nation that would make effective use of social management techniques, technology, and science, specifically biology and eugenics (although the goals of the two groups might have been different). On the sciences see Ute Deichmann, *Biologen unter Hitler: Vertreibung, Karrieren, Forschung* (Frankfurt/New York: Campus, 1992); Benno Müller-Hill, *Tödliche Wissenschaft: Die Aussonderung von Juden, Zigeunern und Geisteskranken 1933–1945* (Reinbek bei Hamburg: Rowohlt, 1984); Monika Renneberg and Mark Walker, *Science, Technology, and National Socialism* (Cambridge: Cambridge Univ. Press, 1993); and Weingart et al., *Rasse, Blut und Gene* (cit. n. 7).

[17] See Schmidt-Waldherr, *Emanzipation durch Professionalisierung?* (cit. n. 14), pp. 41–62; and Robert Proctor, *Racial Hygiene: Medicine under the Nazis* (Cambridge, Mass./London: Harvard Univ. Press, 1988), pp. 118–130. However, the Nazi combination of misogyny and racism could seem attractive to women (of the "correct" race) because of the policy of pronatalism, and even a few feminist interpretations of race elitism sprang up. See Gudrun-Axeli Knapp, "Frauen und Rechtsextremismus: 'Kampfgefährtin' oder 'Heimchen am Herd'?" in *Nationalsozialismus und Moderne*, ed. Harald Welzer (Tübingen: Diskord, 1993), pp. 208–239.

[18] The acceptance of "a party which is likewise a combat unit against the citizenship of women" (Gertrud Bäumer) was not possible, but women in these groups were unable to come to agreement on an appropriate form of resistance; see Schmidt-Waldherr, *Emanzipation durch Professionalisierung?* For an overview on women in the National Socialist state see Lerke Gravenhorst and Carmen Tatschmurat, eds., *TöchterFragen: NS-Frauengeschichte* (Freiburg: Kore, 1990); see also Gisela Bock, *Zwangssterilisation im Nationalsozialismus: Studien zur Rassenpolitik und Frauenpolitik* (Opladen: Westdeutscher, 1986).

[19] See Ulla Bock and Dagmar Jank, *Studierende, lehrende und forschende Frauen in Berlin: 1908–1945 Friedrich-Wilhelms-Universität zu Berlin; 1948–1990 Freie Universität Berlin* (Berlin: Universitätsbibliothek Freien Univ. Berlin, 1990); and Kristine von Soden, "Zur Geschichte des Frauenstudiums," in *70 Jahre Frauenstudium—Frauen in der Wissenschaft*, ed. Soden and Gabi Zipfel (Cologne, 1979), pp. 9–42.

RISKING A CAREER: MORALITY

In 1934 Schiemann wrote an exhaustive obituary note on Erwin Baur that highlighted his work in genetics. From their eighteen years of collaboration she knew well both his field of research and his style of administration. He had been her doctoral advisor, and afterward she became his first assistant at the Institute for Heredity and Breeding Research (Institut für Vererbungs- und Züchtungsforschung), established in 1914. After 1921 she held a tenured position as senior assistant, and her tasks brought her into contact with the whole range of research techniques.[20] Schiemann was responsible for the experimental equipment and, in particular, the plant collections. She conducted the practical investigations of the students, supervised the research of younger colleagues, lectured on plant breeding and the genetics of cultivated plants, and helped organize the Fifth International Congress on Genetics, held in Berlin in 1927. The theoretical basis of the breeding experiments was found in the genetic methods of hybridization and selection. The institute's research program was strongly oriented toward the atomistic approach and experimental pragmatism of the American geneticists who had created the basic structure of classical genetics through a synthesis of cytology and Mendelian factor analysis. T. H. Morgan's theory on chromosomes was taken up promptly as well.[21] (See Figure 2.)

Baur was clearly a representative of the new generation of scientists in Germany. He was one of the innovative young men who built their careers as they built a new science.[22] Schiemann frankly acknowledged the importance of Baur in her academic career. She presented him as a versatile personality, a gripping and resourceful teacher whose strength lay less in routine work than in an "intuitive understanding of the essential." Like his research, his management style was innovative: he constantly reinforced his connections to agricultural associations, to the breeding industry, and to government authorities. In his attempt to utilize scientific genetics, Baur did not limit himself to breeding research on plants and animals. Like many other physicians and biologists of his generation, he saw eugenics as the application of Mendel's laws to society and applied hereditary laws to the human population. At the beginning of

---

[20] For the obituary see Elisabeth Schiemann, "Erwin Baur," *Ber. Deut. Bot. Gesell.*, 1934, *3*(2):51–114. My information on Baur is drawn from this essay unless otherwise noted. The general information on Schiemann's career presented in this paragraph comes from Kuckuck, "Elisabeth Schiemann" (cit. n. 1); Lang, "Elisabeth Schiemann" (cit. n. 1); Elisabeth Schiemann, "Erinnerungen an meine Berliner Universitätsjahre," in *Studium Berolinense: Gedenkschrift der Westdeutschen Rektorenkonferenz und der Freien Universität Berlin zur 150. Wiederkehr des Gründungsjahres der Friedrich-Wilhelms-Universität zu Berlin* (Berlin: De Gruyter, 1960), pp. 845–856; and Schiemann, "Autobiographie," *Nova Acta Leopoldina*, 1959, *143*:291–292.

[21] Harwood underscores the political significance of this congress, the first international scientific congress to be held in Germany after the war; see Harwood, *Styles of Scientific Thought* (cit. n. 9), p. 239. Baur's institute resembled American genetics centers in organizational aspects as well; see *ibid.*, pp. 41, 160.

[22] In 1908 he took the initiative, with others, in founding the *Journal of Inductive Evolutionary and Hereditary Theory* (*Zeitschrift für Induktive Abstammmungs- und Vererbungslehre*), and he was a founding member of the German Society for Genetics (Deutsche Gesellschaft für Vererbungswissenschaft). In 1911 his book *Introduction to Experimental Genetics* (*Einführung in die experimentelle Vererbungslehre*) was published and he succeeded in gaining his own institute. Baur's main research objects were snapdragons; his goal, to produce a gene chart of antirrhinum paralleling Morgan's gene chart of the fruit fly, was achieved in the late 1920s. He then started work with Max Delbrück, N. W. Timofeeff-Ressovsky, and K. G. Zimmer that led to a systematic interpretation of gene mutations and to molecular genetics.

Figure 2. Lise Meitner (standing) and Elisabeth Schiemann in the garden of the Institute for Heredity and Breeding Research in Berlin-Dahlem. (Courtesy of Churchill Archives, Cambridge.)

the twentieth century such ideas were commonplace in political thought, in Germany as elsewhere, on both left and right. But with the institutionalization and professionalization of eugenics after the war came a shift toward more conservative and authoritarian politics; social criticism directed toward improving the lot of the lower classes was replaced by a biological rhetoric aimed at halting national degeneration.[23] Baur's writings and political activities reflect this development. "He compared the German Empire to an antirrhinum-Volk—a nation of snapdragons. Its composition was equivalent to the population resulting from crossing three or four varieties of snapdragons." Baur's diagnosis was that negative selection was threatening the existence of the nation's elite and that measures had to be taken to weed out degenerated population stocks. In a text entitled "The Decline of the Cultivated Nations

---

[23] Schiemann, "Erwin Baur" (cit. n. 20), p. 63. Gisela Bock has described the widespread interest in applying Mendelian laws to human populations as "thinking in hereditary norms [*Denken in Erbwerten*]"; see Bock, *Zwangssterilisation im Nationalsozialismus* (cit. n. 18), p. 40. See also Paul Weindling, *Health, Race, and German Politics between National Unification and Nazism, 1870–1945* (Cambridge: Cambridge Univ. Press, 1989), pp. 399–487; and Weindling, "Weimar Eugenics: The Kaiser Wilhelm Institute for Anthropology, Human Heredity, and Eugenics in Social Context," *Annals of Science*, 1985, 4:303–318.

from a Biological Viewpoint," first published in 1922 and issued again in 1932, he drew on Oswald Spengler's ideas, which were popular in conservative and right-wing circles.[24] He presented a mixture of eugenics views that denigrated urban life and advocated agricultural self-sufficiency as the basis of a planned national economy. Baur combined nationalism, social progress, and biology in a fashion typical for postwar conservatives: biology should dictate national values and be a guide to future legislation, circumventing the chaos of party politics.

Schiemann did not question or object to Baur's views on eugenics.[25] But although she, too, belonged to the cultural elite and held a conservative political stance in general, two important features of her thinking and her behavior distinguish her from Baur: the role of biology in her understanding of cultural and social developments and her pronounced rejection of National Socialism. Both features emerged as the result of the course her career took in the late 1920s.

While Schiemann was collecting information for the obituary of Baur she received several letters that expressed surprise that she had agreed to write the article.[26] Why? She had worked with him for most of his professional life and might have seemed the obvious choice. What had happened?

During 1928, preparations were under way at the Dahlem institute for the establishment of the new Kaiser Wilhelm Institute for Breeding Research in Müncheberg, which was to be headed by Baur. Schiemann had helped plan this new institute and was responsible for moving the extensive collections from Berlin-Dahlem. On 29 September the institute in Müncheberg opened. However, the original plan to place Schiemann in a tenured Kaiser Wilhelm Institute membership post, as director of an independent department for the history of cultivated plants, was abandoned. Her appointment kept being postponed without explanation. After two years a heated argument over this issue terminated Baur and Schiemann's long-standing cooperation. In 1931 a relatively unknown and much younger male scientist was appointed Baur's successor in Berlin-Dahlem, in reaction to which Schiemann left the institute there. Moreover, she resigned her professorship at the Agricultural College of Berlin, which housed the institute, and had her rights to lecture transferred to the Friedrich Wilhelm University of Berlin. She found a place at the Botanical Museum in Berlin-Dahlem, but this unpaid post offered very limited possibilities for breeding and genetics experiments. During the next twelve years she intermittently obtained re-

---

[24] Weindling, *Health, Race, and German Politics*, p. 237; and Erwin Baur, "Der Untergang der Kulturvölker im Lichte der Biologie," *Deutschlands Erneuerung*, 1922, 6:257–268, rpt. in *Volk und Rasse*, 1932, 7:65–79. Spengler was the author of *The Decline of the West;* for the German original see Oswald Spengler, *Der Untergang des Abendlandes: Umrisse einer Morphologie der Weltgeschichte*, 2 vols. (Munich, 1919–1922). Baur expressed his views in Erwin Baur, Eugen Fischer, and Fritz Lenz, *Grundriß der menschlichen Erblichkeitslehre und Rassenhygiene* (Munich, 1920), which was later used by Nazi ideologues to back their "race theory." Baur had been a member of the Society for Eugenics since 1907; he later became chairperson of the Berlin branch and cooperated with the ministry of health and numerous other state agencies. He served as a consultant to the standing committee on eugenics and population affairs in the Prussian parliament and was influential in the establishment and staffing of the Kaiser Wilhelm Institute for Anthropology, Human Genetics, and Eugenics. See Weindling, "Weimar Eugenics."

[25] In 1934 she wrote: "Thus during the years of his collaboration in the eugenics movement great things had been achieved, and steady progress on carefully prepared ground had been set in motion, when the National Socialist revolution took charge of further developments." Schiemann, "Erwin Baur" (cit. n. 20), p. 107.

[26] These letters can be found in the Staatsbibliothek Preußischer Kulturbesitz Berlin, Handschriftensammlung, Nachlaß Elisabeth Schiemann (hereafter cited as **Nachlaß Elisabeth Schiemann**).

search scholarships from the Kaiser Wilhelm Institute for Biology, supported by its director, Fritz von Wettstein.[27]

Schiemann never expressed herself openly on her treatment by Baur. Neither did she completely hide the negative side of working with him: "Baur was . . . 'chemically clean of vanity'; he clung so little to his own ways of thinking that when he saw better ways he was quite prepared to change them, without inner inhibition. Yet he could forget that other people's fate had been determined by his work, and that they were then thrown off track."[28] Her case can be seen, in the first place, as discrimination because of her sex. In the early days Baur employed only women assistants: Schiemann, Gerda von Uebisch, Emmy Stein, and Luise von Graevenitz (some years later Paula Hertwig joined the staff). The first male colleague appointed was Hans Nachtsheim, in 1921. The Institute for Heredity and Breeding Research was not a university institute; rather, it was affiliated with the Agricultural College of Berlin. A decade later, when Baur headed the prestigious and well-equipped Kaiser Wilhelm Institute for Breeding Research in Müncheberg, things were very different, and he had left most of his female assistants behind. Despite the promising beginnings, it was virtually impossible during the Weimar era for a woman to pursue a successful academic career in genetics, whatever her qualifications. Only two women were appointed as full professors in any field—one in pedagogy, one in agriculture; both of these appointments came in 1923, when the economic crisis of the postwar period had abated somewhat. Because the establishment of a new discipline was hindered by the structure of German universities, geneticists had to apply for chairs in one of the traditional biological fields. Competition was particularly intense; specializing in the new field most often meant a position as an assistant at an institution of secondary importance.[29]

But there is more to Baur and Schiemann's disagreement than sex discrimination. She had embarked on a path contrary to the reductionist method of radiation genetics he favored, with its exclusive concentration on the decoding of the molecular structures of genes. Schiemann was aware of the philosophical questions prompted by developments in the sciences. As a student she had heard Oskar Hertwig lecture on the ethical, social, and political problems of Darwinism (he was very skeptical about the promises made by eugenics), Max Planck on positivism and the mechanistic approach toward nature, and Max Hartmann on causality. By combining new

---

[27] Most of the time her sister Gertrud Schiemann, a violinist, supported both of them; when she had no musical engagement Gertrud worked as a masseuse.

[28] Schiemann, "Erwin Baur" (cit. n. 20), p. 78. Others are peculiarly silent on this topic too. See Hans Stubbe, "Elisabeth Schiemann zum 70. Geburtstag," *Züchter*, 1951, 7/8:193–195; Lang, "Elisabeth Schiemann" (cit. n. 1); and Kuckuck, "Elisabeth Schiemann" (cit. n. 1). Personality differences are put forward as an explanation for their breakup, if it is mentioned at all. Further inquiries have been made by Petra Hillmann and Helga Wackwitz, "Elisabeth Schiemann 1881–1972" (unpublished thesis, Carl von Ossietzky-Universität, Oldenburg); among the former assistants of Schiemann they interviewed, only the women would concede sex-based discrimination.

[29] On Baur's early assistants see Harwood, *Styles of Scientific Thought* (cit. n. 9), p. 202. On Mathilde Vaerting, the professor of pedagogy, see Theresa Wobbe, "Ein Streit um die Gelehrsamkeit: Die Berufung Mathilde Vaertings im politischen Konfliktfeld der Weimarer Republik," *Reihe: Berliner Wissenschaftlerinnen Stellen Sich Vor*, 1991, 8:3–30. On Margarethe von Wrangell, the professor of agriculture, see Margarethe von Wrangell, *Das Leben einer Frau 1876–1932: Aus Tagebüchern, Briefen und Erinnerungen dargestellt von Fürst Wladimir Andromikow* (Munich, 1936). For details on the difficulties of the new field in establishing itself in the universities see Jonathan Harwood, "National Styles in Science: Genetics in Germany and the United States between the World Wars," *Isis*, 1987, 78:390–414.

research methods in genetics, Mendelian factor analysis, cross-breeding experiments, hybridization, and selection with cytology, she saw a way to investigate the wealth of biological variations as the basis of both evolutionary development and agricultural practice.[30] She chose barley, other grains, and strawberries as her favorite research objects. In the late 1920s she became more and more interested in the development of cultivated plants from wild forms to present-day selective breeds. She was particularly interested in the history of grain, in tracing back its earliest forms and establishing the biological connection between wild and cultivated plants. This development could only be understood through work that integrated various biological methods and disciplines, including genetics, cytology, systematics, and plant geography. Schiemann was inspired by Nikolai Vavilov's gene center theory, which linked all these aspects "and states that the area where the greatest variety of a cultivated plant is found is also the area of origin and the place where its original wild form should be traced." This theory provided the basis for initiating various collection expeditions and extensive research on cultivated plant populations, which Schiemann followed with interest. At the Botanical Museum in Berlin-Dahlem she could at least continue her work in this field. Questions about the age, origin, and subsequent migration of plants led her to studies in prehistory, anthropology, and archaeology in a fascinating interdisciplinary research field that Meitner once described as "reading human cultural history in the diversity of existing cultivated plants." Schiemann's *The Development of Cultivated Plants* was published in 1932 and has since been recognized as one of the main books in this research field.[31]

Jonathan Harwood's distinction of two styles in genetics helps in situating Schiemann's approach. The pragmatists, among them leading American geneticists but also the group at Baur's institute, were characterized by their use of materialist terms, atomistic theory, and mechanistic explanations and by their strong focus on applied research. Most German biologists, particularly the older generation like Carl Correns, Fritz von Wettstein, and Richard Goldschmidt, were skeptical about this reductionism. Their understanding of genetics was much broader, and they advocated a comprehensive approach that stressed basic research on the role of the gene in evolutionary and embryonic development. Their efforts to study the contexts of hereditary processes and their choices of problems were based on a holistic understanding of nature that saw organisms not as random associations of individual parts

---

[30] Information on Schiemann's student years comes from Schiemann, "Erinnerungen" (cit. n. 20), pp. 846–847. On the combination of insights and techniques from various fields see Elisabeth Schiemann, "Die Rolle der natürlichen Auslese in der Pflanzenzüchtung," *Illustrierte Landwirtschaftliche Zeitung,* 1927, *36* (offprint).

[31] Elisabeth Schiemann, "Biologie, Archäologie und Kulturpflanzen," *Jahrbuch der Max-Planck-Gesellschaft* (Göttingen: Hubert, 1955), pp. 177–198, on p. 189; and Meitner to Elisabeth Schiemann, 23 Oct. 1956, Meitner Papers. See also Paula Hertwig, "Elisabeth Schiemann zum 75. Geburtstag," *Zeitschrift für Pflanzenzüchtung,* 1956, *2:*129–132. For the book see Schiemann, *Entstehung der Kulturpflanzen: Handbuch der Vererbungswissenschaften,* Vol. 3, ed. Erwin Baur and Max Hartmann (Berlin: Borntraeger, 1932). Schiemann also published some essays for the wider public. See, e.g., Schiemann, "Auf den Spuren der ältesten Kulturpflanzen," *Forschungen und Fortschritte,* 1933, *28:* 1–3; Schiemann, "Die Geschichte der Kulturpflanzen im Wandel der biologischen Methoden," *Saertryk af Botanisk Tidsskrift,* 1954, *51:*308–329; and Schiemann, "Biologie, Archäologie und Kulturpflanzen." A list of her publications can be found at the Archiv zur Geschichte der Max Planck-Gesellschaft, Berlin; a selection of her works is presented in Kuckuck, "Elisabeth Schiemann" (cit. n. 1), pp. 534–537.

but as *Wirkungsganzes*. As late as 1934, Paula Hertwig explained why many biologists still had reservations about the atomistic model of the chromosome: "This rejection [of the atomistic model] is mainly without experimental proof. It is, rather, based on the desire to find a holistic principle in organic development. It is the reluctance to understand organisms as aggregates of predispositions . . . whose total independence could not guarantee the unity" of the whole.[32]

Schiemann started her career in botany and genetics within an institute run along pragmatist lines, but she shared the attitudes toward science, culture, and politics of those who favored a comprehensive understanding of biology. Like other outsiders in the German academy, women were more likely to obtain posts in new disciplines and at less (or not yet) prestigious institutions like colleges of agriculture and engineering or in applied research institutes rather than at the established universities. But their social background and education often affiliated them with the dominant group of German scholars whose self-confidence and research programs were determined by ideas and values compatible with the classical humanistic conception of *Bildung*. These tensions that marked the situation of academic women in the postwar period increased with the political events that soon took place.

The rise of the Nazi regime to power in 1933 marked a turning point in the development of eugenics. In combination with anti-Semitism, it became the ideological foundation of the totalitarian state. The Nazis described their political policies as applied biology, and they could in fact use the latest findings in population genetics for their purposes.[33] The coordination of research strategies and social policy developed during the Weimar period was retained and refined; the administrative apparatus of health departments and welfare institutions became the efficient technocratic tools of the extermination policy.[34] No opposition to the sterilization laws or to Nazi racial policy formed among scientists. While only a few were as ready as Fritz Lenz to subordinate their research to the plans and conditions specified by the new rulers, most approved a political move to the right, as did Baur, or soon adapted to the new circumstances despite initial disapproval, as did Eugen Fischer. The conflicts that occurred between the Nazi regime and its scientists were arguments between competing authorities: frictions between different centers of power within academic

---

[32] Paula Hertwig, quoted in Weingart et al., *Rasse, Blut und Gene* (cit. n. 7), p. 334. On the two styles in genetics see Harwood, *Styles of Scientific Thought* (cit. n. 9). *Wirkungsganzes* means, roughly, "effect of the whole," but also refers to the structure of an entity. On this topic see Evelyn Fox Keller, *Refiguring Life: Metaphors of Twentieth-Century Biology* (New York: Columbia Univ. Press, 1995).

[33] See Proctor, *Racial Hygiene* (cit. n. 17), p. 64. The Nazis were unconcerned as to whether they appealed to work of scientists who actively supported them or of those who ran into difficulties because of their criticism of the regime—like Paula Hertwig, for whom Schiemann wrote a letter of recommendation to Hermann Boehm, Reichsführerschule der deutschen Ärzteschaft, 17 Feb. 1940, Nachlaß Elisabeth Schiemann. To the Nazis, the invisibility of genetic defects over many generations meant that practically everyone could be suspected of carrying hereditary diseases or "racial inferiority." This concern led to the plan of registering and controlling the genotype of the entire population. This point has been stressed by Karl Heinz Roth, "Schöner neuer Mensch: Der Paradigmenwechsel der klassischen Genetik und seine Auswirkungen auf die Bevölkerungsbiologie des 'Dritten Reiches,'" in *Der Griff nach der Bevölkerung: Aktualität und Kontinuität nazistischer Bevölkerungspolitik,* ed. Heidrun Kaupen-Haas (Nördlingen: Greno, 1986), pp. 11–63.

[34] This process has been described by Ludger Weß, *Die Träume der Genetik: Gentechnische Utopien von sozialem Fortschritt* (Nördlingen: Greno, 1989); and Weindling, *Health, Race, and German Politics* (cit. n. 23), pp. 441–533.

politics, or wranglings over status between the conservative first generation of geneticists and their successors, to whom the Nazis offered a career boost. The Nazis remained suspicious toward scientists who insisted on the precedence and independence of their expertise and their departments. However, the very fact that the earlier critiques of eugenics had been limited to genetic and biological controversies, never superseding the scientific context, facilitated the reconciliation of biological theory and Nazi race ideology.

The belief that "pure" and "free" science was by definition ethical was shared by Harwood's "comprehensives" and "pragmatists," though their understanding of ethics differed. Whereas the comprehensive ideal saw the ethics of scientific work in its presumed betterment of the German nation and humanity as a whole, modernist reductionism completely stripped science of any concern with social norms or political interests. Ironically, this very disconnectedness from political conflicts, particular social relations, and concrete moral responsibilities meant that "doing science" led to an involvement with the politics of destruction and extermination. The majority of German scientists continued their research under the Nazis as if nothing had changed. Biological and genetics research in Germany during the 1930s met international standards and was funded by the Rockefeller Foundation until 1942. Conservatives contributed to the rhetoric of a national German science. However, in the end modernists proved even more effective for the purposes of the state apparatus and in preparations for war. The role of science in the discourse on eugenics and the professionalization of the eugenics movement initiated a dismissal of morality that allowed the incorporation of many scientists into the Nazi power apparatus—which thereby made the modernization of social management and the use of modern science an integral part of its practice.[35]

During the difficult years at the end of the 1920s Schiemann had become a committed member in the Dahlem congregation of the Protestant Church. After the Nazis came to power, they demanded enforcement of "Aryan laws" within the church itself. Those who refused to abide by this demand formed the Confessional Church (Bekennende Kirche). Schiemann spoke against anti-Semitic attitudes that arose even in the Confessional Church itself. She criticized the church for condemning state intervention into its internal affairs while otherwise acknowledging the legitimacy of the Nuremberg Laws.

> The state takes for itself the right to decide what divine order is, namely: blood, race (specie), soil, and nation. The church accepts this decision, declares that it is not binding for the realm of the church, but allows it in the realm of the state.... Thus the church sanctions all the injustice which is committed in the name of this decision.... The definition of people is wrong! For me, for the church in Germany, these baptized people [she meant Christians of so-called non-Aryan descent] are German people. This is where the question arises, May I and may the church draw a limit at these baptized persons?... Who then is my neighbor?... To the question: who does not understand the intentions of the state? I have to answer as a member of the Christian (B.K.) church: me.[36]

---

[35] The studies I have cited on science under the Nazi regime have shown various aspects of this transformative process.

[36] Elisabeth Schiemann to Martin Niemöller, 4 Mar. 1936, Nachlaß Martin Niemöller, Zentralarchiv der Evangelischen Kirche in Hessen und Nassau. For an extensive account of the formation of the Confessional Church see Kurt Meyer, *Der evangelische Kirchenkampf*, 3 vols. (Göttingen:

Her tone is clearly impatient when she discusses the biological arguments of "race theory": "this flood of confusing dilettantism that has been poured over our nation." In an open letter to priests of the Confessional Church she states that not the "purity of race," as Linnaeus could perhaps still have claimed, but, rather, general change and transformation is the main natural law of biology. Variability is the precondition of development, and it originates only from "mixing." "And thus it is an old and outdated notion, just like the one of heaven and earth, if one takes the story of the Bible literally: each according to his own destiny."[37] In her academic writings Schiemann never draws an analogy between human society and biological heredity. Rather, her approach to "The Relationship between the Phylogeny of Human Races and That of Cultivated Plants" (as the title of one of her articles puts it) is determined by interdisciplinary considerations that take genuine historical perspectives into account. She did not adjust her method of working or her convictions to suit the new doctrines. At the university she expressed her views against the "race theory," even if she stood alone. One of her former students recalls that during a meeting organized by students, "only Schiemann got up and stated, with a clear although slightly breaking voice—as was her wont in times of great stress or passion—that we should acknowledge the contributions of different peoples to German culture and science—French, Italian, and 'Yes, let us say it clearly, the Jews.'"[38]

By the time the Nazis took power Schiemann had become an outsider in the scientific community. Not only was she excluded from the important institutional and informal networks of her profession; she also stood apart from the lack of moral concern—even abandonment of hopes and ideals—that spread among her colleagues. Her public statements against the Nazi regime constrained her professional situation even further, and in 1940 her right to teach at the Friedrich Wilhelm Universität in Berlin was revoked on political grounds.

Schiemann had found her own independent and very particular response to the Nazis' policies by relating science and ethics. In our attempt to understand how she brought her fascination with modern biology and her beliefs about acting responsibly into professional and social relations into thoughtful consistency, Harwood's distinction of two styles of thought again is helpful. The two groups of geneticists differed in other than scientific aspects. Those who advocated a comprehensive approach held to the traditional cultural and ethical values of the German educated middle classes. They can be characterized by the breadth of their interests and their knowledge not only of their own discipline but also of philosophy, history, and fine

---

Vandenhoeck & Ruprecht, 1976–1984). Schiemann suffered from gastric disease at the end of the 1920s, and in their private correspondence during this time Meitner often asks about her health.

[37] Elisabeth Schiemann to Niemöller, 4 Mar. 1936. The letter contains a typescript, from which this quotation is taken. Martin Niemöller went to prison in 1937 and spent the following years in concentration camps; see Wolfgang Gerlach, "Vom Seeteufel zum Friedensengel: U-Bootskommandant, Freikorpsoffizier, Pastor, Widersacher Hitlers, KZ-Häftling, Gewissen der Nation," *Zeit,* 3 Jan. 1992, pp. 33–34. Another well-known cleric who resisted the Nazis is Dietrich Bonhoeffer, who was hanged in Flossenbrück, a concentration camp, on 9 Apr. 1945. The death sentence for high treason was abolished only in 1996; see Heinrich Wefing, "Gerechtigkeit für einen Gewissenstäter," *Zeit,* 12 Apr. 1996, p. 4. After World War II members of the Confessional Church were still notable for their democratic stance and engagement.

[38] Elisabeth Schiemann, "Beziehungen zwischen der Stammesgeschichte der Menschenrassen und der Kulturpflanzen," *Jahrbuch des Naturwissenschaftlichen Vereins für die Neumark,* 1931/1932, *3:*5–14; and Lang, "Elisabeth Schiemann" (cit. n. 1), p. 25.

arts; they espoused a general humanism that positioned itself "above politics" and had a distaste for modernization and democratization.[39]

Schiemann's outspoken opposition to anti-Semitism reveals her humanistic attitude toward personal relations. In her correspondence with Meitner, the wish "to help others" is a constant theme and an element of their mutual understanding. Schiemann's activities in the church were not restricted to theoretical debates; she taught biology to priests and laypeople, and her name is mentioned among those who helped Jews escape from Germany during the war.[40] She saw the anti-Semitism of the Nazis as a direct and manifest threat to the lives of many of her friends and colleagues, and to complete strangers as well. In 1937, a period when the two were especially close, Gertrud Schiemann's answer to a letter in which Elisabeth had given her an account of the conflicts in the Confessional Church reflects her sister's point of view: "By the way, you cannot count on Irmgard in these matters. She avoids everything that could cause her any internal or external problems. One reason why we had a breakup all of a sudden was that she could not stand being together with someone, whose different views she knew. Personally she is after all quite a disappointment to me."[41]

Variability was the key word that linked Elisabeth Schiemann's understanding of science and morality, just as it created a bridge between the two styles of biological thought with which she was affiliated. In her use of the notion, variability served as both a technical concept in her study of the history of cultivated plants and agricultural breeding practices and as a theoretical concept that enabled her to integrate her evolutionary theory and Mendelian genetics. Moreover, it served to broaden her view of the relation between knowledge and ethics in order "to realize the far-reaching nexus between what has been envisioned individually and what takes place in general, between the living and life."[42] This semantic linking of science, politics, and morality, as Schiemann transformed it into her own, stressed personal responsibility; however, because Schiemann—like the majority of the educated middle class—interpreted the comprehensive ideals as in opposition to politics, she had no perception of the power structures that lay behind the developments in the German nation and in German science.

A retreat into reminiscences about better times, an orientation toward the past, was the effect of such an apolitical stance. Elisabeth and Gertrud Schiemann sent congratulations on the sixtieth birthday of Kaiser Wilhelm II, who had long since

---

[39] "While the Institute for Biology under von Wettstein's directorship became a haven for dissidents, the events at Müncheberg during 1933 are a textbook example of the process of Gleichschaltung (forced alignment)"—notwithstanding, as Jonathan Harwood also notes, the political diversity within Erwin Baur's staff; see Harwood, *Styles of Scientific Thought* (cit. n. 9), p. 219.

[40] Schiemann mentioned her teaching of biology in her church in Elisabeth Schiemann to Niemöller, 4 Mar. 1936. A note indicating that she held a seminar for women in the church on 6 June 1938 and a manuscript for a talk on this topic can be found in the Nachlaß Elisabeth Schiemann. There is no evidence as to whether Schiemann helped Jews leave Germany. Some of those I interviewed in preparing this essay mentioned it. I find the suggestion credible because of her ongoing friendship with some members of the Bekennende Kirche, about which a letter from Dr. Ekkehard Loerbroks, dated 23 Apr. 1993, has informed me.

[41] Gertrud Schiemann to Elisabeth Schiemann, 30 Apr. 1937, Nachlaß Elisabeth Schiemann. The phrase I have translated as "personally" is "in menschlicher Beziehung," which also has the sense of "with regard to humaneness."

[42] Schiemann, "Erwin Baur" (cit. n. 20), p. 58.

lost power. When she met former friends on a trip to the southwest of Germany, Gertrud Schiemann wrote to her sister:

> Oettingen is strongly disposed "pro," although he loathes everything except the Jew-baiting, in which he participates with full strength. But since he is no party member, and will not now be admitted, he won't get an important position. . . . The eldest son Eberhardt too is a physician and above all a raving Nazi. The 2nd, originally a lawyer, thereupon became a military man, much more critical. . . . This was in broad outline what I got to know. It is a strange feeling. . . . Somehow I saw all this . . . the Oettingens, like a hundred other people in those days [before World War I at her parents' house], served only as background decoration for the intellectual circle and the general sprightliness of life at that time. An unburdened and yet eventful life it was nevertheless, and wideness of mind formed its ground.[43]

In contrast, during the Nazi period the lives of these women were shaped by the experience of isolation, the spell of social coldness.

GETTING INVOLVED WITH POLITICS

"I had exactly one and a half hours to pack, to leave Germany after thirty-one years." In July 1938 Lise Meitner finally was forced to flee. Many of her friends and colleagues had left after April 1933, when the new regime passed the Law on Reinstatement of the Permanent Civil Service, which resulted in the dismissal of all "non-Aryans" and other unwelcome persons from academic positions, or after passage of the Nuremberg Laws in September 1935. By 1938 Germany had lost a substantial portion of its leading scientists—10 percent of the professors and other scholars in biology, about 60 percent of the nuclear physicists.[44] Meitner had hesitated for a long time, hoping that the "nightmare" of National Socialism would soon come to an end. When she escaped from Germany she could take along nothing more than a small suitcase. She was sixty years old.

Meitner had come to Berlin as a young physicist in 1907 to attend Planck's lectures in theoretical physics. After some negotiating, the director of the Institute of Chemistry, Emil Fischer, agreed to allow her to cooperate with Otto Hahn in conducting experiments on beta rays and to investigate actinium C and thorium D, two radioactive products of atomic disintegration. Later, in 1912, she worked as an unpaid guest in Hahn's department in the brand new Kaiser Wilhelm Institute for Chemistry. At the same time she became Planck's assistant at the University of Berlin. A year later she was awarded a tenured research position at the Kaiser Wilhelm Institute, and by 1918 she headed her own department, where she further studied the characteristics of beta and gamma rays using the cloud chamber.

Though her career advanced steadily, Meitner was acquainted with the prejudices against academic women. When she arrived in Berlin she did not know that Prussian universities would not admit women. In Fischer's institute she was allowed only in the basement, where she and Hahn had their laboratory in the former woodwork

---

[43] Gertrud Schiemann to Elisabeth Schiemann, 13 June 1937, Nachlaß Elisabeth Schiemann.
[44] Kerner, *Lise, Atomphysikerin* (cit. n. 1), p. 82. On scientists leaving Germany see *ibid.;* and Deichmann, *Biologen unter Hitler* (cit. n. 16), p. 310. These numbers do not begin to indicate the damage to German intellectual life.

shop. From time to time she sneaked into the auditorium, where she listened to lectures from under the ascending seats. She had to live on the small amount of money that her family could spare. However, she recalled those early years without regret: "When our own work turned out well, we sang in two voices, mostly songs of Brahms. I could only hum, but Hahn had a very good singing voice. With the young colleagues of the nearby physics institute we had personally and scientifically a very good relationship. Often they came to visit us, sometimes entering through the window of the woodwork shop instead of taking the ordinary path. In short, we were young, cheerful and light-hearted, maybe politically too light-hearted."[45]

Meitner was the first female assistant at a Prussian university. Women in Prussia were given the right to teach at universities and to hold the title of professor in 1920; in 1922 Meitner became the fourth woman to qualify. During these years she succeeded in achieving most of her goals. Her friendship with Schiemann, however, taught her that her case was exceptional. When she became a member of the board of the German Association of Academic Women in 1930, Meitner was leading her own research department at a prestigious institute, teaching at the University of Berlin, and had become a well-respected member of the international nuclear physics community.[46] She had already been nominated, together with Hahn, for the Nobel Prize in chemistry.

Meitner's situation changed dramatically in 1933. In July she was suspended from the university, and in September she was put out of her lectureship altogether. After 1936 public appearances became impossible, even at a colloquium held by a colleague she knew personally. For the moment she was protected from real danger by her Austrian citizenship. She could continue her research at the Kaiser Wilhelm Institute for Chemistry, where her colleagues remained helpful and supportive. She had considered resigning her professorship and had thought about leaving Germany, but colleagues and friends, especially Planck, had convinced her to stay on. Moreover, she had started another project with Hahn in 1934. After reading about Enrico Fermi's new experiments and his plan to discover new artificial elements, the transuraniums, she convinced Hahn that they too should begin bombarding uranium with neutrons. Fritz Straßmann joined them in this work a year later.

After the annexation of Austria in March 1938 Meitner's situation became imminently dangerous. She now counted as a German Jew, and so the racial laws affected her directly. In addition, a Nazi at the institute had started making trouble. At the end of June, her fear that she would not be allowed to leave Germany was confirmed. The Nazis did not want well-known Jews to travel abroad and would make no exception in her case. Hasty preparations, kept absolutely secret, for flight began. Her Dutch colleague Dirk Coster came to Berlin to pick her up, having already arranged with the Dutch border officials that she could enter the country without a visa. Meitner spent her last night in Berlin with the Hahns. The next day she was lucky in that no SS control was on her train; from Groningen she telegraphed to Berlin the code word that signaled her safe arrival. During a visit in Copenhagen Niels Bohr asked her to stay at his institute, but she decided to go to Stockholm.

---

[45] Kerner, *Lise, Atomphysikerin,* p. 37.

[46] Schiemann qualified as a professor in 1924. On Meitner's joining the board of the association see *Rundschreiben des Deutschen Akademikerinnenbundes,* 2 July 1930, Landesarchiv Berlin, Helene Lange-Archiv.

During the following months Hahn and Meitner exchanged letters about the continuation of their experiments in Berlin-Dahlem. Before the Christmas holidays she received word that Hahn and Straßmann had found the chemical element barium by bombarding uranium. Working with her nephew, Otto Robert Frisch, she correctly interpreted the results of the experiments as nuclear fission and theoretically calculated the enormous amount of energy that was set free. In February 1939 their article was published; but Meitner did not feel altogether confident about the outcome of these matters. She had helped to pave the way to a success she could not share, and she feared that others would see her part in the collaboration as unimportant.[47]

In fact, the director of the Nobel institute in Stockholm, Manne Siegbahn, accepted her only with great reservations. To Meitner's disappointment, he agreed to give her a job but provided her with no assistants and very little research equipment. She lived the life of a refugee. With very little money, staying in a hotel, she had to wait almost a year until her belongings were sent from Berlin. When they arrived, she found that many of her books had been confiscated and that the furniture was badly damaged. Her family had left Vienna and was scattered over the United States and Europe, though a sister, Gustl Frisch, had come to Sweden with her husband. Meitner's past life in Germany began to slip away. By writing letters and sending parcels she kept in contact with her friends and colleagues and tried to counter the increasing estrangement. At least once a month she wrote to Schiemann. The letters were short, for there was not much to tell. Meitner felt lonely and depressed and was constantly tired and prone to colds. "What shall I write? What the day brings me superficially has become so irrelevant, and unimportant, I can't sit down and tell it. It means almost nothing to me anymore." Or: "My very own life has the substance = zero. Unfortunately I hear very little from friends . . . and at the same time one always sits and waits longingly for news."[48]

Elisabeth Schiemann had been deeply shocked when she had come to visit Meitner only a few days after her flight and found the house empty. She then learned from Hahn what had happened: "What I do know now! what I did foresee long since! and what indeed has become inconceivable reality." She walked through the garden and the house, packed away some of the books, and talked to the housemaid. Together with Hahn she oversaw the transportation of Meitner's belongings to Sweden. At least once a month she wrote a long letter to her friend, trying to make her feel connected with goings-on in Berlin. Five years later, in summer 1943, she could happily inform Meitner of her appointment at the Kaiser Wilhelm Institute for Research on Cultivated Plants (Kaiser Wilhelm Institut für Kulturpflanzenforschung), where she would have her own department for the history of cultivated plants. "It is strictly speaking precisely what B[aur] laid into my hands in 1928, in order to take it away from me one year later. Since then I have grown fifteen years older, and the times have not exactly made such work easier to begin."[49] Schiemann was sixty-two, and it had been a bad year so far. Berlin was often the target of bomb attacks, and the offices at the Botanical Garden had been severely damaged and partly burned

---

[47] For details see Ruth Sime, "13. Juli 1938: Lise Meitner verläßt Deutschland," in *Das Geschlecht der Natur: Feministische Beiträge zur Geschichte und Theorie der Naturwissenschaften,* ed. Barbara Orland and Elvira Scheich (Frankfurt, 1995), pp. 119–135.
[48] Meitner to Elisabeth Schiemann, 29 Nov. 1938, 30 Oct. 1939, Meitner Papers.
[49] Elisabeth Schiemann to Meitner, 24 July 1938, 25 July 1943, Meitner Papers.

down. During the spring she had been in the hospital, later spent time at a spa, and still had not fully regained her health.

Schiemann welcomed the new opportunity. The institute was located in Tuttenhof, not far from Vienna; she would have to move to Austria. "And yet it lies heavy on me, that I cannot come to you with all my *personal* questions for this new future—it probably will be the rest of my life. Do you know, do you feel, what this will mean to me and how this is now circling simultaneously in all my thoughts?" Meitner's response was double edged:

> That you miss talking with me about your personal questions connected with the new post, I gratefully value as an expression of your amicability; however, whether I could have been useful to you? If I refrain from sharing the joy that you are allowed to realize long-planned work and to count on a glad future, it is because affairs have a completely different aspect for me. I see only the grave, . . . a grave that contains everything that has given formation and joy to my former life.

Schiemann felt misunderstood:

> What I wrote about Vienna, *that* should have said something *completely* different than what you heard—and that nearly hurts me! That you believe that matters would have a completely different aspect for you than for me! Exactly *this* I have meant to say: that for me all this has an edge because it has to be without you.—No, really *no,* I did *not* mean to express regret that you cannot give me useful advice. I thought it would be enough for you to understand me when I say that I miss you:—too, I *cannot* say more and if you don't always have this in mind, you will misunderstand anything. I could tell you about my future work and the preparations now and later. Should I wait until we could speak our minds in person? Shouldn't it also be possible, *without* saying everything—which after all just now, as long as the border lies between us, is not possible—to *understand,* because we ought to know each other, that such a thoughtless passing through life, as you believe me capable of, couldn't by any means be possible between us. It is my request—and may it dare be my Christmas wish—that you credit me with a somewhat more loving and sympathetic heart.[50]

Censorship prevented any further communication on this point. Schiemann's letters to Meitner in 1944 tell about the friends that have been bombed out, about moving her research materials from Berlin to the new institute, about the autumn crops in Austria, and about her plan to start living there at the beginning of the next season.

The following spring the war came to an end. Meitner could now articulate her views more clearly, and she touched upon responsibility for the terrors of the National Socialist regime. She expected her German friends, finally, to take a stand. "I have listened to many discussions in Sweden, America, and England. . . . Many of us scientists, including myself, had hoped that German scientists, who had really remained free of Nazi ideology, would express publicly their regret about the horrific events and their wish to repair what was left to repair." She had learned to see Germany from the outside and had come to the opinion "that it was not only stupid, but also a great injustice, that I did not leave immediately . . . because in the last resort I had supported Hitlerism by staying on." Schiemann did not understand her. She recognized only issues of personal morality and could not follow Meitner's political

---

[50] Elisabeth Schiemann to Meitner, 17 Oct. 1943; Meitner to Elisabeth Schiemann, 25 Oct. 1943; and Elisabeth Schiemann to Meitner, 12 Dec. 1943, Meitner Papers.

views about complicity in a totalitarian system of injustice. She maintained the distinction between political participation and doing science; indeed, she did not see the strategy behind the foundation of an institute for research on cultivated plants by the Nazi administration. The Tuttenhof institute had been part of a general plan to expand the Third Reich far into the east; its purpose was to acquire the knowledge that they assumed would be necessary to improve agriculture there when the "master race" (*Herrenrasse*) would take over, after the extermination of the Jews.[51]

In the spring of 1945 the Allied forces occupied Germany. Travel became almost impossible, and the institutional structure of German science disintegrated. The Tuttenhof institute fell into the Soviet zone of occupation and was dissolved.[52] In July Meitner sent an advertisement to the German Red Cross in Berlin asking for news of Elisabeth Schiemann and her sister Gertrud.

Meitner continued her efforts to maintain the friendships from her past. In December 1946 the Hahns were her guests in Stockholm. Hahn was being honored with the Nobel Prize in chemistry for the discovery of nuclear fission—a clear injustice to Meitner and Straßmann, whose parts in the experiments and in formulating the theoretical interpretation were ignored. Not surprisingly, the reunion was not altogether a happy one. But the subject of conflicts between Meitner and Hahn was not the Nobel Prize but, rather, politics. She could not accept that he deflected any discussion of Germany's crimes, pointing instead to the Allies, especially the Americans, for the production and detonation of the atomic bomb. She reported in a letter to James Franck: "Forgetting the past and instead stressing the injustice that is being done to Germany. Since I am a part of the past to be repressed, Hahn has not mentioned our long cooperation or even my name in those interviews in which he talked about his life's work."[53]

COMING TO TERMS THROUGH SCIENCE

For most of 1947 Elisabeth Schiemann was in England at the invitation of the Commonwealth Bureau of Plant Breeding and Genetics, which collected studies on agriculture from all parts of the world. She was glad for the chance to close the gap in her knowledge of scientific developments outside of Germany. In May Lise Meitner visited London and they had the chance to see each other again, nine years after Meitner's flight from Berlin. Despite their intense exchange of letters over the years, the meeting between the two women was disappointing for both of them. Meitner was the first to comment on this: "I have thought a lot about our meeting in London. Maybe it would have been better if we had been less cautious with each other and had talked more frankly to each other. Persons who are connected through a long

---

[51] Meitner to Elisabeth Schiemann, 3 Nov. 1946, Meitner Papers; and Meitner to Otto Hahn, in Kerner, *Lise, Atomphysikerin* (cit. n. 1), p. 76. On the founding of the Tuttenhof institute see Hans Stubbe, *Bericht über die im Auftrage des OKW und des Reichsforschungsrats durchgeführte zweite biologische Forschungsreise nach dem Peleponnes und nach Kreta 1942*, Archiv zur Geschichte der Max Planck-Gesellschaft; for the "Generalplan Ost" in general see Mechthild Rössler, *"Wissenschaft und Lebensraum": Geographische Ostforschung im Nationalsozialismus* (Hamburg: Reimer, 1990).

[52] Its director, Hans Stubbe, moved with the remaining staff and materials to Gatersleben, in the former German Democratic Republic.

[53] Meitner to James Franck, 16 Jan. 1946, in Kerner, *Lise, Atomphysikerin* (cit. n. 1), p. 111. Franck was a former colleague in Berlin-Dahlem who had emigrated to the United States in 1933. As Renate Feyl has remarked, Meitner's "work was crowned with the Nobel Prize for Otto Hahn": Feyl, "Lise Meitner" (cit. n. 1), p. 162.

common experience, a tie that was a very valuable part of my life, can probably reach an understanding on problems which occupy them both very intensely, even if their points of view are partly very different." Schiemann was hurt; she had felt that Meitner was avoiding her company and her confidence. They had not met until Meitner's tenth day in London, and even then not privately. They talked about physics, traveling, and other neutral subjects. Schiemann could only interpret this as a personal rejection. "*This* was it, I suppose, what you express in saying we were too cautious with each other. And therefore I wish with my whole heart, that the new year will bring us together again once more, that we can really talk at leisure and perhaps even resume a conversation when we have slept on it overnight—to have a few days together! If that could be possible?"[54]

She would not try to vindicate herself. Instead, her sister Gertrud tried to clarify her standpoint for Meitner:

> I fear, the distrust that you show for the political attitude of your friends does not let you feel how much positive resistance Hahn and Elisabeth have offered during these dark twelve years, when every breath one took was protest. What it means, in a war that daily costs the life of dear friends, to hope for the victory of the enemy, that the evil may not gain domination—this is such a hard sorrow and I believe the most reliable proof, that two such warm patriots as those two are and ever were, were on the right side with their outlook and acted, both of them, during the years—which you have thank God not gone through here—without regard for themselves, whenever there was even a small expectation to be useful to others, or to work against the system. . . . Especially Elisabeth has matured inwardly and risen above herself. Her *entire* thinking was devoted to work on behalf of the persecutees and to emergency campaigns, and that has given her much worldly wisdom and stability, which she had previously often lacked.

Meitner wanted to understand the causal connections that led from Germany's past to the National Socialist regime. She was concerned not only with questions of personal guilt but with structural faults as well. She tried to explain this in a letter to Gertrud Schiemann, concluding: "My friends, Otto, Edith, surely also Elisabeth, think differently about it; for them the past is all over and done with. I was prepared for that and have known it for at least eight years. I have learned much in these years and obtained insight one cannot regret, even if it makes life somewhat more complicated."[55]

One legacy of the National Socialist period was an insurmountable and yet elusive division between victims and perpetrators. The extermination policy of the Nazis had left both sides speechless. One side had had experiences that were unspeakable; the other was silent in its guilt. Meitner's friends, even Schiemann, were unwilling to recognize the difference that resulted from the experience of being threatened by genocide. The absence of such acknowledgment cut short their appreciation for one another. Although the tensions between the two women later diminished, their one-time closeness was never restored; the estrangement could not be overcome simply by time. They kept in touch, informing each other of their whereabouts and goings-on. At Christmas 1946 Schiemann knew that she was appointed as a tenured profes-

---

[54] Meitner to Elisabeth Schiemann, 11 Aug. 1947; and Elisabeth Schiemann to Meitner, 1 Nov. 1947, Meitner Papers.

[55] Gertrud Schiemann to Meitner, 21 Mar. 1947; and Meitner to Gertrud Schiemann, 21 Jan. 1947, Meitner Papers.

sor, extraordinarius, at the University of Berlin, but reflected: "Doubtless in the future full professorships for women will not come into question." In December 1949 she celebrated the opening of "*my* little institute," the Research Unit for the History of Cultivated Plants (Forschungsstelle für Geschichte der Kulturpflanzen), in Berlin-Dahlem.[56] Retirement, only seven years later, was not easy for her since her institute was dissolved at the same time by the Max Planck Society (as the Kaiser Wilhelm Society was now called). Meitner, on the other hand, had been glad to stop working in Stockholm in 1954. It had never been the same as in Berlin. She became increasingly engaged in political questions concerning science, including the situation of women in science and the military use of nuclear energy. She had turned down offers of posts in Germany. Meitner had learned to accept the divide between herself and Germany—and the losses that came with it.[57] The intensity of her intimate friendship with Schiemann was one more casualty of the politics of National Socialism.

In order to analyze the context of Meitner's and Schiemann's lives and careers, it is helpful to take some recent and more general reflections on the history of science into consideration. The specific culture of modern science is produced through the combined use of instrumental, social, and writing technologies to establish "pure science" and to secure the separation of nature from society and the separation of science from moral responsibility and politics. It is the irony (and the antinomy) of both modernity and science that the very effort to enforce such separations creates multiple and powerful linkages, mixtures, and mediations between elements that are meant to stay isolated. The history of the sciences during the Nazi regime in Germany reveals many aspects of this hybrid quality of science. The attempt to distinguish science from ideology, rationality from its destructive results, basic research from applications, technological from social management, and so forth, is doomed to fail amid the entanglements of cognitive and institutional connections. But this was no isolated case; instead, the development of German science during this period should be seen as part of the process of modernization in science, especially in biology and in physics.

In post–World War II Germany the ideal of "pure science" holds a special ideological meaning: as a part of a semantic structure to negate the differences created by the Nazi extermination policy, a part of the silence that followed the war, and a part of the political foundations of the Federal Republic of Germany. However, this ideal could express other meanings as well—even meanings directly opposed to the mainstream understanding, as the cases of Schiemann and Meitner show. Schiemann had linked her scientific knowledge with an ethics of care and with her activities in the Confessional Church against the Nazis. Meitner had come to a universal humanism, hoping that science could be an agent in connecting people; from this standpoint she asked her friends to condemn the Nazis. Both women's positions were linked to their experience of otherness, of being different. But these were not the same differences, and they brought about correspondingly different shifts in the network of meanings: discrimination because of her sex had led Schiemann to an individual morality that prompted her to risk personal endangerment by speaking her mind and caring for others. The realities of exile required Meitner to think about her own

---

[56] Elisabeth Schiemann to Meitner, 26 Dec. 1946, 1 Jan. 1950, Meitner Papers.
[57] She remarked, "I feel like a mother who sees clearly—and helplessly—that her favorite child has turned out badly." See Kerner, *Lise, Atomphysikerin* (cit. n. 1), p. 100.

involvement with the social structures that had made her a victim. Both women represent, then, the double aspect of what Max Horkheimer has called the "feeling for morality": compassion and politics.[58] Thus the concept of "pure science" divided and united them at the same time, both linking them to and separating them from their surroundings. Schiemann and Meitner were limited in their reflections on their identity as scientists, their lifelong efforts to succeed as women in science, and their remaining fragile bond.

Lise Meitner and Elisabeth Schiemann shared the central ideals of their academic colleagues and yet gave them a new direction by posing their identification as scientists against their experiences facing discrimination as women and the threats of the Nazi regime. However, further connections between science, politics, and morality remained hidden to them. A subsequent generation of women, in a world deeply changed by World War II, came closer to recognizing these correlations, particularly in understanding their patriarchal dimensions. It is important to think in new ways about how science acquires its social meaning: the ambiguity of its rhetoric and appeals to facts can be employed for the purposes of domination and destruction as much as for emancipation and freedom. Science thus requires of its practitioners and students the "feeling for morality," that is, political ethics—both theoretical insight and individual responsibility—in a world that science itself has rendered too complex to be comprehended in a single framework.

---

[58] On Max Horkheimer's concept of moral and political responsibility see Mechthild Rumpf, *Spuren des Mütterlichen: Die widersprüchliche Bedeutung der Mutterrolle für die männliche Identitätsbildung in kritischer Theorie und feministischer Wissenschaft* (Frankfurt am Main: Materialis, 1989).

Which Science? Which Women?

By Margaret W. Rossiter*

AS IS EVIDENT FROM THE OTHER ARTICLES in this volume, historians of women in science like to study specific persons or groups at a particular time and place—nineteenth-century British botanists, twentieth-century American and Canadian archaeologists, or even a recent Nobel Prize–winning German biologist. Generally such studies reveal that the many fields or specialties within science were and are rather different—they grew up historically at various times and under somewhat different conditions, and each was shaped by various strong personalities, institutional settings, and job opportunities.[1] Each has its own "traditions," is more or less "crowded" in its supply of personnel and resources of various sorts, and has a different proportion of women in it.[2] Other work also suggests that circumstances and chronology (e.g., the importance of the two world wars) were different in countries outside the United States, about whose women we know very little.[3] Thus it is time to sort out what we do know and to set out some categories before we try to pull these case studies into some larger whole.

For the sake of argument here, I will claim that the single most important indicator or predictor of a woman's experience in science is the proportion, though changing over time, of women in her field or subfield. We all know in general that, because the women were often not where the men were, some portions of that collectivity called "science" have more women and higher proportions of them than others. In some fields this pattern has "always" been true; in others, especially in the United States, it is a product of recent affirmative action policies that have changed conditions rather dramatically in some fields and with certain consequences. Yet actual data for any period or country before the 1970s are hard to come by. Tables 1–3 are compiled from the 1956–1958 survey *American Science Manpower,* published by the National Science Foundation in 1961. This survey is imperfect, as most are, but it offers the most complete and most disaggregated data set of its time on scientific men and women. (It was based on questionnaires sent by eight American scientific

---

* Department of Science and Technology Studies, Cornell University, Ithaca, New York 14850.

[1] E.g., Gérard Lemaine, Roy MacLeod, Michael Mulkay, and Peter Weingart, eds., *Perspectives on the Emergence of Scientific Disciplines* (Paris: Mouton, 1976); and Loren Graham, Wolf Lepenies, and Peter Weingart, eds., *Functions and Uses of Disciplinary Histories* (Sociology of the Sciences Yearbook, 7) (Dordrecht/Boston: Reidel, 1983). One of the purposes of writing disciplinary history may be to write the women out of the story; see Margaret Rossiter, "The ~~Matthew~~ Matilda Effect in Science," *Social Studies of Science,* 1993, 23:425–441.

[2] Phyllis Holman Weisbard and Rima D. Apple, eds., *The History of Women and Science, Health, and Technology: A Bibliographic Guide to the Professions and the Disciplines,* 2nd ed. (Madison: Univ. Wisconsin System, Women's Studies Librarian, 1993), has 2,505 entries.

[3] See, e.g., Marianne Gosztonyi Ainley, ed., *Despite the Odds: Essays on Canadian Women and Science* (Montreal: Véhicule, 1990); and Farley Kelly, ed., *On the Edge of Discovery: Australian Women in Science* (Melbourne: Text Publishing, 1993).

Table 1. Number and Percentage of American Scientists, by Field and Sex, 1956–1958

Fields	Total	Men	Women	Percentage of Women
Other specialties	1,160	924	236	20.34
Psychology	11,073	9,026	2,047	18.49
Education	936	780	156	16.67
Biological sciences	18,015	15,701	2,314	12.84
Statistics	203	181	22	10.84
Mathematics	10,030	9,016	1,014	10.11
Astronomy	362	329	33	9.12
Geography	969	889	80	8.26
Medical sciences	1,918	1,799	119	6.20
Chemistry	35,805	33,891	1,914	5.35
Social sciences [economics]	418	398	20	4.78
Physics	12,702	12,391	311	2.45
Meteorology	2,136	2,088	48	2.25
Earth sciences	13,071	12,822	249	1.90
Engineering (chemical, sanitary, and other)	21,469	21,330	139	0.65
Agricultural sciences	9,598	9,561	37	0.39
Total/Average	139,865	131,126	8,739	6.25

SOURCE.—National Science Foundation, *American Science Manpower, 1956–58: A Report of the National Register of Scientific and Technical Personnel* (Washington, D.C.: Government Printing Office, 1961), pp. 80–83.

societies, institutes, and federations to their members and even nonmembers in late 1956. The numbers used here are based only on those responses by women who were employed full time—not the retirees, the part-timers, the students, or the unemployed—and we must assume that even these totals are largely an undercount.[4] Table 1 shows wide variation in the percentage of women practitioners among the

---

[4] National Science Foundation, *American Science Manpower, 1956–58: A Report of the National Register of Scientific and Technical Personnel* (Washington, D.C.: Government Printing Office, 1961), pp. vii, 33–34. The eight entities were the American Chemical Society, the American Geological Institute, the American Institute of Biological Sciences, the American Institute of Physics, the American Mathematical Society, the American Meteorological Society, the American Psychological Association, and the Federation of American Societies for Experimental Biology, which together accounted for "about 200 specialized societies." The U.S. Public Health Service also contributed its registry of sanitary engineers. As the requirements for membership varied with each society (some required doctorates), the comprehensiveness of the *American Science Manpower* data also varied, but NSF officials felt it best to leave the definitions to the societies. For more on the scientific manpower databases of the 1950s and 1960s see Margaret W. Rossiter, *Women Scientists in America: Before Affirmative Action, 1940–1972* (Baltimore: Johns Hopkins Univ. Press, 1995), Ch. 5 and pp. 538–540. Women chemists routinely gave up their membership in the American Chemical Society when they married a fellow chemist (*ibid.*, p. 98 n. 5). Counts of scientists based on the Earned Doctorate File at the National Research Council would omit scientists with only a master's degree, a situation affecting proportionally more women than men.

sixteen fields—from a high of over 20 percent in one down to fewer than 1 percent in two others. Most of the women scientists included, who are probably all retired and may well be deceased by now, were in a very few fields: just four large fields together accounted for 83.4 percent, or 7,289 of the 8,739 female respondents (biological sciences with 2,314, psychology with 2,047, chemistry with 1,914, and mathematics with 1,014). The twelve other sciences had very few women (though in a small field, even a tiny number of women could make up a respectable proportion of the whole: the 33 in astronomy and the 22 in statistics represented 9 percent and almost 11 percent of respondents in their respective fields).

As a prod to clearer thinking, I propose to break down these arbitrary percentages into three slightly overlapping levels of feminization and to characterize each with examples from the expanding literature on particular specialties. First would be those many fields where 8 percent of practitioners or fewer are women. These could be termed "peripheral" fields, in which there would be a cast of individuals with whom we are by now familiar: those known as the "exceptions," "firsts," "pioneers," and—more recently and cynically—"token" women in science. Here access to training and jobs would be the chief difficulty and would vary with the individual. In fact, many of the early lone women were the sisters, daughters, wives, or friends of men already in the field. Such personal connections might have favored a woman's entrance: since she was such an unusual case she could be accepted as a once-only non-precedent-setting exception that necessitated little further institutional change. (Take, for example, the well-connected anthropologist Jean McWhirt Pinkley, the first and for a long time the only woman scientist in the National Park Service. Widowed during World War II, Pinkley was soon hired by the Park Service, in which her father-in-law was a high official, and rose to the position of chief archaeologist of the Mesa Verde National Park. But she was not followed by other women scientists in the Park Service until the 1970s.[5]) It would have helped the first woman to have been an intrepid soul, either oblivious to the problems facing other women (for they were not affecting her) or, more likely, all too aware of them but unable to do anything about them. In many fields the early years were like this, and such stories make up much of the lore of the history of women in science. Before 1970 physics, earth sciences, engineering, and the agricultural sciences—those fields found at the bottom of Table 1—would have fit in this "peripheral" category. There would have been numerous bans and taboos as to what women could and could not do, hardly enough women for many of them to know each other, probably not even the interest or leadership to start a women's organization within the larger group. Recognition and advancement would have been very limited. Most fields in the United States have moved or are moving beyond this trace or pioneer stage, but some remain here, among them entomology and dental science, which has a strong military tradition.

Next would be those fields in which about 5 to 15 percent of participants are women. These areas offer a wider range of possibilities; they might be called "marginal" fields. This is the most interesting and most critical stage, because the women here are no longer just "firsts" but are faced with more possibilities, including some dangers. Access would at this stage be less of a problem (though still restricted in places); there would be more "second" and "third" women in the field; and some of the women here might have had more varied backgrounds and some career choices

[5] Chester A. Thomas, "Jean McWhirt Pinkley, 1910–1969," *American Antiquity,* 1969, *34*:471–473.

or job alternatives. These are fields where some women might know each other; they might form a committee on women or a separate society, in which some might become prominent. Such a club or forum for discussion might in fact be needed, because the women at this stage might be encountering problems and limitations with advancement and recognition. In addition, they would face one particular tension— the threat of incipient ghettoization, if indeed some had not already occurred. Seeing an increasing number and possibly a rising proportion of women entering the field, employers and potential mentors might fear its "tip" into a female enclave: they thus might be eager to find and designate as "womanly" one or a few employment areas, out of the path to any major recognition, to which women could be directed and that would contain them. Especially suitable areas or positions include those that might be designated as or called on attributes that could be construed as "womanly": jobs at women's colleges and those requiring invisible service work or skills were often stereotyped as feminine. Among women so relegated have been "computers," editors, chemical secretaries or librarians, technical writers, schoolteachers, assistants, and computer programmers.[6]

Most sciences in the United States in the 1950s and 1960s fell into this category, including in Table 1 the biological sciences, statistics, mathematics, astronomy, geography, the medical sciences, chemistry, and the social sciences (chiefly economics). Currently even more fields may be entering or are about to enter this stage, especially since many doors to entry-level jobs opened about twenty-five years ago. If these formerly young entrants are now at midcareer, they should be encountering stressful situations of middle management like the "glass ceiling" (a term coined— not coincidentally—in the early 1980s). They may be settling on a "Mommy track" or, when passed over for promotion or sexually harassed, opting for other less stressful or possibly more rewarding pursuits.[7]

Third, and finally, would be those subfields in which 15–40 percent—or even more—of the practitioners are women. These might be thought of as "participatory" fields, relatively feminized compared to other scientific fields, though women are still not near a majority. There would be occasional women leaders, but—chosen for their high standing in "men's work"—they would rarely be feminists. In fact, in some fields with relatively high percentages of women, enough to achieve a kind of "critical mass," many women leaders, rather than becoming more feminist or militant and possibly changing the field significantly, would shy away from such confrontation and become willing collaborators in antifeminism. They might even begin to have some doubts and ambivalences, feeling that it was "unnatural" for women to be so prominent (as did many members of the International Council of Women Psychologists in the United States in the late 1940s) and worrying that men were being *excluded* from positions of leadership, or even from the field itself. The solidarity they might have felt when their percentage was lower and their position somewhat imperiled might begin to wane and their all-female organizations fall into disarray, as their proportion of the total membership increased. Because women are

---

[6] See Toby A. Appel, "Physiology in American Women's Colleges: The Rise and Decline of a Female Subculture," *Isis*, 1994, 85:26–56; and Margaret W. Rossiter, "Chemical Librarianship: A Kind of 'Women's Work' in America," *Ambix*, 1996, 43:46–58.

[7] Anne E. Preston, "Why Have All the Women Gone? A Study of Exit of Women from the Science and Engineering Professions," *American Economic Review*, 1994, 84:1446–1462. I thank Mary Oates for a copy of this essay.

recently becoming more numerous and prominent in fields where they used to be scarce, we need to have more work on the situation in these newly feminized areas. Psychology continues to lead, as nowadays more than half of its doctorates are going to women. Thus we can expect that before long the proportion of women in the field will also be over 50 percent. Is some kind of backlash under way there? How does it start? How far will it go?[8]

But even if we can create such a three-way typology, we should remember that the overall proportion of women in a field is itself the average of their representation in its several subspecialties, for they are not uniformly distributed across all of them. For example, in physics in 1956–1958, as shown in Table 2, women made up 2.45 percent of the field as a whole; but while they represented over 5 percent of those in atomic and molecular physics and just under 4 percent in the combined category "other physics specialties," fewer than 1 percent of those in the subfield of acoustics were women. The situation is even more dramatic in chemistry, where women constituted 5.35 percent of the field overall in 1956–1958, ranging from a high of 16.25 percent in biochemistry on down to a low of 0.94 percent in rubber chemistry. Within the comprehensive rubric of the "biological sciences," where their average was 12.84 percent, they ranged from 35.10 percent of those in "other biological specialties" and 23.60 percent in nutrition and metabolism down to just 1.82 percent of the entomologists. So we have to begin to take stock of these field and subfield differences more systematically than in the past—the situation is not the same for all women in science or even for those in *one* science. We might even begin to entertain the thought that women entomologists have more experiences in common with women physicists (especially those in mechanics and heat, who made up 2.01 percent of the subfield) than with other women biologists in more feminized subfields.

In fact, we can take advantage of the NSF data, presented in the lengthy Table 3, on the ninety-six subfields surveyed in 1956–1958, the one time responses were broken down in such a way, to see several things. First, the proportion of those in a subfield who were women ranged widely, from nearly 46 percent in developmental psychology on down to zero in radiological and health engineering and nuclear engineering. The table also shows, once again, that most women in science were in a very few subfields—three-fourths were in just thirty-three of the ninety-six specialties—and that half of the fields had 3.66 percent or fewer women. Thus the range of opportunities open to women scientists answering the questionnaire was far narrower than that available to the men, even though overall—as shown in Table 1—women represented 6.25 percent of the respondents. Third, the most welcoming fields for women—those with the highest proportion of women—tended to be those prefixed "other," that is, those residual areas outside the principal categories recognized by governmental statisticians of the 1950s. Of the nine such subfields (ranked nos. 2, 6, 7, 9, 27, 46, 51, 60, and 80), four were among the top ten (those with the highest proportion of women), and even "other engineering," in 80th place, had proportionally more women than nine other kinds of engineering.

---

[8] On the International Council of Psychologists see Rossiter, *Women Scientists in America: Before Affirmative Action* (cit. n. 4), pp. 43–49, 345–346. See also Patricia A. Ostertag and J. Regis McNamara, "'Feminization' of Psychology: The Changing Sex Ratio and Its Implications for the Profession," *Psychology of Women Quarterly,* 1991, *15*:349–369; and Linda Marie Fedigan, "Science and the Successful Female: Why Are There So Many Women Primatologists," *American Anthropologist,* 1994, *96*:529–540.

Table 2. Number and Percentage of American Biologists, Chemists, and Physicists, by Subfield and Sex, 1956–1958

Field	Total	Women	Percentage of Women
Physics	12,702	311	2.45
Atomic and molecular physics	756	40	5.29
Other physics specialties	1,959	78	3.98
Optics	1,446	44	3.04
Solid state physics	1,926	45	2.34
Nuclear physics	2,622	56	2.14
Mechanics and heat	844	17	2.01
Theoretical physics	713	8	1.12
Electricity and magnetism	1,574	16	1.02
Acoustics	862	7	0.81
Chemistry	35,805	1,914	5.35
Biochemistry	2,732	444	16.25
Other chemical specialties	923	89	9.64
Analytical chemistry	5,792	484	8.36
Pharmaceutical chemistry	1,035	57	5.51
Organic syntheses	2,148	103	4.77
General organic chemistry	2,374	109	4.59
Agricultural and food chemistry	1,892	83	4.39
Inorganic chemistry	2,505	93	3.71
Physical chemistry	4,021	134	3.33
Other organic chemical specialties	6,785	224	3.30
Resins and plastics	2,507	50	1.99
Petroleum products	1,493	29	1.94
Rubber chemistry	1,598	15	0.94
Biological sciences	18,015	2,314	12.84
Other biological specialties	851	221	35.10
Nutrition and metabolism	1,123	265	23.60
Microbiology	3,628	676	18.63
Anatomy	953	139	14.59
Botany	1,524	218	14.30
Zoology	1,541	190	12.33
Pharmacology	968	104	12.04
Physiology	2,058	207	11.18
Pathology	865	96	11.10
Genetics	682	69	10.12
Biophysics	366	29	7.92
Ecology	451	31	6.87
Hydrobiology	250	11	4.40
Phytopathology	887	24	2.71
Entomology	1,868	34	1.82

SOURCE.—National Science Foundation, *American Science Manpower, 1956–58: A Report of the National Register of Scientific and Technical Personnel* (Washington, D.C.: Government Printing Office, 1961), pp. 80–83.

Table 3. Scientific Subfields, Ranked by Proportion of Women, 1956–1958

Rank	Subfield	Percentage of Women	Number	Cumulative Total
1	Developmental psychology	45.59	124	
2	Other biological specialties	35.10	221	
3	Educational and school psychology	29.39	323	
4	Nutrition and metabolism	23.60	265	
5	Clinical psychology	22.81	887	
6	Other psychology	20.91	60	
7	Other specialties (i.e., miscellaneous)	20.34	236	
8	Microbiology	18.63	676	
9	Other mathematical specialties	18.51	203	2,995 (34.27%)
10	Psychometrics	17.89	105	
11	Geometry	16.98	72	
12	Counseling and guidance	16.92	253	
13	Education	16.67	156	
14	Biochemistry	16.25	444	
15	Algebra and number theory	15.89	139	
16	Personality	15.33	44	
17	Anatomy	14.59	139	4,347 (49.74%)
18	Botany	14.30	218	
19	Theory and practice of computation	13.31	323	
20	Zoology	12.33	190	
21	Pharmacology	12.04	104	
22	Physiology	11.18	207	
23	Pathology	11.10	96	
24	Statistics	10.84	22	
25	Social psychology	10.63	59	
26	Genetics	10.12	69	
27	Other chemical specialties	9.64	89	
28	Experimental, comparative, and physiological psychology	9.59	111	
29	Astronomy	9.12	33	
30	Analytical chemistry	8.36	484	
31	Geography	8.26	80	
32	Biophysics	7.92	29	
33	Probability and statistics	7.64	83	6,544 (74.88%)
34	Analysis and topological algebraic structure	7.01	109	
35	Ecology	6.87	31	
36	Medical sciences	6.20	119	
37	Industrial and personnel psychology	6.16	74	
38	Topology	5.86	16	
39	Pharmaceutical chemistry	5.51	57	
40	Atomic and molecular physics	5.29	40	
41	Social sciences (mostly economics)	4.78	20	
42	Organic syntheses	4.73	103	
43	General organic chemistry	4.59	109	
44	Hydrobiology	4.40	11	

Table 3. *continued*

Rank	Subfield	Percentage of Women	Number	Cumulative Total
45	Agricultural and food chemistry	4.39	83	
46	Other physics specialties	3.98	78	
47	Oceanography	3.75	9	
48	Inorganic chemistry	3.71	93	
49	Logic	3.66	6	
50	Physical chemistry	3.33	134	
51	Other organic chemical specialties	3.30	224	
52	Optics	3.04	44	
53	Actuarial mathematics	3.00	37	
54	Climatology	2.94	3	
55	Mathematics of resource use	2.91	26	
56	Human engineering	2.89	7	
57	Phytopathology	2.71	24	
58	Physical or dynamical meteorology	2.40	4	
59	Geochemistry	2.37	5	
60	Other meteorological specialties	2.36	16	
61	Solid state physics	2.34	45	
62	Aeronautical engineering	2.33	19	
63	Ceramic engineering	2.26	4	
64	Geology	2.16	207	
65	Nuclear physics	2.14	56	
66	Synoptic meteorology	2.10	25	
67	Mechanics and heat	2.01	17	
68	Resin and plastics	1.99	50	
69	Petroleum products	1.94	29	
70	Entomology	1.82	34	
71	Metallurgical engineering	1.58	9	
72	Electronics	1.13	28	
73	Theoretical physics	1.12	8	
74	Surveying, mapping, and photometry	1.09	15	
75	Horticulture	1.08	9	
76	Hydrology	1.03	8	
77	Engineering mechanics	1.02	5	
78	Electricity and magnetism	1.02	16	
79	Rubber chemistry	0.94	15	
80	Other engineering specialties	0.89	9	
81	Geophysics	0.89	20	
82	Industrial engineering	0.87	7	
83	Electrical engineering	0.81	5	
84	Acoustics	0.81	7	
85	Mechanical engineering	0.75	4	
86	Animal husbandry	0.70	7	
87	Agronomy	0.66	6	
88	Sanitary engineering	0.32	11	
89	Civil engineering	0.30	8	
90	Chemical engineering	0.26	13	

Table 3. *continued*

Rank	Subfield	Percentage of Women	Number	Cumulative Total
91	Forestry and range science	0.24	12	
92	Fish and wildlife	0.21	2	
93	Mining engineering	0.14	2	
94	Soil science	0.11	1	
95	Radiological and health engineering	0.00	0	
96	Nuclear engineering	0.00	0	
Total			8,739	

SOURCE.—National Science Foundation, *American Science Manpower, 1956–58: A Report of the National Register of Scientific and Technical Personnel* (Washington, D.C.: Government Printing Office, 1961), pp. 80–82.

To refine the picture still further: these substantial variations among fields and subfields reflect differences in training opportunities open to women. For example, within most fields there may have been some universities that trained many women and thus formed a kind of oasis within a bleak overall picture. This range among universities is largely the result of patterns within particular departments and even the influence of individual professors. In fact, one might suspect that most of the women doctorates were trained by a few notable professors, as happened at New York University in mathematics in the 1950s with Lipman Bers and at Radcliffe-Harvard in the 1940s and 1950s with Bart Bok in astronomy, Kirtley Mather in geology, and Ralph Wetmore in botany. (Unfortunately—and not coincidentally—several of these professors also shared something else: they were considered so liberal or left-leaning as to face charges of Communist sympathies in the 1940s and 1950s.) One could pinpoint other particular laboratories or mentors who merit further study, although the list of prominent scientists who refused to train women graduate students might be far longer.[9] Thus what looks like a subfield pattern can be a reflection of an institutional one that can in turn be reduced to a mosaic of personal protégée networks. If "all politics is local," then perhaps much of a scientific career is personal or at least small-scale phenomena, and all the aggregate statistics in Tables 1–3 are just the result of many different situations.

It has been fashionable to describe fields with many women as "soft" and those without them as "hard."[10] Although the terms refer to tangible physical phenomena,

---

[9] Anne Roe, "Women in Science," *Personnel and Guidance Journal*, 1966, *44*:786. This is discussed further in Rossiter, *Women Scientists in America: Before Affirmative Action*, Ch. 4. Regarding Bers's support of women see *ibid.*, p. 419 n. 33. On Bok see David H. Levy, *The Man Who Sold the Milky Way: A Biography of Bart Bok* (Tucson: Univ. Arizona Press, 1993); and the Bart J. Bok Papers, Harvard University Archives, Cambridge, Massachusetts. On Mather see Kennard Baker Bork, *Cracking Rocks and Defending Democracy: Kirtley F. Mather* (San Francisco: American Association for the Advancement of Science, Pacific Division, 1994); and the Kirtley Mather Papers, Harvard University Archives. On Wetmore see John G. Torrey, "Ralph H. Wetmore, April 27, 1902–April 28, 1989," *Biographical Memoirs of the National Academy of Sciences*, 1994, *64*:421–436; and the Ralph Wetmore Papers, Harvard University Archives.

[10] Norman Storer, "The Hard Sciences and the Soft: Some Sociological Observations," *Bulletin of the Medical Library Association*, 1967, *55*:75–84; Storer, "Relations among the Scientific Disciplines," in *The Social Contexts of Research*, ed. Saad Z. Nagi and Ronald G. Corwin (New York:

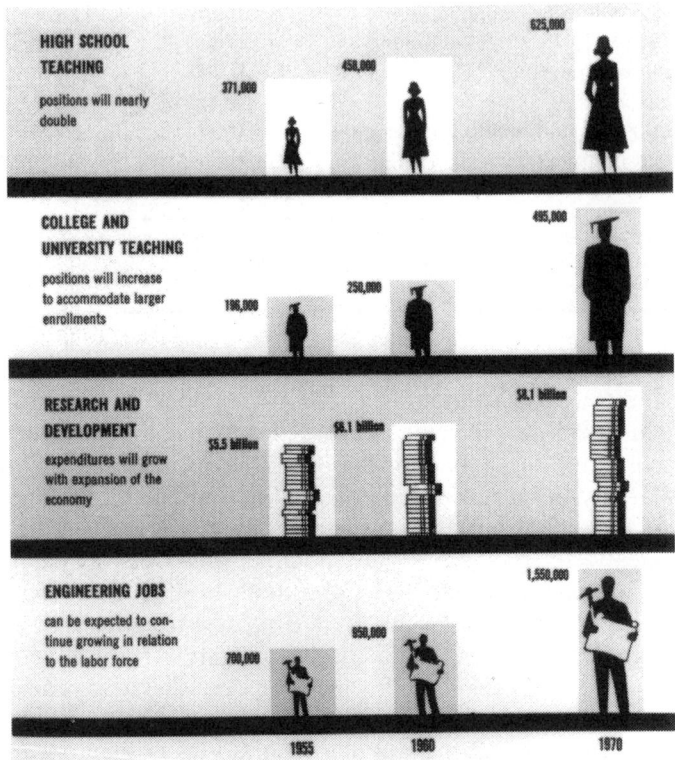

Figure 1. In 1956 the National Science Foundation published a booklet for the National Committee on the Development of Engineers and Scientists emphasizing the pressing national shortage of scientists. This pictograph demonstrates the gender typing implicit in these manpower projections: women were to become schoolteachers, while men became engineers. Interestingly, the chairman of this committee (renamed the "President's Committee" after Sputnik) was Eric A. Walker, then dean of engineering at Pennsylvania State University, who was the author of a 1955 article, "Women Are NOT for Engineering." (National Science Foundation, Trends in the Employment and Training of Scientists and Engineers [Washington, D.C.: Government Printing Office, 1956], p. 21; Margaret W. Rossiter, Women Scientists in America: Before Affirmative Action, 1940–1972 [Baltimore: Johns Hopkins University Press, 1995], p. 68).

they don't get us very far sociologically (and their proponents are in fact reminiscent of those anthropologists of the 1870s who, prejudging their data rather than problematizing them, kept finding female brains to be smaller than males'). Yet the people using these terms seem to know what linked phenomena they referred to.

Interscience, 1972), pp. 229–268; and Anthony Biglan, "Relationships between Subject Matter Characteristics and the Structure and Output of University Departments," *Journal of Applied Psychology,* 1973, *57*:204–213. See also Stephen G. Brush, "Are the Soft Sciences Too Hard?" *Contention,* 1995, *4*(2):3–12.

There is evidence, as was shown in three extensive questionnaires by the sociologist Saul Feldman in the late 1960s, that both undergraduates and graduate students were very aware of the level of feminization of various fields, though men and women differed on the levels they perceived. They were also aware that feminization was linked inversely to the whole idea of "prestige." In fact, among scientists, malcontents in "soft" fields were often so dissatisfied with their image that they developed strategies to make their disciplines "harder." This new look could mean a variety of things: the field could be made intellectually more rigorous, more experimental, or more reliant on high-tech instruments—or, conversely, more abstract, with more reliance on mathematical models. (Although the social sciences are often labeled "soft" and thought to have a high proportion of women, the field of economics has long been a standard exception to this rule. Even within economics there has been a noticeable movement toward greater "hardness" or mathematicization of abstract models in the United States since World War II, as Mary Cookingham's fine study of Jessica Peixotto, Emily Huntington, and the elimination of "social economics" at Berkeley in the 1950s has shown.[11])

Another inverse correlation might be drawn between the proportion of women in a field and its wealth, that is, the quantity of society's resources it is able to command. Women tend to be where the money is not: they have been rare in engineering, agricultural sciences, and fields, like physics, that are favored by the military; they are, by contrast, far more often congregated and persevering in underfunded fields that have lacked a sponsor. In invertebrate taxonomy, for example, several notable women have worked in museums, sometimes in unpaid positions, until well into their eighties.[12] Surprisingly, actual data on funding by field are scarce. The best I have been able to do here is shown in Table 4, which details federal support (a large part of the funding available to a discipline, but not the whole) for twenty large fields and aggregates for fiscal year 1959, the first year such information was broken down even this far.

But numbers do not tell the whole story, and the ones we have are imperfect in any case. We also need a vocabulary to deal with advancement—or the lack of it. One important matter to consider is the hierarchical distribution of women within a field, as the proportion of women usually drops off at each higher level. For instance, consider a field where, despite a low proportion of women overall, some do rise to the top. This situation might be pictured as a kind of tall, thin obelisk. In another, more feminized, field or subfield there may be many women overall—as perhaps botany, psychology, or anthropology—but again fairly few at the top. This could be depicted as a more broadly based pyramid. If there were no women at the top, then we would no longer have a pyramid but a truncated form, like a mesa (this is the shape the "glass ceiling" refers to). The dynamics that lead to these differences

---

[11] Saul Feldman, *Escape from the Doll's House: Women in Graduate and Professional School Education* (New York: McGraw-Hill, 1974), Ch. 3 ("Masculine and Feminine Academic Disciplines: Their Characteristics"); and Mary E. Cookingham, "Social Economists and Reform: Berkeley, 1906–1961," *History of Political Economy*, 1987, *19*:47–65. See also Harry G. Johnson, "Economics and the Radical Challenge: The Hard Social Science and the Soft Social Reality," in *Culture and Its Creators: Essays in Honor of Edward Shils*, ed. Joseph Ben-David and Terry Nichols Clark (Chicago: Univ. Chicago Press, 1977), pp. 97–118.

[12] E.g., Libbie Hyman worked unpaid at the American Museum of Natural History for decades, Dora Henry toiled at the University of Washington into her nineties, and Irene McCulloch was at the University of Southern California almost as long.

Table 4. Federal Funds for Research, by Field of Science, Fiscal Year 1959

Engineering sciences	$461,059,000
Medical sciences	267,647,000
Physics	139,188,000
Space sciences	117,157,000
Biological sciences	87,593,000
Chemistry	67,988,000
Agricultural sciences	64,278,000
Atmospheric sciences	30,990,000
Operations research	25,978,000
Psychological sciences	24,354,000
Economics	23,734,000
Solid earth sciences	22,938,000
Mathematical sciences	16,074,000
Astronomy	9,857,000
Other physical sciences	9,542,000
Oceanography	7,308,000
Other sciences	6,753,000
Other social sciences	3,954,000
Sociology	2,543,000
Anthropology	728,000
Total	1,389,663,000

SOURCE.—National Science Foundation, *Federal Funds for Science, IX: The Federal Research and Development Budget, Fiscal Years 1959, 1960, and 1961* (Surveys of Science Resources Series) (Washington, D.C.: Government Printing Office, 1961), p. 72 (table 18).

ought to be studied more. Lack of advancement may be the result of ghettoization, mentioned earlier, where women spend their careers (or at least their years) in parts of their fields that are not much recognized (e.g., service sectors) or are denied the training that is required for the top positions (e.g., fieldwork for government geologists). Then—having spent their careers on unrewarded "grunt" work—they can be denied promotion and even berated collectively for not having published much or contributed enough to be promotable.[13]

The science of nutrition, often linked with the field of "home economics," provides an extreme case of the dangers of what might be termed "overfeminization" or "hyperfeminization." Established in the 1890s by the MIT chemist Ellen Richards and others as a way for educated women to help immigrants and housewives, the field should be of special interest to those who study women and science. The late Ruth Bleier thought it was refreshingly open to those who wanted to make science

---

[13] Sociologists can do this to them too, particularly those who rank men and women by how much they publish, ignoring the fact that oftentimes women hold jobs where publishing is not a major component. See, e.g., Jonathan R. Cole, *Fair Science: Women in the Scientific Community* (New York: Free Press, 1979). Earlier, however, Jessie Bernard had shown that some women's lower rate of productivity was "a function of their disadvantaged position in the communication system of their disciplines": Bernard, *Academic Women* (State College: Pennsylvania State Univ. Press, 1964), App. C (quotation on p. 263), App. D. Some recent evidence indicates that possibly a disproportionate number of women are perfectionists who publish fewer but better articles than do matched men: Gerhard Sonnert, *Who Succeeds in Science? The Gender Dimension* (New Brunswick, N.J.: Rutgers Univ. Press, 1995), pp. 121, 153.

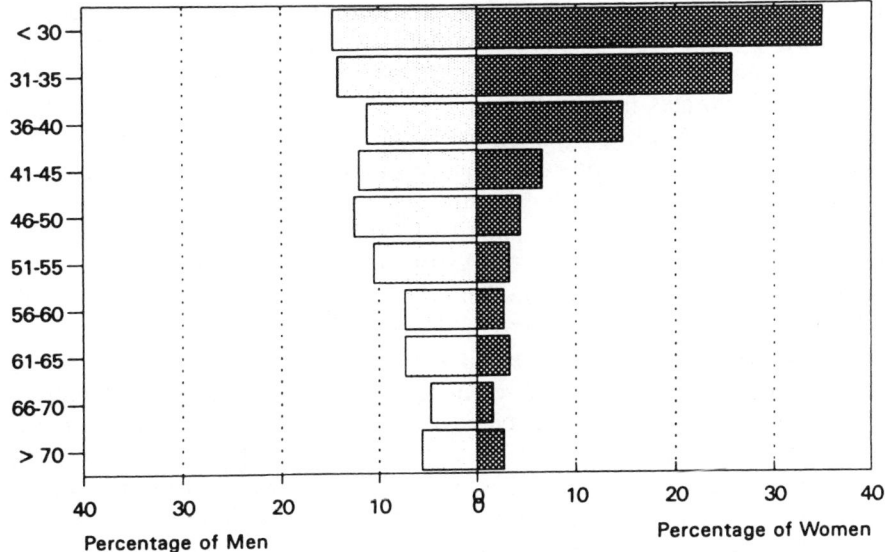

Figure 2. A survey of the membership of the American Physical Society in 1990 revealed that 6.5 percent of the members were women, most of whom were quite young. As shown in this chart, 35 percent were under age thirty. This contrasts sharply with the more uniform age distribution of the male members. One can speculate what will happen to the women's age distributions in the future, if, as one hopes, more young women continue to join, those between thirty and sixty remain members, and only the oldest give up their memberships. ("Gender Survey of the APS Membership, 1990," Newsletter of the Committee on the Status of Women in Physics of the American Physical Society, *January 1993*, 12[3]:5. Reprinted courtesy of the American Institute of Physics.)

socially responsible. Yet home economics is still often trivialized and badly understudied.[14] The field was immediately taken up by administrators at land-grant and other coeducational institutions who felt that they needed a feminine curriculum to offer their increasing numbers of women students. Its popularity was aided by women's clubs and other political groups that held that society needed more (white and college-educated) mothers and thought that teaching home economics in the public schools would help perpetuate the race. In the 1920s the U.S. Congress created a Bureau of Home Economics within the Department of Agriculture and initiated federal support for research in the subject.[15] Thus several external demands joined

---

[14] Ruth Bleier, "The Cultural Price of Social Exclusion: Gender and Science," *NWSA Journal*, 1988, *1*:19. The neglect of home economics is soon to be rectified by Sarah Stage and Virginia Vincenti, eds., *Rethinking Women and Home Economics in the Twentieth Century* (Ithaca, N.Y.: Cornell Univ. Press, 1997). For a thoughtful analysis of the field and its problems as a feminized branch of knowledge see Marjorie East, *Home Economics: Past, Present, and Future* (Boston: Allyn & Bacon, 1980), esp. Ch. 7 ("A Female Field"). See also *The Field of Home Economics: What Is It?* (Washington, D.C.: American Home Economics Association, 1961), mimeographed.

[15] See Jane Bernard Powers, *The "Girl Question" in Education: Vocational Education for Young Women in the Progressive Era* (London/Washington, D.C.: Falmer, 1992); and Carolyn Goldstein, "Mediating Consumption: Home Economics and American Consumers, 1900–1940" (Ph.D. diss., Univ. Delaware, 1994).

together to create a subject especially for women, supported by state and federal funds, where women students and faculty were for a time treated preferentially.

Yet there were limits to the scientific standing of this highly feminized field of "home economics." Although most of the women faculty doing research in the discipline had doctorates in such mainstream sciences as chemistry, biochemistry, economics, and psychology, there were after the early days few male professors of home economics. Over time the feminization of the field had consequences related to funding. Though most state legislatures were willing to fund a college of home economics at their land-grant university to train better wives and mothers and to strengthen the family, and the USDA offered modest research backing, other federal science agencies—the NSF, the National Institutes of Health, and even the Office of Education (which administered the National Defense Education Act of 1958, with its billion dollars for graduate study)—did not recognize home economics as a subject worthy of support (i.e., as a science) and thus refused to grant it funds. (Because the NSF did not consider it a science, data for home economics do not appear in any of the tables presented in this essay.) This denial of support was a serious blow to a field whose leaders were under pressure on campus and from accrediting groups to prove its rigor by training graduate students and publishing research. The level of support was so low and the field itself so feminized that in the 1950s and 1960s the deans of many colleges of home economics tried to hire male faculty to upgrade (or harden or masculinize) their school's image. But such deans found that few male scientists were interested and that those who were often were not particularly distinguished. One frequent strategy to entice better male candidates was to change the name of the college to "human development" or "human ecology."[16]

This is a case of what Tom Gieryn has called a "boundary problem." Evidently, when prominent scientists or officials or legislators or just "common sense" thought that something was too feminized, too feminine, and too "soft," they would deny it the status of a "science," whatever its intellectual content. This has consequences for the wealth and support of a field. In fact, a certain circular process takes place: if the field is perceived as not manly or prestigious enough to be a real science, then scientific agencies will not support it; and if they don't then little significant research is completed and little prestige is earned—thus justifying further decisions to award no new resources. But if a field is held to be manly and—especially during the Cold War—if it was valued by the military services, as were the several subjects surveyed in Stuart Leslie's *The Cold War and American Science*—it was massively funded and rapidly embraced by prestigious institutions.[17]

[16] On the difficulties of establishing the rigor of home economics see Margaret W. Rossiter, *Women Scientists in America: Before Affirmative Action* (cit. n. 4), Ch. 8; for a shorter version see Rossiter, "The Men Move In, 1950–1970," in *Rethinking Women and Home Economics*, ed. Stage and Vincenti (cit. n. 14). See also Maresi Nerad, "'Home Economics Has to Move': The Disappearance of the Department of Home Economics from the University of California, Berkeley" (Ph.D. diss., Univ. California, Berkeley, 1986); and Nerad, "Gender Stratification in Higher Education: The Department of Home Economics at the University of California, Berkeley, 1916–1962," *Women's Studies International Forum*, 1987, *10*:157–164.

[17] Thomas Gieryn, "Boundary-Work and the Demarcation of Science from Non-Science: Strains and Interests in Professional Ideologies of Scientists," *American Sociological Review*, 1983, 48:781–795; Gieryn, "Boundaries of Science," in *Handbook of Science and Technology Studies*, ed. Sheila Jasanoff, Gerald E. Markle, James C. Petersen, and Trevor Pinch (Thousand Oaks, Calif.: Sage, 1995), pp. 393–443, esp. pp. 420–424. See also Kari Whittenberger-Keith, "Exchange on Profes-

If we had a taxonomy of fields and women's usual experience within them, we might be able to make better comparisons, to highlight the unique and unusual, and to develop a better vocabulary for depicting them. For example, there have been many women and scientific couples in the field of demography, which is a mathematically oriented neighbor of sociology, despite a lack of encouragement from such founders of the field as Frank Notestein and Frederick Osborn. There have even been several women presidents of the tiny Population Association of America—more, in fact, than of the very much larger American Sociological Association (at least before 1970 or so, the period I know best). In some ways demography's openness to women may be related to the structure or source of its funding, "soft money" from foundations, which generated temporary research positions rather than "hard money" academic ones. Demography's anomalous setting in universities seems similar to that of crystallography, which also had many couples and much soft money support. Yet Maureen Julian was at pains a few years ago to show us that—despite such famous females as Kathleen Lonsdale, Rosalind Franklin, and Dorothy Hodgkin, and even though William Henry Bragg, the founder of the discipline, was particularly supportive of women—crystallography is not as feminized as we tend to think, at least in the United States (where, according to a 1981 directory, 11 percent of crystallographers were women) and the United Kingdom (where, according to the same source, 10 percent were women).[18] Thus if we had a way to tease out and evaluate the several factors involved and assess their relative importance in comparative cases, we might be better able to understand and explain the overlapping and interlocking processes, to identify what is the pattern (and maybe why) and what the exception or the oddity, if any.

Then we might also be able to identify strategically important research topics—and choose them not just because they fit the interest of the researcher or because materials are available but because they promise to expose some key factors. Moreover, subfields can be small and so easier to study in detail than larger fields; those with many women (such as biochemistry) may have a lot of couples that invite dual biographies.[19]

Then, too, we might also be better able to predict future behavior within a given field, as it becomes more or less feminized, and thus become useful to the scientists we study. Once we recognize, for example, that women in American physics are

---

sionalization as Marginalization: The American Home Economics Movement and the Rhetoric of Legitimation," *Social Epistemology*, 1994, 8:123–132; and (as commentary) Catharina Landstroem, "The Boundaries of Housework," *ibid.*, pp. 133–138. Stuart W. Leslie, *The Cold War and American Science: The Military-Industrial-Academic Complex at MIT and Stanford* (Cambridge, Mass.: MIT Press, 1993). See also Rebecca S. Lowen, "Transforming the University: Administrators, Physicists, and Industrial and Federal Patronage at Stanford, 1935–1949," *History of Education Quarterly*, 1991, *31*:365–388.

[18] John Sharpless, "Prelude to Intervention: Demographers, World Population Growth, and Cold War Politics, 1940–1965," paper presented at the annual meeting of the History of Science Society, Santa Fe, New Mexico, 1993; Jean Donaldson, "Women in Demography," paper prepared for Science & Technology Studies 444, Spring 1994, Cornell Univ.; Linda B. Bourque,"A Biographical Essay on Judith Blake's Career and Scholarship," *Annual Review of Sociology*, 1995, *21*:449–477; and Maureen M. Julian, "Women in Crystallography," in *Women of Science: Righting the Record*, ed. G. Kass-Simon and Patricia Farnes (Bloomington: Indiana Univ. Press, 1990), pp. 335–383.

[19] See Helena M. Pycior, Nancy G. Slack, and Pnina G. Abir-Am, eds., *Creative Couples in the Sciences* (New Brunswick, N.J.: Rutgers Univ. Press, 1996).

approaching the level of 10 percent of the doctorates awarded—up markedly from just 1.06 percent (or just 6 of 564 Ph.D.'s) in 1960–1961 to 6.25 percent (54 of 862) in 1980 and 8.76 percent (102 of 1,165) in 1989—then we might be able to predict where the next set of frictions would appear. There are those who say that the standard pipeline model of manpower analysis is too simple. Advancement to leadership positions might not be as automatic as this analogy suggests. Instead, major snags might be clogging the pipeline, causing pressure to rise until some force sweeps the obstacles aside or the pipe bursts with an efflux of midcareer women. As the cohort of young women who entered science or engineering in recent decades reaches age forty or so, some should be becoming heads of something—their section, their division, or the whole institution—and not just assistant or associate directors or even assistants to the associate director. If they aren't, maybe they should be planning a protest or a lawsuit. Maybe those in fields with high percentages of women should be planning how to fight the backsliding or even backlash that might occur at 20 percent or so.

Furthermore, we know next to nothing about *which* women are in any of these fields. The best information is about those few who have left autobiographies or large archival and manuscript collections. Next come those about whom biographies have been written. Then, and by far the greatest number, are those listed in biographical dictionaries such as *American Men and* (since 1972) *Women of Science* or the many biobibliographies that have appeared in the last ten years or so.[20] Probably few of these women are from what we would call the upper class, which makes the anthropologist Elsie Clews Parsons unusual and important. If her case is any guide, rich women scientists get asked for money, and if they give it they are remembered— and marginalized—as patrons and donors rather than as the full-fledged scientific contributors they may also have been. Other women scientists were born rich and raised with gloves and governesses, only to lose it all in the Depression. Frances Hamerstrom rebelled sufficiently defiantly and definitively (as depicted in three hilarious autobiographies) to become a wildlife specialist (and marry another). Caroline Littlejohn Herzenberg, whose family resources were devastated by the Depression, found that winning the Westinghouse Talent Search in 1949 opened a door to higher education and eventual upward mobility as a physicist.[21] These few examples leave a lot of ground uncovered. My lone impression of American women in microbiology, to suggest an example, is that a lot of them had fathers who were physicians. They aspired to follow in his footsteps, but due to his ill health or early death family finances were exhausted long before they got to medical school. Therefore these

---

[20] E.g., Louise S. Grinstein and Paul J. Campbell, eds., *Women of Mathematics: A Biobibliographic Sourcebook* (New York: Greenwood, 1987); Ute Gacs et al., *Women Anthropologists: A Biographical Dictionary* (Westport, Conn.: Greenwood, 1988), rpt. as *Women Anthropologists: Selected Biographies* (Urbana: Univ. Illinois Press, 1989); Marion Tinling, ed., *Women into the Unknown: A Sourcebook on Women Explorers and Travelers* (New York: Greenwood, 1989); and Agnes N. O'Connell and Nancy Felipe Russo, eds., *Women in Psychology: A Biobibliographic Sourcebook* (New York: Greenwood, 1990).

[21] Rosemary Lévy Zumwalt, *Wealth and Rebellion: Elsie Clews Parsons, Anthropologist and Folklorist* (Urbana/Chicago: Univ. Illinois Press, 1992); Frances Hamerstrom, *Strictly for the Chickens* (Ames: Iowa State Univ. Press, 1980); Hamerstrom, *Is She Coming Too? Memoirs of a Lady Hunter* (Ames: Iowa State Univ. Press, 1987); Hamerstrom, *My Double Life: Memoirs of a Naturalist* (Madison: Univ. Wisconsin Press, 1994); and Barbara B. Mandula, "Caroline Stuart Littlejohn Herzenberg," in *Women in Chemistry and Physics: A Biobibliographic Sourcebook*, ed. Louise S. Grinstein, Rose K. Rose, and Miriam H. Rafailovich (Westport, Conn.: Greenwood, 1993), pp. 243–252.

women, many of whom were Southern, gravitated toward the federal laboratories in Washington, D.C., earned higher degrees at George Washington University, and had careers of some distinction in (medical) microbiology, a feminized field (18.6 percent of practitioners were women in 1956–1958) not taught at many undergraduate institutions until recent decades.[22]

Writings on women and or in science are proliferating at a great rate, as this volume shows. Our continuing goal should be to break down or subdivide the aggregate entity called "science" into its subspecialties and, as authors here and elsewhere are doing, study those intensively, while at the same time retaining some sense of how that particular field differed (or does now) from other fields. Then we may hope to integrate women more fully than is the case at present into "mainstream" history of science, which is already broken down by specialties, chronological periods, and national communities. The result may be a less ghettoized, richer, and more comprehensive history of science than we have had to date.

[22] Elizabeth Moot O'Hern, *Profiles of Pioneer Women Scientists* (Washington, D.C.: Acropolis, 1985). An exception, the Department of Bacteriology and Hygiene at the Mississippi State College for Women, was the result of the driving enthusiasm of Martha O. Eckford, an alumna and Johns Hopkins Sc.D. in 1925. Its most famous graduate was Elizabeth Hazen, '10, of the New York State Department of Health. See Bridget S. Pieschel and Stephen Pieschel, *Loyal Daughters: One Hundred Years at Mississippi University for Women, 1884–1984* (Jackson: Univ. Press Mississippi, 1984), pp. 103–104, 132; and J. McKeen Cattell and Jaques Cattell, eds., *American Men of Science, A Biographical Directory*, 6th ed. (New York: Science Press, 1938), p. 400.

Women's Standpoints on Nature
What Makes Them Possible?

By Sandra Harding*

ARE THERE DISTINCTIVE WOMEN'S STANDPOINTS on nature? Even posing such a question may sound scandalous to those who hear in it echoes of "anatomy is destiny" arguments against the advancement of women in science. Yet a positive answer to it has been the focus of a number of feminist analyses. Women's health movements around the world have argued that women's bodies are one object of scientific scrutiny about which there are such distinctive women's standpoints. Feminist environmentalists have argued that women's socially assigned interactions with their environments give them distinctive repositories of knowledge. Moreover, some have read Evelyn Fox Keller's work on Barbara McClintock as making such claims about the far more abstract topics of genetics.[1] These kinds of studies seem to imply that biological sex differences and socially assigned gender differences can sometimes provide distinctive resources for the growth of scientific knowledge.

What is it about women's situations that could or does make possible these standpoints? Is it biology? Culture? Can men have or take these standpoints? Do all women have them? Do all women have the same standpoints? What about women scientists? If we could get satisfying answers to this second set of questions, it should settle the first one.

Feminist standpoint theory was developed primarily to account for the more comprehensive and empirically adequate knowledge about social worlds that could be generated by starting off research from feminist understandings of women's lives instead of from dominant conceptual frameworks that expressed the interests and values of social institutions from which women's voices had been excluded or in

---

* Department of Philosophy, UCLA, Los Angeles, California 90095.

My thanks to the editors and anonymous referees for helpful suggestions that have clarified and strengthened this essay's arguments. The essay also benefited from comments by Barbara Laslett, Carolyn Merchant, and the other participants in the University of Minnesota workshop on this issue held in May 1995.

[1] On women's biology see Ruth Hubbard, *The Politics of Women's Biology* (New Brunswick, N.J.: Rutgers Univ. Press, 1990); Emily Martin, "The Egg and the Sperm: How Science Has Constructed a Romance Based on Stereotypical Male-Female Roles," *Signs: Journal of Women in Culture and Society,* 1991, *16*:485–501; and Hilary Rose, "Hand, Brain, and Heart: A Feminist Epistemology for the Natural Sciences," ibid., 1983, *9*:73–90. For feminist environmentalism see Joni Seager, *Earth Follies: Coming to Feminist Terms with the Global Environmental Crisis* (New York: Routledge, 1993); and Vandana Shiva, *Staying Alive: Women, Ecology, and Development* (London: Zed, 1989). See also Evelyn Fox Keller, *A Feeling for the Organism: The Life and Work of Barbara McClintock* (New York: Freeman, 1983); and Keller, *Reflections on Gender and Science* (New Haven, Conn.: Yale Univ. Press, 1985).

which they were marginalized. This theory of how the growth of knowledge had occurred in the history of the sciences, and of the best methods to advance the growth of knowledge in the future, contrasted with the familiar view that any claims deserving to be called "knowledge" had permanently shed whatever historical fingerprints might initially have marked them. Where the conventional epistemology argued that real knowledge was by definition free of socially local values and interests, standpoint theories pointed to the androcentric, or bourgeois, or Eurocentric features of purportedly culture-free knowledge claims—some of which clearly had advanced the growth of knowledge, while others had and were restraining it. From the beginning, feminist standpoint analysts took as their domain not only social worlds but also nature and the natural sciences. In addition to women's "bodily knowledge" and women's different understandings of environmental processes, there was the obvious fact that it was mainly (but not exclusively) women historians, biologists, philosophers, and researchers and scholars in other disciplines who were producing the less sexist and androcentrist readings of nature and of what turned out to be culturally local (because gendered) scientific processes and philosophies of nature and of science.[2] So the analysis in this essay addresses an issue that has been touched on but not comprehensively reviewed in a wide array of feminist science studies. What makes possible these women's standpoints on nature?

After reviewing the perfectly understandable reasons proffered for regarding as scandalous the idea that there are such gendered standpoints, I shall argue that, nevertheless, analyses of how it is that women's lives can generate such resources deserve more appreciation than many of us, feminist and prefeminist alike, have given them. The issue is not only about understanding women's past achievements or women's knowledge in premodern societies; it is also about the resources that starting off research from women's lives can provide for increasing human knowledge of nature's regularities and their underlying causal tendencies anywhere and everywhere gender relations occur. It is also, in part, an issue about women making science policy, whether or not they are practicing scientists—a point to which I return in closing.

Here I want to reflect on the kinds of arguments made by feminist science theorists in order to try to specify just what features of women's situations make possible distinctively gendered standpoints on nature. My strategy is to look at the feminist work through the lens of postcolonial cross-cultural studies of science, technology, and medicine, including what is referred to as the study of local knowledge systems.[3]

---

[2] See Sandra Harding, *The Science Question in Feminism* (Ithaca, N.Y.: Cornell Univ. Press, 1986); Harding, *Whose Science? Whose Knowledge? Thinking from Women's Lives* (Ithaca, N.Y.: Cornell Univ. Press, 1991); Nancy Hartsock, "The Feminist Standpoint," in *Discovering Reality: Feminist Perspectives on Epistemology, Metaphysics, Methodology, and Philosophy of Science*, ed. Harding and Merrill B. Hintikka (Dordrecht/Boston: Reidel, 1983); Dorothy Smith, *The Everyday World as Problematic: A Sociology for Women* (Boston: Northeastern Univ. Press, 1988); and Smith, *The Conceptual Practices of Power: A Feminist Sociology of Knowledge* (Boston: Northeastern Univ. Press, 1990).

[3] E.g., see *Appropriate Technology*, June 1995, 22(1), a special issue on gender, science, and technology; Rosi Braidotti, Ewa Chackiewicz, Sabine Hausler, and Saskia Wieringa, *Women, the Environment, and Sustainable Development: Towards a Theoretical Synthesis* (London: Zed, 1994); Susantha Goonatilake, *Aborted Discovery: Science and Creativity in the Third World* (London: Zed, 1984); Wendy Harcourt, ed., *Feminist Perspectives on Sustainable Development* (London: Zed, 1994); David Hess, *Science and Technology in a Multicultural World: The Cultural Politics of Facts and Artifacts* (New York: Columbia Univ. Press, 1994); and United Nations Commission on Science and Technology in Development, Gender Working Group, *Missing Links: Gender Equity in Science and Technology for Development* (Ottawa: International Development Research Center, 1995;

This strategy has the effect of treating women and men as living in different cultures, so I first specify the limited sense in which this is reasonable.

GENDERED CULTURES?

Of course, in an important everyday sense, women and men live in the same cultures. One familiar way to specify cultures is by ethnicity, nationality, or some other category that contains both women and men, as in "Native American culture" or "French culture." However, sociologists and anthropologists also study the cultures of the street corner, locker room, school, laboratory, corporation, and military, and some of these cultures are in fact completely or highly gender segregated. Even when they are not, sometimes one gender's preferred institutions and practices form the local climate—for example, in corporate management and elementary school classrooms. It is in this sense of *culture* that it becomes illuminating to think of women and men as living in at least partially different cultures.

Will middle-class women and men be more resistant than others to the idea that they live in different cultures? Anywhere men and women share more androgynous life resources, gender cultures will be less differentiated. The agendas of liberal feminism have had their greatest success in the educated classes, so this is one group that should be resistant to the idea of gendered cultures. After all, liberal feminism historically was designed primarily to give middle-class women access to the benefits available to their brothers. Until recently, it was in the middle classes that the greatest similarities in women's and men's educations, career opportunities, incomes, and responsibilities for family life were found.

Recently, working-class lives have of necessity moved toward greater androgyny. The effects of the worsening economy on working-class families in the United States has led to these men's greater participation in child care and domestic work as their wives must bear more of the burden of providing family income. Moreover, the jobs available to working-class men increasingly have been deskilled and turned into "McJobs"—into the kinds of temporary and part-time work formerly more characteristic of working-class women. My point here is that wherever androgynous life resources are found there will be "less gender"—since gender is partially a structural division of labor or activity—and where there is "less gender" there will be less difference between men's and women's "cultures."[4]

In none of these cases would it be correct to say that life patterns are by any means identical for women and men or that the struggles of women in these classes are over. My particular issue here is that women and men scientists and university faculty members are in the groups that may well find it less plausible to think in terms of different gender cultures. Members of this class not only in fact live more androgynously, but they have been trying to make the resources of education, financial opportunity, jobs, and the like that are available to middle-class men available also to their sisters. So we who are in these groups should consider the probability that

---

London: Intermediate Technology Publications, 1995; New York: United Nations Development Fund for Women, 1995).

[4] I thank Barbara Laslett for pointing out to me that poverty can create forms of structural androgyny. For a discussion of the importance for social analyses of understanding gender differences as fundamentally structural and symbolic relations rather than simply as matters of individual identity see Harding, *Science Question in Feminism* (cit. n. 2), Ch. 2.

our resistance to the idea of gendered cultures may in part be a product of our politics and our distinctive class situation.

THE SPECTER OF "WOMEN'S SCIENCES"

Thus, for women and men of the professional class, the idea of women's standpoints on nature may call up the terrifying or perhaps merely absurd image of "women's sciences." The reasons for such responses are not hard to detect and need to be acknowledged.

In the first place, even raising such a topic risks predictable "misreadings" of it as (falsely) asserting that women's biology leads them to think differently—that there are genes or hormones or brain organization for sex-different "sciences." The claim that women are likely to have different resources for understanding nature is neither reducible to nor dependent upon claims that their brains are different. (And we need to recollect that, of course, there are biological constraints on all human activities; and, of course, one cannot distinguish the biological from the social contributions to particular patterns of human belief and behavior; and, of course, patterns of behavior can leave their traces in the brain, as they do in other parts of the body, etc.) However, even if there should turn out to be biological differences in the ways women and men think, other differences between them are my focus here.

Second, the idea of "women's sciences" raises the historical specter of the horizontal discrimination that restricted the job opportunities of fully credentialed women scientists to careers in cosmetic chemistry and home economics and women doctors to pediatrics and gynecology.[5] In many countries today, women scientists tend to be clustered in a small number of specialties thought of as women's fields. The causes of this clustering are to be found not only in the stereotypes about appropriate women's and men's activities and concerns that guide career choices and the hiring practices of scientific institutions, but also in the vagaries of local cultural and scientific history. Men, for example, often abandon a research field when the pay and status begin to be higher in others and thus create "women's sciences" by default. I do not mean to suggest that it is unfortunate for the rest of us that pediatrics, nutrition, public health, and such other socially valuable research fields attract and retain women scientists, but only that the idea of distinctive women's standpoints on nature can call to mind patterns of purported feminine "callings" and of career discrimination against women.

However, in the third place, feminists have been troubled by other issues, such as the way claims for distinctive women's standpoints challenge the dogma that the only good or real sciences are culturally neutral ones. Feminism is supposed to be removing sexist and androcentric cultural biases in the sciences, not substituting other cultural presuppositions, values, and interests for them; so the criticism goes. If good science is not culturally neutral, then a host of unattractive consequences seem to follow. After all, women have claimed the right to equal access to scientific education, jobs, publication, membership in scientific societies, and scientific awards on the grounds that they can do precisely the same good, objective, value-neutral

---

[5] Margaret W. Rossiter, *Women Scientists in America: Struggles and Strategies to 1940* (Baltimore: Johns Hopkins Univ. Press, 1982). See also Rossiter, *Women Scientists in America: Before Affirmative Action, 1940–1972* (Baltimore: Johns Hopkins Univ. Press, 1995).

science as can their brothers. It is precisely not their womanly, "feminine" characteristics that have earned them their hard-won places in the sciences but, instead, their transcendence of such cultural features. Equality has meant sameness with men for these feminists, as it has had to mean for all of us dealing with cultures where it is not just a linguistic accident that *man* and *human* routinely can be used interchangeably. Moreover, to venture beyond the claim that women can do just as good science as men to the claim that they can do differently valuable kinds of scientific work lends legitimacy to the long-standing, powerful devaluation of women's beliefs and practices. It also appears to devalue the status of modern sciences by implying that they represent not distinguished human achievements but merely masculine ones. Such an implication seems to ignore the fact that sciences "work" precisely because they enable prediction and control of nature regardless of the gender (and race, ethnicity, religion, and class) of the scientists. I shall explore what it means to claim that women do have distinctive standpoints on nature while denying that these are in fact implications of such a claim.

Fourth, to many feminist thinkers in the social studies of science, the question of women's standpoints appears inextricably mired in various contested assumptions. They think it essentializes women, centering some idealized "woman" or set of them, or some purportedly typical woman's activity, such as mothering, as representing all women and the womanly. Or it directs us to conceptualize scientific authority as grounded in something very different from universally valid knowledge claims, namely, the beliefs about nature of each individual woman in the world—a *reductio ad absurdum* of claims for women's standpoints. These are misreadings of standpoint arguments, but they lead to a resistance to the idea of distinctive women's standpoints on nature.

Finally, there are those who think that such a question distracts from more important questions of whether there can be not women's or feminine sciences but feminist ones. The questions for feminists should be not only about what scientific fields or styles of doing and thinking have been permitted or encouraged for women living in male supremacist societies but, more important, about what kinds of sciences feminists should want in order to end male supremacy and increase women's access to the resources they need to live, and to live well. The questions should be about not women's standpoints but feminist ones. However, I am arguing that one component of feminist standpoints can be a strategic use of the resources that women's distinctive natural and social locations provide.[6]

Some of these queries are more compelling than others. The terrain marked out by my question is a confusing, difficult, and dangerous one, but I don't think feminists or scholars in the social studies of science can afford simply to set it aside for that reason. The next section identifies four categories of differences between cultures that lead to their providing distinctive resources for understanding nature's regularities and their underlying causal tendencies. In each case, these kinds of differences between cultures also are differences between the resources available to sciences that frame their projects from the perspective of men's lives and those that

---

[6] I would argue that this was, in fact, one issue feminist standpoint theorists were trying to articulate from the beginning in their (our!) language about the importance of women's "experiences" of our bodies and of everyday life—language that misled in several ways. This is a topic tangential to the issues of this essay that I shall not pursue further here.

(also) start off from women's lives. This essay concludes with reflections on what this does and does not have to do with women scientists.

CULTURALLY LOCAL SCIENCES: MATERIAL AND SOCIAL CAUSES

What are the features that have provided resources for the historical development of culturally distinctive scientific traditions? This section examines women's and men's exposures to different aspects of nature's regularities, the different interests in and desires about nature's regularities that women and men can have in each culture, women's and men's different relationships to the discursive resources and traditions of their cultures, and the characteristically different ways that women and men tend to organize the social production of knowledge in each culture. (Of course these are only analytic separations of these features since, for example, what counts as an "aspect of nature's regularities" in daily life is itself shaped by cultures' interests and discursive resources.)

Heterogeneous Nature

First, cultures and subcultures are located in different natural environments. The different regularities of nature to which they are exposed offer them possible resources and probable dangers. Some cultures interact daily with high altitudes, mountainous terrains, deserts, oceanic islands, rivers, arctic or equatorial environments, or some other of nature's immensely diverse features. People in each culture need to be able to protect themselves from the natural patterns peculiar to those climates, land formations, plants, animals, and diseases that surround them or through which their travels take them and to figure out how to gain access to the forms of food, clothing, shelter, travel, and exchange that their part of nature offers. Moreover, "biological" differences—dark skins or light, immunity to malaria or lack of it, and so forth—create different interactions with the surrounding environment. Thus, to start with, different cultures are well positioned to understand different regularities of nature and their underlying causal tendencies, as travelers have observed from antiquity through the present day.

Theories that appear plausible in one environment, furthermore, may not in another. For example, plate tectonics was apparently accepted first by geographers and geologists working on environmental phenomena that were not well explained by older theories, such as the fit between the shapes and geological constitutions of the west coast of Africa and the east coast of South America or the Pacific Rim pattern of earthquakes and volcanoes. Theories that identify physical causes of premenstrual syndrome, chronic stress syndrome, or chronic fatigue syndrome may appear more plausible to people in whose bodies these phenomena occur, while others may find psychosomatic explanations of these symptoms more reasonable.

The claim here is not that knowledge based on some set of local interactions is always more accurate; very often it is not. The fact that knowledge is local in the sense we are considering here is no guarantee that it is the most accurate, let alone the most comprehensive. Rather, the claim is that cultures' different locations in heterogeneous nature expose them to different regularities of nature and that exposure to such "local environments" is a valuable resource for advancing collective human knowledge through what initially always appears as local knowledge.

Different peoples are repositories for historically developed and continually refined knowledge about different parts of nature.

A skeptic might well argue here that modern science, in contrast to the mere "ethnosciences" that have developed in these different natural niches, can in principle predict and explain all of nature's diverse features. The standard assumption has been that different modern sciences' representations of different aspects or parts of nature can be fit together, like pieces of a jigsaw puzzle, to form a coherent whole that uniquely represents nature's order. But that assumption is beginning to appear less plausible for many reasons, including that nature itself is far more disunified than modern sciences have expected. As one theorist of nature's disunity puts the point: "the disunity of science is not merely an unfortunate consequence of our limited computational or other cognitive capacities, but rather reflects accurately the underlying ontological complexity of the world, the disorder of things."[7] Thus it would be a mistake to assume that all "local knowledges," whether those of different scientific disciplines or those of different cultures, can be integrated into a coherent whole, not only because of the culturally distinctive incommensurable interests, discursive resources, and ways of organizing the production of knowledge that different disciplines and cultures bring to scientific research, but also because apparently nature's order is not that of a single coherent whole. Thus there have been and still are distinctive contributions that different cultures are able to make to the pool of human scientific knowledge because of their specific location in heterogeneous nature. In this respect, cultures are like scientific disciplines. And modern science no more escapes being "local" than do so-called ethnosciences. The "local" of modern science may extend from England around the Cape of Good Hope to India, or from Cape Canaveral to the moon; but any modern science's prediction and control of nature is still dependent upon exposure to some specifiable range of nature's order and lacks exposure to other such possible ranges.

Are women and men exposed to different aspects of nature's regularities? To start with, obviously women and men are biologically different, though not in all those characteristics of such interest to biological determinists. Not only are their reproductive systems different, but other aspects of their bodies—percentage of body fat (affecting, for example, their tolerance for cold water in long-distance swimming), skeletal construction (affecting their abilities in sports, including their susceptibility to injuries), susceptibility to the effects of drugs—seem measurably distinct, on average. These biological differences expose them to different regularities of nature. Moreover, characteristic gender-segregated socially assigned activities—from tending children, the aged, and the sick to other kinds of domestic labor, local community maintenance, clerical work, gathering food, and maintaining subsistence agriculture, herding, and forestry—bring women into distinctive interactions with natural environments, as the literature on gender and economic development, especially, has stressed.[8] Thus women's "biology" and culturally distinctive activities bring them into interactions with natural environments that are different from those with which their brothers daily interact. Consequently women will tend to be reposi-

---

[7] John Dupre, *The Disorder of Things: Metaphysical Foundations of the Disunity of Science* (Cambridge, Mass.: Harvard Univ. Press, 1993), p. 6.

[8] See, e.g., *Appropriate Technol.*, June 1995, 22(1), special issue on gender, science, and technology.

tories of historically developed knowledge about these aspects of the natural world. Research that starts out from feminist understandings of women's bodies and interactions with nature—not just men's—will arrive at more comprehensive and accurate understandings of nature's regularities and underlying causal determinants. So these gender-distinct locations in nature provide one source of women's distinctive standpoints on nature.

Different Cultural Interests

Different cultures have different interests and desires, even when they are more or less genetically the same and in "the same environment." Thus cultures ask different questions about the natural world. Sciences' problematics are shaped by their funders and sponsors and, more generally, by what is of interest to those groups that are in an economic and political position to have their concerns conceptualized as ones for empirical research. Bordering the Atlantic Ocean, one culture will be interested to fish it, another to use it as a coastal highway for trading, a third to use it for emigration, a fourth to desalinize it for drinking water, a fifth to use it as a refuse dump, a sixth to use it as an underwater military highway for submarines and torpedoes, and a seventh to mine the minerals, gas, and oil beneath its floor. These differing interests and their occasional intersection have created culturally distinctive patterns of knowledge about this part of nature's regularities and how best to explain them.

Many examples of how culturally different interests have shaped distinctive patterns of scientific knowledge and ignorance will spring to readers' minds from historical studies. Two examples are Donna Haraway's well-known account of how different national preoccupations shaped different knowledge in Japanese, Indian, and Anglo-American primatology and Paul Forman's account of how national security interests came to direct the agenda of physics in the United States before and during World War II.[9]

There is nothing controversial about these observations. What is controversial is to claim that science—real science—includes the choice of scientific problems and to point out that the cognitive content of science is shaped by and has its characteristic patterns of knowledge and ignorance precisely because of problem choices. Referring to feminist criticisms of inattention to women's health and medical concerns, Evelyn Fox Keller characterizes the conservative view this way: "This kind of criticism does not touch our conception of what science is, nor our confidence in the neutrality of science. It may be true that in some areas we have ignored certain problems, but our definition of science does not include the choice of problem—that, we can readily agree, has always been influenced by social forces." However, this restrictive "definition of science" is no longer the most authoritative one; even the National Academy of Sciences has made it clear that this older definition must be expanded. The notion of scientific methods, its report recommends, can reasonably be broadened to "also include the decisions scientists make about which

---

[9] Donna Haraway, *Primate Visions: Gender, Race, and Nature in the World of Modern Science* (New York: Routledge, 1989); and Paul Forman, "Behind Quantum Electronics: National Security as Basis for Physical Research in the United States, 1940–1960," *Historical Studies in the Physical and Biological Sciences*, 1987, *18*:149–229.

problems to pursue or when to conclude an investigation. Methods involve the ways scientists work with each other and exchange information. Taken together, these methods constitute the craft of science."[10]

The evidence here argues that women have at least partially different interests in and desires about the natural world to the extent that they are biologically different from men and are assigned activities that bring them into systematically different interactions with their environments. Women need and want to know how our bodies work, how drugs affect us, and how more effectively to interact with the environment on behalf of our own interests and the lives of those dependent on us for whom we have been assigned responsibility. For whom have women been assigned responsibility? In many cultures this group includes children, other household members, other kin (especially in sickness and old age), and often the larger local communities, where women are responsible on an everyday basis for maintaining social networks and social services. That is, both men and women have children, have other kin and sick and aged people around them, and live in communities, but they have characteristically socially distinctive interests in and desires with respect to these people's situations. Of course these vary from culture to culture; each culture has norms for what are appropriate interests and desires for women and for men. These interests are most segregated where adult activities are maximally segregated. For example, gender interests are geographically segregated in cases where men work in distant cities, in migrant agricultural labor, or in other countries as "guest workers," rarely returning to the areas where their wives and families live; this can even occur where professional and managerial men spend long hours on the job in cities and little time in domestic work or in the suburban communities where their wives and children spend their days.

There are many other contexts for thinking about women's differing interests in nature. For example, the vast majority of fatalities in modern wars occur in civilian populations and, especially, among women and children. Moreover, a much greater proportion of women's lifework than of men's is invested in birthing and raising the next generation, including the sons who will become soldiers. It is implausible to presume that women have the same interests and desires as their brothers in supporting militarism and the scientific and technological research agendas that service militaries. The presumption that such sciences represent "human interests" is even more questionable when one considers how ideals of the warrior and the national hero are ideals of masculinity: women's compensation for the costs of war is far less than men's since they share only vicariously in the masculine glory that accrues from military victories.[11] Women have fewer interests in research, basic and applied, that services militarism and nationalism than do men and more interests in research, basic and applied, that services sustainable domestic and local community activities.

---

[10] Evelyn Fox Keller, "Feminism and Science," in *Sex and Scientific Inquiry,* ed. Sandra Harding and Jean O'Barr (Chicago: Univ. Chicago Press, 1987), pp. 233–246, on p. 235; and National Academy of Sciences, *On Being a Scientist* (Washington, D.C.: National Academy of Sciences Press, 1989), p. 6.

[11] See Cynthia Enloe, *Bananas, Beaches, and Bases: Making Feminist Sense of International Politics* (Berkeley: Univ. California Press, 1990); Enloe, *The Morning After: Sexual Politics at the End of the Cold War* (Berkeley: Univ. California Press, 1993); and Sara Ruddick, *Maternal Thinking: Toward a Politics of Peace* (Boston: Beacon, 1989).

Such considerations lead to recognition of two additional kinds of cultural differences that generate distinctive patterns of knowledge and ignorance.

Cultural Discursive Traditions

One can focus on the role of metaphors and models of nature in the formulation of research projects as a central example of this far more complex category. Many observers from postcolonial, feminist, and conventional science studies have pointed out how such cultural elements insure that modern sciences have not been, are not, and could not be value free.[12] It has become clear that the goal of absolute value freedom is counterproductive because the advance of scientific knowledge requires just such cultural elements to direct its theories and subsequent interactions with nature. Thus cultural presuppositions are not the unmitigated defect in the sciences that they have conventionally been thought to be. This conclusion emerges from both the philosophy and the history of northern sciences, and it confirms the claims from both postcolonial and feminist science studies that cultural diversity in conceptualizing both nature and the research process is a necessity for the growth of scientific knowledge.

According to such analyses, presented over the last three decades, scientific theories are underdetermined not just by any existing collection of evidence for them but by any possible collection of evidence. Scientific processes are not transparent; their culturally regional features can sometimes even constitute the conceptual frameworks for descriptions and explanations of nature's order.[13] Thus more than one scientific theory or model can be consistent with any given set of data. Moreover, each such theoretical representation can have more than one reasonable interpretation. Indeed, this looseness or slack in scientific explanation turns out to be a major source of the growth of scientific knowledge. It is this feature that permits scientists to "see nature" in ever-new ways that advance the accuracy and comprehensiveness of their claims.[14]

Thus different cultural elements provide crucial resources for advancing the growth of knowledge. Such elements can be borrowed by a science from other disciplines, directly from the surrounding culture, from adjacent cultures with which the science interacts, from older elements of a culture's own scientific tradition, and, no doubt, from other sources. We could say that cultural elements, such as language,

---

[12] For an example of each see Goonatilake, *Aborted Discovery* (cit. n. 3); Keller, *Reflections on Gender and Science* (cit. n. 1); and Bas Van Fraassen and Jill Sigman, "Interpretation in Science and in the Arts," in *Realism and Representation,* ed. George Levine (Madison: Univ. Wisconsin Press, 1993), pp. 73–99.

[13] See Thomas S. Kuhn, *The Structure of Scientific Revolutions,* 2nd ed. (Chicago: Univ. Chicago Press, 1970); Bruno Latour, *The Pasteurization of France,* trans. Alan Sheridan and John Law (Cambridge, Mass.: Harvard Univ. Press, 1988); Helen Longino, *Science as Social Knowledge: Values and Objectivity in Scientific Inquiry* (Princeton, N.J.: Princeton Univ. Press, 1990); Carolyn Merchant, *The Death of Nature: Women, Ecology, and the Scientific Revolution* (New York: Harper & Row, 1980); Andrew Pickering, *Constructing Quarks* (Chicago: Univ. Chicago Press, 1984); W. V. O. Quine, "Two Dogmas of Empiricism," in *From a Logical Point of View* (Cambridge, Mass.: Harvard Univ. Press, 1953); and Steven Shapin and Simon Schaffer, *Leviathan and the Air-Pump: Hobbes, Boyle, and the Experimental Life* (Princeton, N.J.: Princeton Univ. Press, 1985).

[14] Mary Hesse, *Models and Analogies in Science* (Notre Dame, Ind.: Univ. Notre Dame Press, 1966); Nancy Leys Stepan, "Race and Gender: The Role of Analogy in Science," *Isis,* 1986, 77:261–277; and Van Fraassen and Sigman, "Interpretation in Science and in the Arts" (cit. n. 12).

far from being only the "prison-house" that they have been represented as in conventional accounts, are also part of sciences' toolbox of methods and resources. That is, scientific language necessarily enables and limits what a culture can know about nature's regularities and their underlying causal tendencies. It is a source of "different sciences" even within the history of modern science, as the favored models of nature have changed, and it enables cultures to draw on their own familiar metaphors and models to explore different aspects of nature's regularities; they take the standpoint of their cultural inheritances in order to "see nature" in distinctive ways.

Women and men do not have the same relation to cultural metaphors and models precisely in those cases where the metaphors and models carry sexual and gender meanings. A central project of feminist science studies has been to evaluate critically just these kinds of scientific and technological discursive legacies. Scholars have pointed out how our understandings of nature and of research processes are limited when the favored metaphors and models are restricted to those attractive from the perspective of male supremacist ideologies. We can gain more accurate and comprehensive understandings of both nature and research if we avoid or at least balance such gendered models, since they overvalue "masculine" models of nature and modes of conducting research. They have the effect of turning gendered meanings into evidence for the plausibility of research claims. This is true whether nature is conceptualized as a mother who is endlessly bountiful, as a wild and unruly harridan who must be controlled lest man's fate be threatened, or as a shy maiden whose veils must be stripped away so that science can "discover her secrets"—all highly influential models in the history of European sciences.[15]

Women, like other nondominant groups, are less susceptible to thinking of language as transparent to the world. They tend to be more alert to the presence of cultural metaphors, models, and ways of organizing research that inappropriately devalue women and their activities, as histories of popular culture reveal. They sometimes seek out other ways of using cultural traditions. Or they feel less bound by them—they are less well socialized into seeing nature or ideal research processes through the hierarchical models preferred in dominant scientific discourses. And feminist discourses take such analyses as one of their central projects. However, it is by no means exclusively women who have examined sciences' cultural traditions from a critical perspective on such discourses of male dominance; a number of male historians of science have also been able to make important contributions here by taking the standpoint of women.[16]

Standpoints of women call for other than masculinist models and metaphors in scientific and technological discourses. Nonsexist, woman-valuing models and degendered ones that forgo forcing nature's order into a procrustean gender bed are

---

[15] See N. Katherine Hayles, "Gender Encoding in Fluid Mechanics: Masculine Channels and Feminine Flows," *Differences,* 1992, 4(2):17–44; Keller, *Reflections on Gender and Science* (cit. n. 1); Keller, *Secrets of Life, Secrets of Death: Essays on Language, Gender, and Science* (New York: Routledge, 1992); Emily Martin, "Egg and the Sperm" (cit. n. 1); Merchant, *Death of Nature* (cit. n. 13); Shiva, *Staying Alive* (cit. n. 1); and Londa Schiebinger, *Nature's Body: Gender in the Making of Modern Science* (Boston: Beacon, 1993).

[16] See Brian Easlea, *Science and Sexual Oppression: Patriarchy's Confrontation with Woman and Nature* (London: Weidenfeld & Nicolson, 1981); Easlea, *Fathering the Unthinkable: Masculinity, Scientists, and the Nuclear Arms Race* (London: Pluto, 1983); David Noble, *A World without Women: The Christian Clerical Culture of Western Science* (New York: Knopf, 1992); and Robert Nye, "Medicine and Science as Masculine 'Fields of Honor,'" in this volume.

two categories of alternatives that could enable us all to "see nature" in more accurate and comprehensive ways.

Cultural Organizations of Scientific Work

Last, the cognitive content of sciences is shaped by culturally distinctive favored forms of social organization and, especially, of work. Scientific research is social labor, carried out in culturally distinctive kinds of organizations—laboratories located in industries, universities, physicians' offices, and federal institutes or computer-connected collections of such sites; field stations, farms, collecting and observing expeditions, conferences, learned societies, journals, hospitals, routine visits to healers with culturally diverse credentials; and so on. What we can know of nature's regularities and how we explain them is dependent in part on how communities for systematic observation and explanation of nature's regularities are organized. Some examples here can suggest a range of ways in which this observation can be supported.

The historian Robert Proctor demonstrates that imbalances in the political power of research fields or disciplines—aspects of how research is organized—have shaped what we know about the causes of cancer. The far greater funding for and political power of medical compared to environmental researchers insures that we know much more about the causes of cancer to be found within individuals than about those to be found in environments. It is difficult to avoid the conclusion that our continuing relative ignorance about environmental causes of cancers is due to the way such research threatens not only the interests of medical researchers but also those of governments, militaries, and industries that wish to avoid responsibility for past and present polluting practices.[17]

In the history of European sciences, Steven Shapin and Simon Schaffer show how the scientific experiment was "invented" through careful staging of demonstrations of the air pump to suitable observers. Bruno Latour argues that Pasteur had to turn physicians into scientists in order to demonstrate the validity of his hypotheses to them and the public. In such cases, the very constitution of new fields of research has required the reorganization of scientific work.[18]

One can also read the postcolonial accounts that focus on how European expansion and the growth of modern science depended on each other as drawing our attention to a particular form of organizing the production of systematic scientific knowledge. European expansion required better cartography, astronomy, oceanography, shipbuilding, geology, and mining, better understanding of the plants, animals, diseases, and peoples of other parts of the world, and diverse other knowledge about the natural and social worlds. In turn, those sciences benefited immensely from being developed in the diverse environments and through the cultural borrowings that European expansion made possible. European expansion was a form of organization of the production of modern sciences' knowledge that, in effect, turned the world into a laboratory for European sciences. Peoples that could not benefit from this kind of "collecting" and integration of knowledge from many diverse parts of nature

---

[17] Robert Proctor, *Cancer Wars: How Politics Shapes What We Know and Don't Know about Cancer* (Boston: Basic, 1995).
[18] Shapin and Schaffer, *Leviathan and the Air-Pump* (cit. n. 13); and Latour, *Pasteurization of France,* trans. Sheridan and Law (cit. n. 13).

and cultural traditions "lost knowledge" (and often their lives and cultures) because of European expansion.[19]

Finally, Sharon Traweek's comparative study of Japanese and U.S. high-energy physics shows how cultural models of the organization of work and ideal career trajectories, on the one hand, and nationally established relationships between equipment manufacturers and physicists, on the other hand, converge to generate the pursuit of at least marginally different scientific problems in Japan and in the United States and Europe.[20] Her study also draws attention to other ways in which the characteristic durations of research projects can shape a culture's patterns of knowledge and ignorance. Where research funding is too tightly tied to electoral politics, for example, projects will tend to be shorter than the terms of political office. Few politicians will fund a scientific project that will come to fruition only after they may have been voted out of office and thus cannot reap the political benefits of having sponsored such an advance of knowledge.

Do women and men tend to organize differently research and, more generally, work? One interesting case is reported by Haraway. Japanese women primatologists routinely learn to identify individually huge numbers—hundreds—of the primates they study, a feat that Japanese men find remarkable. This familiarity enables them to learn far more about the complex social relations in these species. Traweek has explained how Japanese women physicists, doubly devalued in the international scientific community because they are not European or American and not men, have ingeniously developed valuable alternative resources for advancing their research projects. For example, as professionals, they tend to retain far stronger links to their colleagues in U.S. and European graduate schools than do their Japanese male peers. Excluded by the male Japanese physics community, they remain in the international networks of their old school chums and, consequently, in different ways can be tied into the prestigious international physics community.[21] There are also indications that women's characteristic patterns of social relations in everyday life tend to lead women scientists to organize their laboratories, their choices of scientific projects, and their publishing strategies differently than do their male peers.[22] Starting off research from women's culturally distinctive organization of scientific and technological work can lead to more comprehensive and accurate scientific and technological claims about nature.

I have been arguing that a wide array of literatures can be read as claiming that

---

[19] Lucille H. Brockway, *Science and Colonial Expansion: The Role of the British Royal Botanical Gardens* (New York: Academic, 1979); Alfred Crosby, *Ecological Imperialism: The Biological Expansion of Europe* (Cambridge: Cambridge Univ. Press, 1987); Goonatilake, *Aborted Discovery* (cit. n. 3); James E. McClellan, *Colonialism and Science: Saint Domingue in the Old Regime* (Baltimore: Johns Hopkins Univ. Press, 1992); and Patrick Petitjean, Catherine Jami, and Anne Marie Moulin, eds., *Science and Empires: Historical Studies about Scientific Development and European Expansion* (Dordrecht: Kluwer, 1992).

[20] Sharon Traweek, *Beamtimes and Lifetimes: The World of High Energy Physicists* (Cambridge, Mass.: Harvard Univ. Press, 1988).

[21] Haraway, *Primate Visions* (cit. n. 9); and Sharon Traweek, *Building Big Science in Japan* (forthcoming).

[22] Marcia Barinaga, "Is There a 'Female Style' in Science?" *Science*, 16 Apr. 1993, *260*:384–391. See also the literature on women in organizations, e.g., Joan Acker, "Gendered Institutions: From Sex Roles to Gendered Institutions," *Contemporary Sociology,* 1992, *21*:265–269; Rosabeth Moss Kanter, *Men and Women of the Corporation* (New York: Basic, 1977); and Albert J. Mills and Peta Tancred, eds., *Gendering Organizational Theory* (London: Sage, 1991).

distinctive "standpoints on nature" are created by the fact that different cultures are exposed to different parts of nature and that cultures examine their parts of nature by way of culturally distinctive interests, discursive resources, and ways of organizing the production of empirical knowledge. Each of these forms of generating culturally "local knowledge" is also a form of generating gendered "local knowledge." From the perspective of these analyses, all sciences and technologies bear the distinctive cultural marks, including gendered ones, of their production processes. Some of these sciences and technologies are immensely more powerful than others at predicting and controlling nature, but not all of the potentially powerful ones are necessarily those generated by European or androcentric histories and conceptual frameworks. The store of human knowledge about the natural world can be expanded if cultures can take advantage of the resources that women's standpoints provide. Indeed, it maximizes the objectivity of scientific knowledge when sciences exploit the diverse cultural resources available to advance the accuracy and comprehensiveness of scientific knowledge.[23]

WOMEN (AND MEN) SCIENTISTS

What does all this have to do with women scientists? One certainly cannot conclude that women's biological differences from men automatically lead them to think differently; that women should go into those sciences focused on issues centered in women's lives; that only women can make significant contributions to fields characteristically thought of as womanly or that all women in those fields automatically do; that sciences not focused on these fields are only masculine sciences, not human ones; that there are typical or essential, or fixed and unchanging, womanly interactions with nature that can define once and for all what "women's standpoints" are; or that women automatically know what other women's standpoints on nature are (or even, without reflection, what their own are). Nor should it be concluded that this issue of women's standpoints should replace important questions about which feminist analyses can and should best frame particular scientific or epistemological projects. After all, these arguments for the importance of women's standpoints on nature are framed within a distinctive approach—namely, feminist standpoint theory—that other theorists may well contest.

Instead, I suggest only that when women or men scientists can figure out how to ask questions about nature's regularities that originate in the kinds of distinctive natural "locations in nature" and in the kinds of cultural resources that women's interests, relations to cultural traditions, and ways of organizing knowledge make available, the storehouse of human scientific knowledge can expand and that knowledge will become more accurate. But for this to happen, women's distinctive natural and cultural locations must be appreciatively recognized by science policy and by the public policy in which the sciences participate. It would help if more women were in positions to make science policy and public policy. And it would help if feminist perspectives on these issues, such as those reported here, were correctly

---

[23] I have discussed the virtues of such a strengthening of standards for maximizing objectivity in a number of places. See, e.g., Sandra Harding, "'Strong Objectivity' and Socially Situated Knowledge," in *Whose Science? Whose Knowledge?* (cit. n. 2), Ch. 6; Harding, "After the Neutrality Ideal: Politics, Science, and 'Strong Objectivity,'" *Social Research*, 1992, *59*:567–587; and Harding, "'Strong Objectivity': A Response to the New Objectivity Question," *Synthese*, 1995, *104*(3):1–19.

perceived in public life more generally to provide important resources for the growth of knowledge. This is a task in which both women and men can participate, inside and outside the sciences. After all, women have had to learn how to ask interesting questions about nature from the perspective of natural and social "locations" that were not "their own." Why can't men now join women in the project of figuring out how to think from the standpoints of women's culturally diverse but always distinctive lives?[24]

---

[24] This essay is part of a larger project that includes Sandra Harding, "Is Science Multicultural? Challenges, Opportunities, Uncertainties," *Configurations*, 1994, 2:301–330, rpt. in *Multiculturalism: A Reader*, ed. David Theo Goldberg (New York: Blackwell, 1994), pp. 344–370; Harding, "Is Modern Science an Ethnoscience?" in *Sociology of the Sciences Yearbook, 1996*, ed. Terry Shinn, Jack Spaapen, and Roland Waast (Dordrecht: Kluwer, 1997); Harding, "Multicultural and Global Feminist Philosophies of Science: Issues and Challenges," in *Feminism, Science, and the Philosophy of Science*, ed. Lynn Hankinson Nelson and Jack Nelson (Dordrecht: Kluwer, 1996); and Harding, *Is Science Multicultural? Feminism, Postcolonialism, and Epistemology* (Bloomington: Indiana Univ. Press, in press).

Creating Sustainable Science

By Londa Schiebinger*

> If we can identify the role of human agency in the making of knowledge, we—as women and as scientists—could know other things in new ways.
> —Joan Gero (1993)

MY PROBLEMATIC is somewhat different from that set by the editors of this volume. My interest lies in the relationship between gender studies of science and scientists, centering on the following questions: What impact has gender studies of science had on the methods and practice of science? What kind of working relationships have been established between science studies scholars and scientists, and what fruitful relationships might be institutionalized? I take issue with Bruno Latour's suggestion that the purpose of science studies is to cultivate an appreciation of science, leaving undisturbed the object of study. Feminist science scholars not only study the "beauty of facts and discipline in science" but often seek to change them.[1]

The question is, How can this be done? The history and philosophy of science have themselves become exacting disciplines. We hold cozy conferences and put finishing touches on nuanced and complex theories. For the most part, however, our work does not reach the intended audiences in the sciences. The question of creating a vital working relationship between historians and philosophers of science and scientists is, for me, tied to the problem of increasing the numbers of women in science. I see the former as a necessary condition of the latter.

We have embarked on a new era in regard to the question of women in science. For the first time in history, institutions that for centuries have held women and minorities at arm's length are now courting them. There is genuine enthusiasm in this regard. As the former editor of *Science* put it, "It may cost some money, some effort, and some understanding, but the voyage to full equality can be even more exciting and worthwhile than the voyage into space."[2] And women have made un-

---

* Department of History, Pennsylvania State University, University Park, Pennsylvania 16802.

[1] Bruno Latour, "Letter to the Editor," *The Sciences*, Mar./Apr. 1995, pp. 6–7.

[2] Daniel Koshland, Jr., in *Science*, 25 Mar. 1988, *238*:1473. For bibliography on women in science, technology, and medicine see Alison Wylie, Kathleen Okruhlik, Sandra Morton, and Leslie Thielen-Wilson, "Philosophical Feminism: A Bibliographic Guide to Critiques of Science," *Resources for Feminist Research/Documentation sur la Recherche Feministe*, 1990, *19*(2):2–36; Margarete Maurer, *Frauenforschung in Naturwissenschaften, Technik und Medizin* (Vienna: Wiener Frauenverlag, 1993); Elisabeth A. Bacus *et al.*, eds., *A Gendered Past: A Critical Bibliography of Gender in Archaeology* (Technical Reports, 25) (Ann Arbor: Univ. Michigan Museum of Anthropology, 1993); and Phyllis Holman Weisbard and Rima D. Apple, eds., *The History of Women and Science, Health, and Technology: A Bibliographic Guide to the Professions and the Disciplines*, 2nd ed. (Madison: Univ. Wisconsin System, Women's Studies Librarian, 1993).

precedented gains. Who, just five years ago, could have predicted that the chief scientist at the National Aeronautics and Space Administration would be a woman (from 1994 to 1996 this post was held by the astrophysicist France Cordova)? Who would have expected that the Surgeon General of the United States would be a feisty woman (though only briefly), that the agency responsible for building U.S. military weapons would be headed by an African-American woman, and that the Secretary of the Air Force would be a female professor of engineering from MIT? More dramatically, who would have predicted that the National Institutes of Health would devote nearly three-quarters of a billion dollars to study neglected aspects of women's health or that entire fields of science—such as primatology—would be overhauled by the feminist critique of science?

Despite these considerable gains, women as a group have not reached parity with men. Women in science and engineering overall continue to face higher unemployment, lower pay, and fewer opportunities for promotion than their male peers. Why is this so? One reason is the tragic divide between three increasingly self-contained groups of experts: those who fashion and fund intervention programs designed to increase the number of women in science, historians and philosophers of women and gender in science, and scientists. Because of the enormity of the task, those who design programs rarely discuss the restructuring of knowledge and institutions required to make them work. The National Research Council's Committee on Women in Science and Engineering, formed in 1990, for instance, narrowly limited itself to questions of education, recruitment, and advancement—that is, questions of how to make women more competitive as scientists. Missing from its bibliographies are the gender critiques of science offered by Sandra Harding, Evelyn Fox Keller, Sharon Traweek, and many others.[3] At the same time, feminist theorists and epistemologists rarely suggest concrete solutions or programs designed to overcome the problems they so ably uncover. Feminist science theorists often display the disdain for applied science characteristic of mainstream science theorists. Even more tragic is that scientists are by and large unfamiliar with the literature on gender in science.

These divides are reproduced in scholarship on women and gender in science, which includes diverse scholarly approaches that are often pursued in isolation from each other. First is the massive statistical literature, whose purpose is to demonstrate that women are underrepresented in science and to chart increases or decreases in their status. Second is the historical and sociological study of women in science, much of which reveals a clash of cultures between women and European and North American science. In 1959, C. P. Snow identified two cultures, scientific and literary, between which loomed a gulf of "mutual incomprehension, ... hostility and dislike, and most of all lack of understanding." Similarly, there exists a gulf between the cultures of science as we know them and women of diverse backgrounds, ethnic and national groups. The history and sociology of women in science has generally

---

[3] National Research Council, Committee on Women in Science and Engineering, *Women in Science and Engineering: Increasing Their Numbers in the 1990s* (Washington, D.C.: National Academy Press, 1991); and National Research Council, Committee on Women in Science and Engineering, *Women Scientists and Engineers Employed in Industry: Why So Few?* (Washington, D.C.: National Academy Press, 1994). On the inequalities faced by women in science and engineering see National Science Foundation, *Women, Minorities, and Persons with Disabilities in Science and Engineering: 1994* (NSF94-333) (Arlington, Va., 1994), p. xxxiii.

emphasized the consequences of the resulting conflicts for women: women have been banned from rarefied intellectual pursuits, their interests and concerns marginalized.[4] We have seen some institutional initiatives to solve some of these problems: spousal hiring programs, parental leave policies, policies for stopping the tenure clock—all of which leave basic academic structures in place.

What I want to focus on here is a third body of literature that analyzes the structure of knowledge crafted within institutions that have historically excluded women. The success of feminist critiques of science in the last ten years has been to reveal concrete examples of the gendering of science. But feminism is ultimately reactionary in the sense that it responds to and is structured by sexism. The critical task now is to turn critique into a resource for generating knowledge. It is not enough to understand how science has been made; we need to develop more practical, constructive ways to employ tools of gender analysis in creating what I will call "sustainable science." Only when gender analysis becomes an integral part of science research programs will the problem of women in science be solved.

GENDERED SCIENCE

Leaving aside for the moment the work of Christine de Pizan, François Poullain de la Barre, Anna van Schurman, Dorothea Leporinin Erxleben, Antoinette Blackwell, Charlotte Perkins Gilman, Hedwig Dohm, and numerous other early critics of science, the modern feminist critique emerged in the 1970s. Much of this early critique sought to identify the distinctive masculine character of Western science. Objectivity and reason were identified not as neutral values but as notions intimately associated with Western masculinity and the public sphere.[5] Overarching critique provided the impetus and context for the fine-grained analyses of gender dynamics in particular scientific discoveries, theories, nomenclatures, instruments, techniques, and objects that began to emerge in the late 1980s and 1990s.

Feminists have enjoyed great success in revealing gender inequalities in the humanities, social sciences, and life sciences, where subject matters are sexed or easily

---

[4] C. P. Snow, *The Two Cultures and the Scientific Revolution* (New York: Cambridge Univ. Press, 1962), p. 4. For the statistical literature, in addition to the National Science Foundation report on the status of women and minorities in science cited in note 3, above, see Betty Vetter, *Professional Women and Minorities* (Washington, D.C.: Commission on Professionals in Science and Technology, Jan. 1994). The literature on the history and sociology of women in science is voluminous. See, e.g., Margaret Rossiter, *Women Scientists in America: Struggles and Strategies to 1940* (Baltimore: Johns Hopkins Univ. Press, 1982); Rossiter, *Women Scientists in America: Before Affirmative Action, 1940–1972* (Baltimore: Johns Hopkins Univ. Press, 1995); Evelyn Fox Keller, *A Feeling for the Organism: The Life and Work of Barbara McClintock* (New York: Freeman, 1983); Margaret Alic, *Hypatia's Heritage* (London: Women's Press, 1986); Pnina G. Abir-Am and Dorinda Outram, eds., *Uneasy Careers and Intimate Lives: Women in Science, 1789–1979* (New Brunswick, N.J.: Rutgers Univ. Press, 1987); Londa Schiebinger, *The Mind Has No Sex? Women in the Origins of Modern Science* (Cambridge, Mass.: Harvard Univ. Press, 1989); Harriet Zuckerman, Jonathan Cole, and John Bruer, eds., *The Outer Circle: Women in the Scientific Community* (New York: Norton, 1991); Evelynn Hammonds, "Science," in *Black Women in America: An Historical Encyclopedia*, ed. Darlene Hine (New York: Carlson, 1992), pp. 1015–1016; and Helena M. Pycior, Nancy G. Slack, and Pnina G. Abir-Am, eds., *Creative Couples in the Sciences* (New Brunswick, N.J.: Rutgers Univ. Press, 1996).

[5] Carolyn Merchant, *The Death of Nature: Women, Ecology, and the Scientific Revolution* (San Francisco: Harper & Row, 1980); Evelyn Fox Keller, *Reflections on Gender and Science* (New Haven, Conn.: Yale Univ. Press, 1985); and Sandra Harding, *The Science Question in Feminism* (Ithaca, N.Y.: Cornell Univ. Press, 1986). For a history of pre-twentieth-century critique see Schiebinger, *Mind Has No Sex?* pp. 1–9, 160–188.

imagined to have sex and gender. We can chant a litany of well-established examples of how the life sciences are gendered. We know, for example, how women's bodies have been read and misread by the medical sciences. We have seen how the long arm of gender has superimposed stereotypical attributes onto apes, plants' pistils and pollen, and cells and cell parts that do not necessarily have sex, let alone gender.[6]

A simple example of how gendered stereotypes have been written into cell biology can be found in textbook accounts of conception, where the active sperm and the passive egg long remained stock characters. After the mid 1980s, biologists no longer characterized the classical "passive" egg as drifting aimlessly along the fallopian tube until captured by the heroic, active sperm. Textbooks now more often portray the egg as an active agent, directing the growth of microvilli (small fingerlike projections on its surface) that tether the sperm and releasing digestive enzymes that allow a sperm to enter it. Critics have warned of problems ensuing from the regendered egg and sperm, which, in tune with more current gender stereotypes, are now often portrayed as "partners"—much like a dual-career couple—working together toward successful fertilization.[7]

The "exact" sciences, however, often claim for themselves a special epistemological status: freedom from social imprint. Confidence in this matter is so firm that

---

[6] On the reading of women's bodies by the medical sciences see, e.g., Ruth Bleier, *Science and Gender: A Critique of Biology and Its Theories on Women* (New York: Pergamon, 1984); Anne Fausto-Sterling, *Myths of Gender: Biological Theories about Women and Men* (New York: Basic, 1985); Ludmilla Jordanova, *Sexual Visions: Images of Gender in Science and Medicine between the Eighteenth and Twentieth Centuries* (Madison: Univ. Wisconsin Press, 1989); Thomas Laqueur, *Making Sex: Body and Gender from the Greeks to Freud* (Cambridge, Mass.: Harvard Univ. Press, 1990); Cynthia Eagle Russett, *Sexual Science: The Victorian Construction of Womanhood* (Cambridge, Mass.: Harvard Univ. Press, 1989); Ruth Hubbard, *The Politics of Women's Biology* (New Brunswick, N.J.: Rutgers Univ. Press, 1990); Nancy Tuana, *The Less Noble Sex: Scientific, Religious, and Philosophical Conceptions of Woman's Nature* (Bloomington: Indiana Univ. Press, 1993); and Nelly Oudshoorn, *Beyond the Natural Body: An Archaeology of Sex Hormones* (London: Routledge, 1994). On gender stereotyping in other fields see Donna Haraway, *Primate Visions: Gender, Race, and Nature in the World of Modern Science* (London: Routledge, 1989); Tuana, ed., *Feminism and Science* (Bloomington: Indiana Univ. Press, 1989); Marina Benjamin, *Science and Sensibility: Gender and Scientific Inquiry, 1780–1945* (Oxford: Blackwell, 1991); Evelyn Fox Keller, *Secrets of Life, Secrets of Death: Essays on Language, Gender, and Science* (New York: Routledge, 1992); and Londa Schiebinger, *Nature's Body: Gender in the Making of Modern Science* (Boston: Beacon, 1993).

[7] See Biology and Gender Study Group, "The Importance of Feminist Critique for Contemporary Cell Biology," in *Feminism and Science*, ed. Tuana, pp. 172–187; Emily Martin, "The Egg and the Sperm: How Science Has Constructed a Romance Based on Stereotypical Male-Female Roles," *Signs: Journal of Women in Culture and Society,* 1991, *16*:485–501; and Bonnie Spanier, *Im/partial Science: Gender Ideology in Molecular Biology* (Bloomington: Indiana Univ. Press, 1995), pp. 61–62. While many have hailed this new rendering of the drama as an example of prejudice vanquished, we might also see it as a narrative of masculinization. Not only is the egg energized; it is masculinized, that is, ascribed the valued "active" characteristics of the sperm. Like women themselves, female biology is here expected to assimilate the values of the dominant culture. Emily Martin warns that as the egg becomes active or masculinized, it is also seen as aggressive—a *femme fatale,* threatening to capture and victimize men. An active female can be valued differently than an active male. "New data," she writes, "did not lead scientists to eliminate gender stereotypes. . . . Instead, scientists simply began to describe egg and sperm in different, but no less damaging, terms" (Martin, "Egg and Sperm," pp. 498–499). The molecular biologist and professor of women's studies Bonnie Spanier interjects further that in this instance the notion of equality between the contributions of the egg and the sperm is misleading, hiding the fact that the egg (as females more generally) contributes more to biological reproduction than the sperm. Emphasizing equality in heredity, she argues, diminishes the actual role of the egg as the larger gamete that contributes nutrients, organelles such as mitochondria and ribosomes, the cell membrane, and proteins crucial to the development of the zygote.

critics of feminism often play "stump the speaker." The challenge goes something like this: Is there a concrete example of gender in the substance of physics or math? Can you point to gender distortion in Newton's laws or Einstein's theory of relativity? If not, then mathematics and the physical sciences are objective and value free, as we have claimed all along. This challenge is problematic, as Sandra Harding has pointed out and as I will discuss in what follows.[8] Considering it for a moment, however, as posed, can we identify gender in math and physics, whose subject matters have no recognizable sex, in the same way that we have done in the life sciences?

Take, first, mathematics, the "critical filter" for careers in science and engineering. Feminists have decoded sexism in student problem sets. Phyllis Rosser's extensive study of the mathematics portion of the Scholastic Aptitude Test (SAT) shows that the fifty-point spread between women's and men's scores results to a great extent from aspects of the test's format that work against women. Problems often exclude women actors and draw from the masculine side of life—sports, business, technology, and so forth. Rosser has also shown how bias at this level could be remedied.[9]

The mathematicians Kenneth Bogart and Peter Doyle have taken the analysis a step further to suggest that certain problems have not been solved (or are not easily solved) because of sexist assumptions. They report on the whimsical "ménage problem," first posed in 1891, which asks for "the number M_n ways of seating n man-woman couples at a circular table with men and women alternating so that no one sits next to his or her partner." Bogart and Doyle suggest that only the tradition of seating ladies first made this problem seem difficult and speculate that, had it not been for this tradition, the problem would have been solved fifty years earlier. The easiest solution requires that both be seated at once, giving preference to neither the women nor the men.[10] Bogart and Doyle do not comment on the rigidly Victorian character of the problem itself.

Other feminist critiques of mathematics have centered on its overwrought abstractness. There is in these critiques nothing peculiar to women or gender. Feminists join others who argue that a sense of certainty in mathematics has sometimes been bought at the price of oversimplification. N. Katherine Hayles has discussed, for example, how differential and integral calculus have difficulty modeling a world in motion and the problems this limitation raised for the development of fluid mechanics. According to Hayles, eighteenth-century calculus could see complex flow only as haphazard movement, as a deviation from its basic models rather than as a

---

[8] To attempt to respond to this question on its own terms, of course, reinforces the privilege accorded physics. See Sandra Harding, "Why 'Physics' Is a Bad Model for Physics," in *Whose Science? Whose Knowledge? Thinking from Women's Lives* (Ithaca, N.Y.: Cornell Univ. Press, 1991), pp. 77–102.

[9] Phyllis Rosser, *The SAT Gender Gap: Identifying the Causes* (Washington, D.C.: Center for Women Policy Studies, 1989); and Rosser, *The SAT Gender Gap: ETS Responds, a Research Update* (Washington, D.C.: Center for Women Policy Studies, 1992). The purpose of the SAT is to predict first-year college grades. Some universities, including the Massachusetts Institute of Technology, have begun admitting women with good academic records, even if they score lower on standardized tests than some of the men candidates, because they have found that these women perform just as well during their first academic year as men with higher scores. On the importance of mathematics see Lucy Sells, "High School Mathematics as the Critical Filter in the Job Market," in *Developing Opportunities for Minorities in Graduate Education*, ed. R. T. Thomas (Berkeley: Univ. California Press, 1973), pp. 37–39.

[10] Kenneth Bogart and Peter Doyle, "Non-Sexist Solution of the Ménage Problem," *Mathematical Monthly*, 1986, *93*:514–518, on pp. 514–515.

dynamic part of the environment. As in any tradition, what can be modeled is taken as the norm; what cannot becomes an aberration. Leonhard Euler's notion of a "fluid particle" (a body treated mathematically as a point having volume, mass, and density) was crucial to understanding hydraulics, since fluids conceived as points could never flow. As Hayles has pointed out, complex flow created difficulties for an analytic tradition that privileged constancy over change and discrete factors over dynamic interaction.[11]

The ultimate challenge to feminist science studies, however, is said to be physics. What is it about physics that so vehemently excludes women? It seems odd that in the biological sciences, where multiple negative images of females have been embroidered into foundational concepts and theories, 38 percent of the Ph.D.'s are now awarded to women, while in physics, where far fewer examples of overt gendering have been brought forward, only about 11 percent of new Ph.D.'s are women.[12] The low number of women in physics has no doubt helped to insulate it from gender analysis.

Another common explanation for the low numbers of women in the physical sciences is that those sciences are "hard." We are told repeatedly that the physical sciences are "hard" and that the life sciences, like the humanities and social sciences, are "soft." It is possible to distinguish at least four meanings of the supposed hardness of physics. First and foremost, the physical sciences are considered *epistemologically* hard. As disciplines, the physical sciences are held to be tough and analytical, yielding demonstrable answers grounded in fact, while the soft sciences and the humanities are characterized as having considerable breadth, permeable boundaries, and open-ended epistemological structure. Second, physics and the physical sciences are said to be *ontologically* hard. They study "hard," inanimate things—matter in motion—while the life sciences and humanities study "soft," animate organisms—plants, animals, humans, and their behaviors. Third, physics, chemistry, and the other physical sciences are thought to be *methodologically* "hard" because they are difficult, requiring a high degree of abstract thinking, strong analytical skills, hard work, and long hours. Finally, the physical sciences are said to be *emotionally* tough. In their ethos and telos, they are thought to be "dispassionate," distant, abstract, and quantitative, while the soft sciences are considered "compassionate" and qualitative, perhaps introspective, and closer to everyday concerns. The elaborate gendering of disciplines has led Robert Westman to suggest (presumably in all seriousness) that the history of science is "androgynous," combining, as it does, the "hardness" of science with the "softness" of history.[13]

---

[11] N. Katherine Hayles, "Gender Encoding in Fluid Mechanics: Masculine Channels and Feminine Flows," *Differences,* 1992, *4:*16–44. On oversimplification in mathematics see Nancy Cartwright, *How the Laws of Physics Lie* (Oxford: Clarendon, 1983); and Philip Davis and Reuben Hersh, *Descartes' Dream: The World According to Mathematics* (Brighton, Sussex: Harvester, 1986).

[12] For gender in physics see Keller, *Secrets of Life, Secrets of Death* (cit. n. 6), Pt. 2; Karen Barad, "A Feminist Approach to Teaching Quantum Physics," in *Teaching the Majority,* ed. Sue Rosser (New York: Teachers College Press, Columbia Univ., 1995); and Renée Heller, "The Tale of the Universe for Others" (unpublished manuscript, Physics and Women's Studies, Univ. Utrecht).

[13] Julie Klein, "Blurring, Cracking, and Crossing: Permeation and the Fracturing of Disciplines," in *Knowledges: Historical and Critical Studies in Disciplinarity,* ed. Ellen Messer-Davidow, David Shumway, and David Sylvan (Charlottesville: Univ. Press Virginia, 1993), p. 188; Zuckerman *et al.,* eds., *Outer Circle* (cit. n. 4), p. 31; and Robert Westman, "Two Cultures or One? A Second Look at Kuhn's *The Copernican Revolution,*" *Isis,* 1994, *85:*79–115, on p. 92.

The hardness of the science—in what it studies, how it studies it, the degree of difficulty attributed to it, and the emotional detachment involved—is also inversely proportional to the number of women in the field.

As with mathematics, the epistemological hardness of physics may be illusionary—the result of carving out a narrow project. The cosmologist Martin Rees has suggested that the Big Bang is "a grand problem but perhaps a more straightforward problem . . . and far easier than anything in the biological world." While evolutionary geneticists are prone to suffer from "physics envy" (the desire to unveil incontrovertible laws governing the evolution of organisms with the same epistemic cash value as the laws of physics), it may turn out that biology is ultimately "harder" in the sense that the problems it undertakes encompass complexity not amenable to reduction to a few simple laws. The physicist Karen Barad has pointed out, further, that only Newtonian physics might be considered epistemologically "hard" in a strictly positivist sense. She argues that quantum physics, like history or literary criticism, depends on extensive theoretical and instrumental interpretation in identifying phenomena labeled "elementary particles."[14]

The epistemological "hardness" of the physical sciences has also been secured by the disciplinary separation of the practice of science from the critical examination of science. Questions of meaning, consequences, or social responsibility are rarely considered part of physics proper but to belong to other realms, such as philosophy, ethics, or sociology. This may help to explain the curious state of modern physics, which, at the highest theoretical end, couples unreflective materialism to high-flying metaphysics. There are physicists who see "the face of God" (George Smoot), seek "the God particle" (Leon Lederman), and strive "to understand the mind of God" (Stephen Hawking), thus endowing their quest with religious verve. As Robert Wilson has remarked, "both cathedrals and accelerators are build at great expense as a matter of faith."[15] Yet the physicists' god is envisioned to be as apolitical as their science. Consequently, physicists can ascribe a higher meaning to their quest while ignoring the social realities of their undertaking.

Asking why there are fewer women in physics than in other fields of science may, however, emphasize the wrong axis of comparison. It might be more appropriate to realign physics with the military, for there are proportionally no more or fewer women in physics than there are in the United States Armed Forces (see Figure 1). I do not mean to suggest that women are by nature peace loving, antimilitary, or antinuclear: Lise Meitner was—fairly or unfairly—called "the mother of the bomb," some eighty women participated in the Manhattan Project, and women continue to number among weapons designers. My argument is that cultural conventions have long prohibited women from joining defense activities and that these attitudes may

---

[14] Martin Rees, "Contemplating the Cosmos," in *A Passion for Science*, ed. Lewis Wolpert and Alison Richards (Oxford: Oxford Univ. Press, 1988), pp. 34–35; and Barad, "Feminist Approach to Teaching Quantum Physics" (cit. n. 12). On the "illusion" that physics is epistemologically hard see Cartwright, *How the Laws of Physics Lie* (cit. n. 11), p. 45; on geneticists' "physics envy" see Virginia Morell, "Rise and Fall of the Y Chromosome," *Science*, 14 Jan. 1994, *263*:171–172, on p. 171.

[15] Robert Wilson, cited in Margaret Wertheim, *Pythagoras' Trousers: God, Physics, and Gender Wars* (New York: Times Books, 1995). On the separation of the practice of science from its critical examination see Barad, "Feminist Approach to Teaching Quantum Physics"; and Robert Proctor, *Value-Free Science? Purity and Power in Modern Knowledge* (Cambridge, Mass.: Harvard Univ. Press, 1991).

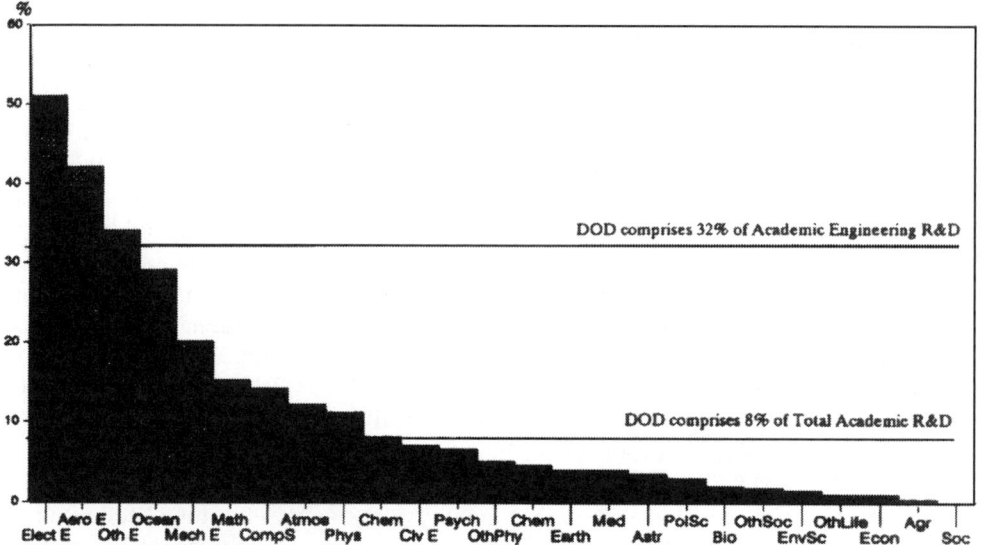

Figure 1. Department of Defense funding by academic field. If we were to superimpose a chart of women's participation in the sciences shown on this chart, we would find that, in most instances, the level of DoD funding is inversely proportional to the number of women in the field (glaring exceptions here are agriculture and economics). No DoD funding goes to the fields where women are heavily concentrated—literature, history, or women's studies. (Adapted from Wim Smit, "Science, Technology, and the Military: Relations in Transition," in Handbook of Science and Technology Studies, ed. Sheila Jasanoff, Gerald Markle, James Petersen, and Trevor Pinch [Thousand Oaks, Calif.: Sage, 1995], pp. 598–626, on p. 608. By permission of Sage Publications.)

well spill over into some areas of physics, which since World War II has made strong contributions to national defense.[16]

Few women become physicists, then, for a number of reasons: its cultural image as a "hard" science, its overtly aggressive culture, its historic ties to the military, its extensive use of abstract mathematics, its status as a "big science," and its use of large and capital-intensive equipment.[17]

CREATING NEW KNOWLEDGE

Scholars of gender have aptly studied epistemic bias in the structure and substance of science; that is the negative program. Critique can also open doors to new ques-

---

[16] Ruth Sime, *Lise Meitner: A Life in Physics* (Berkeley: Univ. California Press, 1996); Charlotte Kerner, *Lise, Atomphysikerin: Die Lebensgeschichte der Lise Meitner* (Weinheim: Beltz, 1986), pp. 102–111; and Caroline Herzenberg and Ruth Howes, "Women of the Manhattan Project," *Technology Review*, 1993, 96:32–40. See also Teri Hopper, "'Radioactive Ladies and Gentlemen': Women and Men of the Radioactivity Community, 1919–1939," paper delivered at the annual meeting of the History of Science Society, Minneapolis, 28 Oct. 1995. On the contributions of physics to national defense since World War II see Peter Galison and Bruce Hevly, eds., *Big Science: The Growth of Large-Scale Research* (Stanford, Calif.: Stanford Univ. Press, 1992).

[17] See Charlene Morrow and James Morrow, "Whose Math Is It, Anyway?" *Initiatives*, 1993, 55:49–59, esp. p. 50; and Sharon Traweek, *Beamtimes and Lifetimes: The World of High Energy Physicists* (Cambridge, Mass.: Harvard Univ. Press, 1988).

tions, projects, and insights—a more positive program. What is new and unprecedented is the growing agitation for change among scientists, especially women. The feminist ferment of the past decade has in many instances reshaped what is known and knowable: the simple process of taking feminists (men and women) seriously as makers of knowledge and a more respectful manner of including females as subjects of research have had a tremendous impact on methods, manners, and priorities in many of the sciences.[18]

The historical process by which gender analysis has come to influence aspects of science theory and practice has yet to be studied. In the absence of such research, it is astonishing how mainstream has become the idea that women (females of the human species) are changing science. While this view perhaps represents an improvement over the decades of assimilation fostered by liberal feminism, the brand of difference feminism (and its variant, standpoint theory) it embodies has begat its own distinctive set of problems.

In spring 1993 *Science* magazine jumped onto the difference feminist bandwagon (probably without realizing it) with its question: Is there a "female style" in science? Apparently not wanting to use the term *feminist,* the editors chose instead to focus on "female style"; unfortunately, in so doing they grounded gender in biology and placed the discussion in the essentialist camp. Nonetheless, the query was similar to that regarding feminist science posed in the late 1970s and early 1980s: When women enter science, do they bring with them different values and priorities? And *Science* encountered problems similar to those faced by many feminists—an all-too-simple notion of a feminist or, in this instance, female science. From the articles in *Science* one can extrapolate the content of this prospective female style. It is warm; it is above all fuzzy. It is caring, relational, at times holistic and nurturing. Surprisingly, of the two hundred women and thirty men who responded to the magazine's follow-up survey, more than half said they believe that there is a female style in science, while only a quarter said that there is not. The respondents were, of course, highly self-selecting.[19]

This same issue of *Science* highlighted primatology as the prime example of a science remade by the influx of women, and in so doing it reinforced the myth that women *qua* women are the leavening agent producing change in the institutions and results of science (it is also significant that this article did not mention Donna Haraway's work).[20]

Is it women or feminists that have brought change to the sciences? It is true that gender ideology has been used historically to lock women (as a class of humans) out of the sciences, but this does not mean that bringing women into science automatically corrects gender biases. Having a significant number of women in a particular field, as Mildred Dresselhaus's theory of "critical mass" suggests, does seem a necessary condition for probing new research paradigms related to gender. (It would be highly paradoxical, if not impossible, to have a feminist science dominated by men.) But to say that women have changed science is overly simple. Many women primatologists, for example, have produced male-dominance theories

---

[18] Cheris Kramarae and Dale Spender, *The Knowledge Explosion: Generations of Feminist Scholarship* (New York: Teachers College Press, Columbia Univ., 1992).
[19] Marcia Baringa, "Is There a 'Female Style' in Science?" *Science,* 16 Apr. 1993, *260*:384–391; and *ibid.,* 23 July 1993, *261*:412.
[20] Virginia Morell, "Primatology," *Science,* 16 Apr. 1993, *260*:420–429.

indistinguishable from those of their male colleagues; by the same token, many men have been instrumental in opening new lines of feminist investigation.[21]

Increasing the numbers of women without increasing an awareness of gender issues will have little impact on science or its institutions. It is rarely mentioned that affirmative action can be abused by the political right. Women who consider themselves "old boys" become the darlings of conservatives; institutions gain respectability by showcasing a few high-profile women, but the fundamentals do not change. To make women the agents of change essentializes gender differences (even when those differences are said to be culturally produced) and unnecessarily excludes men as potential allies. It is not women per se, but women and men who have cultivated a critical awareness of gender, who are making a difference. More important, making women the agents of change depoliticizes the process, reducing to one dimension the multifactorial complex of economic, social, and attitudinal changes required to get women into science in the first place.

Take the example of the biomedical sciences, where the 1990 founding of the National Institutes of Health (NIH) Office of Research on Women's Health and the 1991 Women's Health Initiative represent at least a limited triumph for feminism. Taking women's health seriously did not require new technical breakthroughs or simply more women doctors (though that helped): it required new judgments about social worth and a new political will.

These new attitudes formed in the crucible of an active women's health movement. Since the 1960s and 1970s groups—including the Boston Women's Health Collective, the National Women's Health Network, the Black Women's Health Movement, and consumer lobbies for treatment and prevention of breast cancer—have drawn attention to how the U.S. health care system has failed women. Women's health reform built on the work of women's movements that challenged fundamental assumptions about women's place in the professions and society more generally. These challenges required a host of legislative supports, such as the Civil Rights Act of 1964, the Equal Employment Opportunity Act of 1972, and the Equal Opportunity in Science and Engineering Act of 1980 (Title 42 of U.S. Code, sect. 1885–1885d) that specifically directed NIH and NSF to undertake programs to increase the participation of underrepresented groups in medicine, science, and engineering. The whole was shored up by affirmative action policies that insisted on equal opportunity for women and minorities within governmental agencies, universities, and industries doing business with the federal government.[22]

More specifically, national interest in women's health care required that there be a significant number of people dedicated to women's issues well placed within the medical profession. Florence Haseltine (director of the NIH Center for Population

---

[21] Mildred Dresselhaus, "Women Graduate Students," *Physics Today,* June 1986, *39:*74–75; Rosabeth Kanter, *Men and Women of the Corporation* (New York: Basic, 1977); and, on primatology, Haraway, *Primate Visions* (cit. n. 6), p. 252.

[22] Evelyn White, *Black Women's Health Book* (Seattle: Seal, 1990); Sue Rosser, *Women's Health—Missing from U.S. Medicine* (Bloomington: Indiana Univ. Press, 1994); Eileen Nechas and Denise Foley, *Unequal Treatment: What You Don't Know about How Women Are Mistreated by the Medical Community* (New York: Simon & Schuster, 1994); Anna Mastroianni, Ruth Faden, and Daniel Federman, eds., *Women and Health Research* (Washington, D.C.: National Academy Press, 1994), Vol. 2; Vivian Pinn, *Overview: Office of Research on Women's Health* (Bethesda, Md.: National Institutes of Health, 1995); and Shirley Malcom, "Science and Diversity: A Compelling National Interest," *Science,* 29 Mar. 1996, *271:*1817–1819.

Research), for example, founded the Society for the Advancement of Women's Health Research in 1990; William Harlan, then director of epidemiology and clinical applications at NIH, supported and coined the name for the Women's Health Initiative. Women's health reform also benefited from the emergence of powerful people interested in gender issues, many of them women, in the Congress: in June 1990 the bipartisan Congressional Caucus on Women's Issues—including Democrats Patricia Schroeder and Barbara Mikulski and Republicans Constance Morella and Olympia Snowe—called for a congressional investigation into NIH practices and lack of compliance with its own policies concerning women.[23] This coalition of politicians (including also Henry Waxman) joined with activist physicians to press NIH to found the Office of Women's Health Research, initially headed by Ruth Kirchstein, who is now deputy director of NIH. Responding directly to feminist critiques of biomedical research, the Office of Women's Health Research is mandated to oversee appropriate inclusion of women in epidemiological studies and clinical trials, to encourage women to enter medical research, and to spur research into diseases that hold distinctive risks for women or are unique to women. The Women's Health Initiative, a fourteen-year, $625 million study (the largest ever undertaken by NIH), congealed in 1991 when Bernadine Healy, a Bush appointee, became NIH's first woman director. The initiative funds research into diseases that are more common or found only in women, such as osteoporosis, breast cancer, and cardiovascular disease—the leading causes of death and disability in older women.

The success of the women's health movement also required the opening of the academy to women and their concerns. It relied on gender analyses developed within women's studies and the history and philosophy of science and medicine. Finally, it benefited from the emergence of a new class of professional women, ready to talk openly about and demand care for disorders long hidden behind the cloak of female modesty.

Change for women within the sciences, then, is a complex and broadly social process. It is not uniquely women, but women *and* men with a critical awareness of gender, who are the agents of that change. How this happens in concrete instances requires more study.

SUSTAINABLE SCIENCE

I am suggesting that we move beyond the problems endemic to difference feminism and attempts to create a feminist science to something I call sustainable science. In a sense, a new label is not needed or perhaps even desirable; however, I offer the notion of sustainability as a useful heuristic. My notion of sustainable science resembles other new directions in feminist science theory, such as Donna Haraway's "situated knowledge," Sandra Harding's "strong objectivity," and Carolyn Merchant's "partnership ethic."[24] One element common to these various initiatives is emphasizing gender as one analytic among many required for creating socially and environmentally responsible science.

---

[23] National Institutes of Health, *Problems in Implementing Policy on Women in Study Populations* (Washington, D.C.: Government Accounting Office, National and Public Health Issues and Human Resources Division, June 1990).

[24] Carolyn Merchant, *Earthcare: Women and the Environment* (New York: Routledge, 1996), p. 8 and conclusion. Haraway and Harding are discussed later in this essay.

Much of what I mean by sustainable science is captured in the older notion of "socially responsible science." The movement for social responsibility in science arose after World War II, especially among physicists worried about the compromising of science goals by the militarization of science but also among physicians worried about the health effects of nuclear war and nuclear power. I am interested in broadening the notion to include responsibility toward nature as well as culture. The concept of sustainability comes from sustainable agriculture, which emerged in the 1970s as a challenge to conventional industrial agriculture with its emphasis on chemical fertilizers, monoagriculture, and hybrid seed. To my knowledge, the term *sustainable science* was first used by Helmut Hirsch and Helen Ghiradella in a Native American science journal; it incorporates the Native American notion of undertaking actions to meet the needs of the present in a way that can be sustained for many generations.[25]

What, then, is feminist about sustainable science? One might argue that feminism has to do only with women's equality and that once that is achieved the problem is solved. Most feminists, however, would disagree. Feminists are rarely advocates solely for women. What in the past has been advanced as "feminist science" offers strong elements of environmentalism and humanitarianism that have little to do with women's equality per se. Difference feminism ran amok in attempting to encompass a range of diverse political views—environmentalism, humanism, and pacifism— within feminism. In attempting to join feminism with environmentalism, for example, difference feminism (and much of ecofeminism) faltered on the shoals of essentialism by arguing that women have a special relationship with nature or that the oppression of women is connected with the domination of nature. Instead of being seen as characteristics attached culturally to women, feminist concerns for the environment might be seen as political goals held in common with a number of people whose first allegiance may or may not be to feminism.

Sustainable science shifts attention away from classical epistemology (how we know), which has exercised science and science theory since the seventeenth century, to focus on the goals and outcomes of science (what we know and don't know, and why). Key questions include: Science for whom? How is our knowledge influenced by who is included in science and who is excluded, which projects are pursued and which ignored, whose experiences are validated and whose are not, and who stands to gain in terms of wealth or well-being and who does not? And for how long? It is precisely in the choice of questions, in the priorities set for science, that much is determined. The questions we pose often determine the kinds of solutions we consider. Once a problem is set, there may be one best answer. When, for instance, the question of sexual equality is set into the realm of biological investigation, a particular set of debates and lines of investigation are opened and others closed off.

Donna Haraway's notion of situated knowledge (as a form of critique) is useful in this context. As postmodernists of various stripes have pointed out, feminists cannot, any more than anyone else, produce universal theories of science. In the early 1980s, when the notion of a feminist science arose, feminists were challenged to state precisely what it is or might become. This cannot be done in an abstract way; problems

---

[25] Helmut Hirsch and Helen Ghiradella, "Educators Look at Contemporary Science Teaching," *Winds of Change,* Spring 1994, pp. 38–42.

begin to arise when solutions are grounded in identity politics (the tendency to attach particular qualities to socially defined groups). While cultivating a cross-cultural understanding of the problem of gender in science, situated feminism calls for analyzing gender difference as one among many variables of power within concrete contexts.[26]

Sandra Harding's notion of strong objectivity is also useful in moving the focus from *how* we know to *what* we know and why we know it. Harding's notion of strong objectivity strengthens current notions of objectivity (which she calls "weak objectivity") by extending the concept to include the critical examination of all beliefs and interests forming a scientific project. Weak objectivity, she argues, prematurely cuts off the consideration of values, economics, and politics in the design of research projects. It is not enough to work on a piece of the puzzle; scientists (and other scholars) must also analyze the origins and long-term consequences of their work. Strong objectivity requires that the critique of science be joined to the generation of knowledge and not operate as jeremiad after the fact.[27]

Sustainable science requires tools for gender analysis. Tools for gender analysis are as diverse as the variants of feminism and of science theory and practice. They work in conjunction with critical history and philosophy of science; and, as with any set of tools, some are fashioned and others discarded as analytical circumstances change. Crucial tools for gender analysis (calibrated through race, ethnicity, age, class, sexual orientation, and geographies) include, but are not limited to, the following.

1. Gender analyses of how priorities are set. How are choices made about what we want to know (and what we choose not to know) in the context of limited resources? Who benefits and who does not from a particular research project? A good example is the women's health research discussed earlier. Improving women's health care has not required new technical breakthroughs: it required new judgments about women's social worth and willingness to invest in women's health and well-being.

2. Gender analyses of populations chosen for study. The primatologist Linda Fedigan has discussed the 1950s "baboonization" of primatology, where savannah baboons, one of the most aggressive and male dominated of all primates, became the preferred model for ancestral human populations despite primatologists' knowledge of other, less aggressive primate populations.[28] In this instance, the choice of subject matter interjected a potent antifeminist element into understandings of human origin.

One of the basic tools of gender studies is, of course, the analysis of appropriate inclusion of females as subjects and objects of research. Since the 1980s, additional tools have been forged in this area to refine the analysis of gender in relation to class, race, ethnicity, and sexual preference. These tools have helped researchers become aware of the differences in disease among women and adjust resource

---

[26] Donna Haraway, "Situated Knowledges: The Science Question in Feminism and the Privilege of Partial Perspective," in *Simians, Cyborgs, and Women: The Reinvention of Nature* (New York: Routledge, 1991), pp. 183–203.

[27] Harding, *Whose Science? Whose Knowledge?* (cit. n. 8), Ch. 6. See also Helen Longino, "Can There Be a Feminist Science?" in *Feminism and Science,* ed. Tuana (cit. n. 6), pp. 45–57; and Regine Kollek, "Brauchen Wir eine neue wissenschaftliche Revolution?" in *Fortschritt Wohin?* ed. Hans-Jürgen Fischbeck and Kollek (Münster: Agenda, 1994), pp. 41–49.

[28] Linda Fedigan, "The Changing Role of Women in Models of Human Evolution," *Annual Review of Anthropology,* 1986, *15:*25–66.

allocation and treatments appropriately. Returning to the biomedical sciences, it has been learned that African-American women suffer fewer heart attacks than white women but more often die from them. Osteoporosis, one of the targets of the Women's Health Initiative, occurs most often in white women of non-Hispanic origin; this may mean that the initiative is not responding directly to the needs of minority women and that African-American and Hispanic women may not be screened and educated aggressively about the disease and consequently may be at risk.[29]

Yet other tools of analysis are used to encourage a global perspective when adjusting science and science policy to specific populations. Critics of U.S. women's health reform, for example, point out that fine-grained inequalities in health research are not what haunts the majority of the world's population. Many women around the world suffer and die from diseases induced by poverty, malnutrition, and childbirth.

3. Analyses of how gender structures scientific institutions and the relationship between disciplines. Many modern disciplines have their origins in the German university system, from which women and their concerns were stringently excluded. The hierarchy of disciplines in U.S. universities further correlates with the number of women, inequalities in intellectual authority, and often funding levels (as noted earlier). The archaeologist Joan Gero has shown, for instance, how disciplinary and subdisciplinary status hierarchies have placed women in both the discipline of archaeology and the study of prehistory.[30]

Disciplinary divisions have isolated gender studies of science from science studies (and vice versa) and the history and philosophy of science from science research and education (and vice versa). Solving the problem of women and gender in science will require not only reform of disciplines but deep and sweeping reform of disciplinary divisions.

4. Gender analyses of scientific language. Gender stereotypes are not innocent literary devices used to spice up texts and abbreviate thought. Analogies and metaphors, the theorist Susan Squier writes, function to construct as well as describe— they have both a hypothesis-creating and proof-making function in science. They can determine the direction of scientific practice, the questions asked, the results obtained, and the interpretations deduced.[31] We have already noted that gendering the egg as passive and the sperm as active places them within a predetermined and complex matrix of cultural meanings.

5. Gender analyses of criteria used in both determining what needs explanation and what counts as evidence. The archaeologists Margaret Conkey and Joan Gero discuss how male-identified stone tools figure among highly prized data for tracing the "progress of humankind." These potent symbols of "Early Man" obscure other important aspects of prehistoric life, such as nutting, leatherworking, grain harvesting, and woodworking—all of which were done with nonstandardized stone tools.[32]

---

[29] Vanessa Gamble and Bonnie Blustein, "Racial Differentials in Medical Care: Implications for Research on Women," in *Women and Health Research,* ed. Mastroianni *et al.* (cit. n. 22), Vol. 2, pp. 174–191.

[30] Joan M. Gero, "Genderlithics: Women's Roles in Stone Tool Production," in *Engendering Archaeology: Women and Prehistory,* ed. Gero and Margaret W. Conkey (Oxford: Blackwell, 1991), pp. 163–193.

[31] Susan Squier, *Babies in Bottles: Twentieth-Century Visions of Reproductive Technology* (New Brunswick, N.J.: Rutgers Univ. Press, 1994), Ch. 1.

[32] Margaret W. Conkey, "Making the Connections: Feminist Theory and Archaeologies of Gender," in *Women in Archaeology: A Feminist Critique,* ed. Hilary du Cros and Laurajane Smith (Canberra:

Gero argues that adopting a broader definition of tools will prove fundamental to a more comprehensive understanding of gender and tool use in prehistory.

6. *Analyses of gender differentials in outcomes for the environment.* Vandana Shiva has offered the example of forest management in India, where women developed a technique called lopping. Lopping, the selective thinning of trees, simultaneously provides feed for livestock and increases forest density and productivity. Shiva has suggested that "scientific forestry," with its emphasis on cash crops, has disproportionately displaced women (since traditional divisions in labor assigned this work to them) and undermined sustainable uses of the forest.[33]

7. *Gender analyses of professions.* What is the image of a successful professional in a particular field? Who is recruited? Who is rewarded—and for what reasons? Helen Longino has discussed how communities of researchers form "background assumptions"—the unquestioned givens that serve as the bases for mutual understanding and effective research. She also discusses how including representatives of alternative points of view in such communities can uncover social values and interests that become enshrined in research programs and unconsciously shape observation or reasoning.[34]

8. *Analyses of gender dynamics in what is considered "science."* Voltaire's 1764 proclamation that "all the arts have been invented by man, not by woman," was echoed recently in the assertion by two prominent sociologists of science that women have achieved less than men in science no matter how achievement is measured.[35] Women have generally been considered recipients, not generators, of knowledge. Exploring what is considered "science"—using ethnographic tools—can influence how women's contributions are evaluated.

Thus far I have offered examples primarily from Western-style science. Looking at alternative knowledge traditions may further expand Western definitions and practices of science. Within Western culture, as elsewhere, midwifery offers a key example of women's knowledge traditionally devalued by high science. This devaluing may have resulted more from the fact that midwifery has been practiced by women (not always of the highest classes) than from an evaluation of the knowledge involved or the value of the services rendered.[36] Other practices explored to date have clustered around agriculture and forest management because women have

---

Australian National Univ. Occasional Papers, 1993), pp. 3–15; and Joan M. Gero, "The Social World of Prehistoric Facts: Gender and Power in Paleoindian Research," *ibid.,* pp. 31–40.

[33] Vandana Shiva, *Staying Alive: Women, Ecology, and Development* (London: Zed, 1988), pp. 65–66. See also Shiva, ed., *Close to Home: Women Reconnect Ecology, Health, and Development Worldwide* (Philadelphia: New Society, 1994).

[34] Helen Longino, "Subjects, Power, and Knowledge: Description and Prescription in Feminist Philosophies of Science," in *Feminism and Science,* ed. Evelyn Fox Keller and Longino (Oxford: Oxford Univ. Press, 1996), pp. 264–279.

[35] François-Marie Arouet de Voltaire, *Dictionnaire philosophique* (1764; Amsterdam, 1789), Vol. 5, p. 255; and Stephen Cole and Robert Florentine, "Discrimination against Women in Science: The Confusion of Outcome with Process," in *Outer Circle,* ed. Zuckerman *et al.* (cit. n. 4), p. 205.

[36] Jean Donnison, *Midwives and Medical Men: A History of Inter-Professional Rivals and Women's Rights* (London: Heinemann, 1977); Judith Leavitt, ed., *Women and Health in America* (Madison: Univ. Wisconsin Press, 1984); Ornella Moscucci, *The Science of Woman: Gynaecology and Gender in England, 1800–1929* (Cambridge: Cambridge Univ. Press, 1990); Schiebinger, *Mind Has No Sex?* (cit. n. 4), Ch. 4; Laurel Ulrich, *A Midwife's Tale* (New York: Vintage, 1990); Hilary Marland, ed., *The Art of Midwifery: Early Modern Midwives in Europe* (London: Routledge, 1993); and Adrian Wilson, *The Making of Man-Midwifery: Childbirth in England, 1660–1770* (Cambridge, Mass.: Harvard Univ. Press, 1995).

traditionally been in charge of food and food preparation. A prime example is Andean potato breeding; for centuries Quechua women have bred and preserved potato seeds. (One might reflect on the importance of the potato, imported from this area, for industrial development in Europe; the potato was a necessary foodstuff for Europe's swelling population in the seventeenth and eighteenth centuries.) Andean women do not merely clone potatoes by planting whole potatoes or pieces but actually breed potatoes from seeds. These *semilleras* or "keepers of the seeds," as they are called, meet annually to exchange their produce, find new seeds, and share knowledge about production, conservation, and use. An experienced *semillera* can distinguish dozens of varieties of potatoes and will know about their time of maturation, yield, disease susceptibility, cooking properties, perishability, and the like.[37] A single woman might manage up to fifty-six varieties of potatoes.

There is nothing sacred or mystical about the fact that particular knowledges have been developed by women. Women's work in birthing or seed preservation responds to sexual divisions of labor in particular cultures. The same kinds of knowledge could have been developed by men under different conditions—and may in that instance have been considered "science."

* * *

These tools of gender analysis, along with many others, aid in crafting sustainable sciences, sciences that have built into their research designs analyses of their long- and short-term effects and a consideration of their historical position within particular cultures and value systems. Sustainable science is the best way to realize the feminist goals of achieving equality for women in the sciences and creating sciences that address the concerns and needs of women around the world.

For some years now difference feminism has prescribed a quick and easy recipe for changing science and has in the process neglected the deep historical and philosophical analysis required to understand how science, culture, history, and environment shape one another. Much feminism has focused too narrowly (and reductionistically) on one variable—women—often leaving aside the complexities of the processes by which science is made. Neither changing women to fit science nor changing science to incorporate conventional feminine ideals will be sufficient: feminist goals based on either traditional divisions of labor or conventional gender representations are set in shifting sand. What is needed are collaborations between scientists, historians, and philosophers that will foster not only a diverse community of scholars but scientists critically attuned to their place in nature.

[37] Mario Tapia and Ana de la Torre, *La mujer campesina y las semillas andinas* (Lima: FAO, 1993); Stephen Brush, "Potato Taxonomies in Andean Agriculture," in *Indigenous Knowledge Systems and Development,* ed. David Brokensha, D. M. Warren, and Oswald Werner (Washington, D.C.: Univ. Press America, 1980), pp. 37–47; and Arun Agrawal, "Indigenous and Scientific Knowledge: Some Critical Comments," *Indigenous Knowledge and Development Monitor,* Dec. 1995, 3:3–6.

Notes on Contributors

Estelle Cohen, a historian of gender and science, has been affiliated with the Minnesota Center for Philosophy of Science at the University of Minnesota since 1994. During the past year she taught courses on the history of the body and the politics and cultures of reproduction at Macalester College and Hamline University Graduate School. In 1997–1998 she will be at Harvard University's Department of the History of Science. She is currently preparing a book manuscript called *Constructing Biology as Social Knowledge: Gender, Reproduction, and the State, ca. 1660–1900*.

Sandra Harding is Professor of Philosophy at the University of Delaware and Adjunct Professor of Philosophy and Women's Studies at UCLA. She is the author or editor of seven books, including *The Science Question in Feminism* (Cornell, 1986), *Whose Science? Whose Knowledge?* (Cornell, 1991), and *The "Racial" Economy of Science: Toward a Democratic Future* (Indiana, 1993). With Elizabeth McGregor she coauthored "The Gender Dimension of Science and Technology," in UNESCO's *World Science Report 1996. Is Science Multicultural? Postcolonialism, Feminism, and Epistemology* will appear in 1998 (Indiana).

Evelyn Fox Keller received her Ph.D. in theoretical physics at Harvard University, worked for a number of years at the interface of physics and biology, and is now Professor of History and Philosophy of Science in the Program in Science, Technology, and Society at MIT. She is the author of *A Feeling for the Organism: The Life and Work of Barbara McClintock; Reflections on Gender and Science; Secrets of Life, Secrets of Death: Essays on Language, Gender, and Science;* and, most recently, *Refiguring Life: Metaphors of Twentieth-Century Biology* (Columbia University Press, 1995). Her current research is on the history of developmental biology.

Sally Gregory Kohlstedt is Professor in the Program of History of Science and Technology and Director of the Center for Advanced Feminist Studies at the University of Minnesota. She coedited *International Science and National Scientific Identity: Australia between Britain and the United States* with Roderick W. Home (Kluwer, 1991) and *Gender and Scientific Authority* wth Barbara Laslett, Helen Longino, and Evelynn Hammonds (University of Chicago Press, 1996). She is now working on the history of the nature study movement at the turn of the last century and on museums as sites for public and scientific interaction.

Nina E. Lerman is Assistant Professor at Whitman College, where she teaches U.S. history, women's history, and history of technology. She was a postdoctoral fellow for the "Women, Gender, and Science Question" workshop and conference and has guest edited (with Arwen Mohun and Ruth Oldenziel) a special issue of *Technology and Culture* on gender and technology. She is writing a book about technological knowledge, social structures, and urban industrialization based on her studies of nineteenth-century technical education.

Diana E. Long is Professor of History at the University of Southern Maine and Visiting Lecturer at the University of Central Lancashire. She has edited volumes on the history of American medicine and published on the history of twentieth-century sex endocrinology. Her most recent work, "Scientific Authority and the Search for Sex Hormones," will appear in *A Queer World: A Center for Lesbian and Gay Studies Reader,* edited by Martin Duberman (New York University Press, 1997).

Helen E. Longino is Professor of Women's Studies at the University of Minnesota and a member of the Minnesota Center for Philosophy of Science. She has most recently coedited *Feminism and Science* with Evelyn Fox Keller (Oxford University Press, 1995) and *Gender and Scientific Authority* with Barbara Laslett, Sally Gregory Kohlstedt, and Evelynn Hammonds (University of Chicago Press, 1996). She is working on a book on philosophical issues in social studies of science and another on the contours of a critical/feminist philosophy of science.

Robert A. Nye is Thomas Hart and Mary Jones Horning Professor of the Humanities and Professor of History at Oregon State University. He is completing a project on the history of medical ethics in France and Great Britain and is editing an Oxford Reader on "sexuality."

Margaret W. Rossiter is the Marie Underhill Noll Professor of the History of Science at Cornell University. She is the author of *The Emergence of Agricultural Science: Justus Liebig and the Americans, 1840–1880* (1975), *Women Scientists in America: Struggles and Strategies to 1940* (1982), and a sequel, *Women Scientists in America: Before Affirmative Action, 1940–1972*

(1995). Currently she is also editor of *Isis* and *Osiris*.

Elvira Scheich teaches social theory of knowledge and gender studies at the Technical University of Berlin. She is author of *Naturbeherrschung und Weiblichkeit: Denkformen und Phantasemen der modernen Naturwissenschaften* (Pfaffenweiler, 1993) and editor of *Vermittelte Weiblichkeit: Feministische Wissenschafts- und Gesellschaftstheorie* (Hamburg, 1996). She coedited *Zwielicht der Vernunft: Die Dialektik der Aufklärung aus der Sicht von Frauen* (Pfaffenweiler, 1992) and *Das Geschlecht der Natur: Feministische Beiträge zur Geschichte und Theorie der Naturwissenschaften* (Frankfurt, 1995). Her current studies are concerned with the links between modernization, gender relations, and scientific developments in the twentieth century.

Londa Schiebinger is Professor of History of Science and Women's Studies and former Director of the Institute for Women in the Sciences and Engineering at Pennsylvania State University. She is author of *The Mind Has No Sex? Women in the Origins of Modern Science* (Harvard, 1989) and the prizewinning *Nature's Body: Gender in the Making of Modern Science* (Beacon, 1993). Her current work on gender in science, from which the essay in this volume is drawn, will be published by Harvard University Press in 1998.

Ann B. Shteir is Associate Professor of Humanities at York University. She is author of *Cultivating Women, Cultivating Science: Flora's Daughters and Botany in England, 1760 to 1860* (1996), which was awarded the Joan Kelly Memorial Prize of the American Historical Association. She was Guest Editor of a special issue, "Women and Science," of *Women's Writing: The Elizabethan to Victorian Period* (1995). With Barbara T. Gates she has edited *Natural Eloquence: Women Reinscribe Science* (1997).

Alison Wylie is a philosopher of social science with special interest in archaeology and feminist research methodologies. Her essays on feminist social science appear in *Changing Methods,* edited by Sandra Burt and Lorraine Code (Broadview Press, 1995), and *Women and Reason,* edited by Elizabeth Harvey and Kathleen Okruhlik (Michigan, 1992); and she is a member of the Chilly Collective, which edited *Breaking Anonymity: The Chilly Climate for Women Faculty* (Wilfrid Laurier University Press, 1995). She teaches at the University of Western Ontario.

Index

ALCOVER, Madeleine, 137
Allen, David E., 30
Amar, André, 139
American Medical Association, 113
Anderson, Kathryn, 24–25, 27
Apprenticeships, 50–51
Archaeology: Chacmool conferences in, 89–91, 93–96; feminist critiques of, 80–84, 91–93; gender research in, 88–98; hyperrelativism in, 85–88; and New Archaeology, 80 n. 1, 85–88, 92–93; objectivity in, 80, 98–99; politics of, 84–88
Aristophile, G. S. *See* Suchon, Gabrielle
Aristotle, 130–131, 136
Ashburner, Michael, 21
Astell, Drake, 137
Astell, Mary, 134–135
Authority in science, 19, 41–42; women's claims to, 19

BALBIANI, Gabriel, 64
Barad, Karen, 207
Bauman, Zygmunt, 145–147
Baur, Erwin, 143, 152–155
Becker, Lydia, 38
Benjamin, Marina, 60
Berriot-Salvadore, Evelyne, 130
Bers, Lipman, 177
Bhaskar, Roy, 86
Biagioli, Mario, 60, 68–69
Bickel, Beatrice, 115
Billings, John Shaw, 101–102, 111–114, 116, 118
Biology, career of Lise Meitner in, 143–168
Biology, developmental. *See* Developmental biology
Bismarck, Otto von, 69
Blackwell, Antoinette, 203
Bleier, Ruth, 180
Blondel, James, 128
Bodin, Jean, 121
Boerhaave, Herman, 127
Bogart, Kenneth, 205
Bohr, Niels, 162
Bok, Bart, 177
Bourdieu, Pierre, 62, 77, 79
Boveri, Theodor, 22
Boyle, Robert, 68–69
Bragg, William Henry, 183
Bretonne, Nicolas-Edmé Restif de la, 141
British Medical Association, 73
Broca, Paul, 65 n. 11
Brumfiel, Elizabeth, 82, 90 fig. 2
Bull, Alice, 26–27
Butler, Judith, 101
Bynum, William, 113

CAVENDISH, Margaret, 132 n. 25
Cell biology, gender stereotypes in, 19–22, 204
Châtelet, Émilie du, 135
Chaumette, Pierre Gaspard, 140
Claasen, Cheryl, 81, 90–91
Claparède, René-Edouard, 63–65
Class, relation of, to science and work, 39–59
Cohen, Patricia Cline, 47
Conkey, Margaret, 89–92, 214
Connell, R. W., 62
Cook, Judith, 88
Cookingham, Mary, 179
Cordova, France, 202
Correns, Carl, 156
Coster, Dirk, 162
Cullen, Thomas, 114–115
Cultures: effects of, on knowledge formation, 193; of gender, 188–189; and organization of scientific work, 197–199
Curie, Marie, 71

DENMAN, Thomas, 130
Descartes, René, 126, 135
Desmond, Adrian, 32
Developmental biology: career of Nüsslein-Volhard in, 17, 23–28; gender stereotypes in, 19–22, 204; rivalry between genetics and embryology within, 19–23; women in, 18–19
Diderot, Denis, 138
Difference: and anti-Semitism, 146–147; feminism, 211; and women's participation in science, 147
Dionis, Pierre, 126–127, 136
Discourse: and cultural traditions, 195–197; feminist, 126–142; of gene action, 19–23, 27; of nature in Victorian England, 33–38; of professional medicine, 100; scientific, about women, 124–142; scientific, as attempt to avoid violence, 69–71
Doe, Jane, 118–119
Dohn, Hedwig, 203
Doyle, Helen, 24
Doyle, Peter, 205
Drake, James, 127, 132, 139
Drake, Judith, 127–129, 132–134
Drélincourt, Charles, 129
Dresselhaus, Mildred, 209
Driesch, Hans, 24
Drumont, Edouard, 70

ECKFORD, Martha O., 185 n. 22
Education: Lancasterian movement in, 46; in science and technology, 39–58
Elias, Norbert, 62
Ellis, Havelock, 106

Embryology, 19. *See also* Developmental biology
Erxleben, Dorothea Lepouniu, 203
Ethics and science, 67, 143–68, 211–213
Eugenics, 152–154, 157–158

FAUSTO-STERLING, Anne, 88
Fedigan, Linda, 213
Fee, Elizabeth, 77
Feldman, Saul, 179
Female style in science, 209
Feminism: difference, 211; in Germany around World War I, 150; Nüsslein-Volhard's ambivalence toward, 25–28; women scientists' fear of, 172–173
Feminist: analysis of science, 88, 92; science studies, 80–99, 209; science theory, 211; standpoint theory, 186–187; theory and women scientists, 16–17, 24–25, 209
Fermi, Enrico, 162
Field, Helen, 118–119
Filmer, Robert, 121
Fischer, Emil, 161
Fischer, Eugen, 157
Fletcher, Robert, 101–102, 111–112
Foner, Mary Margaret, 88
Forman, Paul, 193
Franck, James, 165
Franklin Institute for the Promotion of Science and the Useful Arts, 39–40, 42–47
Franklin Rosalind, 78–79, 183
Frevert, Ute, 69

GALEN, 131
Galileo, 68–69
Garrison, Fielding H., 101–102, 111–112, 116
Garrison, Florence, 113, 115–116
Gender: cultures of, 188–189; and math and science, 205–211; and scientific language, 196, 214
Germany, science and women in, 17, 21, 23–28, 143–168
Genetics, 19. *See also* Developmental biology
Gero, Joan, 84, 90, 201, 214–215
Ghiradella, Helen, 212
Gilman, Charlotte Perkins, 203
Glass ceiling for women scientists, 179
Glazer, Penina Migdal, 116–177
Goldschmidt, Richard, 156
Gouges, Olympe de, 127
Graaf, Reiner de, 122, 126–127, 129–130, 139
Gynecology and medical care of women, 107–111

HABER, Fritz, 144
Haecker, V., 22
Hahn, Gertrud, 166
Hahn, Otto, 143, 161–163, 165
Hamerstrom, Frances, 184
Handsman, Russell G., 90 fig. 2
Hanen, Marsha, 95
Haraway, Donna, 88, 193, 198, 205, 209, 211–212
"Hard" sciences, 177–179, 206–208

Harding, Sandra, 88, 202, 205, 211, 213
Harlan, William, 211
Hartmann, Max, 155
Hartsock, Nancy, 88
Harwood, Jonathan, 156, 158–159
Haseltine, Florence, 210
Hastorf, Christine, 82, 90 fig. 2, 97–98
Hawking, Stephen, 207
Hayles, N. Katherine, 205–206
Hazen, Elizabeth, 185 n. 22
Health care, women's. *See* Women's health care
Healy, Bernadine, 211
Herzenberg, Caroline Littlejohn, 184
Hirsh, Helmut, 212
Hodgkins, Dorothy, 183
Home economics and science, 180–182
Honor codes, masculine: effect on women, 75–79; democratization of, 69; as intraprofessional regulation, 72; role of independence and virtue in, 61–62, 67–68
Hooker, William Jackson, 37
Hopkins, Nancy, 24
Horkheimer, Max, 168
Hume, Everett E., 112
Huntington, Emily, 179
Hyperfeminization, 180–181
Hyperrelativism in social sciences, 85–88

IDEOLOGIES OF SOCIAL CATEGORIES, WORK, AND TECHNOLOGY, 51–52
Index Catalogue of the Library of the Surgeon General's Office: effect of, on women in medicine and science, 115–118; and professionalism in medicine, 112–114
Inquiry: effect of standpoint of practitioners on, 96–99; need for interdisciplinary strategies of, 87
Interdisciplinarity, need for, 87

JACKSON, Thomas L., 90 fig. 2
Jacobi, Alexander, 112, 114, 116
Jacobi, Mary Putnam, 76
Jacotot, Joseph, 141
Japanese women scientists, 198
Jex-Blake, Sophia, 76
Johns Hopkins Medical School, 113–114
Julian, Maureen, 183

KELLER, Evelyn Fox, 88, 186, 193, 202
Kelley, Jane, 95
Kelly, Howard Atwood, 114
Kennedy, Mary, 96–97
King, Azuba, 76
Kirby, Elizabeth, 36–37
Kirby, Mary, 36–38
Kirshstein, Ruth, 211
Knowledge: formation of, effect of cultural differences on, 193; kinds associated with science, 42; technological, 41 n. 5, 57–58
Koch, Robert, 113
Kramarae, Cheris, 100–101

LANGEVIN, Paul, 71
Language, scientific, 196, 214

Latour, Bruno, 77–78, 197, 201
Lederman, Leon, 207
Leeuwenhoek, Antoni van, 127–128
Lehmann, Ruth, 24–25
Lenz, Fritz, 157
Leslie, Stuart, 182
Lewontin, Richard, 78
Leydig, Franz, 63
Lindley, John, 29, 31–38
Linnaeus, 159
Locke, John, 121, 134
Longino, Helen, 88, 215
Lonsdale, Kathleen, 183
Loudon, Jane, 38

MACAULAY, Catherine, 142
Mandeville, Bernard, 121 n. 2, 137
Manseau, Lynn, 27
Manual training: as moral training, 56; movement for, 52–57; as opposed to science training, 50–51
Marshall, Joan, 100
Marshall, Paula, 100–106
Martyn, Thomas, 35
Masculine honor codes. *See* Honor codes, masculine
Masculinized aspects of science, relation of women in science to, 7
Math, gender in, 205
Mather, Kirtley, 177
Maugham, W. Somerset, 107 n. 14
McCall, Leslie, 77
McClintock, Barbara, 186
Medical practices of women, 132
Meitner, Lise, 143–168, 207
Merchant, Carolyn, 211
Metaphors of nature, 196
Mikulski, Barbara, 211
Modernity, relation between science and, 146–148
Moore, Henrietta, 90 fig. 2
Morantz-Sanchez, Regina, 115–116
Morella, Constance, 211
Morgan, T. H., 152
Muller, H. J., 20

NACHTSCHEIM, Hans, 155
Nature: as heterogeneous, 191–193; metaphors and models of, 196
New Archaeology, 80 n. 1, 85–87, 92–93
Nielson, Joyce, 88
Nijhout, Fred, 21
Notestein, Frank, 183
Nüsslein-Volhard, Christiane, 17, 21, 23–28

OBJECTIVITY, scientific, 80, 84–87, 98–99, 187, 189–190
Oettingen, 161
Osborn, Fredrick, 183
Osborne, William, 130
Osler, William, 114

PARSONS, Elsie Clews, 184
Pasteur, Louis, 113

Perxotto, Jessica, 179
Philadelphia, science and technology education in, 39–58
Physical sciences as "hard" sciences, 206–208
Physics: career of Elisabeth Schiemann in, 143–168; gender in, 205–208
Pickering, Andrew, 87
Pinkley, Jean McWhirt, 171
Pitt-Rivers, Julian, 67
Pizan, Christine de, 203
Planck, Max, 155, 161–162
Pollock, Susan, 90 fig. 2
Poullain, François de la Barre, 121, 127, 135–140, 203
Poulson, Donald, 26
Pratt, Anne, 38
Price, T. Douglas, 90 fig. 2
Prisch, Otto Robert, 163
Proctor, Robert, 197
Progress, notion of science as, 52

RACE, relation of, to science and work, 42–50
Race theory, 159–160
Reed, Dorothy, 117
Rees, Martin, 207
Reinharz, Shulamit, 88
Reiss, Timothy, 137
Rice, Prudence M., 90 fig. 2
Richards, Ellen, 180
Robinson, Mary, 138
Rosser, Phyllis, 205
Rossiter, Margaret, 116
Rousseau, Jean-Jacques, 35, 66

SABIN, Florence, 117
Sander, Klaus, 26
Schaffer, Simon, 197
Schiemann, Elisabeth, 143–168
Schiemann, Gertrud, 155 n. 27, 160–161, 165
Schotte, Oscar, 19, 22
Schroeder, Patricia, 211
Schüpbach, Trudi, 27
Science: definitions of, 13; and ethics, 67, 143–168, 211–213; female style in, 209; feminist analysis of, 80–99, 88, 92; feminists in, 209; and home economics, 180–182; kinds of knowledge associated with, 42; modernity and, 146–148; as opposed to manual labor, 50–51; as progress, 52
Science, women in. *See* Women in science
Scientific: discourse as attempt to avoid violence, 69–71; language, 196, 214; research as social labor, 197; societies, 66–67; work, cultural organization of, 197–199
Scientific Revolution, 4–5
Seifert, Donna, 81
Séverine, 71
Shapin, Steven, 60, 68–69, 197
Sharp, Jane, 126–127, 130–131
Shiva, Vandana, 215
Shurman, Anna van, 203
Siegbahn, Manne, 163
Siegel, Vivian, 24
Silverblatt, Irene, 90 fig. 2

Slater, Miriam, 116–117
Slye, Maud, 116
Smart, George, 207
Smith, James Edward, 31, 34
Snow, C. P., 202
Snowe, Olympia, 211
Social sciences, hyperrelativism in, 85–88
"Soft" sciences, 177–179, 206
Sophia treatises, 137
Spector, Janet, 89, 90–91
Spengler, Oswald, 154
Squier, Susan, 214
Stacey, Margaret, 72, 76 n. 39
Standpoints, effect of, on inquiry 96, 98–99
Sterne, Laurence, 127
Stevens, Leslie, 24
Straßmann, Fritz, 143, 162, 165
Sturtevant, Alfred H., 20
Suchon, Gabrielle, 136–137

TECHNICAL EDUCATION, 39–58
Technological knowledge, 41 n. 5, 57–58
Technologists, women as, 40–42
Terrail, Gabriel, 71
Terrall, Mary, 135
Téry, Gustave, 71
Traweek, Sharon, 79, 198, 202
Treichler, Paula, 100–101
Trigger, Bruce, 85
Tringham, Ruth E., 90 fig. 2
Turner, Frank, 33
Twining, Elizabeth, 38

UEBISCH, Gerda von, 155
University College London, 31–32

VARIABILITY, 160
Vavilov, Nikolai, 156

Venette, Nicholas, 131
Virchow, Rudolf, 69
Voltaire, 215

WAKEFIELD, Priscilla, 36
Waring, Sarah, 29–30
Watson, James D., 78–79
Watson, Pat, 90, 96–97
Waxman, Henry, 211
Welch, William Henry, 112–114, 116
Westman, Robert, 206
Wetmore, Ralph, 177
Wettstein, Fritz von, 156
Wheeler, Anna Doyle, 127, 141–142
White, Peter, 90 fig. 2
Wieschaus, Eric, 27
Wilson, Robert, 207
Witz, Anne, 35–36, 71–72
Wollstonecraft, Mary, 141–142
Women: medical practices of, 132; as technologists, 40–42; wage work for, 51
Women in science: aims of, and feminist theory, 16–17; authority claims of, 19; effect of *Index Catalogue* on, 115–118; effect of subfield on, 169–185; effect of masculine honor codes on, 75–79; exceptional, 3–4; and fear of feminism, 172–173; in Japan, 198; and relation to masculinized aspects of field, 7
Women's health care, 107–111, 213–214; interest in, 210–211; movements for, 186
Women's Medical College of Philadelphia, 115, 117
"Women's sciences," specter of, 189–191
Woolgar, Steve, 77–78
Wright, Ted, 26
Wylie, Alison, 90 fig. 2

YENTSCH, Anne, 81

4133

ISBN 0-226-30754-9